CRITICAL READINGS IN HUMAN RIGHTS AND PEACE

Critical Readings in Human Rights and Peace

Ram Narayan Kumar
Sonia Muller-Rappard

SAFHR
South Asia Forum for Human Rights, Kathmandu

SHIPRA

ISBN: 81-7541-324-7

First Published in India in 2006

Critical Readings in Human Rights and Peace

Published by:
SHIPRA PUBLICATIONS
115-A, Vikas Marg, Shakarpur
Delhi-110092, INDIA
Phone: 91-11-55277210, 91-11-22500954
Fax: 91-11-22458662
E-mail: info@shiprapublications.com
www.shiprapublications.com

Foreword

The need for developing Human Rights and Peace Studies (HRPS) as an effective means of implementing the Vienna call was quite obvious when the first course was offered in 2000. Subsequent events, especially those of 11th September 2001 and the about-turn on human rights made by some of the most powerful states in the world, have vindicated the Vienna Declaration as well as SAFHR's response to it. The South Asian states' eagerness to follow the all-powerful arbiters of humankind's destiny in developing home-grown strands of anti-human-rights virus has made the HRPS doubly essential. The devices fabricated by almost all South Asian countries to curtail human rights, people's due share in democratic governance, and the protection of the due process to the vulnerable and the marginalized demand that the effort to spread human rights and peace education should address increasingly large audiences.

The South Asian Forum for Human Rights has good reason to look back on the 15 years of its work with some satisfaction. On the one hand time has borne out its conviction that properly informed endeavors "for the protection and promotion of justice, democracy, development, human rights and plural peace within the local contexts become effective only when they are able to draw support from a wider environment of similar initiatives in their neighborhood in harmony with universal objectives." And, on the other hand, participation in HRPS course has enabled activists from the South Asian countries to rediscover the bonds that unite them and the vision of a shared destiny that has been blurred by the selfish and exclusivist policies of their ruling elites. Thus, HRPS has become a vehicle for developing a South Asian identity on the basis of a common and joint pursuit of the ideals of peace, justice, human rights and a genuinely democratic management of their people's affairs.

That there are no final texts on human rights and peace the authors and the editors of the present volume will themselves readily concede. Not only they but all others associated with SAFHR's project under reference, rightly described as the organization's flagship, will look forward to the coming engagements involving course participants, faculty members, and readers of the present publication and hope that the experience of working together will enable them to refurbish their concepts better and make their methodologies even more effective.

The publication of a text that covers the entire range of preparatory studies for an intensive course in human rights and peace education represents an important stage in SAFHR's plan to raise a strong regional cadre of human rights thinkers and activists. Future participants in Human Rights and Peace Studies (HRPS) courses can now have in a single publication nearly all the material they need to equip themselves for the task of promoting human rights and peace across South Asia.

April, 2006

I.A. Rehman,
Director,
Human Rights Commission
of Pakistan,
Lahore

Preface

There have been a number of interesting developments in recent years in designing and conducting new courses within and outside the university, which seek to unshackle social sciences from the orthodoxy of academia and the restrictions it tends to impose on the range and the depth of enquiry and research. The introduction of courses like women's studies and human rights has made it possible to redefine somewhat narrow parameters of social science disciplines as well as to critique their reliance on high canonical works that have traditionally defined knowledge for us. These works have rarely done justice to the experiences, needs and concerns of those sections of society who are unable to claim the rights granted to all citizens, weighed down as they are by the structural constraints that operate on the lives of the marginalised groups: as women, as the underclass, as Dalits, tribals and ethnic communities in the peripheral regions of south Asia. A course on human rights is not only appropriate but also a significant way of bringing all the marginalised groups of society into the framework of analysis, and further, bringing state actions — or inactions, and laws into scrutiny. Even more innovative and challenging is the attempt to conduct a rigorous course which participants can access online, enabling them to continue working in their normal fields and yet be part of an intensive process of study. What is critical for such a venture to succeed is the availability of a solid set of resources which this volume seeks to provide: it comprises a series of references on various topics that can be accessed online complemented by lucid and exhaustive introductions to the scheme of studies under various modules of the course. It also contains hints of assignments that can be undertaken and developed in useful dialogic mode of interaction between the participants and the faculty. The manner in which the reader is organised seeks to democratise interactions by breaking down the hierarchies of contemporary classroom practices operating in universities. For activists and academics working in the field of human rights, an emerging area of study, this volume is both a resource book and a workbook of sorts.

The study of human rights in this volume also goes beyond a linking of the margins as it acts as a complement to fields of study such as international relations, international law, international history, and jurisprudence, all of which have remained state centred in their approaches. The work of feminists in contributing to the understanding of human rights and of redefining ways of thinking about concepts has been significant and this has informed the design of the course as well as the making of this resource book: For example the module on women in peace and conflict provides a discussion of women's role in these processes and flags important dimensions of feminist conceptualisations of war: gendering war and other types of conflict is part of the search for expanding the scope of a human rights perspective and the legal redress that such an expanded perspective offers. One significant attempt by feminist theorists that has succeeded has been to bring rape and sexual violence into the definition of genocide. Feminist jurisprudence has thus inflected and expanded international law and joined the collective attempt of human rights theorists and activists to refuse impunity to violations of human rights and provide a means by which both state and non-state actors who have committed crimes may be brought under judicial scrutiny. Feminist scholars have also worked creatively to think about human rights in non-segmented ways by redefining concepts such as 'security' and 'violence' as normally understood in the social sciences: for example women have linked the violence at home, with violence in the street to the violence on the borders; indeed, borders themselves have been redefined from a feminist perspective as operating on women's lives at different levels and different spaces rather than through the sole axis of the territorial borders of the nation-state. Similarly the notion of 'security' itself has been transformed from the dominance of the 'national security' model of territorial states to food security and more importantly to security against all types of violence that women are routinely subjected to.

Issues such as these and other suggestive lines of enquiry are contained in embryonic form in this important initiative in creating a reader for human rights courses; it is the product of considerable labour but one which is well worth the effort as the volume will be of use to students, academics and activists thinking about human rights.

April, 2006
Delhi

Uma Chakravarty

Contents

Contents

Introduction

The age of global recession of rights together with the cultural and political doctrines on the march, which seem to have set in at the end of the Cold War, must be especially hard on those who have been involved with human rights and peace education within the countries of South Asia. Their task has never been easy. Education to ameliorate social practices, from caste restrictions to rules of honour that come from ugly mutations in old cultures, has its stumbling blocks that are not always apparent to untrained minds. Human rights and peace educators have to deal with them, despite their unsavoury character and against backlashes, because they destroy the fundamental rights and the meaning of peace of millions of women and men outside the reach of state agencies. The arrogance and the attitudes towards people and their histories, which the ruling classes, Macaulay's archetypes, imbibed from the colonial experience, do not help the task of promoting human rights and peace education. These words, "human rights and peace", have for long been central to the political and constitutional discourse in all the countries of South Asia. Yet, savage atrocities, violent repression of political dissent and impunity remain the stock-in-trade of State policies unsusceptible to education. The complex ethos of denial that obtains, makes the task of generating an effective consciousness to influence these policies rather onerous and psychologically crippling. In the face of adamant denial of justice and democratic dialogue, popular struggles for socio-economic justice, echoing aspirations of people, tend to go down the violent ways. Education against violence, under the circumstances, becomes difficult. Now, the cultural theories on the march, which have become more strident since 11 September 2001, seem to place people from large parts of the world in Asia and Africa along fault lines that bind them, so it is said, insuperably to conflicts. Rights themselves, under a near total grip of the positivistic tradition of interpretation, have become no more than the dead letters of law in which the State decides to express or stifle them. Rights as aspirations, led by intuitive understanding of their inalienability and by faith seem to have no place. There, we see some challenges for human rights and peace educators in South Asia. And, on the top of it all, our intellectuals seem determined to enhance our predicaments with their scholarly contributions.

Historians of human rights give us various views on their origins and evolution. Those scholars who attempt to trace the evolution of the human rights terminology in the linguistic resources of the world cultures, as a way to establish their histories, suggest that they had no existence before the waning of the Middle Ages. Alasdair MacIntyre has clearly said: "there is no expression in an ancient or medieval language correctly translated by our expression 'a right'..." By the curious wisdom of such scholars human rights are modern inventions. By the same logic, the established laws and the facts of all sciences must also be modern inventions because they are not available within the linguistic resources of the pre-industrial world.

The wisdom seems to be questionable because existence cannot be linked to the linguistic capacity of expression, which merely conveys the state of knowledge. If humans did not have rights before they came into languages then it would become difficult to explain ancient 'prohibitions' and 'commandments': "Thou shall not steal" must also translate itself to mean that Jesus of Nazareth was entitled to keep his tunic, that he had a right over it, and that his brother James was under the obligation not to violate it by taking it away without his permission. The commandment within the ancient Hindu tradition that a *Brahmin* must not be killed even for a crime otherwise punishable with death surely must have implied an absolute right to life for all Brahmins, even though there was no term, phrase or locution in Sanskrit for it. The commandment must also have conveyed that members of the lower castes did not possess that absolute right and, of course, that *shudras*, who did not at all count as humans, were free game. Kautilya composed *Arthashastra*, around 300 B.C., when notions of rights had not become lexical. Yet, *Arthashastra* commands that judges and magistrates "shall not impose a fine that is not prescribed; they shall not increase or decrease a fine against the rules; they shall not impose corporeal punishment when it is disallowed." [*Arthashastra*, 4.9.17-18] Surely, the commandments convey the existence of rights as well as some principles for their enforcement even when the classical Sanskrit did not have the rights' terminology. The same meaning can be inferred from the Quranic injunction: "take no life, which Allah had made sacred, except by way of justice and law" [Surah 6:151].

The point of this argument is not to contend that all ancient cultures were, by our contemporary standards, human rights conscious. That would be an absurd line of contention to follow because human rights awareness, like their articulation in languages and laws, is a matter of historical evolution. The argument merely aims to suggest that the positivistic approaches to human rights, which recognize their epistemic value and justiciability only on the basic of terminological clarity, fail to see them in their evolutionary and historical contexts. They also seem to be lacking in the capacity to appreciate the dynamics of human rights as political aspirations that permeate ideas and efforts under diverse cultural milieus to different degrees depending on specific historical factors that also influence whether or not they become part of linguistic resources. This position also implicates those authoritarian and lawless states of the South that rebuff entreaties for accountability and the end of impunity by arguing that human rights norms belong to the arsenal of cultural imperialism. Such arguments rationalize destruction of human rights of people in historically disadvantaged societies. They also subserve the preposterous claim, still resonating within some scholarly circles, that the sensitivity, awareness and actualization of human rights are unique to western cultural contexts.

As a positivistic concept in law, 'human rights', like Alasdair MacIntyre, Kenneth Dover, Zygmunt Bauman, Michel Villey and some other famous scholars point out, is of recent origin. We know from our experiences in South Asia that positive recognition in law does not ensure that human rights become real. The Indian Constitution is probably one of the most pernickety of all the Constitutions in the world, not only listing out the fundamental human rights, but also binding the judiciary down to obligatorily receive complaints of violations and to provide effective remedies. But those who have studied the contradictions, between the constitutional guarantees and the institutional practices within the country, know that abuses are pervasive, that they can be ghastly and that impunity prevails. We know that the eighteenth century notions of natural rights went out of currency for the reason that their understanding of 'nature' has been linked to beliefs about the creation that overlook apparent inequities of human existence from their convictions in the redemptive intentions of an unknowable Creator. The transfer of 'nature' to the secular sphere of scientific knowledge, which initially upset the religious forces, does not really seem to help the human rights cause: 'Nature' of sciences is not based on 'rights'. Its equilibriums as well as its inequalities seem to belong to mutative and selective processes under a morally blind power that cannot be planning for redemptive ends of human existence. Therefore, it is no longer considered right to invoke 'natural rights'. All insist on 'human rights'. Meanwhile, we know that 'humanity', guided by the pursuits of its own follies and delusions of grandeur, can eclipse or even extinguish itself. The rhetorical anxieties about the 'weapons of mass destruction' and 'terrorism', as well as the extraordinary regression from the established norms of procedural freedom and fairness in law worldwide that these anxieties have been used to engineer, suggest that human rights, within the positivistic tradition, are again under mutation.

South Asia Forum for Human Rights [SAFHR], which has been engaging with these issues at the regional level, holds the view that aspirations for human rights and peace as also the realities of the abuse of authority, violent strife and suffering have very complex local contexts that are not always obvious to votaries of universalism. SAFHR believes that the ideals and standards contained in Universal Declaration of Human Rights (UDHR) stand better chance of realization if they move from the local to regional and on to the global. Having remained engaged with human rights and peace research as well as the practical work of human rights documentation, public interest litigation, advocacy, building solidarity networks and civil-society initiatives in all the countries in South Asia, SAFHR holds the view that knowledgeable initiatives for the protection and promotion of justice, democracy, development, human rights and plural peace within the local contexts become effective only when they are able to draw support from a wider environment of similar initiatives in their neighbourhood in harmony with the universal objectives. That is the *raison d'être* of SAFHR as a regional forum.

SAFHR's initiative in developing a framework for the South Asian Orientation Course in Human Rights and Peace Studies [HRPS] followed the Vienna Declaration of 1993, which devotes its Articles 33, 34, 36, 38, 78-82 to stress the importance of human rights education and to call on the governments to establish programmes to impart it. The initiative was based on the recognition that human rights and peace education should not become a monopoly of the States, which not only commit widespread human rights violations but also stimulate, with their socio-political, economic and military policies, endemic situations of violent conflict and wars within the region. Also, the complex ethos of denial that obtains in most countries in South Asia, make their universities and quasi-governmental organizations including statutory human rights commissions inappropriate forums to lead the Vienna call. Under these circumstances, a non-governmental regional network of human rights organizations, which does not depend on the local governments for funding, seemed to qualify as a forum to initiate a regional human rights and peace education programme.

Developing a structure and the substance of the programme, its pedagogic principles and a framework of inquiry which resonate the universality of ideals and represent the uniquely regional concerns has not been an easy task. SAFHR engaged in intense deliberations with frontline human rights and peace thinkers and activists; academics and other highly-experienced persons of the region to develop a design to fill the obvious lacuna within the world of education in providing space and voice to the rights of the oppressed, the discontented and the marginalized and to obtain for them the necessary recognition and significance within the human rights and peace discourse. Ranabir Samaddar, the Director of Maulana Azad Institute of Asian Studies in Calcutta, who gave up his position to become the founder-director of the programme from 2000 to 2003, and his faculty members were able to ensure that the course makes the conscious effort to move away from the banking model of education in which the participants receive deposits of knowledge into their learning accounts to a structurally reciprocal and dialogic system. The modules under the structure of the course, selection of the reading material, the engagement during the distance learning period and the format for presentations and discussions in the classroom environment ensured that the reciprocal engagement between the participants and the faculty members served the dual purpose of generating critical understanding about the issues under inquiry as well as to interrogate the systems of knowledge in ways that lead to possibilities of mutating policies and practices of power through social action.

From the beginning of the HRPS course, SAFHR has been selecting between thirty to thirty-five participants every year. Each applicant is required to send a filled in application form with two references, and a 1000-word essay explaining the relation of the applicant's work to human rights and peace studies and the reason for applying for the course. The selection process is guided by the necessity to have a balanced representation from all the countries in the region, including women activists; refugee activists, media practioners, members of minority groups, researchers, academics and leaders of non-governmental organizations. Participants come from the age span of 25 to 40.

The interactive nature of the course has, over the years, influenced the structure, the content and the pedagogic approaches. In its current format, the course has three distinct components: [1] a three month long distance learning part (May, June and July) conducted mainly on a secure E-learning platform that has been designed as an electronic agora where text, sound, moving and still images, maps and graphs converge in flexible formats and lead to cognitive apprenticeship in multiple thinking; [2] a clinical component that brings the participants as well as the members of the permanent faculty in joint research projects with strong emphasis on field work (August); and [3] a three-week long Direct Orientation (September) when the participants, the faculty and independent resource persons come together for intense discussions and interactions. Participants are encouraged to combine their experiences and assignments from all the three components of the course to write their term papers as joint or individual projects.

Having completed five courses, SAFHR's HRPS programme needs to reach out to the larger community of people involved in human rights and peace education within South Asia and to begin a systematic exchange and evaluation of ideas on the principles of pedagogy, their epistemological assumptions, curricula and methodologies for a regional approach to human rights and peace education. This volume, which offers glimpses into the engagement that the distance learning process of the 5th Course in 2004 became, is a step in that direction.

The first part of the volume includes four comprehensive introductory notes which aim to help the participants with main issues of inquiry under various modules, to introduce them to the main body of literature under the subjects as well as to have them pose questions that inform course readings and assignments. The papers included in the second part of the volume were written originally as comments to the review papers, which the participants of the fifth course had sent before coming to the direct orientation part of the programme. These papers have been thoroughly edited to make them relevant to the future participants of the course. The volume has been evaluated and refereed by three eminent scholars. They are: Godfrey Hodgson, former Director of Reuters Foundation Programme at Oxford and a well-known writer who has taught at several universities including Berkeley and Harvard; Satish Jain, Professor of Economics at the Centre for Economic Studies and Planning, Jawaharlal Nehru University, New Delhi; and, Ranabir Samaddar, Director, Calcutta Research Group and former Director of SAFHR's Human Rights and Peace Studies Programme. Satish Jain has also contributed a thought provoking paper titled "Globalization and Human Rights".

We are immensely grateful for the effort they have put in to make this volume useful to independent human rights and peace scholars, researches, educators and activists worldwide. The volume has been thoroughly revised in the light of the evaluation reports. Vasudha Dhingra, M. Phil., scholar at the Centre for International Politics, Organizations and Disarmament, JNU, interned with the programme for a month to assist the editorial work in its final stages. We are grateful for her association and assistance. Thanks are due also to the participants of the 5th Course who contributed to this volume by writing their review papers and, thereby, encouraging the flow of comments that constitute its second part. The following deserve special mention for the intensity and the quality of their engagement: A.C.M. Nafeel, A.K.M. Mahfuzul Haque, A.S. Nurullah Awal, Gunjan Veda, Johanne Fortin, Jyotsna Poudyal, Manjita Gurung, Mohan Karna, Mohan Tamang, Mohna Ansari, Nusrat Sheikh, Prahlad Dahal, Prashan Thalayasingam, Shampa Chakraborty, Smriti Shrestha Pradhan, Suleman Kakar, Suman Khadka, Sylvie Graenicher, Talib Jan, Tek Bir Chhetri, and Vanita Sharma.

Thanks also to Meher Ali, our Research Associate, for doing the tedious work of proof reading.

Tapan K. Bose	**Ram Narayan Kumar**
(Secretary General, SAFHR)	(Director, HRPS)

Chapter One

Basic Concepts of Human Rights, Society and the State

Some Fundamental Questions

What are human rights? Conceptually, do they belong naturally, inalienably, to all persons irrespective of their historical origins, political systems and geographical and cultural milieus under which they live, as a matter of natural and civilian entitlement by virtue of being human beings? Are human rights the same as civil rights, civil liberties, or natural rights? What are the connotations of *negative* conceptions of rights that require States to abstain from infringing actions? What are the obligations under *positive* concepts of rights that entitle citizens to equality before the law and to the equal protection of the law in terms of opportunity, employment, and social welfare? What is the meaning of the belief that governments, irrespective of their character, may not, cannot, or should not deny or deprive persons of their human rights? What are the intended consequences of this belief? What are the unintended, but foreseeable fallouts when the expectations generated by the belief fail, remain unfulfilled, or become infringed?

Can we compile a list of human rights that covers inalienability, naturalness, and immanence? Typically, a recital of human rights includes freedom of speech, of religion, of family, of movement, dignity and equality before the law and equality of opportunity irrespective of individual socio-political, economic, and sexual status or propensity. Freedom from arbitrary arrest, detention, execution, inhuman punishment, and the right to free and fair trial are also included. Some definitions divide these rights into the categories of basic and political rights. Others distinguish procedural rights, including the right to equality before the law and non-discrimination in social opportunity, from substantive rights that seek to commit the State to minimum standards of provision to citizens as, for example, education, work, and welfare. Some emphasize the contradistinction between individual and collective rights and the tendency of the former to impinge on the latter as, for example, the tendency of the right to freedom of expression to become offensive. Recognition of collective rights raises the problem of contingent restrictions on individual rights. The rights of organized groups of working people to strike, picket, and bargain have been legally recognized in the UK since 1906. Regulations on trade, the dumping of toxic wastes, and environmental controls as well as the rights to health care, food, and education stem from the recognition of collective rights. Cultural rights and the right to enjoy benefits of scientific progress and its applications though connected, are independent areas. Many categorize human rights in three generational terms: the first generation rights include civil and political rights; economic, social and cultural rights fall under the category of second generation rights; and the third generation rights, normally, encompass collective rights. All these categories require clarity regarding their "reportive", "stipulative", and "contextual" definitions. A "reportive" definition signifies the attribution of a meaning to a linguistic expression and, it thereby becomes contestable. A "stipulative" definition binds a linguistic expression to a specific meaning as a proposition. A "contextual" definition depends on the totality of meaning conveyed by the expressions to be defined.

Human rights are generally described to be inalienable, natural, and immanent in human life. If so, are these rights also time immemorial? What is the evidence of human rights in history? Why do we rely on declaratory listings of domestic constitutional provisions and international proclamations, covenants, and treaties to claim them? Why are there such tensions between the claims of human rights and the laws dealing with their enforceability? Why is there such a gap between the laws of enforceable rights and practices and perceptions of their actual implementation? Why do violations constitute the principal theme of the discourse on human rights? Does the pre-eminence of the theme suggest human rights belonging to an arena of contest between societies and the power of States?

What is society, or in contemporary parlance civil society? What is a State? Are society and the State universally synonymous? Or, are they historically specific to the heterogeneity of geographical and cultural travails of human existence? What are the dynamics of tensions between the notions of universal human rights and sovereign State systems? Where do we locate the concept of nation within the rubric of society and citizenship? The concept of nation is generally understood to mean a body of people with common characteristics of identity and references of historical or cultural traditions connected with a common belief of origination in an identifiable geographic location. How does this concept relate to contexts of identities generated by linguistic, racial, and religious affinities? Why and when do their manifestations and demands for socio-political and legal safeguards connected with them, lead to social and political tensions? How is this process different from the tensions associated with the politics of "minorities" against dominant interests and their pleas of protection through affirmative action? What are the differences of their contexts? What is the politics of national identity and how does it convert itself into the politics of Nation-State? When, why, and how do they coincide? What is hegemony and does it have any meaning within the politics of a Nation-State? Why is the concept of hegemony, signifying domination of one over others, mainly used to signify systemic tensions in international relations? What are the ideals and the realities of universal rights, the principles of their enforcement and accountability in international relations? Why do human rights abuses remain so pervasive and global when powerful States like the United States and its European allies claim to be linking their offers of economic and military aid to developing countries with the conditionality of progress they make on human rights?

Discussions and reflections on these questions would lead us back to the first question with a new thrust of inquiry: What are human rights? Are they not the claims of civil society constituents to obtain moral and legal entitlements, in both *positive* and *negative* terms, against the power of State systems? In that case, do not human rights become power concepts? Is not the notion of right a concept of control? Does not a notion of right permeate with the duality of permissibility without interference and possession without the threat of deprivation? In this sense, the notion of human rights does not necessarily stand in logical contradiction with the conception of power and politics. What are the implications of this possible symmetry between notions of the rights of people and the wrongs of the power structures associated with States, which the human rights community wants to redress? The question that follows is: does the notion of human rights inform the political ideas and attitudes of the vast majority of people susceptible to actual abuses and deprivation? How strong is the political culture that seeks to enforce rights and accountability on the strength of popular mobilization and by bringing to bear democratic attitudes towards authority, social discipline, governmental responsibilities, and expectations of substantive provisions to effect policy changes?

Some Western Philosophers of Human Rights

These are the questions that have inspired thinkers, philosophers, and statesmen from ancient days in all cultures to intuitively muse, speak, and write about them. But these questions for us have new interfaces that have been shaped by the complexities of our own times and the histories of our struggles for rights within the matrix of State systems that have evolved under the influence of the industrial revolution and imperialism. Familiarity with the works listed under the footnote in alphabetical order by the author, will help the participants to recognize the philosophical and social significance of these issues for the current situation of human rights in the world. The list has no ideological bias and merely tries to incorporate the variety of important voices on the subject.[1] Participants may already be familiar with some of the names and the works in the list. The following brief introductions merely aim to highlight the ideas and the issues that engaged some of these philosophers, and that remain central to human rights inquiries to this day.

Jean-Jacques Rousseau, the first eloquent champion of popular sovereignty, understood as the prophet of the French Revolution, and an influence on M.K. Gandhi, published his *Discourse on Inequality* in 1755. The work is a hypothetical history of the human race, postulated on the notion of an originally benign character of human nature, which gradually became corrupted as the institutions of family, property, and political power interfered against its spontaneous sociability and its capacities for sharing and goodness. Rousseau held the interventions of the State and the laws of private property to be primarily responsible for the metamorphosis of the human condition from the state of natural freedom and spontaneous association to relations of superiors and subordinates. A fierce opponent of all form of political authority, including of a parliamentary rule that does not rest on direct governance by the people, Rousseau refined and developed his ideas of direct democracy in his *Social Contract*, published in 1762, under his doctrine of **general will.** The doctrine, borrowed substantially from the historical experiences of ancient republican traditions, including the Republic of Geneva of which Rousseau was a citizen, and advanced the idea of a citizens' council as a sovereign legislative assembly. In Rousseau's opinion, moral and civil liberties can flourish only in conditions of economic and political equality maintained on the strength of laws that the people themselves create. Presumably, the idea inspired Gandhi's own dream of *Gram Swaraj*. Rousseau was also a stern opponent of violence in any political form and rejected it in absolute terms, even if that was to be the only way to secure liberty for all humanity. Rousseau, inspite of his eccentric views of human history, wrote in a very sophisticated and emotionally seductive style, and his *Confessions*, published posthumously, and the *Reveries of a Solitary Walker*, published in 1782, offered insights into a mystical personality which, like St. Augustine's, was philosophically complex. Kant read and admired Rousseau's prose.

Immanuel Kant, a popular teacher of philosophy from Germany, who stayed in the town of his birth Koenigsberg all his life, unmarried, was appointed a professor at the local university in the year 1770. In 1794, he was forbidden by the Prussian king, Frederick William II, from writing or lecturing on religion because of the views he expressed in his *Religion within the Limits of Reason Alone* in 1793. Arguably the most important philosopher of Germany whose inquiries followed three simple questions—"what can one know?", "what can one do?" and "what can one hope for?" Kant left an imprint on all branches of abstract thinking which are alive to this day. The pervasiveness of his influence is related to the nature of philosophical propositions he made: "substantive knowledge" without experience, or "outside cognitive apparatus" is impossible; all knowledge is confined within "presuppositions of experience"; only *a priori* epistemic guidance, or transcendental ideals, can help knowledge and effort towards goals beyond appearances. To paraphrase Kant's philosophy this way might actually be trivializing it and, in any case, we can only be concerned here with his theory of morality, or 'goodness-without-qualification' that is coterminous with his theory of freedom and "universal rights". In 1795, Kant published an essay called *Perpetual Peace* to argue that universal democracy is a condition for peace.

Johann Gottlieb Fichte, a German philosopher and a contemporary of Kant, who had to vacate his professorship at Jena in 1799 because of his strict adherence to the theory of morality, in interpreting both religious and political life, published *Foundations of Natural Right* in 1796. The work is recognized as the first coherent theory of individual rights and the State's obligations to ensure welfare of its people. Fichte was also involved in mobilizing German resistance to Napoleonic conquests and the arguments which he developed in his speeches during the period not only appeal to "freedom" and "character" but also to the dignity of resistance.

Thomas Paine, a British idealist, whose fame spread with his 1776 pamphlet *Common Sense*, made America his home to develop emotionally moving arguments for its independence. His *Rights of Man,* published in 1791, defends the ideals of the French Revolution and introduces a programme of social-welfare coupled with democracy, to be provided by the State, which he believed would result in the end of wars and the establishment of perpetual peace in the world.

Karl Marx, a German revolutionary thinker and political philosopher, who lived 40 out of his 65 years of life from 1818 to 1883 in exile in Paris, Brussels, and London, is known as the father of dialectical materialism, often referred to as Marxism. *The Communist Manifesto*, which Marx wrote jointly with his collaborator Friedrich Engels in 1848, and *Das Kapital*, whose first volume came out in 1867, are the two most famous of his published works. His more philosophical writings include *The Poverty of Philosophy*, a critique of French anarchist Pierre-Joseph Proudhon's theories on poverty published in 1847; *The Economic and Philosophical Manuscripts*, written in 1844; and *The German Ideology*, written in 1846.

Dialectical materialism is an approach to understanding the evolution of human society by locating it in the dynamics of economics determined by developments of productive forces and the social relations that they foster. This approach views political, social, and legal systems of thought and practice as the corresponding reflections of the dominant economic interests. Within this worldview, productive activity or labour receives a philosophically essential instrumentality that also drives history to its emancipatory end. Private property is explained as labour alienated from the human labourer. In this sense, private property is human exploitation personified. Capitalism converts labour into a commodity and compels an ever-increasing number of persons to enter the market with nothing to sell but their labour. Thus, capitalism becomes instrumental in the creation of a strong working-class and of its class-consciousness with a political will to abolish private property. This, in a nutshell, is the Marxist analysis of the historical process, which posits the goal of emancipation from exploitative relations and their political superstructures on a materialistic interpretation of history and not on utopian speculations.

Detractors accuse Marxism of being a deterministic philosophy, meaning that it posits all occurrences on antecedent causes. **Friedrich Engels** explained the philosophical principles of the Marxist system in *The Dialectics of Nature*, published in 1925, 30 years after his death. The work explains that a revolutionary leap from a condition of quantity into a difference of quality requires suitable material conditions; that contradictions and opposites interpenetrate in ways that are not strictly regulatory; and that the negation of a negation does not result in a return to the starting point but to a synthesis within a new spiral. Engels' work shows that Marxism is not a hard deterministic theory operating on a regulatory view of causation and an "incompatible" understanding of relations between freedom of action and material outcome, but on a probabilistic notion of causation and predictability "in principle".

Alasdair MacIntyre, a Scottish teacher of philosophy at several British and American universities, is influenced by the teachings of Gottlob Frege and Ludwig Wittgenstein, two great philosophers of language and mathematical logic. In the first phase of his inquiries, sustained in 1960s, MacIntyre struggled with the social and historical validity of orthodox Christian and Marxist tenets, publishing such works as *A Short History of Ethics* in 1966 and *Against the Self-Images of the Age* in 1971. His later work, *After Virtue* in 1981, marks the return to a more classical approach to ethics. *After Virtue* rejects the Marxist theory as being relevant to understanding late the twentieth-century social and political practices, but remains firm in a stern view of consumer capitalism and the associated ideology of liberal individualism, which MacIntyre holds responsible for perverting relationships between individuals and the products of their labour as well as virtuous associations between individuals and social constructs, including family. *Whose Justice? Which Rationality*?, published in 1988, is an attempt to analyze the meaning of justice and truth by adopting a comparative approach to principles of rationality, existential commensurability, and integrity that follow from different systems of moral philosophy. MacIntyre is a harsh critic of the tautological tendencies of human rights rhetoric, its evangelic fervour, its talismanic enunciations, and its portrayal of all perceptions of needs, both individualistic and collective as "rights". He points out that to coalesce fragments of different conceptual schemes, resting upon incommensurable moral premises, is a recipe for mischief.

John Rawls, an American professor of philosophy at Harvard, is widely recognized as one of the most creative and influential political thinkers from the hemisphere in our period, mainly on the strength of his book *A Theory of Justice*, published in 1971. The book is a sophisticated renewal of the social contract theory, first advanced by Rousseau, which develops a logically efficient analysis of the utilitarian notions of political obligation and order by exposing the fallacies of their cost-accounting methodologies that ride roughshod over considerations of justice and fairness. Rawls' theory of justice also aims to disprove the positive law approaches that purport to take a value-free stance to life and human behaviour as objective phenomena, denigrating all arguments of natural rights in the process. The uniqueness of the theory is, at least partially, epitomized by a methodological tool that Rawls calls the "veil of ignorance" argument. It requires a hypothetical expunging of all social, temporal facts of a situation to arrive at a view of fairness and justice of a given rule and requirement. The argument, it would seem, is a sophisticated reconstruction of Rousseau's state of nature theory and allows a measure of inequality in the distribution of all social primary good, if that advantages the conditions of the least favoured lot. The central concerns of Rawls' theory of justice are social and distributive justice and the advancement of the underprivileged sections of the society without destroying the primacy of liberty. Inevitably, Rawls' theory has come under attack from many quarters which he has tried to deal with in his *Political Liberalism*, published in 1993.

Friedrich August von Hayek, an Austrian like Karl Popper and, like him, a defender of individualism against "enemies of open society", was essentially an anti-socialist economist who received the Nobel Prize in Economics in 1974. An implacable enemy of economic planning, regulation, and intervention, and also of social welfare by governments, Hayek championed free market in a really free sense. But he argued against the freedom of trade unions, which he described as "monopolies of labour", to operate and obstruct capital operations in the market. A favourite with the Reagan and Thatcher administrations in the USA and the UK, Hayek's *The Constitution of Liberty*, first published in 1960, is an interesting work because it posits liberty as a market value. The work does not explain whether or not liberty enters the market as a commodity or as a watchdog for the freedom of other transactions.

Herbert Lionel Adolphus Hart, a professor of jurisprudence at Oxford from 1952 to 1968, published *The Concept of Law* in 1961. In this work, Hart tries to develop strong philosophical arguments against the theories of legal positivism, deriving from the writings of John Austin, that explain law as rules of conduct sustained by the threat of force. Hart's later work, especially *Law, Liberty and Morality* published in 1963, was devoted to advance the position that law should not encroach upon the private lives of consenting adults to regulate their lives under the cover of preserving social morality.

Ronald Dworkin, who succeeded Hart as a professor of jurisprudence at Oxford in 1968, published *Taking Rights Seriously* in 1977 to argue that divorced from the principles of morality the laws, hinging on precedent and legislative enactments, become fundamentally irrational and cease to serve the commonweal under the realm of judicial discretion. The argument taxes the principle of judicial discretion to relate to the spirit of political morality, inherent in laws, rather than to conventions of precedence. Dworkin developed these ideas of "interpretative integrity" of the judicial process further in *A Matter of Principles*, 1985, and *Laws of Empire*, 1986. His later writings, including *Life's Dominion,* 1993, deal with more controversial issues of human rights, including pornography, abortion, and euthanasia.

Simon Weil, an intuitively brilliant French Parisian born in 1909, studied philosophy under Emile Charter, known as Alain, and abandoned her teaching position to become a factory worker in 1930s Paris to understand the restoring power of meaningful labour. A subscriber of left-wing syndicalism in her student years, Simon Weil, with her Jewish family background and having been through a mystical Christian experience, became a harsh critic of the communist ideal of "the revolution" as the "opium for the masses" that substitutes the old religious promise of salvation. She, also, remained a radical enemy of capitalism, its production modes, and the consumption cultures it promoted. Moreover, she critiqued the State and the increasing power it obtained and used against the basic human "needs" of freedom, security, order, and truth. Simon Weil, who died in 1943 at the young age of 34, as an active member of the Free French resistance against the German occupation of France, is a relatively unknown but important figure within the world of human rights discourse. *Oppression and Liberty,* first published in 1955, is one of the collections of her posthumously published writings.

Michel Foucault, one of the most enigmatic French thinkers on the predicaments of human entrapment in modern history, was a psychologist by training. He moved to Paris from a provincial town Poitiers in 1945 at the age of 18. A student under Jean Hyppolite, a Hegelian philosopher at the Ecole Normale Superieure, Foucault discovered his homosexuality and grew up under its thrill, shame, despair, and challenge. He left for a teaching position in Uppsala, Sweden, in 1955, to escape his lonesomeness in Paris, and published his first major work *Madness and Civilization* in 1961. After spending some years in Poland and then in Germany, Foucault came back to France in 1960 to publish *The Birth of the Clinic* and the biography of a surrealist writer Raymond Roussel in 1963. Foucault's *The Order of Things* came out in 1966. These books, which explained the categorization of "experiences" and "practices" into respectable and repressible groupings in Europe beginning from the 17th century, were instantaneously successful. French intellectuals immediately recognized their allegorically historical character and their power of new interpretations, and Foucault became a celebrity. Stunned by his popularity, despite his homosexuality, Foucault escaped France once again in 1967 to become a teacher in Tunisia and came back to France in May 1968 excited by the reports of students' unrest aided by the surging proletariat and to be joined by the "non-proletarian masses of women, prisoners, homosexuals, psychiatric patients" to bring about a new de-centralized, *de-constructed* society. The following two decades, till his retirement into his private struggle against the "shadows of death" by little understood AIDS, were Foucault's most political. In a televised debate in 1971, as a professor of the *College de France*, Foucault was heard telling Noam Chomsky: "The proletariat doesn't wage war against the ruling class because it considers such a war to be just. The proletariat makes war against the ruling class because, for the first time in history, it wants to take power." His recipe against the "categorizing power" of history, in the period, was "popular justice." Foucault declared: "One should start with popular justice with acts of justice by the people, and go on to ask what place a court should have in this." In 1978, Foucault again responded to the call of "limit experience" of politics by travelling to Iran to absorb and report on the "political spirituality" of the revolutionary movement and to praise its leaders for their "religion of combat and sacrifice." Foucault had by then discovered the subculture of homosexuality and its fringe sadomasochism in California and had been spending extended periods in the company of the like-minded. His *Uses of Pleasure*, the second volume of *The History of Sexuality*, published in 1984, shows a quieter man, inspite of his philosophical rebelliousness, much like Nietzsche in *The Birth of Tragedy*, still disenchanted with the world, disillusioned with friends, ready to marry death in the dusk of gods. He still complained about his gay friends who were being "reclaimed" by the clinic whose birth he had discussed in 1963, before leaving for Sweden to escape his fame in France. In 1983, with the knowledge that AIDS would take him to death, Foucault declared: "To die for the love of boys: what could be more beautiful?" Foucault, like Nietzsche, is difficult to understand without some knowledge of his life outside his writing.[2]

Foucault and his writings provoke controversy and incomprehension. The difficulties of his style of writing are also criticized. Foucault rejects the modern European construction of history and refuses to adopt a cloak of self within its contexts. His understanding of "social discipline", acting on subjects, is such that it leads to facets of power unrecognized by the conventional construction of political history. Foucault's history is fundamentally non-Marxist and, despite his condemnation of "subjectivity" of deviant people and the use of terms like "proletariat" and its urge for power, the philosophical tendencies of his work knock at the doors of new inquiries about the limits of rights, given the "practices of the self", in historically twisted societies, and the challenges of resisting "what we are." Significantly for the discourse on human rights, Foucault's work redirects the critique of political power and authority towards the established knowledge of society as the source of abuse: it does not really matter if someone operates from within the structure of State authority or from outside. What matters is the knowledge base and whether an operating person is conforming or questioning the categorization of relations within the society.

State and Society

Available literature on rights, the State, society, democracy, justice, development, conflict, and peace is aplenty and even the most voracious reader cannot cover, within three months between the start of the distance learning and the commencement of the direct orientation programme, even a tiny part of it. The selection of what to read can become a dilemma and answers to the issues of inquiry raised in this note may not easily follow. There is little agreement and clarity in scholarship. We do not even know what is exactly conveyed by such commonly used concepts as "State" or even when, where, and how it originated. We know it is more than the government, which can come and go without affecting the State. The State is supposed to encompass all the components of a political system that orders and organizes collective life. Yet, it is, inexplicably differentiated from civil society that includes schools, religious establishments, hospitals, work places, and trade unions. The State is understood to embrace the parliament, the judiciary, the civil administration, the police, the army, and jails. But it is supposed to exclude political parties that control parliament and fill offices including the offices of Prime Minister and President who command all the institutions of coercion.

A large number of political thinkers differentiate the State and civil society as if postulating the State to be outside. Notable among them are: Thomas Hobbes [1588-1679], who authored *Leviathan* under the influence of the English Civil War; John Locke [1632-1704], the author of the *First and Second Treatises on Civil Government* that inspired the writers of the US Constitution; Jean-Jacques Rousseau [1712-1778], the author of *Social Contract, Discourse on the Origin of Inequality* and *Emile* widely recognized as the inspirer of the French Revolution; Georg Wilhelm Friedrich Hegel [1770-1831], probably the second most influential political philosopher from Germany after Immanuel Kant [1724-1804]; Karl Marx [1818-1883], the philosophical father of modern communism; and John Rawls, one of the most influential political theorists from Harvard; and several others.

Hobbes argued for a draconian State to curb the "innate" human tendencies of lawlessness, greed, and cruelty that, in his view, belonged to the "state of nature". Marx introduced the concept of "alienation" to describe a transformation of human nature alien to the self in the capitalist phase of human evolution and visualized its culmination in a true democratic communism attending on the withering away of the State. For both of them, the State stands outside human society. Can it be that this apparent agreement among these varied scholars followed from a recognition that whereas the State and all institutions of coercive authority and control are, conceivably, expendable, stable associations and arrangements of collective life to operate economic, religious, and family relations and structures, theoretically on social agreement, are indispensable and capable of survival in a Stateless conception of human life? If so, the political theory, across a wide spectrum of opinion, would seem to relegate institutions of authority to a secondary status before a voluntary understanding of primary social relations. However, it is difficult to see how the State, drawn from society, can be a construct, even in theory, outside the society and the implications of such a construct in understanding interactions between institutions of authority and people on the one hand and interpenetrations of political and social actions on the other, should themselves become issues of inquiry.

Involved discussions on the issues of the State, society, politics, their implications for justice and the future dynamics of relations between political power and the people presuppose a fairly comprehensive understanding of political theory. It is easy to cite the basic literature that constitutes the syllabus of political studies at advanced levels.[3]

Two Difficult Thinkers: Hannah Arendt and Jacques Derrida

We have already introduced some of the thinkers who have contributed substantially to the evolution of human rights discourse. Students of human rights and peace studies should also become familiar with the works of Hannah Arendt and Jacques Derrida who, in our opinion, encapsulate the diversity and the ambivalences of the discourse and its contrapuntal positions, in relevant ways.[4] The following brief introductions merely aim to highlight the historical contexts and the intellectual perspectives that the two thinkers represent.

Hannah Arendt (1906-1975) came from a Jewish family background in Koenigsberg in Germany and studied philosophy under three eminent philosophers of the period. They are: (1) Edmund Husserl, the founder of the phenomenological school in modern philosophy; (2) Karl Jaspers, an existentialist who understood philosophy as a tool of self-discovery and understanding; and, very significantly, (3) Martin Heidegger, widely acknowledged as one of the most original thinkers of the century, who extended open support to the Nazi regime.

Only 18 when she began to attend Heidegger's lecture in Marburg, Hannah Arendt fell passionately in love with his intellectual personality. The relationship continued until her own death in 1975, surviving inner torment, doubts, and humiliation, and also the ordeals of her own exile first to France when Hitler came to power in Germany and then to the USA when Germany invaded France in 1940. Hannah knew that Heidegger silently connived in the persecution of Jaspers, her own teacher, who had to quit his position at Freiburg University because his wife was Jewish. Jaspers lived under the constant dread of deportation or death, barred from leaving the country, until the end of the Nazi era. Heidegger was the Rector of Freiburg University when Jasper was forced to quit. Heidegger had studied philosophy under Edmund Husserl, to whom he had dedicated his first major work *Being and Time*, published in 1927. Heidegger, not only removed the dedication in the edition of the book published after Hitler's rise to power, but also signed a circular banning him from the university. Hannah Arendt worked intensively for the last eight years of her life, closely with Heidegger, in bringing out the English translations of his writings.

Hannah Arendt's own work is marked by her extraordinarily lucid capacity to analyze the rise of imperialism and totalitarianism under several ideological systems and the impact of capitalism in its modern variants essentially from the perspective of the downtrodden, political pariahs, victims of State persecution, immigrants and refugees, and the future of their aspirations for justice and dignity in public life. Her first major work, published in 1951, is titled *The Origins of Totalitarianism*. The next three books that represent the range of her basic concerns are: *The Human Condition*, 1958; *On Revolution*, 1963, and *On Violence*, 1970.

Her book titled *Eichmann in Jerusalem: A Report on the Banality of Evil*, which came out in 1963, was criticized by many for its central thesis of *banality* by which she analyzed the evil personified by Eichmann. The work, probably, conveys her ambiguity towards the human tendency to collaborate with evil that she must have also felt towards Heidegger. In an article titled "What is Existential Philosophy", published in the *Partisan Review* in 1946, Hannah characterized Heidegger's fling with Nazism as "a spiritual playfulness that stems in part from delusions of grandeur and in part from despair". Hannah Arendt's books, as also her life, remain extremely valuable in our own contemporary context of examining the State, society and the processes of politics relevant to the ideals of human development, peace, and justice.

Jacques Derrida, born in Algiers in 1930, grew up reading philosophy at the *Ecole Normale Superieure* in France and then teaching the subject at the *Ecole Normale Superieure* and the *Ecole des Hautes Etudes en Sciences Sociales* at the Sorbonne. Universally acknowledged as the father of "deconstruction", Derrida had an extraordinary amount of influence on the academic postmodernists dealing with cultural studies, postcolonial theory, feminist, gay, and lesbian issues, normative law, and critical theories. Derrida, like, Foucault, is not easy to read and understand without a basic grounding in the philosophical legacies of structuralism in Europe. However, Derrida and his "deconstruction" are now so rooted within the rhetoric of emancipatory politics that some understanding of his ideas and their relevance to our discourse is almost essential.

Derrida grew up in an environment of left ebullience in France that was dependent on the philosophy-figures who reposed much faith in the socialist promise of the Soviet Union. Disillusionment connected with the demise of Jean-Paul Sartre, his existential humanism and his defence of freedom within the Soviet Union, which attended on Khrushchev's speech to the Twentieth Party Conference in Moscow, delivered in February 1956, was not conducive to left politics. The events and exposures about the world beyond the Iron Curtain not only shattered the hopeful engagement with Marxism as "the unsurpassable horizon of emancipation", which many existentialists had developed, but they also exacerbated the cynicism and calculated deception within the rhetoric of the Cold War in Europe. Derrida had not been very politically active but identified himself as a leftist and developed his "philosophy of deconstruction" in this environment.

Derrida placed the structuralist theory developed by Claude Levi-Strauss to study cultures as autonomous processes on its head, hung Edmund Husserl's phenomenology, especially its threads of inquiries into structures of language and the world of meaningful communication, upside down, and began to design his philosophy of deconstruction by bizarre effects of the scaffolding. Derrida's first major work *Speech and Phenomena*, published in 1967, attacked the idealistic theory of meaning, which Husserl developed in his *Logical Investigations*. Husserl's 1901 work suggests that *meaning* actually transcends the temporal and external limitations of language by relating to a mental apprehension of intentionality and transcending the sensation of objects. Derrida attacked the theory and tried to show that Husserl's arguments critically depended on the resources of language that are external and historical. Derrida accused Husserl and others, influenced by his theories, of promoting *logocentrism*, a privilege of speech that allows its users to advance private intentions and idealistic objectives against temporal and material aspects of language and their public meaning. According to Derrida, this is an endemic trait within the Western philosophical tradition making all utterances dodge determinable meaning and the relationship of truth within the world of material reality.

Derrida's other works such as *Of Grammatology*, 1967; *Margins of Philosophy*, 1972; *Dissemination*, 1972; *The Truth in Painting*, 1978; and *Of Spirit*, 1989, develop and build on this primary repudiation of the possibility of truth and rational discourse through language. He combined this with the inverted imagery of Levi-Strauss's cultural relativism to raise an "ultrastructuralist" pedestal for the ever-growing agenda of "deconstruction." The history of this development is not only politically convoluted but is also mired in the philosophical quarrels that started with a 1946 public spat between Jean-Paul Sartre and Martin Heidegger over their use of "humanism". Derrida took full advantage of the confusion to push his agenda of deconstruction as a playful wheedling of paradoxes within all texts and as a long prolegomenon to the end of logocentrism and all associated wickedness of intentionality of language.

The publication of Derrida's *Politics of Friendship* in 1997 marks a new, seemingly activist phase in the programme of deconstruction. The book examines the affiliations between the intentionality of meaning in language, within the Western philosophical tradition, and the politics and history of "identity" that it fosters. The book shows how these affiliations tend to first promote "membership of the like", then impose hierarchies on idealized fraternities, and finally turn them into essentially hostile politics of friends against enemies. Shorn of the usual textual wheedling, the book introduces an interesting paradigm to examine coercive arrangements of a social order, including nations and borders, as well as the politics of conflict they breed as conventions. The same perspective is palpable, although less manifest, in two books that appeared in 1992 and 1994.[5]

There are obvious difficulties in this approach of seeing all abuses in history and society originating in "logocentric" intentionality within the Western philosophical tradition. If countries, nations, states, and citizens are meaningless, it becomes difficult to see how democracy and its associated values can be meaningful. If intentionality, consciousness, and will are the terminological tools of "hegemony" how should we distinguish the politics of friendship from the politics of prejudice, rights from wrongs, and justice from iniquity?

In a 1989 lecture given in New York, Derrida addressed the issue of justice. However, he did so in terms that not only appear to contradict basic tenets of his deconstruction doctrine, but in a numinous state of revealing that leaves little scope for doing or dialogue. The lecture *Deconstruction and the Possibility of Justice*, which is now available within the covers of a book under the same title, examines the operation of law on the basis of authority and violence, its linkages with economic and political interests, and its development through dubious calculations and interpretations. That leaves us without any hope. But Derrida talks about the concept of justice, "outside and beyond the law", as an "infinitely irreducible" idea, which is "invincible to all scepticism". He goes on to explain: "One can recognize, and even accuse it of madness. And perhaps another sort of mysticism. Deconstruction is mad about this justice, mad with the desire for justice."

Is there a programme of action here? What does a messianic declaration of justice as an idea beyond law do to the doctrine of deconstruction? Socrates' dialogues, as they survive in Plato's writings, are pervaded with the idea of justice. Derrida traces the original sin of logocentrism to Plato. Deconstruction claims to be a programme to undo the entire tradition of Western philosophical thinking and discourse that has since developed. How does the idea of justice survive this programme and even become an irreducible infinity? Can it be that the actual problem that hampers a logical resolution to the question is the theoretical excess that the doctrine of deconstruction has been engaging in? That itself should be an interesting issue for inquiry and perhaps, our resource persons can turn for hints to yet another philosopher, Michael Dummett, a professor at Oxford, who also engages with the interconnected problems of language and metaphysics, realism and logic, meaning and metaphor, and truth-conditions and intuitionism.

The State and its Contestants in Contemporary South Asia

An essential field of inquiry is the origins of the modern State, its apparatus to order, organize, and enforce obedience, and the interests, understanding, and self-consciousness on which it rests in South Asia. It is acknowledged that the State in South Asia emerged after remaining subsumed under British imperialism, *sans* citizenship, for more than 150 years. The history of the State in South Asia is, in our view, also important to understand mutually dependent relationships between mercantile trade and the militarization of the modern State that ensured the European colonization of the world and, at the same time, consolidated the understanding of human rights as positive recognitions under the law. The monopoly of violence that the modern State holds is a corollary of these parallel processes. John Locke's idea of social contract and his list of basic human rights to "life, liberty, and property" were influenced by the interest he took in the affairs of the colonies. His theories on property developed out of the work he did as the secretary of the Board of Trade and Plantations, to which he had been appointed by Charles II in 1666 at the recommendation of Lord Ashley, one of the richest Englishmen of the period and a powerful defender of the British East India Company. The political philosophy of the liberal State, which John Locke pioneered, not only contributed to the success of the "Glorious Revolution" but also to the rise of a new leadership of the British East India Company, exemplified by men like Josiah Child who pioneered and implemented the policy of colonization as a necessity for the success of British trade interests. As Karl Marx pointed out in an article published in the *New York Daily Tribune* on the 11th of July 1853, the era of apparent liberty in Britain was "in reality the era of monopolies... authorized and nationalized by the sanction of Parliament". Liberal democracy, in this historical sense, represented "the first decisive victory of the bourgeoisie over the feudal aristocracy coinciding with the most pronounced reaction against the [common] people..." We must recall in this context that the Union between the Constitutional Monarchy and the monopolization of commercial interests in Britain was achieved with the East India Company offering enormous loans to the British State at the lowest possible interest rates. These loans could not be offered under the authoritarian regimes of Cromwell and even Charles II. The British Crown began to elbow the Company in India out of its imperial responsibilities only after loosing the American War of Independence. The process of negotiation to affect the transition between the landed aristocracy, leaders of the mercantile trade, and the new industrial bourgeoisie, and the leaders of a liberal State under a constitutional monarchy in Britain, which took seven and a half decades from 1783 to 1857 to be completed, played an important part in the development of legal guarantees of private property. Many important political voices involved in the so-called Reform Process, including Edmund Burke, who introduced the India Bill in 1783, James Mill and his son John Stuart Mill, as well as Jeremy Bentham, had themselves been important share-holders in the East India Company. When such are the historical foundations of the philosophy of human rights, it does not make sense for us to engage in the human rights discourse without paying attention to the histories of State-systems and their constitutional relations with citizens as they developed in the region.

South Asia became a British colony for the intertwined objectives to increase the money and the might of the conquering power under a trading company with a royal warrant. In 1699, even as Guru Govind Singh inaugurated the community of the *Khalsa* in Punjab, Josiah Child, the Governor of the East India Company, died in London after pioneering the position that the company's mercantile trade would fail against European competition unless it secured India as a colony. Child was the first Governor of the Company to inspire the English garrison in India to attack the Mughal forces under Aurangzeb at Surat in 1688. Although the clash ended with a temporary fiasco for the English, it led in 1696 to the establishment of a new base in Calcutta that inaugurated the English Empire in India in the real sense.

The British Empire in South Asia, unlike the Roman Empire in Europe and the Middle East, held its inhabitants as subject peoples without the rights of citizenship. Ironically, the modern concepts of "the rule of law", contrasted with arbitrary power, and constitutional governance, as the obverse of the rule of force, are attributed to the historical and political experiences emerging from the relations between the conquerors and the colonized. These experiences, their interpretations and interrogations are critical for our understanding of the politics of conflict and peace rampant across the subcontinent and we propose to introduce here a framework to be tested and debated on the canvass of narration and commentary, which the fifth Reader provides.

It is widely acknowledged that "identities" of politics were engineered and evolved even as the Indian subcontinent, as a British colony, emerged into the political commotions of modern times from the twilight years of the Mughal Empire. The transformations required the colonial masters to profess respect for popular claims to political rights. The umpteen diversities that characterized the sub-continent's society must have made the task rather difficult. To associate popular leaders with the government, it was necessary to arrange the kaleidoscopic mass of people into clearly definable sections. To the western political mind, reared in the consciousness of crusades and inquisitions, the religious identity of people was by far the most obvious basis for an independent social status. The introduction of the elective principle for representation in the government triggered off a self-assertive competition among various religious communities. Appealing to history to claim distinction over one's rivals became a technique of their competitive strategy.

The Hindu and the Buddhist sense of history had been forged largely by the eighteenth and early nineteenth century oriental scholarship that the English and other European scholars had pioneered. The Asiatic Society of Bengal, founded in 1784 at Calcutta, was the forum for the publication of their researches. Early Brahmos, Theosophists, Arya Samajists, and Ramakrishna missionaries had become acquainted with the merits of Sanskrit literature while Goethe and Herder were discovering them in Europe. The writings and translations of Sanskrit works by William Jones, Charles Wilkins, Henry Thomas Colebrooke, Jonathan Duncan, and later from other Europeans like Rudolf Von Roth and Max Muller were their common source. Ashoka was a mythological figure, also for the Indians, until James Prinsep deciphered the Brahmi and Kharoshti scripts to read his pillar and rock edicts. Indians did not know Buddha as a historical person before Alexander Csoma de Koros and B.G. Hodgson had opened the avenues for textual studies in Buddhist history and philosophy. Without men like Alexander Cunningham there would have been no archaeological corroboration of pre-Islamic Indian history. Discoveries in the Indus Valley culture had to wait the excavations carried out by John Marshall in 1920s. The leaders of the Hindu renaissance, beginning with Rammohan Roy, derived their philosophical attitudes and reformism from the works of these scholars.

There were also others, like the founders of Arya Samaj, whose attitude about the European contribution to the discovery of the "wonder that was India" was ambivalent, bordering on hostility. Conscious of their suffering under the Muslim conquest, fostered by historical discoveries of their original greatness, gave a new sharpness to the feelings of resentment they already nurtured against them. The Muslim and Sikh populations, unlike the Hindu, had not received their history from the English. On the contrary, the English arrival had ruined their supremacy. The English had usurped their kingdoms, and were distributing political rights to their rivals who were numerically stronger. When the British, in early 1900, began to move towards the ideals of representative democracy and self-rule, the leaders of the minority communities, conscious of the demographic realities and their political implications, began to insist and obtain special constitutional safeguards and regional autonomy. For the Hindus, of course, the Muslims were tyrants of yesteryears who, their tongue in jowl, were demanding constitutional safeguards as a religious minority.

The conspicuous leaders of the people in the period, across all communities, were mostly lawyers who had received their education in England. They believed in the unity of all people and recognized the importance of communal harmony and political accommodation. The critical question that guided their politics for a constitutional framework of State in the colonial era, and which remains pivotal to the contemporary political discourse in the subcontinent, can be paraphrased as follows: Can a people who claim their entitlement to national resources on the basis of an imagined religious identity, that also makes them numerically the strongest, ever succeed in harnessing the forces of democracy for their long-term interests, without ensuring the protection of religious minorities and the defence of human rights of politically discontented segments of the population as well as the non-dominant communities in the sub-continental peripheries? The answer, with any knowledge of the regional history, was and remains a clear no.

In order to become a moving force of history, this consciousness required clear constitutional principles to guide the process of participatory democracy into an evolving institutional matrix of relations between the rulers and the ruled. The process gained impetus following Curzon's 1905 partition of Bengal, and by 1916 succeeded in crystallizing the constitutional principles around which the subcontinent, with all its diversity and problems, had a good chance to become a united, federal, and strong nation.

The annulment of Bengal's partition and the transfer of India's capital to Delhi embodied the principle that the provinces, organized as autonomous units on the basis of regional, linguistic, and cultural unity, would federate under a centre that would not interfere in their internal administration except in emergencies and to protect minorities from persecution. This was, by the standards of political thinking of our own times, an enlightened view of the State, conceived not in monolithic terms but as "an agency for recognizing groups, determining what legal status and rights they shall have, supervising and coordinating their interrelationships, and itself conducting certain kinds of functions in which all have a common interest."[6]

The second principle, which found expression in the Lucknow Pact of 1916 between the Congress and the Muslim League leaders, suggested that the religious minorities would receive constitutional safeguards against their anxieties about the majoritarian tyranny through agreement among responsible leaders of various communities. As an example of historical synchronicity, the Pact conveyed the same sentiment which pervaded the draft Treaty of Versailles with Poland and was expressed in French Prime Minister Georges Clemenceau's letter of the 14th of June 1919 to the Polish Prime Minister Ignace Jan Paderewski, also a famous pianist: "Unfortunately, the races have been estranged by long years of bitter hostility. It is believed that these populations will be more easily reconciled to their new position if they know that from the very beginning they have assured protection and adequate guarantees against any danger of unjust treatment of oppression."[7] The Lucknow Pact of 1916, like the Minorities Treaties in East Central Europe and the Balkans in the aftermath of World War I, was inspired by two clear political objectives: [1] to guarantee equality for members of the minority groups with the majority population, and [2] to ensure that they could preserve their distinct identities and cultural traditions against threats of assimilation. The 1916 Pact was based on the recognition that if the elective principle was to be the basis for Indian political reforms, minority communities would have to get constitutional safeguards against the majority rule of Hindus. The Pact conceded a separate electorate to the Muslims with a "weightage system" that guaranteed their representation in the Councils in greater numbers than their democratic strength allowed.

With this concession, the Hindu leaders made them withdraw their support for Bengal's partition, which had been done primarily to assuage the Muslim political anxiety that the introduction of the elective principle through the *Indian Councils Act of 1892* would further reinforce the Hindu dominance. The partition of what was then an extremely large State of Bengal had created an eastern conclave with Dacca as its capital that had an overwhelming Muslim majority. Bal Gangadhar Tilak, the most popular Hindu leader of the period and the architect of the Lucknow Pact of 1916, on this occasion announced: "It has been said that we, Hindus, have yielded too much to our Muslim brothers. I am sure I represent the sense of the Hindu community all over India when I say that we could not have yielded too much…."[8] Experience had taught the Hindu nationalist leaders of the period that they should show magnanimity to win over the Muslim population into the nationalist camp. Given their overwhelmingly superior numbers, Hindus could not lose much by making concessions to the groups that feared their domination. They recognized that given the history of sub-national hostilities, there simply was no other way of welding India into one democratic Nation-State.

Fundamental human rights, especially the political ones, became part of the sub-continental paradigm of Statehood through the first fervent *Satyagraha* against the British rule in 1919, which Gandhi led against the enactment of *the Rowlatt Act* in that year. The British government had passed the *Rowlatt Act*, to create special courts for the trial of revolutionary suspects, on the recommendations of a judicial committee, which had examined the evidence bearing on the revolutionary conspiracies then rife in the subcontinent. Gandhi did not impugn the findings, but opposed the Act on the principle that "elementary rights of individuals" were more important than the political interests of the Empire. Gandhi also argued that a State that takes away fundamental human rights and legal safeguards against malicious prosecution would draw more people to revolutionary conspiracies than it could curb through such legislation.

These were the three fundamental constitutional principles—provincial autonomy, constitutional safeguards for minorities, and fundamental human rights—that guided the search for independence and self-rule within South Asia. Gradually over the next three decades, these ideals acquired clearer constitutional forms through developments that drew strength from both official and citizens' initiatives. The two *Government of India Acts of 1919 and 1935* developed from the recommendations of private constitutional bodies like All Parties Conferences, the Motilal Nehru Committee Report of 1929 and the Muslim League's Charter of fourteen points, also of 1929, the two Round Table Conferences of 1930 and 1931, with Gandhi attending the latter. The Cabinet Mission Plan of May 1946 itself evolved from difficult negotiations involving diverse political groups throughout the war years and thereafter. A Constituent Assembly was formed on the basis of this Mission Plan which promised independence for the Indian subcontinent as a decentralized federation with substantial safeguards for minority populations, including territorial autonomy in regions where they constituted a considerable proportion of the population. The Mission Plan was endorsed, albeit reluctantly, by proponents of Pakistan.

With the benefit of hindsight, it is possible to assert that if the Hindu leaders had kept the Muslims on their side, pledging to them the safeguards they wanted, the postcolonial politics within the subcontinent might have taken a different course. However, we must consider their failure in a larger historical context: the antipathies that divided various communities, the "curse of ignorance"; all that dead wood was not easy to ride over. The Muslim minority, still hankering after its lost glory, was not willing to accept the majority rule. The political parties were divided, no matter what their disclaimers, by sectional interests rather than by broad issues. There was no tradition of debating the burning issues of the day, in a spirit of detachment from narrow political loyalties. The masses were lacking in formal education and were completely innocent of any experience in participatory democracy—except in village councils. The social restrictions, which compartmentalized the Indian people into a myriad of autonomous units, were formidable obstacles in the way of promoting coexistence through accommodation. The deeply ingrained feelings of distrust, which were pitting one group against the other at the popular level, tended to defeat all attempts at conciliation at the top.

The Lucknow Pact became possible precisely because its authors on both sides were self-appointed leaders who did not thrive on the cultivation of popular prejudice or following. Tilak was a popular leader and a staunch Hindu. But in his intellectual makeup he was nearly as aloof from the common Hindu as Jinnah was from the common Muslim. As the two were alike in this respect, they could afford to sit together and reach a deal. Gandhi's rise on the political scene would soon make such deals impossible. Gandhi represented *the people's power*, but he also carried with him much of the peoples' atavistic inertia, ignorance, and introversion. He disliked Jinnah for his Western manners and his use of English. He also disdained Tilak for his lofty intellectual airs. As chance would have it, Tilak died on the 1st of August 1920, the very day fixed by Gandhi for the inauguration of his first non-cooperation movement.

The arousal of masses under Gandhi's leadership is a separate story. He preached non-violence and Hindu-Muslim unity, and came to be recognized as a *Mahatma*. But the realities of social fragmentation, communal distrust, and the politics of division manifested themselves in recurrent cycles of communal carnage. Outbursts of physical violence followed a regular pattern triggered by simple techniques of instigation. Muslims slaughtered cow, revered by Hindus as a holy animal, and the Hindus retaliated by putting pork, considered unholy by Muslims, in mosques to stir up communal mayhem. Any other trivial provocation would serve the purpose just as well. British officials dealt with these problems by the book, with feelings of amused complacency, except when they threatened to escalate into big troubles.

These outbursts of violence, known by the queer name of communal riots, provided the backdrop for the momentous constitutional developments that led to the transfer of power and the division of the subcontinent into India and Pakistan in 1947 amid a bloody carnage and a colossal displacement of people across the new borders. While the British had meant to rule India, they had viewed communal riots from an administrative angle. When the time came for them to leave, the communal frenzy and its consequences did not seem to bother them much. Pendral Moon, once Secretary to the Governor of Punjab, expressed the English attitude in a letter addressed to a colleague on the 24th of November 1946: "...The importance of our cutting the cables and leaving Indians [*read people of the subcontinent!*] to manage their own affairs [with our help if they request it] becomes all the more urgent as the strife of parties out here increases. In fact the worse the threat of chaos, the more pressingly incumbent on us it is to depart. Please make the powers that be understand this simple paradox...."[9]

When Mountbatten's proposal of partition went before the British Cabinet for approval in May 1947, Pethik Lawrence, the Secretary of State for India, conveyed the official position in a letter dated the 9th of May 1947: "Under your proposals they [the Sikhs] will be divided and I do not think that any subsequent adjustment of boundaries can possibly begin to satisfy the claims they put forward... But if you are satisfied that a Boundary Commission, with terms of reference such as will help to keep the Sikhs quiet until the transfer of power, can be set up without provoking the hostility of the two major communities, I shall be very ready to support your view to my colleagues."[10]

Thus was the decision to partition the subcontinent taken. Sarvepalli Gopal, a noted historian of the period, suggests that in 1947 Indian leaders did not know what they were doing: "The most striking feature of the negotiations for partition and the transfer of power in the summer of 1947 was the ambiguity on most of the vital issues. Was secession to be total or partial; would power be handed over by the British wholly or only in a measure, and what were the implications of a referendum in the Frontier province?—on none of these matters was there any clear understanding. The Congress, in its eagerness for finality, lost hold of certainty..."[11]

The leaders who precipitated the surgical creation of India and Pakistan developed retrospective "histories" for popular consumption to blame the partition on the intransigence and the treachery of their notional enemies. Jawaharlal Nehru and his Congress colleagues did not even accept the creation of Pakistan as a final and irreversible reality. On the 29th of April 1947, Nehru wrote to his friend K.P.S. Menon: "I have no doubt whatever that sooner or later India will have to function as a united country. Perhaps the best way to reach that stage is to go through some kind of a partition now."[12] The same day, he wrote to General Cariappa: "Of one thing I am convinced that ultimately there will be a united and strong India. We have often to go through the valley of the shadow before we reach the sun-lit mountain tops".[13] Nehru did not keep his thoughts on the subject confined to his own small circle of friends and colleagues but shared them with the people. In his radio broadcast on the 3rd of June 1947, by which he appealed to the nation to accept the partition plan, Nehru said: "It may be that in this way we shall reach that united India sooner than otherwise and then she will have a stronger and more secure foundation."[14]

What did the two countries of India and Pakistan as "territories" exemplify? Did they represent intergenerational memories of people residing in them; their mythical roots; histories; locations of "identity formation"? Did they fulfil *instrumentally* effective standards of "territoriality" as viable and defensible demarcations?

The oldest human settlements located in the floodplains of the river Indus, which gives the Indian subcontinent its name; the later Indus Valley cities of Harappa and Mohenjodaro; the lands associated with the hymns of *Rig Veda* and high Sanskritic culture, all became part of Pakistan. The vast numbers of Muslims in Uttar Pradesh, Assam, Bengal, Bihar, and in the southern peninsula, who had customarily voted for the Muslim League and had enthusiastically supported the call for Pakistan as a confederal idea, became India's hostages There was no territorial connection between West Pakistan and East Pakistan, which broke away, with India's support, to become the independent State of Bangladesh in 1971. Cited by India as a historical refutation of the ideology of religious nationalism that constituted Pakistan, Bangladesh remains mired in societal conflicts too overwhelming for the State institutions to legitimately control. India, on the strength of its size, its superior military capabilities and more alluring rhetoric of secularism and socialism, tried to hide its people-geography mismatch especially in its peripheries by modelling itself as an "organic state", expanding with its growing strength as in Kashmir and Nagaland, and marrying its expansionist nationalism with a romantic concept of indivisibility.

It is probably futile for us to speculate about how events might have developed if the mirage of a centralized political economy, and the game of sectarian manipulation, had not combined to destroy the vision of a federal democratic State which would have substantial safeguards for the minority communities and fundamental human rights for all. However, a discussion on the distortions of democracy and human rights, and the plight of minorities within the subcontinent today, which is animated by a restorative intent, requires an explanation that accounts for their prevalence. In the preface to his monumental work on the Indian constitution, H.M. Seervai points out that by rejecting the basis on which the subcontinent had become politically united since 1857, the Indian leaders had abandoned the path of "peaceful construction, cooperation and ordered progress". Seervai argues that the Constituent Assembly created a strong centre under the conviction that it would put down the fissiparous tendencies in the provinces. The conviction, according to Seervai, was misplaced: once the basis of political unity of the subcontinent in the division of powers and the communal safeguards was dissolved, a strong centre by itself was inadequate to eliminate the civil strife, disunity, and confusion that are rooted in the heterogeneous nature of the society in South Asia.[15] This is a conclusion that appears helpful to us not only to understand the forces of history that have contributed to the mess South Asia has become, but also to broadly indicate the outlines of what can be done to remedy the situation.

Also, Seervai's arguments, at least partially, explain why India, notwithstanding its image as a regional power, its aggressive foreign policy engagements within South Asia and the claim of being the largest constitutional democracy in the world, has failed to ferment a democratic political culture in its neighbourhood that can at least hold the forces of social discontent away from violent channels.

Jawaharlal Nehru interfered in the affairs of Nepal in November 1950 by rescuing King Tribhuvan from Rana captivity, engineering an armed rebellion to force the abdication of the regime, and commanding a constitutional settlement between King Tribhuvan, the Ranas, and the Nepali Congress, in February 1951, known as the Delhi Agreement. The Agreement paved the way for the first democratically elected government in Nepal, formed under B.P. Koirala in May 1959. Forty-five years down the line, Nepal is reeling under a state of insurgency and a royal takeover that has developed out of political disillusionments about the possibilities of social justice within the parliamentary system that had been established in 1990.

There are clear Indian imprints on Sri Lanka's travails of constitutionalism, beginning with the introduction of its official language policy in 1956, as well as its ordeals with extremism, ethnic violence, and the peace processes. By proclaiming Sinhala the official language of Ceylon in 1956, Bandaranaike, the fourth Prime Minister of the country who came from a wealthy Christian background and had the advantage of higher education at Cambridge and Oxford, was doing what Jawaharlal Nehru did to deal with the agitations for linguistic reorganization of the states within India. Since then, Sri Lanka appears to be intimately emulating India's own infatuations with State intransigence, extremism, ethnic violence, and peace processes that remain oblivious to the substantial issues of social and political discontent and exhaust themselves in discussions over power-sharing mechanisms with warlords.

Bhutan too appears to be under India's shadows. A small country between the eastern Himalayas and Tibet with a population of less than 2 million, estimated by others to be as low as 600,000, Bhutan first came under the British sphere of influence in April 1774 when the East India Company took away its independence in foreign relations. With the treaty of Sinchula, signed in 1865, Bhutan became a virtual protectorate. In 1907, Ugyen Wangchuk, a feudal warlord, supportive of British policies, took over the government of Bhutan after subduing other territorial governors, known as Penlops, who resented the British intrusions. The treaty of Punakha, signed in January 1910, bestowed the title of *Maharaja* on the first Wangchuk ruler of Bhutan who was received with a 15-gun salute, like all heads of princely states within the Indian subcontinent, at the Imperial Coronation Durbar in Delhi on 12th December, 1911.

With the departure of the British from the Indian subcontinent, Bhutan first approached Sikkim, Nepal, and Tibet with the idea to form a larger confederation to counterbalance India's size and significance. The initiative remaining fruitless, Bhutan signed a treaty of perpetual peace and friendship with India at Darjeeling in August 1949. The treaty did not say anything about Bhutan's foreign policy and defence. Jawaharlal Nehru visited Bhutan in September 1958 to assure the kingdom that India had no design against Bhutanese independence; only the urge to safeguard their good neighbourhood against threats from outside. China loomed in the background. The Chinese military action in Tibet, in the spring of 1959, impelled Bhutan to withdraw its representative from Lhasa and to close all trade and commerce with China. Over the next two years, the Bhutanese King visited New Delhi several times and went back with India's promises of economic assistance. India also went out of its way to introduce Bhutan, as a full-fledged Monarchy, to the wider world outside, procuring for it membership in the UN in September 1971.

In 1973, India absorbed Sikkim, an independent kingdom ruled by a *Chogyal* or King belonging to the Namgyal dynasty since the early 1600s, as an associate member of the Indian Union. Sikkim became India's 22nd State in 1975. Sikkim's merger into India created political anxieties within Bhutan, precipitating anti-democratic schemes of self-consolidation. In 1985, Bhutan introduced a new Citizenship Act, which was implemented retroactively to take away the citizenship rights of the Nepali-speaking people in the south of the country, constituting more than a quarter of the total population.

Sections of the Nepali-speaking population were forced to leave the country reportedly to loosen their demographic hold in the South. Nepal endures more than 100,000 Bhutanese refugees.

This is the broad panorama of conflict between the State and some of its contestants on the South Asian scene today.

Notes

1. Dworkin, Ronald, *Taking Rights Seriously*, 2nd ed. (Cambridge: Harvard University Press, 1977); Fichte, Johann Gottlieb, *Foundations of Natural Right* (Cambridge: Cambridge University Press, 2000); Foucault, Michel, *Politics, Philosophy, Culture: Interviews and Other Writings*, 1977-1984, ed. by Lawrence D. Kritzman (New York: Routledge, 1988); Hart, H.L.A., *The Concept of Law* (Oxford: Clarendon Press, 1997); Hayek, F.A., *Law, Legislation and Liberty*, 2 vols. (Chicago, IL: University of Chicago Press, 1978); Kant, Immanuel, *Political Writings*, ed. by H. Reiss, transl. H.B. Nisbet, (Cambridge: Cambridge University Press, 1991); MacIntyre, Alasdair, *Whose Justice? Which Rationality?* (London: Duckworth, 1988); Marx, Karl and Friedrich Engels, *The Communist Manifesto* (Oxford: Oxford University Press, 1998); Paine, Thomas, *Common Sense and the Rights of Man* (New York: NAL-Dutton, 1984); Rawls, John, *Justice as Fairness* (Cambridge, MA: Harvard University Press, 2001); Rousseau, Jean-Jacques, *Discourse on the Origin of Inequality* (Oxford: Oxford University Press, 1994); Weil, Simone, *Oppression and Liberty* (Amherst, MA: University of Massachusetts Press, 1988).
2. His other works, not cited in our list, are: *The Archaeology of Knowledge*, (New York: Routledge, 1990); *The Birth of the Clinic* (New York: Routledge, 1990); *The History of Sexuality*, 3 vols. (London: Penguin 1988); *Madness and Civilization* (New York: Routledge, 1990); and *The Order of Things* (New York: Random House, 1994); *Religion and Culture*, (Manchester: Manchester University Press, 1999).
3. Aristotle, *Politics*, trans. T. Sinclair, rev. T. J. Saunders (London: Penguin, 1981); Bentham, Jeremy, *Handbook of Political Fallacies* (New York: Harper Bros, 1962) and *An Introduction to the Principles of Morals and Legislation* (New York: Hafner, 1970); Bodin, Jean, *On Sovereignty*, ed. J.H. Franklin (Cambridge: Cambridge University Press, 1992); Burks, Edmund, *Reflections on the Revolution in France* (Oxford: Oxford University Press, 1993); Cicero, *On Duties*, ed. M. Griffin and M. Atkins, (Cambridge: Cambridge University Press, 1991), and *On the Commonwealth and on the Laws* (Cambridge: Cambridge University Press, 1999); R.G. Collingwood's *The Idea of History* (Oxford:

Clarendon Press, 1994), *Essays in Political Philosophy* (Oxford: Oxford University Press, 1995), and *The New Leviathan* (Oxford: Clarendon Press, 1993); works of Karl Marx, and Friedrich Engels, primarily their *Communist Manifesto* (Oxford, OUP, 1998); Ferguson, Adam, *Essay on the History of Civil Society* (New Brunswick, NJ: Transaction, 1980); Gramsci, Antonio, *Letters from Prison* (New York: Columbia University Press, 1994); Habermas, Juergen, *Legitimating Crisis*, (Cambridge: Polity, 1988), *Philosophical Discourse of Modernity*, (Cambridge: Polity, 1990), and *The Structural Transformation of the Public Sphere* (Cambridge: Polity, 1992); Hegel's political writings, mainly *Philosophy of Right*; *Leviathan* by Thomas Hobbes; *The Limits of State Action* and *The Sphere and Duties of Government* by Wilhelm von Humboldt,; David Hume's *Political Essays*; *Political Writings* by Immanuel Kant and Leibniz; John Locke's *Two Treatises of Government*; Machiavelli's *The Prince*, *The Discourses*, and *Selected Political Writings*; Mill, John Stuart, *On Liberty* and *Utilitarianism*; Montesquieu's *The Spirit of the Laws*; Plato's *The Republic* and *The Laws*; William of Ockham's *Short Discourse on Tyrannical Government*; Thomas Paine's *Political Writings* and *Common Sense*; Vilfredo Pareto's *The Mind and Society*; Karl Popper's *The Open Society and Its Enemies*; John Rawls' *Political Liberalism*; Rousseau's *Discourse on the Origin of Inequality* and his *Government of Poland*; Bertrand Russell's *Principles of Social Reconstruction*; *The Man versus the State* and *Other Political Writings* by Herbert Spencer; Spinoza's *Theological-Political Treatise*; Voltaire's *Letters Concerning the English Nation*; Max Weber's *Oppression and Liberty* normally figure as essential reading.

4. Hanna Arendt's *The Human Condition* (Chicago: University of Chicago Press, 1990); *On Revolution* (New York: Viking Penguin, 1991), and *On Violence* (New York: Harcourt Brace, 1970) should be easily available in any good library. Jacques Derrida's *Politics of Friendship* (New York: Verso, 1997), and "Deconstruction and the Possibility of Justice", Drucilla Cornell, *et al.*, eds. (New York: Routledge, 1992) should not be very difficult to find.
5. *The Other Heading: Reflections on Today's Europe* (Bloomington: Indiana University Press, 1992); and *Specters of Marx: The State of the Debt, the Work of Mourning, and the New International* (New York: Routledge, 1994).
6. Kymlicka, Will, *The Rights of Minority Cultures* (Oxford: Oxford University Press, 1995) 52.
7. Rodolfo de Nova, "The International Protection of National Minorities and Human Rights", *Howard Law Journal* 11 (1965) 278.
8. H.F. Owen, "Negotiating the Lucknow Pact," *Journal of Asian Studies* (May 1972) 561-87.
9. Extract from the Letter of EP Moon, November 24th 1946, Short

Collection, Mss. Eur. F. 189/14, Correspondence & Papers on the Indian political problem, IOR:L, London.

10. Private and Secret Letter from Secretary of State for India to His Excellency the Viceroy, dated 9 May 1947, MC, Mss. Eur. F.200/140, IORL, London.
11. Sarvepalli Gopal, *Jawaharlal Nehru*, Vol. I (Delhi: Oxford University Press, 1979) 357.
12. *Ibid.*, 343.
13. *Ibid.*, 344.
14. Nehru's Broadcast, 3 June 1947, *Framing of India's Constitution*, Vol. I (New Delhi: Indian Institute of Public Administration, 1966), pp. 527-529.
15. Seervai, H.M., *Constitutional Law of India, A Critical Commentary*, Vol. I, 4th ed. (Bombay: Tripathi, 1991) I-IX.

Chapter Two

Citizenship: Its Hierarchies, Ambivalences and Exclusions

As we already observed, a discourse on human rights, their rationale and reach within the established framework of politics requires a fairly comprehensive understanding of State-systems and their constitutional relations with citizens and others who come under their sovereign domains but are excluded from the protective bulwark of citizenship. This presupposes an examination and analysis of a number of problematic issues. Some of them, to illustrate the range, are:

- tensions between the demands of discipline by the institutions of authority and their capacity to enforce governmental responsibilities;
- the framework of citizens' entitlements and associated arrangements;
- the explicit and veiled hierarchies of citizenship;
- the stratifications of society into "class", "caste", "religious", "ethnic", "nationalistic" and "linguistic" groups and their implications on political cultures;
- the realities of exploitative dominance of men over women, their impact on the ethos of governance, and the dynamics of the movement for gender justice; and
- the normative standards that define the limits of the State's sovereign exercises, principles and practices of participatory democracy, and the space for dissent.

What is Citizenship?

The list of problematic issues that comes under discussion within the rubric of citizenship, its hierarchies and "exclusions" is redoubtable and this essay can aim at no more than to state the principal themes of investigation and make a rapid appraisal of the main stances of inquiry, pivotal to the discourse on human rights and peace. We shall do so primarily from the perspectives of religious minorities, women, immigrants, and refugees with reference to our contemporary experiences.

Etymologically, citizenship means membership in the political community of a city. However, it is used almost exclusively to mean political membership of a State and is often used synonymously with *nationality* even though the membership of a nation has a wider, meaning and may or may not come with citizenship. But let us not get into these complexities from the very start. Citizenship is supposed to come with common rights and common obligations, including the obligation to defend the country. Most constitutional democracies state these rights and obligations, also called duties, in their constitutions. But as we shall notice, constitutional professions do not make them always real. For example, Article 7 in Part 2 of the Nepali Constitution, adopted in 1962, defined citizenship as follows:

> "Every person who has his domicile in Nepal and—(a) who was born in Nepal; or (b) either of whose parents was born in Nepal; or who, as a woman, has any kind of relation with a citizen of Nepal constituting matrimony in accordance with the laws and customs of Nepal; or (d) who has already obtained a certificate of citizenship in accordance with the laws of Nepal; shall be a citizen of Nepal at the commencement of the Constitution." Curiously enough, Article 8(3) of the Nepali constitution also provides that "citizenship of a person may be terminated if—(a) he has raised arms or has made an attempt to raise arms against Nepal or has committed any other offence against the State; or (b) he has not served or avoids serving the State, during war or any other emergency, in the manner prescribed by law."[1]

Article 7 of 1962 Constitution remained valid until the promulgation of the November 1990 Constitution when the provisions for the annulment of citizenship were removed. However, Article 9(7) of the New Constitution says: "The termination of the citizenship of Nepal shall be as determined by law."[2] The law is the *Nepal Citizenship Act, 1964* whose section 10[2], (a), (b) and (c) not only retain the terms of disqualification under Article 8(3), but include the additional clause allowing annulment of citizenship when a person is found to assist an enemy State in a situation of war.[3]

We shall consider the significance of these constitutional provisions of citizenship for the obtaining environment of widespread insurgency in the country during our discussion on the crisis of deliberative democracy in Nepal. For a more introductory purpose, let us continue here with our inquiry into the general principles of citizenship.

Is citizenship merely a legal recognition of domicile and the attendant rights to participation and protection within the political system that people inhabit? What are the normative criteria for the exclusion of many who dwell within a territory, like immigrants and refugees, from the status of citizenship? Is it possible to conceive of permanent members of a society who are, however, not citizens? Is it possible to conceive of permanent members of a society who are citizens but are excluded from the decision-making processes of the political system, or who are admitted to them only partially? What are the roots of such apparent anomalies in the histories and knowledge systems that support the political enterprises of the Establishment?

In its old usage, citizenship applied to equal participating members of the city States of Greece and later within the Roman Republic. Citizens were actually the elite. The vast majority of the permanently resident population, including all women, slaves, and foreigners, were not covered by the recognition of citizenship, which meant exclusion from participatory rights.

The segmental divisions, hierarchies, and civil as well as religious segregations within the caste system in South Asia, whose working was first reported by an independent foreign observer Megasthenes in the third century B.C., excluded the vast majority of inhabitants from the very framework of humanity. The laws of Manu, which codified these exclusions on the basis of a curious theory of pollution through contact, have informed the caste practices in the subcontinent right up to our own times. The exclusions within the caste system were without remedy. They were, in principle, contingent on birth and, therefore, absolute.[4]

These exclusions meant deprivation of the sense of belonging that comes from being welded to a framework of common values and purposes within a community; in other words, full membership within a community with attendant stakes in preserving and promoting common interests. What are the vestiges of this tendency of exclusion and how do they survive and take new forms within modern societies? How do the notions of belonging to a society in this larger sense and the appending conception of loyalty harmonize with the essentially individualistic orientation of modern laws that define both the duties and rights in narrow and mechanical terms as the instruments of self-interest?

The Rule of Equality and the Underdog

The guiding principle of a modern inquiry about the facets of citizenship is the rule of equality, generally pledged by constitutions. The rule arises from the histories of popular mobilization for freedom from subjugation, inequalities, and exploitation, which inaugurated the era after the European empires. The histories of the caste system in South Asia; the consciousness of cruelties against women; the annals of religious persecution and violence begotten by intolerance and bigotry; and the legacies of slavery and subjugation in the age of European empires: all contributed to the naissance of a presumptive pledge in all modern Constitutions that all individuals within organized societies, irrespective of their class, caste, colour, sex, and religion, are entitled to equal terms of participation, respect, and responsibility. But the old attitudes, despite new laws, survive, and exercises of power, with their roots in the dominant knowledge-systems, find new ways to block the realization of rights.

The State of Massachusetts first outlawed slavery in 1783 with reference to the Bill of Rights, which said: "all men are born free and equal." The Thirteenth Amendment to the US Constitution in 1865 abolished slavery altogether. But according to an estimate given by the US Secretary of State Colin Powell in 2001, at least 7,00,000 people every year, the vast majority of them female, are victims of forced human trafficking, known as the modern slave trade.[5]

Racial segregation and discrimination in the United States thrived under the Supreme Court's innovative theory of "separate but equal" citizenship propounded through *Plessy v. Ferguson* in 1896. Segregation in educational institutions supposedly came to an end with the Supreme Court's May 1954 decision in *Brown v. Board of Education* and the Omnibus *Civil Rights Bill*, passed by the US Congress in June 1964, in the wake of the movement for black rights that started from Alabama in 1955 and then spread all over the Untied States under Martin Luther King's leadership. The *Civil Rights Bill* supposedly ended all forms of discrimination against colour and race. But several recent studies on the role of race and its influence on the criminal justice system within the United States show how entrenched racially motivated violence remains and why so little can be done to remedy the situation despite the new laws and an active judiciary. Clearly, old prejudices continue to taint the judicial processes of interpreting the law and the evidence.[6]

The same must be evident to those who pay attention to the plight of *Dalits* in India. Savagery and violent discrimination against 160 million of them, who continue to be described interchangeably as *harijan* meaning "god's people", and "untouchable", remains rampant 59 years after the country's independence. The National Commission for Scheduled Castes and Scheduled Tribes reports a total of 98,349 cases of violent crime against members of the lowest caste. The hold of the caste system, with its emphasis on colour and social hierarchy, remains firm. Yet untouchability is a crime under Articles 14, 15, and 17 of the Indian Constitution. The *Scheduled Castes and Scheduled Tribes Prevention of Atrocities Act of 1989* (1989 Act) prescribes prosecution and punishment for crimes against *Dalits*. But the Act, without an active and committed agency for enforcement, remains inefficacious.[7]

The principle of affirmative action is an established principle of legislative and administrative endeavour under Article 16 of the Indian Constitution. But the law, as the reference to rights, can achieve very limited results when established social traditions nullify its intent. For example, it is hardly meaningful to discuss women's reproductive rights, practices of polygamy, female genital surgeries, and laws and practices impacting dowry murders, prostitution, and human trafficking without reference to socio-religious customs and opinions and their influence on State policies notwithstanding their secular pretensions. Likewise, the principles of equality before the law and equal protection of the law, to have a minimal secular relevance require a legal regime that does not make distinctions between men and women and their sexual preferences in matters affecting marriage, divorce, parental rights, and property.

The working of equality principles in law becomes a puzzling question when we examine how the rules of nationality apply differently for men and women, arising out of a male construction of dominance and dependence. Until fairly recently, a woman automatically gained her husband's nationality on marriage, involuntarily moving onto other nationalities if her husband changed his citizenship, her own personal preferences having absolutely no relevance in the matter. The example highlights the power of patriarchy within the cross-connections of the society and the State.

A discourse and enunciation of rights that takes place outside such an exhaustive repertoire of issues of inquiry may have very little relevance within the praxes of politics and its emancipatory possibilities.

The guarantees of equality in law apply to individuals. However, is it not so that every complaint of discrimination and claim of right to equality, almost invariably, points to groups and classes of people who are exposed to injustice from better organized, dominant, and politically powerful groups? Why does the process of adjudicating complaints and claims of discrimination, as well as "affirmative action", within the framework of a presumptive guarantee of equality appear to reinforce the collective identities of the disadvantaged and, more often than not, seem to perpetuate the stigma associated with the realities of subordination?

It is common to invoke the imagery of hierarchy to express the gradations and the line-up of social subordination and control within the canvass of citizenship. The imagery suggests a static arrangement with a dominant group on the top and the group singled out for maximum injustice, like the *Shudra* within the Hindu system of caste, at the rock bottom. The imagery may be helpful for understanding the equations of power within an insular social system without mobility, which is also impervious to external influences. But the modern concept of citizenship is dynamic and, often, seems like a movement within a spiral. Certainly, the static imagery of hierarchy fails to capture the complexity, inner tensions, and external influences bearing on social clusters within. We must also recognize that the principle of equality is a hypothetical imperative, premised on the assumption that it remains a societal end-objective. We should try to discover whether or not this is so through dispassionate observation and analysis of the social phenomena.

The Significance of the Ahmadi Experience in Pakistan

The history of State formation in South Asia, as we observed in the first part of the introductory note, witnessed a parallel accumulation of statements of political principles, constitutional pledges and internal law codes professing respect for the freedom of religion and protection for the adherents of different religions from persecution by the forces of intolerance. Yet, extant realities belie these professions. States and their instruments in South Asia, including the legislature and the judiciary, appear to have become increasingly susceptible to the currents of intolerance surging and subsiding in the shifting alliances within the majoritarian politics. The experience of Gujarat in India is still fresh. Here, we should briefly refer to the significance of the Ahmadi religious community's experience in Pakistan for the framework of citizenship in the country.

Tayyab Mahmud, Associate Professor of Law at Cleveland-Marshall College of Law, has closely examined the Pakistani judicial attitudes towards the Ahmadi religious community to outline the relationship between majoritarian attitudes and State practices.[8] Followers of Mirza Ghulam Ahmad [1835-1908], who considered himself to be a prophetic successor of Muhammad, the promised *Mehdi*, are stigmatized by the adherents of mainstream Islamic sects as heretics. The Ahmadis themselves are a divided lot about the status of Mirza Ghulam Ahmad. One segment of the followers from Qadian, the birthplace of Ahmad, regard him as the promised Messiah and a successor to Muhammad. Others, known as "Lahori" regard him as a reformer. However, all followers of Ahmad, irrespective of their position on his prophet-hood, are condemned by the conventional Islamic establishment to be a blasphemous lot. A report by the National Human Rights Commission of Pakistan on the *State of Human Rights in Pakistan 1993*, published in 1994, highlights the plight of Ahmadis under political persecution in the country. The footnote below lists out the basic literature that covers the origins, the current practices and the problems of the Ahmadi religious minority in Pakistan.[9]

Zaheeruddin v. State, a case decided by the Supreme Court of Pakistan in 1993, upheld the validity of the *Anti-Islamic Activities of Quadiani Group, Lahori Group and Ahmadis (Prohibition and Punishment) Ordinance, 1984*, which criminalizes Ahmadi religious practices in contradiction with the guarantee of freedom of religion in the Pakistani Constitution.[10] The case arose from an Ahmadi attempt to challenge the constitutional validity of the Ordinance, popularly known as *Ordinance XX*, on the plea that its prohibitions vitiated the guarantees of freedom of speech, equality of citizenship, and equal protection of the law under Articles 19 and 25 of the Pakistani Constitution. Tayyab Mahmud's paper traces the history of judicial capitulation before fundamentalist mobilization in Pakistan whose creation was inaugurated by Jinnah's famous speech before the first session of Pakistan's Constituent Assembly. Jinnah had said: "You are free; you are free to go to your temples, you are free to go to your mosques or any other place of worship in this State of Pakistan... You may belong to any religion or caste or creed—that has nothing to do with the business of the State... We are starting in the days when there is no discrimination, no distinction between one community and another, no discrimination between one caste or creed and another. We are starting with this fundamental principle that we are all citizens and equal citizens of one State."[11]

Tayyab Mahmud shows how Jinnah's speech was rooted in the history of the Muslim struggle for constitutional safeguards for religious minorities within the framework of a representative government, and how the post-partition transformations of polity destroyed those ideological roots. The analysis raises several intriguing questions.

Migrations and their Meanings

In a separate work, Tayyab Mahmud examines the phenomenon of migration in South Asia and the complex ways in which it implicates the organizing principles of the dominant political wisdom in the region concerning society, the state, sovereignty, citizenship, identity, and borders.[12] The following questions encapsulate the positions of inquiry that Tayyab Mahmud adopts: "Are the causes, sources and processes of migration uniform and predictable? Is the migrant available for sovereignty's demand for complete allegiance? Can the migrant partake of a pre-existing imagined community, the nation? Is the migrant compatible with the institutional designs of the State? Is migrant identity commensurable with requisites of citizenship?"

Tayyab Mahmud explores these questions within the framework of colonial encounters between "people" and "power" that has for long been dislocating the populace in the process of developing a global system of accumulation founded on the age-old principles of division of labour. As examples of this process, Tayyab Mahmud takes up three instances of population movement from colonial South Asia: [1] the movement of indentured labour from colonial India to other parts of the British empire that carried approximately 30 million "coolies" away to develop plantations, mines, railroads, canals etc., in the period from 1834 to 1937; [2] the movement of people in response and resistance to the colonial rule, including the 1920 self-banishment of more than 1,00,000 Muslims from the colonial

Dar-ul-Harb [House of war] to *Dar-ul-Islam* [House of Islam] in the Middle East and Central Asia under the inspiration of *hijrat;* and [3] the movement triggered by the "divide and quit" endgame of the British Empire accompanying the transfer of power process in 1947 that witnessed the uprooting of more than 14 million people across the newly created States of India and Pakistan.

Assembled Imaginations Around the Stateless and the Uprooted

Refugees are not new to human history. But the modern discourse about refugees and their rights, revolving around the metaphors of assembled imagination as public nuisance, social parasitism, and political peril, exhibit unprecedented levels of callousness towards human misery of an oceanic scale that is historically unprecedented.

In early 2001, more than 22 million people, escaping from the zones of conflict worldwide, lived under the UNHCR's umbrella as refugees and internally displaced persons. The host countries, as all know, treat them with contempt as an unwanted burden and flotsam, although the UNHCR and other international agencies pay for their upkeep. Inspite of Article 13(2) of the Universal Declaration of Human Rights, which says that "everyone has the right to leave any country, including his own, and to return to his country", voluntary repatriation, resettlement, and the right to return are not binding obligations under international law. This does not reflect very luminously on the impact of ideals on the realities of human development in our age.

Article 41 of the Magna Carta, adopted in 1215, like the Universal Declaration, refers to the right of citizens to "go out of our kingdom, and to return, safely and securely, by land or water, saving his allegiance to us". The French Constitution of 1791, likewise, pledged the "freedom of everyone to go, to stay or to leave, without being halted or arrested." The UNHCR, created in 1951 under the mandate of the Convention Relating to the Status of Refugees, is a busy organization working in more than 46 countries, from Afghanistan to the Democratic Republic of Congo, to realize the ideal of Article 13(2). *The International Covenant on Civil and Political Rights* (*ICCPR*), under Article 12(4), supposedly binds its signatories not to arbitrarily deprive anyone of the right to enter his own country. The obligation is derogable. States can use the argument of national emergencies, permissible under 4(1) of the ICCPR itself, which is always handy to dodge the obligation. Even when there is no apparent "recitable" emergency, countries like Israel, Bhutan and Kenya do not allow the return of those displaced by their policies of aggression which target their own people. The endnote suggests useful readings on the realities and the laws involving refugees and the stateless worldwide.[13]

"The Right of Blood" & "The Right of Territory": The Issues of Dual, Multiple, and Plural Citizenship

The concepts and problems of "dual", "multiple", and "plural" nationality or citizenship are relatively modern and involve permutations in the laws originating from the principles known as *jus sanguinis* and *jus soli*, meaning "right of blood" and "right of territory". *Jus sanguinis* or "right of blood" operates in ideologically different variations to impact conferment of nationality. The main variations are: (1) patrilineal transfer, meaning a conferment of nationality through the father; (2) matrilineal shift, meaning a bequest of nationality through the mother, and (3) bilineal assignment, meaning both the father and the mother donating their nationality to the child. As legal principles, they cast interesting shadows on multiple meanings of nationality and citizenship and the tensions of identity and authority inherent in them that animate their legal permutations.

Traditionally, the notions of "perpetual allegiance" and undivided loyalty to one's country guided the law of nationality around the "one person one nationality principle". The notions had their origins in medieval Europe when persons residing within a territory pledged personal allegiance to the local feudal lords and claimed personal rights in return. The nationality principle developed within the same mould of consciousness even after larger territories came under individual sovereigns. Those who came within the sovereign domain were bound to an irrevocable nationality as perpetual subjects.[14] Marriages between partners of different nationality and parents with a nationality arising from a common *jus sanguinis* rule with children qualifying for a second naturalized nationality under the *jus soli* principle were relatively uncommon. The rules of naturalization, even where they existed, were grossly discriminatory. For example, the Act of 1790 in the United States categorically restricted eligibility for naturalization to aliens who were "free white persons." The legal requirement, with minor variations, remained in force from 1790 to

1952 and locked the doors of citizenship on foreign immigrants. Persons "of African nativity or descent", who were there by the dint of the slave commerce, came within the scope of naturalization only after the Civil War. New prohibitions, on racial grounds, aimed to control migrations from China and Japan.

There were also laws that encouraged "desirable" immigrants to shift to the track of "intending citizens"; for example, the *Homestead Act of 1863*, which required immigrants to file a declaration of intention to qualify for the ownership of property. By dint of this declaration, they also became qualified to vote. The *Alien Land Law* in California, passed in 1913, prohibited "aliens ineligible to citizenship" from acquiring ownership of land. The prohibition tightened with the passing of the 1920 *Alien Land Law*. The passing of the *Immigration Quota Law* in 1924, mainly aiming to exclude the Japanese from entering the United States for permanent residence, made the process of assimilation and naturalization more difficult.[15]

Assimilation and plural citizenship, within the dominant construct of international relations, were detested concepts. The Preamble to the 1930 *Hague Convention* states that "each person should have a nationality and should have one nationality only" and goes on to postulate "the ideal towards which the efforts of humanity should be directed" to abolish all cases of double nationality.[16] Within the framework of this thinking, the citizenship that came with birth was inevitably extinguished when someone acquired a foreign nationality. Birth abroad, too, precipitated an automatic loss of citizenship that otherwise came through parental bequest unless parents expressly retained it. The birth of dual nationality in the age of global movement and global wars exposed its possessors to the effects of tensions between national identities and national authorities; dramatically epitomized in the case of *United States v. Kawakita*.[17]

Tomoya Kawakita was born in California to a Japanese couple in 1921. Under the US law of citizenship by birth, Kawakita became a US national. In 1939, his parents sent him to Japan for education where he declared his US citizenship and registered himself as an "alien". Japan and the US went to war while Kawakita was yet in school. In 1943, Kawakita cancelled his "alien" registration and took a job as a translator with a Japanese industrial firm that used American prisoners of war for mining and other hard industrial labour. After the war, in 1946, Kawakita came back to the US, obtaining a passport from the American Consul at Yokohama by declaring his earlier US nationality. One year later, Kawakita was recognized and reported by a former US prisoner of war resulting in his arrest and prosecution on the charges of treason and subjecting American prisoners to torture. In 1952, the Supreme Court upheld its conviction on the charges and also the sentence of death. In 1953, President Eisenhower commuted Kawakita's death sentence to life imprisonment and in 1963 he received Presidential pardon on the condition that he permanently return to Japan. The case highlights the problematic nature of "dual citizenship" within a framework of citizenship obligations and attendant requirements of loyalty, in which conflicting State interests can literally deface its possessors.

There are many examples of this phenomenon within the histories of growth of nationalism with the attendant expansion of mobility and naturalization. In the early nineteenth century, the British navy is reported to have routinely stopped US flagships to seize their crew members on the grounds that they had not been redeemed from their essential loyalty to the Crown. Naturalized Americans who came back to Britain were under constant risk of being forced to fulfil their subject duties, including the call to military service. Only in 1870, with the passing of the *Naturalization Act of 1870*, did Britain formally recognize the right of British subjects to expatriate and to withdraw from British citizenship. In the years before World War I, France enlisted naturalized French-Americans who returned to France in its military and, ignoring the remonstrations of the US government, called upon all persons of French origin, naturalized as American citizens, to come back into its fold. During World War I, Switzerland too, despite protests from the US, compelled all persons of Swiss origin with a dual nationality who returned to the country to join its army. A more recent and uncanny variant of the "Kawakita syndrome" is provided by the case of Alberto Fujimori, former Peruvian President, who has taken refuge in Japan on the ground of his "ethnic nationality" to escape the process of accountability for human rights crimes committed by him in the country which he ruled for ten years from 1990 to 2000.[18]

The Utopia of a Global Citizenship

Many may dismiss such examples as old history that are of little relevance within the ethos of modern times. Many argue that modern technological advancements, mainly in the areas of transportation and communication, blur borders. Globalized finance, commerce, and culture are not only supposed to efface the old notions of exclusive loyalties, but also to promote cumulative identities against the old, restrictive ones within a functional perspective of universal rights and obligations. The coordination of State-practices through bilateral, multilateral, and universal treaties and agreements on matters concerning individual and collective rights and obligations, irrespective of nationality, is expected to keep the arbitrary elements of sovereignty under control.

Within the framework of this visualization, the term "global nomads" refers to those who, as agents of multinational corporations, international financial and developmental institutions, diplomatic and military corps, as well as non-governmental organizations, academia and religious missions, etc., grow up and feel comfortable in multiple societies. The global regime of law founded on international treaties and conventions is supposed to be fostering a new transnational paradigm of global citizenship. By 1999, seventy independent nations of the world are said to have liberalized their nationality laws to permit their expatriates to regain their citizenship without renouncing their newly acquired nationalities. The *1976 Citizenship Act* of Canada explicitly encourages its people to acquire additional citizenships without losing their nationality rights. Canada's official position is: "For some people dual citizenship... may... enhance their feeling of belonging, because they have personal ties to more than one country."

The interconnectedness of economic processes, intimate linkages and worldwide effects of the processes of production, technology, finance, information, and commerce, etc., are supposed to be decimating the old notional demarcations of sovereign territories. The arenas of politics, human rights, culture, and environment too are envisioned to become universal under the system of global governance heralded by the instrumentality of the United Nations, with its Charter mandate to delegitimize war as a means to resolve international conflicts. The evaporation of the fear of a nuclear Armageddon with the conclusion of the Cold War; the expansion of liberal democracy to countries behind the former Iron Curtain; and the rise of a Third World elite, embedded in "enlightened values" to guide their national affairs, are discussed as indices of a new world in the making in which the State and its sovereign regulations will no longer dictate human identities, aspirations, and endeavours.[19]

The "Terrorism Discourse" and the Devaluation of Citizenship Concepts

The vision of a global citizenship is, indeed, exhilarating and appears to excite discourse despite the evidence of a global return to the dichotomies of war and a virtual fragmentation of the world into enclaves of civilization and savagery. As is common knowledge, the "terrorism discourse" has significantly affected the regime of citizenship and immigration within the Western world, as well as the policies of selection based on profiles and stereotypes of who 'belongs' and who does not, and their hierarchical gradations. Apart from the 'rightness' or 'wrongness' of the "war on terror" and its ideological objectives, its influence on the citizenship debate, and the power it confers on law enforcement agencies to deflect "undesirables" conveys more fundamental cleavages within the larger discourse on the principles of societal organization.

The "war on terror" is a metaphorical expression that has nothing to do with a rational measurement of its threat to the imperatives of national or societal survival. It is a shorthand term to give expression to a sense of crisis that requires the suspension of normal political, legal, and ethical principles for its management. It justifies "excesses" that creep into the crisis management process as, for example, in the working of military tribunals, or in the introduction of new detention laws or new immigration laws that would be considered abhorrent in 'normal' times. The "war" as well as its "costs" are evaluated against simplistic standards of how they affect "us" and "them"; "them" meaning those who come within the concentric circles of exclusion: "enemies", "aliens", "unlawful immigrants", "suspect citizens", etc. The logical, even if unintended, implications of these rankings are "homogenization" and "social purity". The following footnote lists some of the current writings on the topic.[20]

Even before the drastic changes in the human rights environment in the wake of 9/11, the vast majority of "aliens"—immigrants, naturalized citizens, and even second and third generation descendants of settlers from Africa, Asia, and Latin America—living in the prosperous western countries were hardly enjoying the idealized concept of equal citizenship.

Authors like Arthur M. Shlesinger Jr., who published *The Disuniting of America* in 1992, and J. Harvie Wilkinson III, whose *One Nation Indivisible: How Ethnic Separatism Threatens America* came out in 1997, were immensely influential with the policy and political establishment within the United States long before the Twin Towers collapsed under the suicidal aerial mission. The US Congress passed *Illegal Immigration Reform and Immigrant Responsibility Act of 1996* long before racial profiling and discrimination of non-white residents of the United States and curtailment of their human rights acquired justifications in the name of the global "war on terror".[21]

The influence of racial prejudice on the devaluation of national identity and citizenship rights; the treatment of people of colour in the Western world as "perpetual foreigners" and, of course, the Black-White relations and the hierarchies of racial citizenship, are much documented and debated. It is generally agreed that if Whites take the top position with Blacks lying at the bottom, other "colours", yellow, brown, "Latino" shuffle into various rungs within the hierarchical construction of multiracial-citizenship. There is no dearth of literature reflecting on the complex dynamics of racial subordination, shifting alliances, and conflicts among various racial groups and the manners in which white majorities retain their dominance.

The critical legal scholarship that examines the ways of domination is wide ranging. However, the overriding view within the political establishment as well as popular consciousness is graphically conveyed by Robert Bork in his *Slouching Towards Gomorrah: Modern Liberalism and American Decline*: "the arrival of groups of non-European backgrounds would make the task of assimilation much harder in any event, but what bids fair to make it impossible is the recent phenomenon of groups who do not wish to assimilate but to live in America as indigestible lumps in our society." The following footnote is a representative compilation of the master narrative and its critical evaluation under various race theories.[22]

The Problematic and the Predicaments of Feminity

Having briefly examined the issues of citizenship from the perspectives of the downtrodden, the marginalized, the migrant, the disenfranchised, and the demonized, we shall now turn to the problematic and the predicaments of the "female" within its rubric. The inquiry aims to outline the multiple connections and internal processes of recognition, repression, resistance, resilience, and reconciliation that engage the "female" not only with reference to the State but also in relation to other categories of identity within the societal orbit of citizenship.

Talking about categories of identity, it is necessary to ask: is there anything like an "essential" understanding of women's nature? The word "essential" is a term that presupposes some inherent qualities common to all within the category under discussion to be distinguished from their "accidental" qualities. So: are there qualities associable with the nature of womanhood, not contingent on social customs, conventions of knowledge, and historical changes, that is open to cognitive recovery and, therefore, objectively knowable? The question is important not only for an examination of social stereotypes of the "feminine" self, but also for a politically meaningful theory of gender. It has been taken up under a wide range of perspectives and the modern literature on the subject is profuse. The footnote lists out the literature that receives obligatory mention.[23]

Understanding Radical Feminism

A mention of radical feminism requires us to recognize that the subject itself provokes many, including some vocal defenders of women's rights, to harp on its supposedly negative impact on solidarities constituted for the promotion of class, caste, race, religious, and political interests. But is it not so that all varieties of social solidarities, in history, stand tarnished by practices of gender-discrimination?

The feelings surge passionately in the feminist writers who engage with the issue. Celina Romany, Professor of Law at the City University of New York Law School, complains about women being "the paradigmatic alien subjects" not only within their states and within an exclusive international club of states, but also inside the human rights framework. In a paper titled "Women as Aliens: A Feminist Critique of the Public/Private Distinction in International Human Rights Law", which appeared in *The Harvard Human Rights Journal* in 1993, Professor Celina Romany takes on the issues of "contradictions inherent in a human rights discourse". The paper accuses the discourse of excluding women from both "consensual" and "transcendental" accounts through its "controlling metaphors, the notions, and the categories that develop and delimit the conceptions of truth and knowledge", and of coupling patriarchal values with its liberalism to deny its benefits selectively to women.

Apart from accusing the liberal State of being founded on "the standpoint of male power on the relation between law and society", the paper accuses the State of being "in complicity with private actors who infringe human rights of women"; of conniving in the creation of "a parallel state with its own system of justice"; and of abandoning women—"stateless aliens"—to the terror within "the patriarchal family." "Patriarchal domination", the paper explains, "is a state of being which goes beyond material conditions of subordination"; women are also stripped of the "psychic, linguistic and textual vehicles of resistance". After highlighting "the one-dimensionality" of the human rights discourse and its rooted-ness in "patriarchal domination", the paper concludes with a severe indictment of the international society: "International society is an enveloping silence where actors who mirror masculine worldviews operate unhindered by the need to provide discursive justifications of their authority and who do not disclose to the "citizens-readers" (by mystifying legal discourse) the exclusionary nature of the master script."[24]

Those who find Celina Romany's views as extreme should attempt to envisage their relevance to situations of violence against women that represent a convergence of institutional complicity and patriarchal approval as, for example, in the case of so-called dowry deaths in India. In a paper "Rights under Fire", Meghna Shah compares various statistics from governmental and non-governmental sources to suggest that 17 women die every day from dowry-related violence with husbands commonly joining their extended family members in dousing their wives with kerosene before setting them afire, and then succeeding in portraying the murders as kitchen accidents. The laws like the *Dowry Prohibition Act, No. 28 (1961),* amended in 1984 and again in 1986, remain meaningless largely because the enforcement agencies and the criminal justice system remain complicit in violence against women.[25]

The Marginal Woman

Let us now reflect on male dominance within the rights movement: It is known that the civil-rights campaign in the United States in the later 1950s, led by black Baptist minister Martin Luther King, was triggered off when Rosa Parks, a black woman worker, travelling in a bus in Alabama refused to give up her seat in the bus to a white passenger. That was an act of courage showing qualities of leadership. How many admirers of the civil rights movement in the US, triggered by this incident, even know the name of Rosa Parks?

Martin Luther King received the Nobel Peace Prize in 1964 for his charismatically non-violent leadership of the movement before getting assassinated. We are not raising these points to pick issues with Martin Luther King's recognition and his place within the civil rights movement in the United States. Our inquiry is only guided by the possibilities of capturing politically liberating aspects and the ideological moorings of a solidarity that was large and diverse and included men and women of colour. A partial success of the movement under Martin Luther King's leadership, as all know, had much to do with its evocative power in mobilizing Americans across the colour barrier towards a visionary proclamation of ideals that had been made by America's founders like James Madison and Thomas Jefferson. As all know, the civil rights movement in the United States got divided when the radicals like Malcolm X challenged this evocation by announcing that the American ideals are fundamentally tainted by racism and that the declaration of equality of all men had no meaning before the facts of "black" life in America.

Malcolm X and others in his camp and outside actually stood for a radical "segregation" of blacks against Martin Luther King's appeal for the "integration" of all Americans. In the words of Malcolm X: "As long as our people here in America are dependent upon the white man, we will always be begging him for jobs, food, clothing and housing... The Negro here in America has been treated like a child. A child stays with the mother until the time of birth! When the time of birth arrives, the child must be separated, or it will destroy its mother and itself... The child cries for and needs its own world!"[26]

We shall not tax the point beyond inquiring about its allegoric relevance to the realities of the relationship between feminism and patriarchy that never quite came to the fore within the civil rights movement in America. Is the relationship between the "black" and the "white" necessarily very different from the relationship between the "man" and the "woman"? What are the psychological implications of juxtapositions that are so sharp and singular as to be obscuring distinctions between some and all? Do not the "white" and the "man", as singular "reportive" terms for tyranny and injustice, involve the transformation of the entire category of people into dehumanized items of hate? Martin Luther King said: "There is some good in the worst of us and some evil in the best of us. When we discover this, we are less prone to hate our enemies."[27]

Does this mean that although most men and whites may inhere within the systems of tyranny and injustice against women and blacks, some of them can also be partners in the struggles for liberation and justice? If this is so, can it also be that with effort and time all men and whites can be united in the ideals of freedom, justice, and equality for all? What influence can this proposition have on attitudes of action towards political enemies? What may be the ways of expediting the process of attaining social unity in the ideals of freedom, justice, and equality for all? Should we avoid hate only because it is too abhorrent to one's own self? What is the main merit in the virtue of non-violence? Does it lie in an objective avoidance of destruction? Or, does it recommend itself as a good value because it also assures self-preservation? Or, is it so that these qualities of non-violence are symbiotically so related that their separate evaluations can only lead to absurd conclusions?

Of course, there is no dearth of examples to illustrate the power of patriarchy and the way it subordinates and eclipses the role of women in shaping and sustaining social solidarities for justice and reform. Aphra Behn, who lived from 1640 to 1689, was the first English novelist to frontally attack slavery in her 1688 novel *Oronooko*. But she only received heaps of abuse for her avowal as a feminist and for being sexually explicit.

Caroline Norton was a British writer who published *Voices from the Factories* in 1836, exposing the brutalities of child labour, before Friedrich Engels published his *Conditions of the Working Class in England.* Immediately after *Voices from the Factories* came out in 1836, Caroline Norton's husband accused her of sexual promiscuity and not only obtained custody of their children but also the profits from her books.

Sarah Gertrude Millin, a South African novelist, published *God's Step-Children* in 1924 to attack the system of apartheid in her country. In the United States, Elizabeth Stanton, the founder of the National Woman Suffrage Association in 1869 and the author of *Degradation of Disenfranchisement and Solitude of Self,* was also an ardent campaigner for the abolition of slavery. But their contribution and leadership are hardly celebrated.

The name of Spartacus, the leader of a slave revolt at Capua in 73 BC, which was ruthlessly put down, survives in historical memory across scores of centuries. How many have heard of Harriet Ross Tubman, a female black slave from Maryland who in 1849 escaped to Philadelphia, where slavery was legally banned, to set up an organization called *Underground Railroad*, a secret network of sympathizers to help slaves escape to the northern States and Canada? Harriet Ross is not an iconic figure in the American consciousness of the anti-slavery struggle. Nat Turner, who led 60 slaves in Southampton to revolt in 1831 and was hanged along with 16 others, occupies a more prominent niche.

This says something about the history of politics and the dominance of patriarchal consciousness. Even revolutionary movements and schools of thought have not been immune from its effects. Jeanne Manon Roland de la Platiere established a salon in Paris to promote democratic discussions during the politically turbulent years leading to the French Revolution. Jeanne was condemned to the guillotine in 1793, without a right to defence, for opposing Robespierre and Danton. Her last words were "O liberty! What crimes are committed in thy name!"

Rosa Luxemburg's influence within the Bolshevik movement suffered when she began to criticize Lenin after the October 1917 revolution in Russia. Rosa was a committed Marxist who gave her life to bring about although unsuccessfully, a proletarian revolution in Germany. But she advocated democracy within the party and its implementation within the decision-making processes of the post-revolutionary regime in Russia. Lenin was not impressed and ignored her. Lenin's party adversary, Leon Trotsky, also ignored her during her lifetime.

Is male intolerance of feminist self-assertion the trademark of politics alone? Does not the historical evidence point to the permeation of male intolerance of feminist performance in all realms of intellectual and pragmatic pursuits? The famous library at Alexandria was burnt down in 415 AD, supposedly by Christian fanatics, because it was headed by Hypatia, a woman philosopher who was murdered.

Death through oblivion appears to have been a more favoured method of punishing female talent. Shikibu Murasaki is known as the writer of *The Tale of Genji*,[28] a masterpiece of fiction widely acknowledged as a classic work of Japanese literature written around 1000 AD. In reality, no one knows the name of the author. Later scholars, recognizing female authorship, named her after a character in the book, Murasaki.

Alexander Solzhenitsyn became widely known and respected for his anti-communist literature, written inside and outside the concentration camps in Siberia. Not many have heard of Irina Ratushinskaya, a dissident poetess who was sentenced to seven years in a labour camp plus five years in internal exile in 1983 for criticizing the regime, outside the Russian literary circles.

The history of sexual norms hides a more sordid side of male power and its mercilessness. Plato's works openly reflect homosexual preferences. His standing as a philosopher did not suffer for that reason. Sappho was a Greek poetess and the founder of a female literary circle at Mytilene, called Lesvos, the term that gives name to lesbianism. Sappho, who lived around 580 BC, committed suicide. Only fragments of her poetry survive.

Valeria Messalina was the third wife of the Roman emperor Claudius, who had her executed in 48 AD when she tried to get out of the marriage and live with a Roman noble she fell in love with. Have not the times and social values changed? Bertrand Russell's marriage with Dora, the founder of the National Council for Civil Liberties in the UK, was open and she chose to have children with another man without inspiring in him the kind of wrath Messalina faced. Lucy Stone, the founder of the American Suffrage Association and the editor of *Woman's Journal*, married Henry Blackwell in 1855 after a mutual declaration of legal equality of man and woman in marriage, retaining her surname. The epithet "Lucy Stoner" was coined to mean a woman who does the same. For example, Rita Manchanda, who keeps her name despite her marriage with Tapan Bose, and Indira Jaising who is married to Anand Grover are "Lucy Stoners". But is this a common social norm anywhere in the world? Martha Beatrice and Sidney James, two liberal left-wing reformers in Britain, worked closely, like Rita and Tapan, to establish the London School of Economics. When they got married in 1892, Beatrice took the surname of her husband Webb.

The levity of these anecdotal illustrations of feminism, as a complex paradigm of discourse within the rubric of citizenship, merely aims to provide an easy transition to the gravity of the issues of inquiry under the subject. From a feminist perspective, more than the capacity to enunciate rights, an understanding of fundamental rights presupposes an insight into the existential realities that nullify them.

The right to life, as a guarantee to live it out to its natural end, without premature termination and the attenuation of its qualities that makes it unworthy, is not always as naturally available to women as it is to men. Women's health is intertwined with the issues of reproductive health that men fail to recognize. The integrity of the human body presupposes security against assault, including sexual assault, and domestic violence, and affable circumstances of sexual satisfaction. Freedom of thought and expression are connected not only with the equal opportunity to education but also with the freedom from intellectual and imaginary coercion and tyranny, and with the freedom to feel, imagine, think, reason, and express oneself without fear. Freedom of association in both familial and political terms means, first and foremost, the freedom of affiliation and choice. Freedom of opportunity, in economic, educational, and political terms, and in the field of employment, has no meaning if the freedom to develop capacities and talent is non-existent or decisively restricted. Freedom of movement can hardly have any meaning if the weight of social custom ties women down to home and hearth. The right to property is hardly ever available to women on an equal basis with men, notwithstanding Constitutional proclamations. Even the right to recreation and playfulness is decisively restricted to the vast majority of women in the world, not only because of repressive laws but also because of the power of patriarchy.

Life as a concept, within the imagined world of human rights, presupposes the freedom to avail the plurality of all these rights to an irreducible measure. For this to happen, women have not only to battle for the right governmental policies and laws, but also to liberate social consciousness from the patriarchal mould in which it has remained trapped for thousands of years. The miscellany of the feminist discourse and the variegated voices within the field represent the complexity and the multiplicity of historical, social, and political circumstances in which women of the world must struggle to obtain their fundamental rights against State systems and the patriarchal constructions of knowledge and social mores.

"Global Critical Race Feminism"

In addition to the problems that plague the feminist discourse from the outside, participants must also become aware of those plaguing it from within. For example: what is the "Global Critical Race Feminism", which Adrien Katherine Wing champions?[29] According to Professor Wing, women across Africa, the Caribbean,

Asia, and Latin America share a potentially common position of opposition to sexist, racist, and imperialist structures of power for being politically at the lowest rung of the social ladder regardless of the country they live in. The word "race" is to distinguish all women of colour from white women. What is its significance?

Professor Angela P. Harris talks about the role played by white men and women in bringing about the conditions of subjugation of women of colour.[30] Professor Kimberle Crenshaw discusses the phenomenon of globalization in terms of a two-way traffic to explain the flow of capital and management from the developed to the developing world and of intellectual, labour, and material resources the other way round to explain why a feminist perspective cannot bridge the world of discrimination that marks the relations between the white and the colour races.[31]

Taking a different tone, Vasuki Nesiah argues for a "gendered" understanding of the regulation of sexuality, class, race, ethnicity, and nationality across the Third World and First World women without the impediment of colour.[32]

These are challenging intellectual positions that raise many awkward questions: Are the experiences of white women, confronted with the miasma of patriarchy within their own societies, very different from the comparable experiences of non-white women throughout the world? Is the multiplicity of experiences and identities of white women historically so determined that they, in relation to coloured women in a global context, always become privileged and dominant? If that is so, what explains the convergence of perceptions and politics of left radicals across the world of whiteness and colour? How about the world of white women in the Balkans? What about the coloured, women domiciled in the white world in positions of relative privilege who get involved with the issues of justice, human rights, and peace in the lands of their ancestry as intellectual initiatives and acts of empathy? How and why, for example, can a coloured Muslim woman with a "gendered" perspective domiciled in the United States fail to identify herself with the legal Constitution of the American State that does not allow a Saudi Arabian Sheikh to enter the land with his four wives because of its law against polygamy? What may be the "gendered" perspective and existential equations of a coloured lesbian woman employed as a waitress in a small American town towards: (1) fellow coloured women colleagues who are heterosexual; (2) fellow white women colleagues who are homosexual; (3) white feminist intellectuals and activists within the United States who are homosexual; and (4) coloured feminist intellectuals and activists within the United State who are heterosexual?

Last but not least, we must pay attention to the critics of human rights rhetoric who come under many hats.

Some may be transparently dishonest; for example, protagonists and defenders of abusive regimes who posit their arguments on the sovereignty of police powers or who, more spuriously, advance theories of the structural relativism of historical cultures and their autonomous processes. More responsible critics refer, sometimes very harshly, to the tautological tendencies of human rights rhetoric, its evangelic fervour, its talismanic enunciations and portrayal of all perceptions of needs, both individualistic and collective, as "rights". Prominent among them are: Alasdair MacIntyre, a British philosopher currently teaching at Duke University; Zygmunt Bauman, a sociology professor at the University of Leeds; Michel Villey, a French historian and philosopher of law; and Makau Mutua, professor of Law and Director of the Human Rights Centre at the State University of New York at Buffalo School of Law. Their arguments, philosophically dissimilar, are important to understand the logical consequences of socially and historically unconnected arguments of rights in this age of global capitalism, in which international trade and commercial interests, multinational corporations, and international finance impact global political practices and their preferences more decisively than are obvious to all. As claims of "universal reason", they carry the legacies of a "civilizational burden" and classical rationalizations of historical experiences of colonialism. More significantly, a language of rights that is at odds with the epistemologically and historically valid basis of political possibilities runs the risk of getting trapped in cycles of claims and counter-claims that can have no future without patronage and mediation from instruments of authority. Rights conferred by instruments of authority, not emanating from reasons immune to logical and historical refutation, are political privileges that remain authority bound, at best. As claims of recognized rights, they are contradictions in terms.

It is, therefore, important that the South Asian Orientation Course in Human Rights and Peace Studies does not shy away from examining the points of criticism that the very fundamental propositions of the discourse encounter on both philosophical and historical grounds. Mary Ann Glendon, a Harvard Professor of Law widely regarded as one of the "fifty most influential women lawyers in America"[33], compares the universal rights project to that of the "ill-fated tower built by the men of the Valley of Shinar who wanted their very own staircase to heaven"[34], the account of Babel described in *Genesis 11: 1-9*. According to Michel Villey, the Universal Declaration of Human Rights is a compilation of mutually negative rights. Alasdair MacIntyre points out that to coalesce fragments of different conceptual schemes, resting upon incommensurable moral premises, is a recipe for mischief. MacIntyre compares claims of natural rights and human rights with statements of belief in witches and unicorns. Makau Wa Mutua's critique of the Eurocentric universalism of the human rights discourse; the linguistic symbolism of its metaphors that divide the world into the trinity of 'savages', 'victims', and 'saviours' and the manners in which they become 'epistemic' frameworks for the global politics of hegemony and domination is especially important for our inquiries into the binaries of universalism vs. cultural relativism and rhetoric vs. realities.[35]

Notes

1. For the text of the Nepali Constitution (1962) see *Encyclopedia of SAARC Nations*, edited by Verinder Grover, vol. 5 (New Delhi: Deep and Deep Publications, 1997).
2. Nepal Constitution (Adopted on 9 November 1990). See http://www.oefre.unibe.ch/law/icl/np00000_.html.
3. Ram Narayan Kumar, "The Constitutional Monarchy and the Maoists of Nepal", *Contemporary Issues and Ideas in Social Sciences* (July 2005) 21. See at http://www.ciiss.net/html/downloads/publications/kumar0705.pdf.
4. Doniger, Wendy and Smith, Brian K., trans., *The Laws of Manu* (New Delhi: Penguin, 1991); Wilson, John, *Indian Caste*, 2 vols. (Bombay: Times of India, 1877); Ketkar, S.V., *History of Caste in India* (New York: Ithaca, 1909); Ghurye, G.S., *Caste and Race in India* (London: Routledge and Kegan Paul, 1932).
5. State Department News Conference, 12 July 2001, "Colin Powell Announces Release of the 2001 Trafficking in Persons Report", cited in Tiffany St. Claire King, "The Modern Slave Trade", U.C. Davis *Journal of International Law and Policy* 293, 8 (Spring 2002)
6. Anthony v. Alfieri, "Prosecuting Race", *Duke Law Journal* 1157, 48 (April 1999); Amnesty International, United States of America: "Police Brutality and Excessive Force in the New York City Police Department",

1996; Cynthia Kwei Yung Lee, "Race and Self-Defense: Toward a Normative Conception of Reasonableness", *Minnesota Law Review* 367, 81 (1996); Paul Butler, "Racially Based Jury Nullification: Black Power in the Criminal Justice System, *Yale Law Journal* 677, 105 (1995); Andrew D. Leipold, "The Dangers of Race-Based Jury Nullification: A Response to Professor Butler", *UCLA Law Review* 109, 44 (1996); Juan F. Perea, "The Black-White Binary Paradigm of Race: The "Normal Science" of American Racial Thought", *California Law* Review1213, 85 (1997); David Lyons, "Moral Judgment, Historical Reality and Civil Disobedience", *Philosophy and Public* Affairs 31, 27 (1998); Jennifer Wriggins, "Rape, Racism and the Law", *Harvard Women's Law Journal* 103, 6 (1983); Angela J. Davis, "Prosecution and Race: The Power and Privilege of Discretion", *Fordham Law Review* 67, 13 (1998); Kermit L. Hall, "Political Power and Constitutional Legitimacy: The South Carolina Ku Klux Klan Trials, 1871-1872", *Emory Law Journal* 921, 33 (1984); Ian F. Haney Lopez, *White by Law: The Legal Construction of Race* (New York: New York University Press, 1997); J. Clay Smith, Jr., "Black Women Lawyers: 125 Years at the Bar: 100 Years in the Legal Academy", *Howard Law Journal*365, 40 (1997); Phyliss Craig-Taylor, "To be Free: Liberty, Citizenship, Property, and Race", *Harvard Blackletter Journal* 45, 14 (1998); Richard Thompson Ford, "The Boundaries of Race: Political Geography in Legal Analysis", *Harvard Law Review* 1841, 107 (1994).

7. Bina B. Hanchinamani, "Human Rights Abuses of Dalits in India", *Human Rights Brief* 15, 8 (Winter 2001); Smita Narula, "Overlooked Danger: The Security and Rights Implications of Hindu Nationalism in India", *Harvard Human Rights Journal* 41, 16 (Spring 2003)
8. Tayyab Mahmud, "Freedom of Religion and Religious Minorities in Pakistan: A Study of Judicial practice", *Fordham International Law Journal* 40, 19 (1995).
9. Friedmann, Yohanan, *Prophecy Continuous: Aspects of Ahmadi Religious Thought and Its Medieval Background* (New Delhi and New York: Oxford University Press, 2003); Lavan, Spencer, *The Ahmadiyah Movement: A History and Perspective* (New Delhi: Manohar Publications, 1974); Keneddy, Charles H., "Towards the Definition of a Muslim in an Islamic State: The Case of Ahmadiyya in Pakistan" in Dhirendra D. Vajpeyi and Y. Malik, eds., *Religious and Ethnic Minority Politics in South Asia* (GlenDale: RiverDale Company Publishers, 1989).
10. Zaheeruddin v. State, 26 S.C.M.R. (S. Ct.) 1718 (1993) (Pak).
11. Jinnah, Mohammad A., "Address to the First Meeting of the Constituent Assembly of Pakistan", 11 August 1947 in Stanley Wolpert, *Jinnah of Pakistan* (Oxford: OUP, 1984) 337.
12. Tayyab Mahmud, "Migration, Identity and the Colonial Encounter", *Oregon Law Review Fall* 76, 633 (1997).

13. UNHCR homepage at http://www.unhcr.org/cgi-bin/texis/vtx/home; Ullom, Vic, "Voluntary Repatriation of Refugees and Customary International Law", *Denver Journal of International Law and Polity* 115, 29 (Spring 2001); Zick Marjoleine, *UNHCR and Voluntary Repatriation of Refugees: A Legal Analysis* (Boston: Martinus Nihhoff Publishers, 1997); Rosand, Erick, "The Right to Return Under International Law Following Mass, Dislocation: The Bosnia Precedent?", *Michigan Journal of International Law* 1091, 19 (1998); Nanda, Ved, "The Right to Movement and Travel Abroad: Some Observations on the U.N. Deliberations", *Denver Journal of International Law and Polity* 109, 1 (1971); Frelick, Bill, "Refugee Rights: The New Frontier of Human Rights Protection", *Buffalo Human Rights Law Review* 261, 4 (1998); Quigley, John, "Displaced Palestinians and a Right of Return", Harvard International Law Journal 171, 39 (1998); Plender, Richard, *International Migration Law* (Boston: Martinus Nijhoff Publishers, 1988); Hannum, H., *The Right to Leave and Return in International Law and Practice* (Boston: Martinus Nijhoff Publishers, 1987); Major Ary, Vaughan A., "Concluding Hostilities: Humanitarian Provisions in Ceasefire Agreements", *Military Law Review* 186, 148 (1995).
14. Spiro, Peter J., "Dual Nationality and the Meaning of Citizenship", *Emory Law Journal* 1411, 1417-1421, 46 (1997).
15. Haney Lopez, Ian F., *White by Law: The Legal Construction of Race 1850-1990* (New York: NYU Press, 1996); Ong Hing, Bill, *Making and Remaking Asian America Through Immigration Policy* (Stanford: Stanford University Press, 1994); Ferguson, Edwin E., "The California Alien Land Law and the Fourteenth Amendment", *California Law Review* 61, 35 (1947); McGovney, Dudley O., "The Anti-Japanese Land Laws of California and Ten Other States, *California Law Review* 7, 35 (1947).
16. Hague Convention on Certain Questions Relating to the Conflict of Nationality Laws, Apr. 12, 1930, pp. 179-80 League of Nations Treaty Series [LNTS], 89.
17. *Kawakita v. United States*, 343 US 717 (1952).
18. Bar-Yaacov, Nissim, *Dual Nationality* (London: Stevens, 1961) 151-152; Kent Anderson, "An Asian Pinochet? Not Likely: The Unfulfilled International Law Promise in Japan's Treatment of Former Peruvian President Alberto Fujimori", Stanford *Journal of International Law* 177, 38 (Summer, 2002).
19. Pendleton, Michael D., "A New Human Right—The Right to Globalization", *Fordham International Law Journal* 2052, 2054, 22 (1999); David Held Anthony McGrew, David Goldblatt and Jonathen Perraton, eds. *Global Transformations: Politics, Economics and Culture* (Cambridge: Polity Press 1999); David Held and Anthony McGrew eds.,

The Global Transformations Reader: An Introduction to the Globalization Debate, (Cambridge: Polity Press, 2000); Micheling Labelle and Franklin Midy, "Re-Reading Citizenship and the Transnational Practices of Immigrants, *Journal of Ethnic and Migration Studies* 213, 217, 25 (1999); Delphine Matthieussent, "Global Nomads Live the Future, *Japan Times*, 29 August 1999; Dr. Alejandro Portes, "Globalization From Below: The Rise of Transnational Communities", Address before the Department of Sociology Advisory Board and Sociology Alumni Association, University of Washington, 2 November 1999; Thomas M. Franck, "Is Personal Freedom a Western Value?" *American Journal of International Law* 593, 91 (1997); Alesander Aleinikoff, "Between National and Post-National: Membership in the Stated States, *Michigan Journal of Race and Language* 241, 4 (1999); Anne-Marie Burley, "Toward an Age of Liberal Nations", *Harvard International Law Journal* 393, 33 (1992); David Jacobson, "New Border Customs: Migration and the Changing Role of the State", *UCLA Journal of International Law and Foreign Affairs* 443, 443, 3 (1999); David A. Martin, "The Civic Republican Ideal for Citizenship, and for Our Common Life", *Vancouver Journal of International Law* 301, 315, 35 (1994); Thomas M. Franck, "Clan and Superclan: Loyalty, Identity and Community in Law and Practice", *American Journal of International Law* 359, 380, 90 (1996); Randall Hansen, "A European Citizenship or a Europe of Citizens? Third Country Nationals in the EU", *Journal of Ethnic and Migration Studies* 751, 24 (1998); Rey Koslowski, "European Migration Regimes: Emerging, Enlarging and Deteriorating", *Journal of Ethnic and Migration Studies* 735, 24 (1998); Thomas M. Franck, "Community Based on Autonomy, *Columbia Journal of Transnational Law* 41, 45, 36 (1997); Russell Menyhart, "Changing Identities and Changing Law: Possibilities for a Global Legal Culture", *Indiana Journal of Global Legal Studies* 157, 10 (Summer, 2003).

20. Charles Nesson, "The Evidence or the Event? On Judicial Proof and the Acceptability of Verdicts", *Harvard Law Review* 1357, 98 (1985); Samuel R. Gross and Debra Livingston, "Racial Profiling Under Attack", *Columbia Law Review* 1413, 102 (2002); Kevin Sullivan and Glenn Kessler, "Fox Says It's Time to Reopen Talks on Immigration Concerns", *Washington Post*, 27 November 2002; Robin Toner and Janet Elder, "Public is Wary but Supportive on Rights Curbs", *New York Times*, 12 December 2001; Hiroshi Motomura, "Immigration Law After a Century of Plenary Power: Phantom Constitutional Norms and Statutory Interpretation", *Yale Law Journal* 545, 100 (1990); Hiroshi Motomura, "The Curious Evolution of Immigration Law: Procedural Surrogates for Substantive Constitutional Rights", *Columbia Law Review* 1625, 92 (1992);

Hiroshi Motomura, "Federalism, International Human Rights, and Immigration Exceptionalism", *University of Colorado Law Review* 1361, 70 (1999); Hiroshi Motomura, "Immigration Policy, Immigration and We the People after September 11", *Albany Law Review* 413, 66 (2003); Jamin B. Raskin, "Legal Aliens, Local Citizens: The Historical, Constitutional and Theoretical Meanings of Alien Suffrage", *University of Pennsylvania Law Review* 1391, 141 (1993); Soysal, Yasemin, *The Limits of Citizenship: Migrants and Postnational membership in Europe* (Chicago: University of Chicago Press, 1994); Jacobson, David, *Rights Across Borders: Immigration and the Decline of Citizenship* (Baltimore: Johns Hopkins University Press, 1996); Samuel P. Huntington, "The West: Unique, Not Universal", *Foreign Affairs* November-December 1996; James F. Hollifield, "Immigration and Integration in Western Europe: A Comparative Analysis" in Emek M. Ucarer and Donald J. Puchala eds., *Immigration into Western Societies: Problems and Policies,* (London: Pinter, 1997) 28-69; Weiner, Myron, *The Global Migration Crisis: Challenge to States and to Human Rights* (New York: HarperCollins, 1995).

21. Antiterrorism and Effective Death Penalty Act of 1996, Pub. L. No. 104-208, 110 United States Statutes at Large [Stat.] 1214.
22. Peter H. Schuck, "Membership in the Liberal Polity: The Devaluation of American Citizenship" in William Rogers Brubaker ed., *Immigration and the Politics of Citizenship in Europe and North America* (New York: University Press of America, 1989) 51-66; Chistopher L. Eisgruber, "Birthright Citizenship and the Constitution", *New York University Law Review* 54, 72 (1997); Michael Gunlicks, "Citizenship as a Weapon in Controlling the Flow of Undocumented Aliens: Evaluation of Proposed Denials of Citizenship to Children of Undocumented Aliens Born in the United States", *George Washington Law Review* 551, 63 (1995); Schuck, Peter H. and Smith, Rogers M., *Citizenship Without Consent: Illegal Aliens in the American Polity* (New Heaven: Connecticut 1985); Dorothy E. Roberts, "Who May Give Birth to Citizens? Reproduction, Eugenics, and Immigration" in Juan F. Perea ed., *Immigrants Out! The New Nativism and the Anti-Immigrant Impulse in the United States* (New York: New York University Press, 1997); Drimmer, Jonathan C., "The Nephews of Uncle Sam: The History, Evolution, and Application of Birthright Citizenship in the United States", *Georgetown Immigration Law Journal* 667, 671, 9 (1995); Brimelow, Peter, *Alien Natiion: Common Sense About America's Immigration Disaster* (New York: HarperPerennial, 1996); Stephen H. Legomsky, "É Pluribus Unum: Immigration, Race, and Other Deep Divides," *Southern Illinois University Law Review* 101, 108 (1996); Natsu Saito, "Alien and Non-Alien Alike: Citizenship, 'Foreignness', and Racial Hierarchy in American Law", *Oregon Law Review* 261, 76

(1997); Keith Aoki, "Foreignness and Asian American Identities: Yellowface, World War II Propaganda and Bifurcated Racial Stereotypes", *UCLA Asian Pacific American Law Journal* 4 (1997); Pat K. Chew, "Asian Americans: The 'Reticent' Minority and Their Paradoxes", *William And Mary Law Review* 1, 36 (1994); Cynthia Kwei Yung Lee, "Race and Self-Defense: Toward a Normative Conception of Reasonableness", *Minnesota Law Review* 367, 81 (1996); Delgado, Richard and Stefancic, Jean eds., *The Latino Condition: A Critical Reader* (New York: New York University Press, 1998); Richard Delgado, "Rodrigo's Fifteenth Chronicle: Racial Mixture, Latino-Critical Scholarship, and the Black-White Binary," *Texas Review* 1181, 75 (1997); Mari Matsuda, "Voices of the Community", *Asia America Pacific Island Law Journal* 79, 1 (1993); Robert S. Chang, "Toward an Asian American Legal Scholarship: Critical Race Theory, Post-Structuralism, and Narrative Space", *California Law Review* 1243, 81 (1993); Lisa C. Ikemoto, "Traces of the Master Narrative in the Story of African American/Korean American Conflict: How We Constructed Los Angeles", *Southern California Law Review* 1581, 66 (1993); Tanya Kateri Hernandez, "The Construction of Race and Class: Buffers in the Structure of Immigration Controls and Laws", *Oregon Law Review* 731, 76 (1997); Juan F. Perea and Los Olvidados, "On the Making of Invisible People", *New York University Law Review* 965, 70 (1995); Orfield, Gary, *The Growth of Segregation in American Schools: Changing Patterns of Separation and Poverty since 1968* (Cambridge, Mass: Harvard University Graduate School of Education, 1993); George A. Martinez, "The Legal Construction of Whiteness: Mexican-Americans and Whiteness", *Harvard Latino Law Review*, 2 (1997); Kevin R. Johnson, "Racial Restrictions on Naturalization: The Recurring Intersection of Race and Gender in Immigration and Citizenship Law", *Berkeley Women's Law Journal* 141, 11 (1996); Lawrence H. Fucks, "The Reactions of Black Americans to Immigration" in Virginia Yans-McLaughlin ed., *Immigration Reconsidered: History, Sociology, and Politics* (New York: Oxford University Press, 1990) 295-96; Randall L. Kennedy, "Racial Critiques of Legal Academia", *Harvard Law Review* 1745, 102 (1989); William R. Tamayo, "When the 'Coloreds' are Neither Black Nor Citizens: The United States Civil Rights Movement and Global Migration, *Asian Law Journal* 1, 2 (1995); Leamon Robinson, Reginald, "The Other Against Itself: Deconstructing the Violent Discourse Between Korean and African Americans", *California Law Review* 15, 67 (1993); Deborah Ramirez, "Multicultural Empowerment: It's Not Just Black and White Anymore", *Stanford Law Review* 957, 47 (1995); Kevin R. Johnson, "Race, The Immigration Laws, and Domestic Race Relations: A 'Magic Mirror' Into the Hear of Darkness", *Indiana Law Journal* 73 (1998); Delgado, Richard and Stefancic, Jean, *Failed*

Revolutions: Social Reform and the Limits of Legal Immigration (Colorado: Westview Press, 1994); Richard Delgado and Jean Stefancic, "Images of the Outsider in American Law and Culture: Can Free Expression Remedy Systemic Social Ills?" *Cornell Law Review* 1258, 77 (1992); Francisco Valdes, "Under Construction: LatCrit Consciousness, Community and Theory", *California Law Review* 85 (1997); Haunani-Kay Trask, "Coalition-Building Between Natives and Non-Natives", *Stanford Law Review* 1197, 43 (1991).

23. de Beauvoir, Simone, *The Second Sex,* (Harmondsworth: Penguin, 1984); Silverman, Kaja, *Male Subjectivity at the Margins* (London: Routledge, 1992); Stimpson, Catherine R., *Where the Meanings Are: Feminism and Cultural Spaces* (New York: Routledge, 1990); Dworkin, Andrea, *Our Blood: Prophecies and Discourses on Sexual Politics* (London: Women's Press, 1982); Firestone, Shulamith, *The Dialectic of Sex* (New York: Bantam Books, 1970); MacKinnon, Catherine, *Towards a Feminist Theory of the State* (Cambridge: Harvard University Press, 1991); Daly, Mary, *Beyond God the Father: Toward a Philosophy of Women's Oppression* (Boston: Beacon Press, 1973); Gayle Rubin, Deirde English and Amber Holibaugh, "Talking Sex", *Socialist Review* 11, 4 (1981) 43-62; Wolf, Naomi, *The Beauty Myth* (New York: Harper Perennial, 2002); Friedan, Betty, *The Feminine Mystique* (New York: Dell Publications, 1974); Mia Campioni and Elizabeth Grosz, "Love's Labours Lost: Marxism and Feminism" in Marx Gunew ed., *A Reader in Feminist Knowledge* (London: Routledge, 1991); Davis, Angela, *Women, Race, and Class* (New York: Vintage Books, 1983); Eisenstein, Zillah, *Capitalist Patriarchy and the Cast for Socialist Feminism* (New York: Monthly Review Press, 1979); Perkins Gilman, Charlotte, *Women and Economics* (Boston: Maynard and Co., 1898); Phillips, Anne, *Divided Loyalties: Dilemmas of Sex and Class* (London: Virago, 1987); Frankerberg, Ruth, *White Women, Race Matters: The Social Construction of Whiteness* (Minneapolis, MN: University of Minnesota Press, 1993)
24. Celina Romany, "Women as Aliens: A Feminist Critique of the Public/ Private Distinction in International Human Rights Law", *Harvard Human Rights Journal* 87, 6 (1993).
25. Meghna Shah, "Rights Under Fire: The Inadequacy of International Human Rights Instruments in Combating Dowry Murder in India", *Connecticut Journal of International Law* 209,19 (Fall 2003).
26. Luther King, Martin, *A Testament of Hope: The Essential Writings of Martin Luther King, Jr.*, ed. James M. Washington (San Francisco: Harper, 1986) 219; Malcolm X, *The Autobiography of Malcolm X* (New York: Grove Press, 1965) 246, 273-81.
27. Ayres, Jr. Alex ed., *The Wisdom of Martin Luther King* (New York: Meridian, 1993) 26.

28. *The Tale of Genji*. For its summary see — http://mcel.pacificu.edu/as/students/genji/summary.html
29. Adrien Katherine Wing, "Violence and State Accountability: Critical Race Feminism", *Georgetown Journal of Gender and Law* 95, 1 (1999)
30. Angela P. Harris, "Race and Essentialism in Feminist Legal Theory", *Stanford Law Review* 581, 42 (1990); and "Gender, Violence, Race, and Criminal Justice", *Stanford Law Review*, 52, 4 (April 2000).
31. Kimberle Crenshaw, "Demarginalizing the Intersection of Race and Sex: A Black Feminist Critique of Antidiscrimination Doctrine, Feminist Theory, and Antiracist Politics", *University of Chicago Law Forum* 139 (1989).
32. Vasuki Nesiah, "Towards a Feminist Internationality: A Critique of US Feminist Legal Scholarship, *Harvard Women's Law Journal* 189, 16 (1993).
33. From Wikipedia — http://en.wikipedia.org/wiki/Mary_Ann_Glendon (Last visited on 11 February 2006).
34. Dr. Mary Ann Glendon, "Rights Babel: Thoughts on the Approoaching 50th Anniversary of the Universal Declaration of Human Rights" [Revered Thomas J. Furphy Lecture, 1996], De Sales University: at http://www4.desales.edu/~philtheo/Glendon.html (Last visited on 11 February 2006).
35. MacIntyre, Alasdair, *Whose Justice? Which Rationality?* (London: Duckworth, 1991); Michel Villey, *Law and Human Rights* (Zagreb: Disput Publishing House, 2002); Makau Mutua, "Savages, Victims, and Saviors: The Metaphor of Human Rights", *Harvard International Law Journal* 201, 42 (Winter, 2001); Mary Ann Glendon, *Rights Talk: The Impoverishment of Political Discourse* (New York: The Free Press, 1991).

Chapter Three

Conflicts and the Politics of Peace in South Asia*

If human development is about expanding choice and advancing rights, then violent conflict is the most brutal suppression of human development. (UNHDR 2005)

A third of the world's population is estimated to be exposed to armed violence[1] with a clear shift of security risks towards the poorest countries; a shift in geographical locus of violent conflicts towards the global south and conflicts breaking out within countries and producing regional systems of conflict. Some recent studies[2] suggest that from a high of 51 in 1991, conflicts have come down to 29 ongoing wars in 2003. However, today's conflicts last longer and cost more in terms of human and especially civilian lives and are characterised by a multi dimensional crises. While earlier conflicts tended to be characterized as mono dimensional political/military or humanitarian, today's involve State failure, rise of quasi State actors, privatization (and globalization) of militaries, societal and economic breakdown and humanitarian crises. The international conflict and development literature has coined the concept 'Complex Emergencies' to capture the changing nature of today's conflicts.[3]

Post cold war, the sense is that the world has become a more dangerous place to l ive in with burgeoning civil wars and frequent references to 'failed' states, prompting an increasingly militarised interventionism as reflected in December 2001 Report of the International Commission on Intervention and State Sovereignty titled *The Responsibility to Protect*.[4] The report has been followed up with the 2 December 2004 UN GA Resolution [A/Res/59/35] innocuously titled "Responsibility of States for Internationally Wrongful Acts"[5] and the 26 May 2005 report from the Secretary-General to the President of the General Assembly that talks about the State's "collective responsibility to uphold the principles of

* Rita Manchanda

human dignity, equality and equity at the national and the global levels."[6]

Security strategies, both nationally and internationally, suffer from an overdeveloped military response to perceived security threats and an underdeveloped human security response. UN policy analyst Antonio Donini, writing on the wave of 'humanitarian intervention' in the global South since the 1990s, draws attention to the globalization of the market and interventionism in the South as being parallel historical processes. Donini flags three aspects that are characteristic of the contemporary modes of international intervention: (i) militarization of humanitarian aid; privatization of social welfare with governments deemed incapable of providing basic services to their citizens; and (ii) the diversion of long term development funds to quick fix emergency relief programmes. Whatever the form of intervention the decisions concerning it are likely to bypass the leadership and the populations concerned, reinforcing the crisis of (state) legitimacy.[7]

Whereas for much of the 20th century, the meta narratives of international relations and conflict studies focused on conflict as a product of the breakdown in relations between states, today's wars are presented as the product of the failure of states to prevent, contain and resolve conflicts between groups. Conflict theory posits that the frictioning of the geo-strategic conflict paradigm that structured the contours of conflict along the cold war confrontational axis, has given way to civil wars produced by 'ethnic' conflicts or as P Sahadevan analyses in the case of south Asia, 'ethnic militarism'.[8]

Processes of or at least aspirations to 'democratic' governance and development has seen the mobilization of new social groups contending for a share of power and resources. Conflict theory has conceptualized today's multi-faceted civil conflicts as largely 'ethnic' conflicts, de-historicising and essentializing them. In the focalization of histories of social injustice, political exclusion and socio economic grievances into ethno-nationalist conflicts, the questions that get sidestepped are—to what extent are ethno-national and cultural differences a creation of elite led politics, i.e. the mobilization of collectivities by political entrepreneurs? To what extent does ethnicization of conflicts displace and distract from other conflict fault lines?

Mary Kaldor, one of the most influential contemporary theorists of war, while drawing attention to the significance of what she characterises as 'new wars', nonetheless emphasises that contemporary conflicts like in Bosnia, were political conflicts, involving state power as well as various 'private' forces, in which 'identity politics' was a means by which political elites reproduced their power.[9]

Kaldor, analyzing the political economy of 'new wars', examines the significance of globalization and privatization in transforming conventional modes of warfare, and producing wars "in which a range of new militaries—the decaying remnants of state armies, paramilitary groups (often financed by governments), self-defence units, mercenaries and international troops—all engage in new forms of violence. These include disappearances, systematic murder of 'others', forcible population expulsion known as ethnic 'cleansing' (linked ironically to electoral legitimation), and rendering areas uninhabitable—all of which are genocidal. It is estimated that 80 per cent of victims in current wars are civilians; over 80 per cent of victims were from the military in wars earlier this century.[10] In the 'new wars' the codes of conduct of war that were evolved in 19th and 20th centuries are being sidelined as war by state and quasi state actors becomes 'genocidal'.

However, in recognising the significance of change in modes of warfare, there is need to emphasise continuity with the issues that animated the discourse of 'old wars'. Issues related to democratic governance, social identities, development and welfare and territorial security continue to characterise conflicts in our region. Indeed in the south Asia region, the dominant axis of conflict remains inter state—India and Pakistan conflict is braided on to communal violence in particular and the distrust of competing claims of collective identities and territorial insecurities.

The ethno-geographic mosaic of the post colonial states of South Asia predicates a politics of pluralism and inclusion, instead state consolidation has been towards majoritarianism and structures of governance that are coercive and hegemonic. The region is a mesh of multiple conflicts lines–ethno-nationalist conflicts, revolutionary insurgencies for takeover of state power, caste and sectarian conflicts and indigenous peoples' struggles, etc. Within South Asia are conflicts that epitomize the 'new wars' as in the case of conflicts in Sri Lanka and Nepal. Whereas these state structures are contoured as ineffective, weak and failing, there is the behemoth of the 'strong' Indian State. On the eve of the SAARC summit in November 2005, Indian Prime Minister Manmohan Singh referred to the danger of 'failed' states in the region.[11] What the South Asian states have in common is a militarized response (trailing human rights atrocities) to political struggles relentlessly reproducing (weaker) militarized reactions (and human rights abuses).

The protracted conflicts in Sri Lanka, India's Northeast, Kashmir, Pakistan's Baluchistan and Nepal, demonstrate the state's insecure control of territory, occupation, the pursuit of power and identity politics mobilization—that is, 'grievances' against economic inequalities, histories of social injustice, discriminatory structures of power. These protracted conflicts have increasingly got mired in the politics of extremism in which the cause of justice, freedom and humanity have been destroyed. The causes of the conflict have got overwhelmed by the violence that has become an end.

At the global level, the 'privatization' of the mode of warfare and its globalization has spawned a genealogy of conflict theorists, who in a reductionist 'one size fits all' approach, structure conflict as driven by *greed* rather than *grievance*. A World Bank financed study of contemporary conflicts by Paul Collier assesses the predominance of greed (predatory political economy) as driving conflicts with the loud discourse of grievance as an excuse by political entrepreneurs to manipulate collectivities.[12]

Such a paradigm seems over-determined by conflicts such as in Liberia, Afghanistan and Iraq but how meaningful is it for Palestine, Kashmir, Nepal and Sri Lanka. However, it is useful in drawing attention to the political economy that sustains protracted conflicts. The problem is that the 'greed over grievance' formula has dangerous policy implications—it de-politicises and de-legitimizes political protest and militarizes state and international community response. More insidiously, it gets braided onto the loud discourse of 'terrorism' that further hollows out politics from protest and renders illegitimate the assertion of self determination. It produces conflict resolution technologies predicated on stopping the violence, side stepping realities of power and ignoring injustices. Little wonder then that such conflict resolution 'fixes' result in more than half the countries emerging from conflict relapsing into violence within five years.

What is Conflict?

Conflict per se, and particularly social conflict is integral to human relations and is posited on 'difference'. Conflict has a positive dimension and is an essential catalyst of social and political change. Conflict theory which is animated by the emerging conflict & development discourse acknowledges conflict both as an agent and an outcome of change, recognising the demands of justice and power. Marxist social theory, for one, views class conflict as the main dynamic that propels human society towards progress and higher stages of development. Conflicts are not synonymous with violence though they can become violent. Within the 'conflict resolution' field, theorists and practitioners have conceptualised the way oppressive relationships are changed through increased awareness leading to confrontation.[13]

Our focus here is on 'destructive' conflicts that generate practices characterised by organised violence—riots, civil conflicts, inter-state wars. The 17th century philosopher Thomas Hobbes used the term quarrel as the cause of violent conflict—the motive force of a quarrel being a) competitive gain, b) a desire for security and c) glory. Later day theorists have elaborated conflict as "a relationship between two or more parties (individuals or groups) who have or think they have incompatible goals"[14] The dominant motive-competition over scarce resources, has been tweaked to add "opposition among social entities directed against one another".[15] James Laue synthesises these various elements defines conflict as "escalated natural competition of two or more parties who believe they have incompatible goals and whose aim is to neutralize injure or gain advantage over the other party or other parties."[16]

At the level of social and political relations when human interaction takes place as groups, communities, states—conflicts arise due to incompatibilities in power, resources, wealth and status. There are several influential frameworks that seek to analytically structure the causes and processes of conflicts:

One of the most influential structures for analysing conflicts or rather violence is that developed by Norwegian peace researcher Johan Galtung.[17] He draws attention to three different forms of violence:

- Direct violence: physical aggression (emphasis is on organised political violence);

- Structural violence: refers to endemic violence that exists owing to inequalities in societal structures—where there are gross power imbalances that affect people's quality of life which therefore varies substantially. In this particular instance the societal structure refers to an institution (the State) or to a system that bears down on every aspect of social and political life (e.g. apartheid in South Africa). These inequalities can produce direct violence.
- Cultural violence: this involves the use of linguistic, religious and or ethnic symbols/myths that assert superiority to justify violence. Cultural violence also manifests itself in the dehumanization of the other, i.e. Slobodan Milosevic was called 'pig', the Vietnamese 'gooks'.

Kumar Rupesinghe and Sanam Anderlini in *Civil wars, Civil Peace*[18] develop a typology of conflicts around three broad categories:

- Resource conflicts based on competition for economic power and access to natural resources.
- Conflicts over governance and authority based on competition for political power and participation in political process.
- Ideological conflicts based on competition between rival ideologies and value systems.

Michael Brown[19] proposes to organise the root causes of conflict around structural factors, political factors, economic and social factors and cultural and perceptual factors:

- Structural factors: weak States, intra State security concerns and ethnic geography; weak states lack political legitimacy and political institutions capable of exercising meaningful control—State structures weaken—ethnic groups hitherto oppressed become assertive and raise intra security concerns and violent suppression.
- Political factors: discriminatory political institutions, exclusionary national ideologies, inter group politics and elite politics;
- Economic and social factors: economic problems, discriminatory economic system and negative consequences of development and modernity.

- Cultural and Perceptual factors: cultural discrimination against minorities.

Perceptual factors refer to group histories and group perceptions of themselves and others; ethnic mythology and group stereotyping.

More recently, conflict discourses are focusing on the phenomenon of weak, 'ineffective' and 'failed' states as being at high risk of spilling into violent conflict. The *Commission on Weak States and US National Security*[20] identifies three common characteristics of weak states at high risk:

- the security gap;
- the capacity gap; and
- the legitimacy gap.

Poverty[21] and inequality can exacerbate tensions created by these three gaps. Research conducted by the Clingendael Institute argues that there is no clear and persistent relationship between poverty and violent conflict, although it is recognised that economic factors constitute an important mobilizing force.[22] The crucial factor according to the Institute is the degree to which socio-economic categories overlap with specific ethno-linguistic or regional boundaries. Where there is a convergence of poverty-discrimination and categories of ethnicity and region, as in Nepal, compounded by an ineffective state, the situation is at high risk of violence as manifest in the Maoist insurgency in the country.

Nepal illustrates how inequalities across different dimensions can create the conditions for violent conflict. In 1996 when the insurgency began the poverty rate was 72 per cent in mid and far western regions and 4 per cent in Kathmandu. Overlying these regional disparities are disparities in human development status with Human Development Index (HDI) of the upper caste Nepalese 50 per cent higher than that of hill ethnic, *terai* ethnic and occupational caste groups. And while indigenous people constituted 36 per cent of the population and dalits 15 per cent, they held 8.42 and 0.17 per cent of the government posts, respectively. In the heartland of the Maoist insurgency poverty braids with inequality, as well as regional and ethnic discrimination.[23] Moreover this area has the least political voice. The 1990 pro democracy movement had mobilized the ethnic communities but the elite compromise produced between the palace and the upper middle classes created a widening chasm between democratic expectations and democratic practice.[24]

Poverty and inequality — urban: rural; indigenous: upper caste; metropolitan: periphery, and inequitably gendered roles of men and women — all feed the conflict.

The UNDP Human Development Report succinctly captures the relationship between poverty and conflict, "Poverty is part of the cycle that creates and perpetuates violent conflicts — and that violent conflict feeds back to reinforce poverty".[25] Poor societies are at risk of falling into no exit cycles of conflict in which ineffective governance, societal warfare, humanitarian crises and the lack of development, perpetually chase each other.[26]

It is critical to locate contemporary conflicts in the socio-historical context of the dominant development paradigm. International financial institutions push development paradigms in the global south that perpetuate poverty and democratic exclusions. States have become 'complicit' partners in enabling these anti-people policies. There is a need to understand the multiple linkages between the 'development' strategies of global capital, structural adjustment programmes, privatization of basic needs and the State's abdication of social responsibility and its transfer to NGOs, thus further undermining the State's capacity and legitimacy, and producing the self fulfilling discourses of 'failed' State and conflicts.

Contemporary Conflicts: 'New Wars' & Complex Emergencies

Historically, violence has been defended as being instrumental to the maintenance and restoration of order with the state monopolizing legitimate violence. Violence, as evinced above, is also a category of analysis. Social scientists have examined the instrumental use of violence as constitutive of community; and of violence serving the important function of producing and distributing power, wealth and destitution during protracted violent conflict. There is a tradition of 'just war' and the violence of the oppressed. Violence here is liberating.[27]

However, the changing dynamics of contemporary conflicts, its destructive capacity and the consequences for the survival of human communities, States and humankind, has made violence increasingly unacceptable, especially as the 'new wars'—civil wars with multiple non State armed actors—have civilians as the primary direct targets and indirect targets of conflict induced famine, disease, displacement and destruction of social community.[28] In the 'new wars', the rules of war and principles of international law are being flouted by State and non-State actors with both engaged in crimes of disappearances, extra judicial killings, ethnic cleansing, etc. Mary Anderson argues that 'the absorption of civilians and civilian life into warfare as both combatants and primary targets challenges the claim that wars promote justice'.[29] Identity conflicts position women as the bearer of community identity, making the material existence of women highly vulnerable and the target of systematic attack. Rape as an instrument of war has a long historical legacy but in today's ethno-nationalist wars the rhetoric and practice of violence has become exceedingly brutal and sexualized.[30]

Feminist scholarship has established the linkage between patriarchy and violence and posited a continuum of violence between the everyday violence in women's lives and the violence women experience in conflict and in the aftermath. UN Security Council Resolution 1325 is the first international recognition of the gendered nature of conflict, security and peace building.[31] It is also a formal acknowledgement of the role of civil society in peace building.

Characteristic of the new modes of warfare is the induction of women into the armed forces of both State and non State actors and there is need to understand the implications of this phenomenon. Does it have the capacity to be liberating, of promoting rights? Is there only an instrumental use of women who are denied decision making authority? Is it producing a total militarization of society? Also, there is the heinous phenomenon of the induction of child soldiers, made possible by the revolution in small arms in civil wars. These civilian based wars are fought in everyday living spaces—targeted because they are the spaces in which civilians live and work.

Complex Political Emergencies (CPEs)

Researchers Goodhand and Hulme [32] argue that the classical conceptual framework based on 'conflict is war' model has become virtually redundant. These civil conflicts are characterised by the breakdown of political, economic and social order and by the targeting of violence on civilian populations. The most distinctive aspect of Complex Political Emergencies (CPEs) is the horrifying shift in the distribution of suffering towards civilians. At the beginning of the century, 90 per cent of the casualties were combatants whereas the majority of causalities now are intentionally inflicted on civilian resulting in millions uprooted and displaced.

The phenomenon of state collapse provides the context of CPEs in which humanitarian crises 'suddenly' erupt. Somewhat parallel to State collapse is the condition of 'ineffective' State or the 'failure of governance'. Cliff and Luckham identify four dimensions of State failure that lead to CPEs:[33]

- Development policy failures of government and international donor community:
  - failures in conflict management;
  - defects in or absence of democratic process, and
  - systemic crises or failure in state capacity and process of governance.

The concept CPE describes a hybrid conflict that encompasses both internal and trans-national characteristics. Conflicts have always been complex and had political characteristics but frequently protracted conflicts take on the aspects of CPE, characterized by collapse of political, economic and social order prompting an intervention to mend matters. The difference about the post cold war era is the complexity of the politics of humanitarian intervention. The meaning of CPE, argues political scientist Jayadev Uyangoda, is in that it draws our attention to multi-dimensional crises produced by contemporary post Cold War internal conflicts. It attempts to accommodate many aspects of contemporary conflicts that are not accounted for in traditional approaches to conflict: development failure; State failure; political economy of war; the impact of conflict on social structures; the cultures of violence produced by protracted conflicts and the sudden eruption of massive humanitarian crises.[34]

Afghanistan is a classic case of CPE, characterised by a 'failing' State and multiple and overlapping (quasi legal) centres of authority and militarized humanitarian intervention (and subsequent targeting in the war on terror). In protracted civil wars we see the creation of a new type of economy in which violence serves the important function of conferring benefits on certain groups and individuals. A political economy approach towards conflict is all about analysing the production and distribution of power, wealth and destitution during violent conflict, in order to explore the motives and responsibilities of those involved. These motives may change during the course of conflict. Once violent conflict emerges, it transforms itself and all around it — the State; livelihoods; the national economy and social relations.[35]

Drawing upon the Sri Lanka experience of two decades of 'ethnic conflict', Darini Rajasingham-Senanayake argues that it is not simply an ethnic conflict but a Complex Emergency. Here we are not talking about a conflict but an extremely complex, multi-layered conflict system in which a number of different conflicts interact with each other. The conflict, as with other struggles for ethno-national self determination, was fought to change the power-property status quo. Economic inequality and poverty cleavages tended to get ethnicised and politicised due to the circular dynamics of poverty and identity that characterises resource based ethno-religious identity conflicts in the global South.[36]

The conflict dynamics was sustained and fuelled by a range of global and local actors and factors including rural poverty, unemployment, caste marginalization, particularly in northern Tamil society and in the deep South:[37] "In the last decade a war economy that developed self sustaining momentum, emerged as a number of trans-national actors and networks, from the diasporas to the military, humanitarian and development industry, stabilized and sustained the conflict dynamic as the economy structured into a war economy. While a range of political actors and elites made profits through corruption, terror and taxation, the military became the leading employer of a class of marginalized youths from low caste communities in the south and north alike".[38]

The 'no war no peace' interregnum in the wake of the 2002 ceasefire has resulted in violence being franchised to the para-militaries.

Recent literature on internal conflicts has demonstrated the protracted nature of internal conflicts, especially those based over ethno-nationalist/religious identity conflicts and radical insurrections. In South Asia, the ethno-nationalist Naga conflict in Northeast India has been going on for over five decades. Sri Lanka's 'ethnic conflict' is over two decades old while Nepal's Maoist insurrection is spanning a decade.

The Sri Lankan conflict and the Naga conflict are in ceasefire-peace process mode, while Nepal has had an interregnum of two collapsed ceasefires and has currently moved on to 'war' following the end of a Maoist initiated unilateral ceasefire. Scholars have found that ethnicity based rebellions and radical insurrections are less amenable to negotiated settlements than inter-State wars.[39] Sri Lanka has experienced four cycles of negotiations and war — 1987: Indo-Sri Lanka agreement; 1989: LTTE-Premadasa peace talks; 1995: LTTE-Kumaratunga ceasefire peace talks and the latest phase of the Norwegian facilitated 2002 LTTE-GoSL talks in which a tenuous ceasefire is holding but substantive peace talks broke down in 2003.

The Naga conflict represents an exercise in peace building through a series of flawed peace accords that served to divide the Naga peoples and produced greater militarization: 1960, 1975 and currently the 1997 ceasefire-peace agreement which has got log-jammed due to the lack of progress on political issues.

Why do so many ceasefire — peace processes relapse into conflict? Is there a sidestepping of the root causes of conflict in the desperate keenness to stop the violence? Can the realities of power, justice and human rights be ignored if a sustainable peace is to be built? Are these 'flawed' negotiated settlements/peace accords (for example, Chittagong Hill Tracts 1999) likely to prove more stable and effective than a military victory (for example, East Pakistan 1971) or suppression of the conflict (as in Baluchistan and in East Punjab)? Licklider's statistical study of ethnic conflicts finds that "Seventy-nine per cent of the identity wars that ended in military victory were not followed by violence ... as compared to only 33 per cent of identity wars that ended in negotiated settlements".[40] Presumably a critical factor would be the extent to which the peace accord is able to balance perceived notions of 'grievances' and co-optation of elite groups through sharing of power and resources. Is it that the asymmetric structure of power in these internal conflicts makes conflict resolution so intractable? Are these peace accords, these negotiations of power but a pause in the trajectory of violent conflicts?[41]

In the genealogy of conflict theory literature, there is the expanding lexicon of conflict management, conflict resolution and conflict transformation and within the conflict resolution discourse is the paradigm of negotiation theory, influential exemplars being Roger Fry & Willian Ury.[42] In the field of conflict theory, there is substantive existing literature and critical analysis of concepts and practices, including tool kit approaches developed within the dominant paradigm of liberal democracy and paradigmatic shifts away from a statist approach to one that shifts emphasis to reconciliation, i.e.

building relationships and restoring community as the foundation for a sustainable peace as exemplified in the work of John Lederach.[43]

My concern here is to emphasise the important of peace building approaches that address the root causes of conflict; that incorporate technologies of justice and processes of building reconciliation; that seek to democratize peace processes, inscribe the language of rights and inclusion as well as strive to build a vision of peace that is maximalist. Within South Asia, the ineffectiveness or collapse of myriad peace accords and the relapse into militarization of conflicts and policies of 'waging war for peace'—has to do with the wide gap between prescription and reality in peace building. SAFHR's experimental peace audits of the Naga peace process, Chittagong Hill Tracts (CHT) accord and the suppression of the struggle in Punjab and Baluchistan, reveal the weaknesses and limits of peace making.

Ceasefires and Peace Building

Globally, since 1990 over three hundred peace agreements have been signed between adversaries in over 40 jurisdictions. But it has been very hard to deliver a peace that lasts beyond a ceasefire and delivers substantive democracy and tangible benefits to local communities. It is important to politically locate ceasefires and negotiations as a prelude to peace building, and not confuse them as a substitute for the mesh of processes that make up peace building during the conflict, in the ceasefire—negotiations interregnum and in the post conflict aftermath.[44]

Conflict resolution theorists and practitioners, in the overwhelming desire to stop or prevent outbreak of violence, surrender to sidestepping the realities of power and the demands for justice. This invokes the criticism of being status quoists and neo-colonialists, especially as the conflict resolution paradigm prescribes a significant emphasis on the role of third parties. Indeed, the South Asian field of conflicts is singled out as particularly resistant to third party involvement.[45] The Norwegian facilitation of the Sri Lankan ceasefire-peace process, backed by an international 'safety net', is an exception in the region. The earlier 1987 experiment involving the Indian Peace Keeping force exposed the limits of a 'power mediated' settlement that in the end was rejected by both parties.

The conventional wisdom is that internal conflicts, especially ethnic conflicts, are intractable and intrinsically zero-sum. A study of a decade of internal conflicts from 1989 to 99, found that out of 110 conflicts, 75 terminated before the end of 1999, but only 20 per cent of these were terminated by peace agreements. Most conflicts simply ceased being violent without a comprehensive resolution having been reached.[46] There was no resolution or elimination of 'grievances'.

Mary Kaldor has argued that in the course of protracted asymmetric conflicts there comes a stage when the reasons for the conflict get subsumed under the violence and the desperate desire to stop the violence overwhelms all else. The danger is that resolution of the conflict will provide the desired cessation of violence but could sidestep the vital issues of justice and rights that were originally at the core of the conflict. In such cases the peace achieved predicates another cycle of violence with peace in interregnum.

In a prescient analysis, William Zartman hones on to the structure of the asymmetry of power in internal conflicts as contributing to the protracted nature of ethnic conflicts in particular and the difficulty of arriving at a negotiated settlement. Asymmetry of power is a characteristic generally considered non conducive to negotiations and the attempt to redress asymmetry may complicate the negotiations dynamics further. Asymmetry means that one party is stronger (usually the government) and the other (insurgents) is weaker. It compels the rebels to redress asymmetry by greater commitment to the armed struggle. Zartman argues that negotiation is possible when grievances and commitment are in balance. If commitment to continuing the rebellion becomes stronger than grievances, insurgents have no incentive to continue negotiations. In the case of Sri Lanka, the government's strategy of weakening the LTTE militarily and making it amenable to negotiations instead produced a determination on the part of the LTTE to maximize military gains and achieve parity. In short, commitment has overtaken grievances, making for highly unstable negotiations.

Peace settlements should be moments of great opportunity but they become moments of great vulnerability especially when peace gets reduced to a 'one size fits all' formula of providing security, rebuilding institutions, and supporting social and economic recovery. Crucial issues of equity and justice as well as inclusive and participatory politics rarely find a place on the peace table. The root causes of conflict get displaced and suppressed setting the scene for renewed conflicts.

As the ICHRP draft report on the *Role of Human Rights in Peace Agreements* observes, the 'end of history' logic posits the liberal democracy paradigm as the one-size-fits-all solution to internal conflicts and has prescribed common elements to conflict resolution and therefore peace agreements. For instance, for internal conflicts aimed at the seizure of state power by violent means or regional/ identity conflicts, a 'big 'constitutional fix' would be found. In revolutionary insurrections, it would involve "moving to democratic elections and the constitutionalisation of power to prevent its abuse. In ethnically divided societies democracy would take on a group rights spin, with the 'constitutional fix' involving ethnically-based territorial divisions (usually falling short of statehood) or power-sharing, and cultural autonomy within unitary states, or indeed a mix of both. Add to these, a raft of human rights measures and the reconstruction of key legal institutions aimed to provide for accountability through legal checks and balances. These were intended to provide safeguards against abuse of power, which would solidify newly elected democracies as legitimate in a deep sense, and in ethnically divided societies crucially ensure the equal treatment of minorities *vis-à-vis* the majority".[47]

In contemporary peace processes the high table of peace negotiations is structured to seat only the armed protagonists, whereas the 'unarmed' multi-stakeholders in the peace process — civil society, women's groups, the church, business community, (all of whom may have been involved in 'informal' peace making activities), are excluded. Ceasefire monitoring mechanisms (in both third party facilitated and bilateral negotiations) do not provide for a structured civil society involvement, e.g., in the Naga and Sri Lankan peace processes. Peace negotiations become opportunities for brokering elite arrangements for sharing power and apportioning resources rather than envisioning a just and inclusive society. Gendered perspectives in peace building are ignored and basic needs and welfare concerns not prioritized and resourced; conflict is displaced or diverted, processes of reconciliation and mechanisms for recognition of grievance and delivering justice bypassed. There is power sharing; there is security—but for whom? There is peace—but what kind of peace?

Peace should be a maximalist concept, sustained on the twin pillars of human rights and substantive democracy, if it is to have meaningful content and survive. Several of the peace agreements signed in the last 15 years refer extensively to human rights norms and principles. However, in many ceasefire peace processes, as in the case of Sri Lanka, the armed protagonists and the international community facilitating the process have accepted to keep human rights principles in abeyance, as they are deemed an obstacle to the peace negotiations.[48] In the case of the Sri Lankan processes the compromise of an imperfect ceasefire peace process over a perfect war is proving to be extremely untenable and corrosive to the peace process itself.

As peace activist Branka Rajna from Bosnia observed at the conference on 'Women and Violent Conflict', "what was peace and security for the ostensible victors of the conflict who had not been displaced, raped or widowed, if it meant unemployment, bankrupt social funds, no housing and a media full of hate and aggression?"[49]

In defining a holistic peace, it is useful to look at a recent Declaration adopted by a group of South Asian activists at the Dhaka meeting of PISA (2005): "Peace must be more than an absence of direct violence, and must mean freedom from the fear of insecurity in our own homes, security of livelihood and political voice for the excluded. Peace building cannot be just stopping the violence. This has consequences for the relapse back to violence if basic grievances are not addressed."[50]

The CHT accord and the Sri Lankan peace processes[51] represent the limits and weaknesses of such exclusions in building a democratic peace. By contrast the South African peace process represented an effort at democratization of the peace process by providing for a (secondary) long table to enable multiple constituencies to impact on the peace process. The Naga peace process also is singular in the level of mobilization of civil society groups and in particular women's groups in support of the ceasefire and peace process. Indeed, it is likely that the two armed protagonists — the government of India and the NSCN (I-M) leadership — would have walked away from the table were it not for the constant pressure of civil society groups in support of peace.[52]

Contemporary peace agreements are animated by a human rights discourse either by its inclusion or its absence. In the case of conflicts in Sri Lanka or the abortive Nepal ceasefire–peace process (2003), the formal framework of negotiations does not contain specific references to human rights commitments, but there is an active human rights discourse surrounding the process and impacting upon it. Human rights protection is vital to peace-making. According to the study on the role of Human Rights in Peace Agreements, at its strongest, the argument for human rights in peace negotiations is an argument for peace to have some content. What is peace if it is not having fair and accountable government, and, when things go wrong, having access to police, courts and justice systems that do not discriminate or treat people cruelly? Ignoring human rights in the short term, it is argued, cannot lead to peace in the long term.

However, during negotiations, in the interest of stopping the violence and not jeopardizing a fragile process, human rights are kept in abeyance as in the case of the Sri Lankan ceasefire–peace process. Indeed ceasefire agreements, e.g. Naga (NSCN I-M) and GoI and the LTTE-GoSL, concern themselves primarily with the security concerns of armed actors and do not provide for protection of civilians.[53] Every civilian killed in a conflict is a human rights violation. For peace to have meaning human rights concerns need to be inscribed and given priority in peace processes both during and in the aftermath.

Concepts of 'transitional justice' and technologies of truth and reconciliation are an integral part of conflict resolution-peace building theories. South African and Guatemalan experiences with the Truth and Reconciliation Commission represent important landmarks in the development of theory and practice of rebuilding social community, trust and reconciliation. Why is it important to undertake a process of 'truth and reconciliation'? Is it enough to have truth and reconciliation and not justice?

The tension between pursuing truth and justice for human rights abuses and consolidating a *non violent* status quo is evident in the controversy over justice for state engineered disappearances in the Punjab (India). Thousands were disappeared by the state in the counter insurgency operations to suppress the identity conflict/'separatist' violence in the Punjab. In 2004, the efforts of a human rights group, the Committee for Information and Initiative on Punjab, resulted in the National Human Rights Commission of India (a statutory body) taking the unprecedented step of publishing a list of 2,097 'disappeared' people illegally cremated by the police and asking for compensation. It prompted an agitated and hostile reaction. Is it better, as many argued, to avoid disturbing the (albeit imperfect) 'peace' by raking up old, better forgotten injustices? And, if so, for whom is it better — the victims' families? Will such a move demoralize the police/security forces in fighting terrorism? What is the implication of perpetuating a culture of impunity that legitimizes systematic human rights violations in the name of fighting terrorism? What kind of peace has it delivered in the Punjab? What are the implications of this new battle line between human rights on the one hand and security/terrorism on the other? Are the international law frameworks, that uphold human rights as universal and indivisible, to be derogated from when it comes to fighting 'terrorism' (that collapses violent political resistance and terrorist activities as one)?

Multiple Stakeholders

There are multiple actors (interest groups) in a conflict apart from the obviously identifiable armed protagonists—the international community and multilateral agencies, the diasporas, refugees, 'minorities' within ethno-nationalist/identity conflicts, business community—national and transnational, civil society groups including women's groups and the media. The capacity to understand and transform the conflict hinges on identifying the relevant interest groups, especially the 'spoilers' who fear peace. In the Naga conflict, the Indian government had fostered a collaborationist political leadership and bureaucracy through the creation of the state of Nagaland in the Indian Union. Their power and authority is dependent upon the continuation of the status quo.

Also, as we examined above, protracted conflicts produce war economies in which while some are made destitute, there are others who profit and have a vested interest in the war continuing. Particularly in conflicts which are based on access to natural resources/minerals, predatory war economies develop which drive the conflict, as in the case of diamonds in Sierra Leone, heroin in Afghanistan, etc. In the words of Paul Collier 'greed rather than grievance' drives these conflicts. In the case of Sri Lanka, 30 per cent of all revenue flows to the (underdeveloped) rural areas are related to the war machinery, soldiers, salaries, pensions etc.[54] These interest groups, the 'spoilers' have to be neutralized if the peace process is to survive. Increasingly in the humanitarian-development industry, the discourse has attempted to focus on the sensitivity to not reinforce the strength of these predatory interest groups and inculcate development strategies that counter their control.

It is a comprehensive approach that recognises that in addressing poverty and deprivation, the prevention of violent conflict should be the cornerstone of development policy.[55] Whereas earlier the international humanitarian aid and development industry discourse avoided or at best worked around conflict,[56] the development paradigm has been remodelled and made conflict sensitive as reflected in Mary Anderson's influential ready reckoner for development practitioners, 'Do No Harm'. She argues for working 'in' and 'on' conflict, because if you are working in a conflict prone or conflict environment, you are already part of the context. Consequently, there is the necessity for development policy makers and practitioners to develop an understanding of the historical and socio-economic roots of conflict as well as to build local capacities to manage tension and differences in a non violent manner.[57]

In internal conflicts, the role of civil society is most crucial. Given that protagonists of violence are increasingly non-state or sub-state groups emerging from within society, it makes sense to explore the peace making potentials of people from within those societies. Furthermore, in an internal conflict, where it is the government itself that is facing dissent from its own people, it is even more crucial that citizens and communities have a voice in the processes of peace building.

Peace building is seen as a multi-track process and no longer seen as the preserve of governments. It needs to be built at the societal level as well as negotiated by politico-military elites.[58] Civil society actors are increasingly asserting their right and responsibility in mobilizing support for the ceasefire-peace processes; to be part of ceasefire monitoring mechanisms and to sit at the peace table and participate in democratizing the negotiating process and in determining the peace agenda. The peace table is a metaphor for the process of determining the configuration of post conflict socio-political arrangements and the voices of women, civil society groups, minorities, etc. should be enabled to impact on the processes. For instance, women's voices must be heard when rights are being constituted and constitutions drawn up if they are not to be trapped in the category of second class citizenship or find themselves subject to two states—in the public sphere governed by public law and the private sphere (the sphere of women) governed by personal laws that are often iniquitous to women.

At issue here is not only the involvement of civil society and the democratization of the peace process as mentioned above, but also the argument that women's mobilization contributes different perspectives and different ways of doing politics and peace building.

Many of you in South Asia will have seen the dramatic pictures of naked Manipuri women demonstrating in protest against *the Armed Forces (Special Powers) Act* in July. This particular instance not only shows women mobilizing against human rights violations committed by the security forces (and the culture of impunity symbolized by the AFSPA) but also serves to highlight women's particular strategies of intervention in situations of violent conflict.

Today, the meta narrative — of history, of nationalism, of international relations, and of conflict — which is presumed to be 'gender' neutral — has been paralleled by multiple, fragmented narratives, i.e. the narratives of women, *dalits*, *janajatis* (tribals), *adivasis* (the indigenous), etc. Feminist scholarship has explored gender as an important category of analysis in understanding the state, the nation, citizenship, minority rights, and refugees.

It is argued that women's experience of conflict is different from that of men and that, consequently, their perspectives and responses to conflict too are different. It is a truism that women are the worst affected by conflict: it is women and their dependent children who make up the bulk of the world's Internally Displaced Persons (IDPs) and refugees. The focus on women begs the question: Do women exist as a constituency for mobilizing against conflict and for peace building? Gender is only one aspect of a woman's identity and is itself intersected by race, ethnicity, religion, language, caste, and class. Women as the subjects of peace politics may have to be brought into being, i.e. politically mobilized into being.

Feminist historiography of the rape of women in Canton; the rape of women in the 1947 Partition of the subcontinent, in the 1971 Bangladesh war, in the Chittagong Hill Tracts, during the Indian Peackeeping Forces (IPKF) operation in Sri Lanka, in Kashmir, and in Nagaland, has added to the huge body of analysis on the use of rape as an instrument of war. It has resulted in the International Criminal Code recognizing rape as a war crime. War and the culture of militaries are not only masculine but misogynist as well. War places great value on the reproductive role of women and either denies them any degree of autonomy of control over their bodies or ideologically manipulates them. Conflict starkly brings out a continuum of violence from the 'field of battle' to inside the home. Identity-centered conflicts configure women as the physical markers of the community, thereby subjecting them to greater community control while at the same time also rendering them more vulnerable to sexual transgression by the 'other' as a symbol of transgression of the community or nation.

However, our emphasis lies less on women as victims of conflict and more on the ways in which to make the many faces of women's agency visible. Broadly speaking, women's role in conflict manifests itself by i) managing to survive, and this in a sustained manner, ii) reducing and minimizing violence, iii) mobilizing for peace, and iv) reaching out across conflict-torn societies, and by assisting in the reconciliation, healing, and the reconstruction of society. Arguments in support of the connection between women and peace range from the biological, to the social (role as caregivers), to the radical, i.e., for justice and inclusive politics. The connection between women and peace is based on the premise that since women's historical experience is that of inequality and exclusion, they have greater empathy in understanding the dynamics of unequal relationships. South Asian conflicts have seen myriad interventions for peace by women. The question, however, still needs to be empirically addressed: Is there any organic relationship between women and peace? Have women been able to transcend their community identity and reach out across conflict divides following the logic of 'some mother's son'?

UN Resolution 1325 argues for mainstreaming gender in peace making. Why is there a need to do so? Do women make a difference or is it because women make up half the population and need to be represented? Do women bring different perspectives to the peace process? Do they bring different ways of negotiating—do they make a difference?

Finally, as a last point worthy of mention, is the black hole for feminist politics, in other words the possibility of an emancipatory politics for women joining militant struggles. In such circumstances, these women are steeped in cultures that are masculine, hierarchical, and authoritarian, for example LTTE women, Maoist women in Nepal, and NSCN women in Nagaland.

Notes

1. Stewart, F. and Fitzgerald, E.V.K. Eds. *War and Underdevelopment*, Vol. 1: *The Economic and Social Consequences of Conflict*, (Oxford: OUP, 2000).
2. United Nations, *Human Development Report 2005*, (New York: United Nations Development Programmeme, 2005).

3. Jonathan Goodhand & David Hulme, "From wars to complex political emergencies: understanding conflict and peace-building in the new world disorder", *Third World Quarterly*, (Vol 20, No 1, 1999), pp. 13-26
4. *The Responsibility to Protect*: Report of the International Commission on Intervention and State Sovereignty, (Ottawa: the International Development Research Center, December 2001) . at http://www.iciss.ca/pdf/Commission-Report.pdf
5. http://www.un.org/Depts/dhl/resguide/r59.htm
6. UN General Assembly, A/59/2005/Add.3, Fifty-ninth session, 26 May 2005, Agenda items 45 and 55 at http://www.ohchr.org/english/docs/A.59.2005.Add.3.pdf p. 19 of 31 (Last visited on 10 February 2006)
7. Donini, Antonio, Norah Niland and Karin Wermester, "Introduction", in Antonio Donini, Norah Niland and Karin Wermester, eds., *Nation-building Unraveled? Air, Peace and Justice*, (Bloomfield Connecticut: Kumarian Press, 2004).
8. P. Sahadevan, *Ethnic Conflict and Militarism in South Asia: Kroc Institute Occasional Paper # 6:OP:4*, (Joan B. Kroc Institute for International Peace Studies, University of Notre Dame, June 1999).
9. Kaldor, M., *New and Old Wars*, (Cambridge: Polity Press, 1999); Mary Kaldor, "Europe at the Millennium", *Politics* (2000) 20(2), pp. 55-62.
10. Martin Shaw, *Theory of the Global State: Globality as Unfinished Revolution*, (Cambridge: CUP, 2000).
11. Indian Prime Minister Manmohan Singh's key note address at IDSA seminar in New Delhi, November 2005.
12. Ian Bannon and Paul Collier, eds., *Natural Resources and Violent Conflict: Opinions and Actions*, (Washington D.C.: The World Bank, 2004); Paul Collier *et al.*, *Breaking the Conflict Trap: Civil War and Development Policy*, (Washington, D.C.: The World Bank, 2003); Paul Collier, "Rebellion as a Quasi-Criminal Activity," *Journal of Conflict Resolution* 44, No. 6 (2000): 839-853; Paul Collier and Anke Hoeffler, *On Economic Causes of Civil War*, Oxford Economic Papers No. 50 (Oxford: Center for International Studies, 1998); Paul Collier and Anke Hoeffler, *Green and Grievance in Civil War*, Politicy Research Working Paper No. 2355, (Washington D.C.: World Bank, 2000); Paul Collier, "Demobilization and Insecurity: A Study in the Economics of the Transition from War to Peace," *Journal of International Development* 6, No. 3 (1994): 245-351.
13. Diana Francis, *People, Peace and Power: Conflict Transformation in Action*, (London and Sterling, VA: Pluto Press, 2002); Chris Mitchell, "Recognizing Conflict", in Tom Woodhouse, ed., *Peacemaking in a Troubled World,* (Oxford: Berg, 1991).
14. Chris Mitchell, *Ibid.*
15. Greg Russell, *Hans J. Morgenthau and the Ethics of American Statecraft*

(Baton Rouge and London: Louisiana State University Press, 1990), pp. 212-13; Quincy Wright, *A Study of War*, Vol. 1 and 2 (Chicago: University of Chicago Press, 1942).

16. Jimmy Carter and James Laue, *A Conversation on Peacemaking with Jimmy Carter* (Washington, D. C: National Istitute for Dispute Resolution, 1992); James Laue and Gerald Cormick, "The Ethics of Intervention in Community Disputes" in Gordon Bermant, Herbert C. Kelman, and Donald P. Warwick eds., *The Ethics of Social Intervention* (Washington, DC: Halsted Press, 1978); Jaue, James H., *Direct Action and Desegregation, 1960-1962: Toward a Theory of the Rationalization of Protest* (Brooklyn, NY: Carlson Publishing, 1989).
17. Galtung, Johan, "Cultural Violence", *Journal of Peace Research*, 1990 27(3): 291-305.
18. Kumar Rupesinghe with Sanam Anderlini, *Civil Wars, Civil Peace: An Introduction to Conflict Resolution* (London: Pluto Press, 1998).
19. Brown, Michael, "The Causes of Internal Conflict: An Overview", in Michael Brown et al, eds., *Nationalism and Ethnic Conflict* (Cambridge: MIT Press, 1997), 3-25.
20. Commission on Weak States and US National Security Report, 2004: *On the Brink: Weak States and US National Security*: at http://www.cgdev.org/doc/books/weakstates/Full_Report.pdf (Last visited on 10 February 2006).
21. A shift away from the traditional income based definition of poverty is in a minimum basic needs approach, which defins poverty in quantifiable terms and views it as a condition characterised by severe deprivation of basic human needs including food, safe drinking water, sanitation facilities, health, shelter, education and information It depends not only on income but access to social services. Marginalization and social exclusion are other terms used to describe poverty. See, Lipton M & Ravillion M., "Poverty and Policy" in J. Behrman and TN Srinivasan, eds., *Handbook of Development Economics*, Vol. 3B, (Rotterdam, The Netherlands: CEPA, 1995) pp. 2553-2657.
22. Goor, L. van de and S. Verstegen, *Conflict Prognosis: A Conflict and Policy Assessment Framework, Part Two* (The Hague: Clingendael Institute, 2000).
23. *Human Development Report 2005* (New York: UNDP, 2005), p. 163 at http://hdr.undp.org/reports/global/2005/pdf/HDR05_complete.pdf [Visited 12 January 2006].
24. Jonathan Goodhand, *Conflict Assessments—A Synthesis Report: Kyrgyzstan, Moldova, Nepal and Sri Lanka* (London: The Conflict, Security and Development Group, Centre for Defence Studies, King's College, University of London, 2001), p. 25.
25. *Human Development Report 2005* (New York: UNDP, 2005), p. 163.
26. Gurr, Ted Robert, *et al.*, *Peace and Conflict 2001: A Global Survey of*

Armed Conflicts, Self-Determination Movements, and Democracy (Maryland: Center for International Development and Conflict Management, University of Maryland, 2001).

27. Frantz Fanon, *The Wretched of the Earth*, English translation by Constance Farrington (London: MacGibbon & Kee, 1965).
28. Kaldor, M., *New and Old Wars*, (Cambridge: Polity Press, 1999).
29. Mary B. Anderson, *Do No Harm: How Aid Can Support Peace—Or —War* (Boulder: Lynne Rienner Publishers, 1999)
30. Sarkar, T., "Semiotics of Terror: Muslim children and women in Hindu Rashtra", *Economic and Political Weekly*, 12 July 2002.
31. UNSC Resolution 1325 (2000): at http://www.un.org/events/res_1325e.pdf
32. J. Goodhand & D. Hulme, *NGOs and complex political emergencies*, Working Paper No. 1 (University of Manchester and INRAC, October 1997).
33. L. Cliffe and R. Luckham, "Complex political emergencies and the state: Failure and the fate of the state", *Third World Quarterly*, 20(1), 1999, 27-50.
34. Uyangoda, Jayadeva, "Transition from Civil War to Peace: Challenges of Peacebuilding in Sri Lanka", Colombo: Social Scientists' Association, What Kind of Peace Project paper.
35. L. Cliffe and R. Luckham, "Complex political emergencies and the state: Failure and the fate of the state", *Third World Quarterly*, 20(1), 1999, 27-50.
36. Markus Mayer, Darini Rajasingham-Senanayake & Yuvi Thangarajah, eds., *Building Local Capacities for Peace: Rethinking Conflict and Development in Sri Lanka* (Delhi: Macmillan, 2003).
37. Darini Rajasingham-Senanayake, "Sri Lanka and the Violence of Reconstruction", *Development*, Vol. 48: 3, September 2005.
38. Markus Mayer, Darini Rajasingham-Senanayake & Yuvi Thangarajah, eds., *Building Local Capacities for Peace: Rethinking Conflict and Development in Sri Lanka* (Delhi: Macmillan, 2003).
39. Zartman, I.W., ed., *Elusive Peace: Negotiating to End Civil Wars* (Washington, DC: Brookings, 1995); Zartman, I. W., and Rubin, J.Z., eds., *Power and Negotiation* (Ann Arbor: University of Michigan Press, 2001); I. Wiliam Zartman, "Negotiating Internal Conflict: Incentives and Intractability", *International Negotiation* 6: 297-302, 2001.
40. Licklider, Roy, "How civil wars end: Questions and methods", in Roy Licklider ed., *Stopping the Killing: How civil wars end* (New York: New York University Press, 1993); Licklider, Roy, "The consequences of negotiated settlements in civil wars, 1945-1993", *American Political Science Review* 89: 681-90, 1995.
41. Samaddar Ranabir, 'Those bunch of accords', SAFHR Paper Series-4 (Kathmandu: SAFHR, 1999).

42. Fisher, Roger, and William Ury, "Don't Bargain over Positions" in Fisher, Roger and William Ury with Bruce Patton, eds., *Getting to Yes: Negotiating Agreement Without Giving In*, 2nd edition (Boston: Houghton Mifflin, 1991), pp. 3-14
43. Lederach J.P., *Preparing for Peace: Conflict Transformation Across Cultures* (Syracuse: Syracuse University Press, 1995); John Paul Lederach, *Building Peace: Sustainable reconciliation in divided societies* (Washington: United States Institute of Peace, 1997); Lederach, John Paul, Janice Moomaw Jenner, eds, *A handbook of international peacebuilding: into the eye of the storm* (San Francisco: Jossey-Bass, 2002); Lederach, John Paul, *The moral imagination: The art and soul of building peace* (New York: OUP, 2005).
44. Porter, Toby, "Mechanisms for Monitoring Ceasefire and Peace Agreements: Background Paper, Case Studies", (Geneva: Centre for Humanitarian Dialogue, 2003).
45. P. Sahadevan, *Ethnic Conflict and Militarism in South Asia: Kroc Institute Occasional Paper # 6:OP:4*, (Joan B. Kroc Institute for International Peace Studies, University of Notre Dame, June 1999).
46. Wallensteen, P., and M. Sollenberg, "Armed conflict 1989-1999", *Journal of Peace Research,* 37 (5), 635-649, 2000.
47. Draft Consultation of the International Council of Human Rights Policy, *Role of Human Rights in Peace Agreements,* (Versoix, Switzerland: ICHRP, 2005).
48. International Council Human Rights Policy *Role of Human Rights in Peace Agreements* 2005.
49. Testimonies presented at the Conference on "Women and Violent Conflict: Global Perspectives", International Altert, London, April 1999.
50. Adapted from PISA Declaration, adopted by South Asian participants at a Peace in South Asia Conference in Dhaka November 2005.
51. There are second track subcommittees, including the gender subcommittee but they have lacked political leverage.
52. Rita Manchanda, *We Do More Because We Can: Naga Women in the Peace Process* (Kathmandu: SAFHR, 2004).
53. Ram Narayan Kumar & Laxmi Murthy, Four Years of Ceasefire Agreement between the Government of India and the National Socialist Council of Nagalim: Promises and Pitfalls (New Delhi: Other Media, 2002); Rita Manchanda, *We Do More Because We Can: Naga Women in the Peace Process* (Kathmandu: SAFHR, 2004).
54. Gunetilleke, N., Abdul Cader, A., Fernando, M., *Understanding the Dimensions and Dynamics of Poverty in Underserved Settlements in Colombo* (Colombo: Centre for Poverty Analysis (CEPA) & Participatory Improvement of Undeserved Settlements in Colombo (PRIMUSS), 2004); Ganepola, V. and Thalayasingam, P., *Poverty and Conflict: A Review of Literature* (Colombo: Centre for Poverty Analysis, 2004).

55. *Human Development Report 2005* (New York: UNDP, 2005), p. 12.
56. Jonathan Goodhand, *Conflict Assessments—A Synthesis Report: Kyrgyzstan, Moldova, Nepal and Sri Lanka* (London: The Conflict, Security and Development Group, Centre for Defence Studies, King's College, University of London, 2001).
57. Mary B. Anderson, *Do No Harm: How Aid Can Support Peace—Or —War* (Boulder: Lynne Rienner Publishers, 1999).
58. John Paul Lederach, *Building Peace: Sustainable reconciliation in divided societies* (Washington: United States Institute of Peace, 1997.

References

Anderlini, Sanam; Shereen Karmali and Rita Manchanda, "Women, Violent Conflict, and Peacebuilding: a Global Perspective", London: International Alert Conference, May 5-7, 1999.

Bose, Tapan, "Global War on 'Terrorism' and Democratic Rights", key note presentation at SAFHR's fifth South Asian Workshop on Sensitizing Media Reporting Conflict, New Delhi, December 10-12, 2004: http://www.safhr.org/Media%20Report%20Fifth.doc

———, *The Current History of Peace Politics; the Other Side of the War in Kashmir*, SAFHR Paper Series-13, Kathmandu, 2002.

Brown, Michael, "The Causes of Internal Conflict: An Overview", in Michael Brown et al, eds., *Nationalism and Ethnic Conflict* (Cambridge: MIT Press, 2001), 3-25.

Chris Mitchell, "Recognizing Conflict", in Tom Woodhouse, ed., *Peacemaking in a Troubled World,* (Oxford: Berg, 1991).

Commission on Weak States and US National Security Report, 2004: *On the Brink: Weak States and US National Security*: http://www.cgdev.org/doc/books/weakstates/Full_Report.pdf

Darini Rajasingham-Senanayake, "Sri Lanka and the Violence of Reconstruction", *Development*, Vol. 48: 3, September 2005

Das, Veena, "Our Work to Cry: Your Work to Listen" in Veena Das, ed., *Mirrors of Violence: Communities, Riots and Survivors in South Asia* (Delhi: OUP, 1990), pp. 345-398

Diana Francis, *People, Peace and Power: Conflict Transformation in Action,* (London and Sterling, VA: Pluto Press, 2002).

Donini, Antonio, Norah Niland and Karin Wermester, "Introduction", in Antonio Donini, Norah Niland and Karin Wermester, eds., *Nation-building Unraveled? Air, Peace and Justice*, (Bloomfield Connecticut: Kumarian Press, 2004).

Draft Consultation of the International Council of Human Rights Policy, *Role of Human Rights in Peace Agreements,* (Versoix, Switzerland: ICHRP, 2005).

Fisher, Roger, and William Ury, "Don't Bargain over Positions" in Fisher, Roger and William Ury with Bruce Patton, eds., *Getting to Yes: Negotiating Agreement Without Giving In*, 2nd edition (Boston: Houghton Mifflin, 1991), pp. 3-14.

Frantz Fanon, *The Wretched of the Earth*, English translation by Constance Farrington (London: MacGibbon & Kee, 1965).

Galtung, Johan, "Cultural Violence", *Journal of Peace Research*, 1990 27(3): 291-305.

Ganepola, V. and Thalayasingam, P., *Poverty and Conflict: A Review of Literature* (Colombo: Centre for Poverty Analysis, 2004).

Goor, L. van de and S. Verstegen, *Conflict Prognosis: A Conflict and Policy Assessment Framework, Part Two* (The Hague: Clingendael Institute, 2000).

Greg Russell, *Hans J. Morgenthau and the Ethics of American Statecraft* (Baton Rouge and London: Louisiana State University Press, 1990), pp. 212-13.

Gunetilleke, N., Abdul Cader, A., Fernando, M., *Understanding the Dimensions and Dynamics of Poverty in Underserved Settlements in Colombo* (Colombo: Centre for Poverty Analysis (CEPA) & Participatory Improvement of Undeserved Settlements in Colombo (PRIMUSS), 2004).

Gurr, Ted Robert, et al, *Peace and Conflict 2001: A Global Survey of Armed Conflicts, Self-Determination Movements, and Democracy* (Maryland: Centre for International Development and Conflict Management, University of Maryland, 2001).

Human Development Report 2005 (New York: UNDP, 2005), p. 163. http://hdr.undp.org/reports/global/2005/pdf/HDR05_complete.pdf [Visited 12 January 2006] .

I. Wiliam Zartman, "Negotiating Internal Conflict: Incentives and Intractability", *International Negotiation* 6: 297-302, 2001.

———, and Rubin, J.Z., eds., *Power and Negotiation* (Ann Arbor: University of Michigan Press, 2001).

———, ed., *Elusive Peace: Negotiating to End Civil Wars* (Washington, DC: Brookings, 1995).

Ian Bannon and Paul Collier, eds., *Natural Resources and Violent Conflict: Opinions and Actions*, (Washington D.C.: The World Bank, 2004).

James Laue and Gerald Cormick, "The Ethics of Intervention in Community Disputes" in Gordon Bermant, Herbert C. Kelman, and Donald P. Warwick eds., *The Ethics of Social Intervention* (Washington, DC: Halsted Press, 1978).

Jaue, James H., *Direct Action and Desegregation, 1960-1962: Toward a Theory of the Rationalization of Protest* (Brooklyn, NY: Carlson Publishing, 1989).

Jehan Perera, *Peace Process in Nagaland and Chittagong Hill Tracts*, SAFHR Paper Series-5, Kathmandu, 1999.

Jimmy Carter and James Laue, *A Conversation on Peacemaking with Jimmy Carter* (Washington, D.C: National Institute for Dispute Resolution, 1992).

John Paul Lederach, *Building Peace: Sustainable reconciliation in divided societies* (Washington: United States Institute of Peace, 1997).

———, *Preparing for Peace: Conflict Transformation Across Cultures* (Syracuse: Syracuse University Press, 1995).

———, *The moral imagination: The art and soul of building peace* (New York: OUP, 2005).

———, and Janice Moomaw Jenner, eds, *A handbook of international peacebuilding: into the eye of the storm* (San Francisco: Jossey-Bass, 2002).

Jonathan Goodhand., & David Hulme., *NGOs and complex political emergencies*, Working Paper No. 1 (University of Manchester and INRAC, October 1997).

———, "From wars to complex political emergencies: understanding conflict and peace-building in the new world disorder", *Third World Quarterly*, (Vol 20, No 1, 1999), pp. 13-26.

Jonathan Goodhand, *Conflict Assessments—A Synthesis Report: Kyrgyzstan, Moldova, Nepal and Sri Lanka* (London: The Conflict, Security and Development Group, Centre for Defence Studies, King's College, University of London, 2001).

Kumar Rupesinghe with Sanam Anderlini, *Civil Wars, Civil Peace: An Introduction to Conflict Resolution* (London: Pluto Press, 1998).

L. Cliffe and R. Luckham, "Complex political emergencies and the state: Failure and the fate of the state", *Third World Quarterly*, 20 (1), 1999, 27-50.

Licklider, Roy, "How civil wars end: Questions and methods", in Roy Licklider ed., *Stopping the Killing: How civil wars end* (New York: New York University Press, 1993).

Licklider, Roy, "The consequences of negotiated settlements in civil wars, 1945-1993", *American Political Science Review* 89: 681-90, 1995.

Lipton M & Ravillion M., "Poverty and Policy" in J. Behrman and TN Srinivasan, eds., *Handbook of Development Economics*, Vol. 3B, (Rotterdam, The Netherlands: CEPA, 1995) pp. 2553-2657.

Markus Mayer, Darini Rajasingham-Senanayake & Yuvi Thangarajah, eds., *Building Local Capacities for Peace: Rethinking Conflict and Development in Sri Lanka* (Delhi: Macmillan, 2003).

Martin Shaw, *Theory of the Global State: Globality as Unfinished Revolution*, (Cambridge: CUP, 2000).

Mary B. Anderson, *Do No Harm: How Aid Can Support Peace—Or—War* (Boulder: Lynne Rienner Publishers, 1999).

Mary Kaldor, "Europe at the Millennium", *Politics* (2000) 20(2), pp. 55-62.
—*New and Old Wars*, (Cambridge: Polity Press, 1999).

P. Sahadevan, *Ethnic Conflict and Militarism in South Asia: Kroc Institute Occasional Paper # 6:OP:4*, (Joan B. Kroc Institute for International Peace Studies, University of Notre Dame, June 1999).

Paul Collier and Anke Hoeffler, *On Economic Causes of Civil War*, Oxford Economic Papers No. 50 (Oxford: Centre for International Studies, 1998).

Paul Collier and Anke Hoeffler, *Green and Grievance in Civil War*, Policy Research Working Paper No. 2355, (Washington D.C.: World Bank, 2000).

Paul Collier *et al.*, *Breaking the Conflict Trap: Civil War and Development Policy*, (Washington, D.C.: The World Bank, 2003).

Paul Collier, "Demobilization and Insecurity: A Study in the Economics of the Transition from War to Peace," *Journal of International Development 6, no. 3* (1994): 245-351.

Paul Collier, "Rebellion as a Quasi-Criminal Activity," *Journal of Conflict Resolution* 44, No. 6 (2000): 839-853.

Porter, Toby, "Mechanisms for Monitoring Ceasefire and Peace Agreements: Background Paper, Case Studies", (Geneva: Centre for Humanitarian Dialogue, 2003).

Quincy Wright, *A Study of War*, Vol. 1 and 2 (Chicago: University of Chicago Press, 1942).

Ram Narayan Kumar, *A Complex Denial: Disappearances, Secret Cremations & and the Issues of Truth and Justice in Punjab*, 2001.

Ram Narayan Kumar with Laxmi Murthy, Four Years of Ceasefire Agreement between the Government of India and the National Socialist Council of Nagaland: Promises and Pitfalls (New Delhi: Other Media, 2002) .

Rita Manchanda, *We Do More Because We Can: Naga Women in the Peace Process* (Kathmandu: SAFHR, 2004).

Ranabir Samaddar, *"Those Accords": A Bunch of Documents*, SAFHR Paper Series-4, Kathmandu, 1999.

Ranabir Samaddar, Shahid Faiz, *Peace Process in Sri Lanka*, SAFHR Paper Series 8, Kathmandu, 2001.

Sarkar, Tanika 2002 'Semiotics of terror: Muslim Women and Children in Hindu Rashtra *Economic and Political Weekly*, Vol. 37. 28, July 31 2002.

——, "Semiotics of Terror: Muslim children and women in Hindu Rashtra", *Economic and Political Weekly*, 12 July 2002.

Shahid Faiz, *The Peace Question in Baluchistan*, SAFHR Paper Series 16, Kathmandu, 2003.

Jagat M. Acharya, Manjita Gurung, Ranabir Samaddar, *No-Where People on the Indo-Bangladesh Border*, SAFHR Paper Series 14, Kathmandu, 2003.

Stewart, F. and Fitzgerald, E.V.K. Eds. *War and Underdevelopment*, Vol. 1:

The Economic and Social Consequences of Conflict, (Oxford: OUP, 2000).

The Responsibility to Protect: Report of the International Commission on Intervention and State Sovereignty, (Ottawa: the International Development Research Centre, December 2001)—http://www.iciss.ca/pdf/Commission-Report.pdf

UNSC Resolution 1325 (2000):—http://www.un.org/events/res_1325e.pdf

Uyangoda, J. "Understanding Conflict and Conflict Resolution" in *Conflict, Conflict Resolution & Peace Building*" Jayadeva Uyangoda, ed., (Colombo: University of Colombo, 2005).

——, "Transition from Civil War to Peace: Challenges of Peacebuilding in Sri Lanka", Colombo: Social Scientists' Association, What Kind Of Peace Project paper, November 2005.

Wallensteen, P., and M. Sollenberg, "Armed conflict 1989-1999", *Journal of Peace Research,* 37(5), 635-649, 2000.

Wright Quincy, 'The Nature of conflict' in John Burton and Frank Dukes (eds) *Conflict: Readings in Management and Resolution* (London: Macmillan, 1990), pp. 15-33.

Chapter Four

The "War on Terror" and the Challenges to Democracy and Human Rights from the Emergent World Order

The 'war on terror', declared by President Bush following the 9/11 attacks on the World Trade Centre, not only reflects the dominant geo-political interests of the sole Superpower in the aftermath of the Cold War but also augurs a radical reshaping of the New World Order under its influence. It highlights the subordination of law to political interests and reveals the shortcomings of the current corpus of the laws of war. It also signifies the limitations of existing international enforcement mechanisms, which are notionally committed to ensure international peace and security, in combating violations and impunity. The depth and the dimensions of the new global war are best conveyed by the proclamation that President Bush made in his 20th of September 2001 address to a joint session of the US Congress:

"Our war on terror begins with Al Qaeda, but it does not end there. It will not end until every terrorist group of global reach has been found, stopped and defeated... They are the heirs of all the murderous ideologies of the 20th century. By sacrificing human life to serve their radical visions, by abandoning every value except the will to power, they follow in the path of fascism, Marxism and totalitarianism. And they will follow that path all the way to where it ends in history's unmarked grave of discarded lies... We will direct every resource at our command—every means of diplomacy, every tool of intelligence, every instrument of law enforcement, every financial influence, and every necessary weapon of war—to the destruction and to the defeat of the global terror network... Our response involves far more than instant retaliation and isolated strikes. Americans should not expect one battle, but a lengthy campaign unlike any other we have ever seen. It may include dramatic strikes visible on TV and covert operations secret even in success... Every nation in every region now has a decision to make: either you are with us, or you are with the terrorists."[1]

The purpose of this introductory note is to examine the "war on terror" and its implications for the New World Order by analyzing it in the context of the evolution of the existing corpus of law governing armed conflict and the use of force, including the current UN system.

Past Legal order

The "just war" doctrine [4th-16th century]

War belongs to human history and has shaped its directions. Attempts to regulate and limit armed conflict and the use of force can be traced to many historical traditions. A comparative study of these traditions would be fascinating to conduct. However, that is beyond the scope of this introductory note. The philosophical and ethical underpinnings of the modern laws of war seem to draw mainly from the distinctions between 'just war', *bellum justum*, and 'unjust war', *bellum injustum*[2], made in ancient Rome and then developed by later Christian theologians and jurists. The prominent among them are St. Augustine [354-430]; St. Tomas Aquinas [1225-1274]; Stainslaw of Skarbimierz [1360-1431], rector of Jagiellonian University in Cracow, Poland; Francisco de Vitoria [1492-1546], who led the Prime Chair of Theology at the University of Salamanca; Francisco Suarez [1548-1617], who taught theology in various cities of Spain and Italy; Hugo Grotius [1583-1645], the Dutch theologian and lawyer famous for *On the Law of War and Peace*; Richard Zouche [1590-1661], Regius professor of law at Oxford from 1620 who became the chancellor of the diocese of Oxford in 1625; Samuel baron von Pufendorf [1632-1694], the son of a German pastor who abandoned theology to advance the first modern articulation of the right to equality; Emerich de Vattel [1714-67], a Swiss jurist known for his *Law of Nations;* and others. The following endnote lists out the main works of some of these theologians and thinkers relevant to the doctrine of 'just war'.[3] Obviously these Christian thinkers of 'just war', who spanned a period of nearly 1500 years, used the term with different connotations. However, the meanings that have crystallized into principles that still echo in the modern laws of war can be summarized as follows:

1. Just war requires proper justification; in other words, substantive grounds to explain the decision to wage war. Self-defence from an armed attack and punishment for aggressive violence, for example, constitute proper justifications.
2. Proper justification also requires that the substantive grounds be officially iterated for satisfaction or warning, with a reasonable time allowed to elicit a meaningful response.
3. Iteration of the substantive grounds is necessary to establish the just intention, which means the objective to correct a wrong and not to inflict a wrong, no matter what the provocation. Just war can be waged only after its formal declaration.
4. Just war can be waged only under a legitimate authority.
5. Proper justification and right intention apart, just war must avoid senseless waste of human life and must be pursued only as a last resort.
6. Just war is conducted with sufficient attention to avoid harm, pain and death to civilian populations, irrespective of the side they belong to. Lethal force, even when directed against armed combatants, must not exceed the military objectives and necessity.
7. Prisoners of war must be treated humanely and with respect.

These seven principles, which can be culled out of the doctrine of 'just war', constitute the nucleus of the two branches of the law of war known as *jus ad bellum,* the law or the standards that legitimize the recourse to force, and *jus in bello*, the law or the guidelines to direct or conduct the use of force.[4]

For more than twelve centuries, before and after the 16th century Reformation marked by the split between the Catholic and the Protestant churches, the 'just war' tradition remained under the influence of Christian theology. This meant that the Christian Church exercised the authority to declare whether or not a war was just. However, the Reformation and the religious wars it precipitated destroyed the moral authority of the Church to do so—there was no longer a single arbiter. Simultaneously, the Peace of Westphalia [1648], which aimed to end the religious wars in Europe, heralded a radically new approach to the understanding of the 'world order' "based on a plurality of independent States, recognising no superior authority over them", in other words, on the sovereign equality of all states.[5]

However, this Westphalian construct of the 'world order' is but theoretical. In reality, the period from the 17th to the beginning of the 20th century witnessed the framing of international norms and principles that suited militarily powerful States able to build up extensive colonial empires by the dint of conquest and expansion. Belligerent violence without restraint remained a part of the reality during this time. Nonetheless, European States, in competition among themselves for conquest and expansion over the non-European world, did agree on some rules of the imperial game. Such rules as, for example, freedom of the high seas, the designation of lawful combatants, restrictions on the use of weapons causing inhuman suffering, diplomatic and consular immunity, choice of neutrality, etc., worked their way into the realm of International Law.[6] The intention of the law was to prevent anarchy by providing a common ground of interest among all nations. The politics of power nonetheless dictated that even laws based on this common ground were observed more in the breach by nations involved in the regime of law. Treaties not to wage war against each other and to seek an amicable settlement of disputes became common among nations that considered themselves militarily on an even pegging. They also had the advantage of allowing parties to these treaties to exploit weaker nations by agreeing to the demarcation of areas of influence. Perceptions changed intermittently and treaties broke down or underwent new permutations. The following is an example:

In 1823, forty-seven years after the declaration of American independence and thirty-eight years before the commencement of the Civil War, James Monroe, then President of the USA, issued a stern warning to the European powers asking them to curb their colonial ambitions within the hemisphere, especially in South American colonies that previously belonged to Spain. The issuance was presumably provoked by the 1815 joint declaration of the 'Holy Alliance' by Austria, France, Prussia, and Russia to uphold the interests of the Christian religion world-wide. The Monroe Doctrine also promised to abjure American meddling in Europe's political affairs. With the development of American interests in Central America and the Caribbean, the doctrine became a tenet of the American hegemony and self-assumed responsibility for the security of North and South America. Latin American countries resented the interventionist position that the USA maintained under the guise of Monroe Doctrine. In 1868 Carlos Calvo, an Argentinean jurist, challenged the right of any foreign state to intervene in the affairs of another sovereign state in the name of protecting the rights of aliens. In 1902, when Britain, Italy, and Germany joined hands to impose a naval blockade on Venezuela, ostensibly to force the country to pay up its debts to foreign investors in its oil exploration, another Argentine statesman and lawyer, Luis Maria Drago, proposed that no country could militarily intervene in any sovereign American state for the purpose of collecting debts. The Drago doctrine eventually found its way into the Hague Convention of 1907, in Article 1. However, the US interventions in Latin America did not cease. The military weakness of the US in 1833 and the diplomatic ties it nurtured with the UK did not allow it to intervene when British troops occupied the Falkland and Malvinas islands against loud protests from Argentina. But the situation changed slowly and even before the declaration of WW I, Roosevelt turned the Monroe Doctrine into an imperialist theory that 'misgovernment' in any Latin American republic would invite active armed intervention by the United States. The doctrine was forcefully invoked to justify the blockade of Cuba in 1962. After WW I, the American role in Europe itself became vital. For more information on Carlos Calvo and Luis Maria Drago, please, refer to the web links mentioned under the footnote[7].

The Lieber Code [1863] and the Hague Conferences [1899 and 1907]

An important development towards the crystallization of the laws of war took place in the US during the Civil War [1861-1865], which claimed more than 6,00,000 lives within a period of five years. Soon after its outbreak, Henry W. Halleck, General-in-Chief of the Union Armies, approached Professor Francis Lieber, a German born professor of law at the Columbia University, to request him to draft a code of laws applicable to the conduct of the civil war. The Code was promptly drafted and it was adopted by the Union Army as General order No. 100 in 1863. The code defined 'military necessity' as those measures which are indispensable for securing the ends of the war, and which are lawful according to the modern law and usages of war." According to the code, 'military necessity' "admits all direct destruction of life and limb of armed enemies, and of other persons whose destruction is incidentally unavoidable in armed contests of the war..." But the code required both the defenders and the aggressors to secure classical works of art, museums, scientific collections and libraries for "all avoidable injury, even when they are contained in fortified places whilst besieged and bombarded." The code also prohibited rape during armed conflict.[8]

The Lieber Code, a product elaborated on the basis of humanitarian concerns during the American Civil War, which had been fought with a ruthless determination of "total war", as William T. Sherman, Commander of the Union army for Tennessee, characterized it, inspired the Russian Czar to issue the St. Petersburg Declaration in 1868. Under this declaration, the fading aristocracy of Europe tried to place restrictions on the conspicuously destructive power of military technology under notions of chivalry. The declaration says: "the only legitimate object which States should endeavour to accomplish during war is to weaken the military forces of the enemy." A strong view against such military technological equipment as bullets that exploded on contact and also on the use of asphyxiating gas was taken. The spirit of the declaration to clearly distinguish civilians from military targets and provide a clear framework of necessity and proportionality for the conduct of military violence during wars, made progress in developing a code, first in Brussels in 1874, and then in the Hague Conventions of 1899 and 1907.[9]

The Hague Conventions of 1899 and 1907 represent the first attempt to codify both the *jus ad bellum* and the *jus in bello*, and therefore constitute an important landmark in the development of the laws governing war and its conduct.

With regard to the *jus ad bellum*, the first Hague Peace Conference, in 1899, led to the Convention for the Pacific Settlement of International Disputes and to the establishment of a Permanent Court of Arbitration, a forerunner of the Permanent Court of International Justice and the International Court of Justice, to arbitrate cases submitted to it. States, however, remained free to choose whether to opt for an amicable dispute settlement or the use of force.

The second Hague Peace Conference, in 1907, tried to remedy this weakness but failed to secure general acceptance on a convention making resort to arbitration — compulsory in certain cases. It also sought to address the Drago doctrine with the elaboration of the rule that States were not to have recourse to war to recover contract debts unless certain conditions were met.

In sum therefore, the decision to resort to force remained largely discretionary and the Big Powers were therefore able to continue to dominate the scene.

The two conferences achieved more progress with regard to the *jus in bello*. Amongst the most notable of successes was the insertion of the Martens clause by unanimous vote into both the Conventions of 1899 and 1907.[10] Other rules agreed upon during the conferences included provisions prohibiting the employment of expanding bullets (so-called dum-dum bullets) and of projectiles for spreading harmful gases. The conference also produced rules relating to conduct in war, the treatment of prisoners of war, and the rights of neutrals, as well as conventions relating to land and sea warfare.

As noted above, since *jus in bello* principles were applied reciprocally and were dictated by the demands of humanity, all States, however powerful, had an interest in abiding by them; thus, explaining the success achieved by the conferences in this field. Despite these successes, the Hague conferences failed to prevent WW I or even to limit the use of lethal weapons.

League of Nations [1919]

It is only after World War I, when a conflict had involved all major members of the international community for the first time that more comprehensive restrictions on the resort to war were laid down in the Covenant of the League of Nations in 1919 and then later in the Kellogg-Briand Pact of 1928.

Following WWI, the allied victors set up an international institution designed to prevent the recurrence of worldwide armed conflict. Its Members were required to "respect and preserve as against external aggression the territorial integrity and existing political independence of all Members of the League"[11]. Recourse to war was not prohibited as such but was made subject to the limitations designed to avert it[12]. Amongst others, disputes were to be submitted to arbitration, judicial settlement or inquiry by the League Council. Having submitted a dispute to the League Council or to the Permanent Court of International Justice, war could only be resorted to three months after the decision or the report, i.e. after a "cooling-off" period. Members were obligated to carry out the decision or award in good faith; and Members agreed not to resort to war against another Member complying with the decision or award[13]. Gaps in this legal regime nonetheless remained significant[14].

For instance, members were free to resort to war if the Council could not come to a unanimous decision[15], or if the Council did not come to a decision within a given time frame.[16] There was no ban on the use of force short of war. Moreover, whatever the restrictions, they only applied to Members *inter se*.[17] The US was also conspicuously absent. No collective system was set up to enforce the law against a contravening Member. Lastly, no monopoly of force was granted to the League organs; and no army for the maintenance of peace was set up.

In practice, Britain and France came to use the League of Nations as a political instrument, and even when Members did resort to war in violation of the Covenant provisions, the League was unable to react effectively. Thus, although the Covenant sought to limit the recourse to war, its effectiveness was irreparably hampered by its lack of "clear-cut obligations", its lack of "teeth", and the fact that it left the international customary law right to wage war, untouched.

Kellogg-Briand Pact [1928]

The General Treaty for the Renunciation of War as an Instrument of National Policy of 1928, otherwise known as the Kellogg-Briand Pact or Pact of Paris, banned war for the first time. It condemned "recourse to war for the solution of international controversies" and got Contracting Parties to agree to renounce war "as an instrument of national policy with one another"[18]. War nonetheless remained lawful under the following circumstances: (1) in cases of self-defence, (2) in international (as opposed to national) relations, and (3) in relations with third parties. And these exceptions were interpreted broadly. For example, the concept of self-defence was understood to include the right to defend "vital interests" abroad. How were these "vital interests" defined, if at all? During the Cold War the US's "vital interests" gave it the right to prevent an infringement of the Monroe Doctrine! And once again, the prohibition only covered war — not the use of force falling short of war.

Current Legal Order

The corpus of law that emerged from the ashes of the Second World War echoed a number of principles of the "just war" doctrine, of course in purely legal terms. The corpus of law developed into three distinct, yet inevitably linked, fields: first, the *jus ad bellum*, designed to put an end to war; second, the *jus in bello*, intended to ensure the retention of a degree of humanity in conflict[19] ; and third, international criminal law, introduced to punish those responsible for war and those who carried out the law in contravention of the dictates of humanity.

Jus ad bellum[20]

The post-1945 international community's discussions on the establishment of a new international institution to address the weaknesses and shortcomings of the League of Nations and the Kellogg-Briand Pact echoed Saint Augustine's focus on peace as a starting point of the morality/legality of war. The result was the establishment of the United Nations and the elaboration of the UN Charter. As the cornerstone of the current *jus ad bellum,* Article 2(4) proclaims: "All Members shall refrain in their international relations from the threat or use of force against the territorial integrity or political independence of any state, or in any other manner inconsistent with the purposes of the UN."

The only two exceptions under the UN Charter are: (1) where the Security Council specifically authorizes the use of force under its collective security mandate stated in Chapter VII, Articles 39 and 42, and (2) where actions are taken in self-defence under Art. 51. Member States also agree to "confer on the Security Council [SC] the primary responsibility for the maintenance of international peace and security… on their behalf".

The UN Charter thereby directly addresses some of the gaps inherent in the previous legal regimes in place. It prohibits resort to war as well as its threat *and* the use of force. It applies to relations with third states, with the result that the prohibition articulated in Article 2(4) is now part of the international customary law. The legality of the use of force in international relations is governed by the Security Council. And, there are only two explicit exceptions to the prohibition in Article 2(4), only one of which falls within the purview of the States.

Despite the evident progress achieved, the UN Charter still enables room for manoeuvre and therefore scope for abuse. Most notable is the fact that the prohibition in Article 2(4) is limited to: (1) inter-State relations—the use of force in intra-State relations remains intact and beyond the reach of the Charter's provisions[21], and (2) military force-economic coercion is not covered[22]. Furthermore, the very structure of the UN undermines the system it establishes. For instance, the over-reliance on agreement among the five Permanent Members of the Security Council led to the ineffectiveness of the collective security system for the entire duration of the Cold War with no provision for an alternative decision-making body or procedure. Thus, the idea that various Member States would place their army contingents, through special arrangements, at the disposal of the Security Council never materialised. Compounded with the structure and composition of the Security Council that undermine its credibility[23], the UN's record of dealing with contravening States and more generally, its record of enforcement, is mixed, arbitrary, and self-contradictory[24].

Jus in bello and the Geneva Conventions[25]

Following the establishment of a system monopolising the use of force in international relations, the post-1945 international community turned its attention to the *jus in bello*. The existing international customary law principles of necessity, proportionality and distinction (rooted in the "just war" doctrine) and the Hague Conventions of 1899 and 1907 were expanded upon by the four Geneva Conventions of 1949[26] and the two Additional Protocols of 1977[27]. Thus, whereas the Hague laws cover the overall means and methods of combat, the Geneva Conventions seek to safeguard combatants (members of the armed forces) who are wounded, sick, and prisoners of war, and civilians. Common Article 2 of the four Geneva Conventions states that they are applicable in "all cases of war or any other international armed conflict... even if the state of war is not recognised by one of them". In other words, regardless of the legality of the use of force, States are obligated to abide by the laws of *jus in bello* as soon as a war has been embarked upon in inter-State relations[28]. Common Article 3 of the four Geneva Conventions extends their coverage to internal conflicts. It provides that parties to the conflict shall, at the very least, be bound to apply certain provisions guaranteeing the safety of non-combatants (this evokes the law's roots in the medieval chivalric code). The two Additional Protocols further expand on the rules applicable to international and non-international conflicts respectively.

The *jus in bello* which was developed post-WWII was geared to address the conduct of states in inter-State wars. Since the end of the Second World War, however, internal conflicts have been increasing and have remained largely unregulated. As non-international conflicts pit State forces against its own citizens, States have traditionally wanted a free reign to crush any rebellion. In view of the increasing technological capacity of rebels and the need of States to protect their troops, States are becoming more open to the promulgation of minimum rules in non-international conflicts, as evidenced by the terms of the Additional Protocol II to the Geneva Conventions of 1949.

International Criminal Law[29]

The third pillar of the current international legal order pertaining to war is international criminal law. International criminal law seeks to attribute individual responsibility for mass violations of human rights committed in times of peace and/or in times of war. Individual responsibility, including that of "state officials", was indubitably established by the Nuremburg and Tokyo Tribunals, post-WWII, for war crimes, crimes against humanity, genocide, and torture. The Tribunals also established that obedience to superior orders[30], state immunity[31], or the lawfulness of the acts committed under domestic law[32] can no longer serve as defences to a charge or as a bar to prosecution and punishment for these crimes[33]. Furthermore, domestic courts have jurisdiction over the perpetrators of these crimes (for torture only when it qualifies as a crime against humanity) on the basis of the universality principle — in other words — irrespective of where they were committed, by whom, and against what category of victims[34]. However, this jurisdiction is only mandatory with respect to certain crimes, whether under treaty law or international customary law[35]. Nonetheless, the creation of the International Criminal Tribunal for former Yugoslavia [ICTY][36] and Rwanda [ICTR] in 1993 and 1994 respectively, and more recently for Sierra Leone and Cambodia[37], the establishment of the Permanent International Criminal Court [ICC], the crowning achievement, are expressions of a growing consensus that these crimes can no longer go unpunished[38]

At the same time, although their establishment is laudable, these bodies clearly reflect politically sensitive choices and selective enforcement, and thus selective justice, and are, arguably, subject to "tribunal fatigue"[39].

Why was no tribunal established for Burundi? Why is one being considered for Cambodia, though decades later? Why was East Timor's wish for such a tribunal refused but a truth commission, that was not asked for, was established instead? What is the rationale explaining such differential treatments? Similarly, why are only certain heads of State brought to justice, such as Slobodan Milosevic or Saddam Hussein, both of whom were incidentally defeated in an international war involving a Western victor, whereas others, such as Augusto Pinochet, are allowed to walk scot-free? It is worth noting that incidentally—or (perhaps) not—both Milosevic and Saddam headed States that were defeated in an international war involving a Western victor, whereas in the case of Chile, no external forces were overtly involved.

Furthermore, one has to question why the same Western powers are treating Milosevic and Saddam so differently: Milosevic is being tried in an international tribunal[40]; Saddam in the so-called "War Crimes Tribunal"[41]. Although the trial of Saddam by Iraqi authorities, rather than the US ones, should discourage claims of "victor's justice", it is not, on its own, sufficient to allay either the concerns of a sham trial taking place or the fears of tainted justice. The authorities responsible for Saddam's trial are political appointees handpicked by the US. Salem Chalabi, Ahmed Chalabi's nephew and a US-educated lawyer with links to the Bush Administration, was the first head of the US-formed tribunal[42]. He was replaced by Judge Ammar al-Bakri in October 2004 when he resigned amid allegations of corruption[43]. Further nagging doubts about the rationale for having Saddam tried by Iraqi authorities persist considering that: (1) He is to be tried in accordance with existing Iraqi penal codes[44] and not with the more benign international laws, and perhaps more importantly, (2) the death penalty has been re-introduced[45] in Iraq in time for his trial. What explains the US's decision to establish such a tribunal? Why not set up an international tribunal on the lines of the ICTR and ICTY to try Saddam and his cronies? After all, the establishment of such a tribunal to try Saddam for crimes against peace (invasion of Kuwait) was already discussed in the 1990s. Today, he could be tried for other international crimes as well. Arguably, one valid explanation for the US's refusal to consider a full-fledged international tribunal today is the fear that Hussein will follow in Milosevic's footsteps by calling former Western governments to account for the support they showed Saddam before the first Gulf War in 1991, and for their actions in Iraq ever since.

In this context, it is worth pointing out that due to this very real fear of universal jurisdiction being used to bring its own men to account for violations, in particular of the *jus in bello*, the US has systematically attempted to crush efforts by the international community to end impunity for international crimes. For example, Belgium enacted a very progressive law in 1993[46] granting Belgian courts universal jurisdiction over acts of torture, crimes against humanity and war crimes as per the Geneva Conventions. In the course of a campaign of intense pressure on Belgium by the US to alter its law, US Defence Secretary Donald H. Rumsfeld "threatened Belgium that it risked losing its status as host to NATO's headquarters if it did not rescind the law."[47] Belgium altered the law. Its courts still have universal jurisdiction over these crimes but only in certain circumstances that make it more difficult for victims to file complaints for crimes committed abroad[48]. Furthermore, not only has the US revoked its signature of the Rome Statute of the ICC and of course refused to ratify it[49], but it has also started a campaign of pressure on States that have ratified it, to also ratify US Bilateral Immunity Agreements (BIAs)[50]. These Agreements render US troops operating on the territory of the specific country immune to prosecution by the ICC and therefore significantly reduce the ICC's reach and its effectiveness in combating impunity worldwide. As of July 2004, 92 such agreements got signed[51]. Countries that refuse to sign these agreements may see US support for their entry into NATO withdrawn and may be cut off from US military aid[52]. Twenty-two ICC States Parties have refused to sign the BIA despite losing US aid by December 2004[53].

This brief overview of the major developments in the field of international criminal law since the end of the Second World War highlights the political character of prosecutions and extraditions for crimes against humanity, genocide, grave breaches, and torture.

However, it is also abundantly clear that the levels of tolerance for unfettered impunity for these crimes are diminishing. The first prosecutions in the ICC (in 2004, ICC Chief Prosecutor Luis Moreno Ocampo formally announced the beginning of investigations on the Democratic Republic of Congo and Uganda; the UN SC referred Darfur to the ICC in March 2005[54]) are likely to have a significant bearing on the court's future impact as well as on legal developments in the field[55]. In the meantime, there is at least some satisfaction in the knowledge that the likes of Pinochet, Kissinger, Bush Sr., and Mobutu have to keep abreast of judicial and legal developments in each and every country to which they may wish to travel. Finally, in view of the US's open hostility to the notion of accountability, and individual or state responsibility, it is likely that the US will continue to stand as the main opponent to the application of international criminal law to its own men as this would go against the grain of its "expansionist" agenda.[56]

A Case Study: Iraq

The experience of Iraq, from the Gulf War in 1991 to the Iraq war in 2003, as well as the recent Afghanistan war, serves to illustrate some of the weaknesses of the post-1945 legal regime governing *jus ad bellum* and *jus in bello* and its real and practical consequences/ impact. These wars also point to a number of questions of a moral, philosophical, political, economical, and legal order which must be raised in the context of the post-Cold War era and in relation to the New World Order.

We are aware that by moving from the immediate post-WWII era to the immediate post-Cold War era, we have practically skipped the whole Cold War era and the experience of the UN during that time. We believe, however, that the inherent weaknesses of the post-WWII UN system will be made all the more apparent by considering how it functions and what it has achieved in the context in which it was designed to operate; in other words, in a world where the SC is not radically divided along political cleavages.

Reference will of course be made to the Cold War era whenever appropriate.

The Gulf War, 1991, represents a first test case of what the Security Council, the UN body primarily responsible for the maintenance of international peace and security, can do and is willing to do, in the post-Cold War era.

Collective enforcement action in the name of sovereignty

Iraq invaded Kuwait on the 2nd of August 1990[57]. On the very same day, the SC, in Resolution 660, acting under Articles 39 and 42, determined a "breach of international peace and security" by Iraq. To put this in perspective, it should be recalled that during the entire Cold War era, the SC only determined three such breaches[58] owing to the abuse of the right of veto by its Permanent Members in pursuit of their respective political agendas. Four days later, the SC imposed economic sanctions on Iraq under Article 41, Chapter VII[59]. In November 1990, the landmark resolution 678 authorised "all necessary means to uphold and implement resolution 660 and all subsequent relevant resolutions and to restore international peace and security in the area"[60]. Pursuant to this resolution, an American-led force started military operations in Iraq in January 1991.

Dinstein, a prominent Israeli scholar of law, argues that Resolution 678 constituted a specific mandate for the exercise of collective self-defence under Article 51, but that the armed forces of the coalition did not "constitute a UN force predicated on genuine collective security". Be that as it may, Resolution 678 and the enforcement action that followed reveal that, in the post-Cold War context, the SC is coming into its own and is taking seriously its role as "a board of directors of the world" responsible for, to borrow President Roosevelt's words, "enforcing the peace against any potential miscreant".[61] However Resolution 678 and the ensuing enforcement action also reveal some of the weaknesses of the UN system and the tensions that flow from the UN not having its own army. Here we highlight four conspicuous problems:

1. The Security Council's overtly political character (subjective) vs. the need to justify action in legal terms (objective);
2. The need for effectiveness in military terms by garnering the support of States who are 'able and willing' vs. the need for legitimacy, which may require excluding the support offered by certain States;
3. The dependence on a few 'willing and able' states vs. an emphasis on 'collective' action; and
4. Troops under the command and control of individual Member States yet acting under the UN flag.

The tensions arising from these problems inevitably raise a host of questions, not least whether these binaries can be reconciled and, if so, how. How can a political body be 'just' in decisions involving the use of military force against a sovereign State? What is the ambit of the SC's powers in relation to maintaining international peace and security? Is the SC under any type of legal restraint in the discharge of its responsibilities? Was the SC acting within its competence when it prevented Bosnia-Herzegovina from exercising its "inherent right of self-defence" by imposing an arms embargo on it? Does any body hold the SC accountable for its decisions? Should the International Court of Justice be entrusted with controlling the legality of SC Resolutions? Can SC Resolutions actually be illegal? In that case, could one envision that the SC itself could authorise a violation of the *jus ad bellum*? Is there any system to review the rationale for the enforcement action decisions taken by the SC? How do we ensure that the Permanent Members of the Security Council do not simply hijack the body to pursue their own interest? Can the SC be forced to act in cases of flagrant breach of the peace? And if it does not, can it be held to account for acts of omission? Can the SC be made to account for imposing sanctions that may be considered to amount to international crimes[62] ? Is the SC to be held responsible in any way for violations of *jus in bello* by troops acting pursuant to a Resolution authorising the use of force against a Member State? Can the UN actually be held responsible for such violations even though it is not a party to the applicable *jus in bello* conventions?

In addition to concerns falling within the realm of *jus ad bellum,* the Gulf War also raises issues pertaining to the *jus in bello* and point in particular to some of its failures in banning specific weapons which have drastic long-term impacts.

One weapon of this kind used extensively by the US in Iraq is the "cluster bomb", referred to as "steel rain", which has a huge destructive force. Their devastating impact continues to this day, maiming and killing hundreds of civilians. This is due to cluster bombs having a sixteen per cent failure rate and therefore lying dormant until touched. Could no other weapons or methods have achieved the same intended military effect but inflicted less suffering and resulted in lesser long-term hazardous consequences for the people of Iraq?

Another weapon used in Iraq with drastic long-term impacts is depleted uranium [DU]. As it is radioactive waste, DU is free. Tungsten on the other hand, which could be used to replace DU for all its military uses, is neither radioactive nor free. In any event, Iraq served as the US's battle test for DU ammunition. The US's silence, covering up and finally minimizing of the long-term health consequences of the use of DU amongst its own and British soldiers, known as the "Gulf War syndrome", testifies to its knowledge of the terrible consequences of unprotected contact with DU[63]. Evidence of these consequences is now also starting to emerge from Iraq and tells the tale of the suffering past, present and future, of the Iraqi people[64].

Did the situation in Iraq warrant the use of radioactive waste? Did the use of DU fulfil the necessity and proportionality principles? How is one to reconcile the use of radioactive substances, even if they do fulfil these tests, with the principle of distinction? Can the US be held responsible in any way for the human and environmental damage wrought by DU in Iraq? How do the UK's obligations differ from the US's in view of the fact that the UK has ratified the two 1977 Additional Protocols to the Geneva Conventions of 1949 whereas the US has not? After all, API specifically rules out means or methods of war which are of a nature to cause "superfluous injury or unnecessary suffering or can be expected to cause widespread, long term and severe damage to the natural environment". How far-reaching is this obligation? What are the responsibilities of the UK in such an instance?

The principles of necessity, proportionality and distinction apply not only to the choice of weapons but also to the choice of targets. It is claimed that the US war in Iraq was one of chastisement: structures targeted included so-called mixed targets, in other words structures used by both the military and the civilians, but appear to have failed to fulfil the legality criteria. Increasingly, it *is* almost impossible to differentiate targets that are strictly military or civilian. This is prompting the US-led forces to focus on immobilizing the enemy's military machine, or otherwise induce a reaction from the civilian population to resist the regime. In Iraq, the US destroyed the water treatment and power generating facilities in the knowledge that: (1) Iraqis would be unable to repair these structures in the future owing to the sanctions regime in place; (2) parallel power generating structures were being used by the military underground; and consequently (3) the destruction of these structures would predominantly/disproportionately bring about civilian suffering. Can these attacks be legitimized on the grounds of "military necessity"? Did the concrete and military advantage anticipated by attacking such targets outweigh the expected incidental civilian injury or damage as required by the proportionality principle? How workable is the proportionality principle in practice? How does it stand in relation to the principle of military necessity?

In the knowledge of the difficulties already facing civilians, did the imposition of a stringent sanctions regime itself not constitute a violation of the principles of necessity, proportionality, and discrimination which apply both in *jus ad bellum* and in *jus in bello*? Can the Iraqi people seek a legal remedy against these pervasive and perverse violations? If so, against whom should they bring the case and in what court of law? And if not, are they then not entitled to any form of redress?

Humanitarian intervention in Iraq?

Shortly after they were removed from Kuwait, Iraqi troops were once again used, this time against the Shiites in Basra and the Kurds in northern Iraq who, encouraged by the US, staged a rebellion against Saddam Hussein's regime. In the event, the SC passed Resolution 688 determining the existence of a threat to "international peace and security in the region". The question we wish to consider here is whether a State could have intervened unilaterally in Iraq in the name of 'human rights'. In other words, would a State have been justified in using force in Iraq in the name of humanitarian intervention? What are the origins of humanitarian intervention? Does humanitarian intervention constitute an authorized use of force under the UN Charter? If so, what are the requirements for humanitarian intervention to be legal?

Succinctly put, the debate over humanitarian intervention is one of sovereignty vs. the protection of human rights. The roots of the modern concept of sovereignty can be traced back to the 13th century in parts of Europe. However, it was not until the Treaty of Westphalia, in 1648, which ended the Thirty Years' War, that the "emerging concept of the State in Europe" was given "formal institutional status"[65]. The Treaty of Westphalia, by determining that the people within a territory must take the religious faith of their prince, laid the cornerstone for what became the modern notion of sovereignty; in other words, the principle that a sovereign state is virtually unfettered in its actions towards the people within its territory. At the same time however, Hugo Grotius[66] developed the argument for a right to intervene unilaterally in the domestic affairs of a foreign State for humanitarian purposes. According to him, because the intervening State's bond with its neighbouring citizens, based on their common humanity, superseded the relationship between sovereigns, a nation could justifiably attack its neighbour to protect the neighbour's citizens from the atrocities of their ruler[67].

Following the Second World War, the maintenance of international peace and security was uppermost in the minds of the drafters of the UN Charter and became the first of the four "purposes and principles"[68] of the UN, and the primary responsibility of the Security Council[69]. The maintenance of peace and security was premised on the notion of law and order, in other words on non-intervention with the two exceptions under Article 39 and Article 51. Simultaneously, mention of human rights was made, first in the Preamble[70] of the UN Charter and then in Articles 55 and 56 which obligate each Member to "take joint and separate action" to insure the "universal respect for, and observance of human rights and fundamental freedoms". Member States therefore retained the primary responsibility for the promotion and protection of human rights. During the Cold War, the UN rarely intervened in cases of human rights abuse, which often corresponded to one of the superpower's-sphere of influence, for example in Nicaragua, Panama, or Haiti. With the collapse of the Soviet Union, and the increase in the number of intra-State conflicts, rather than inter-State ones, the UN was left sitting on the fence. This inherent tension to the UN system partly explains the apparent lack of cohesion, homogeneity, and therefore predictability of UN interventions in the name of humanity. It is further exacerbated by the UN's dependence on the financial and human resources of its members, and therefore on the political will of its members to act, including the Permanent Members of the SC. But the political will of members is fickle.

Views on humanitarian intervention remain mixed. Some argue that nothing in the UN Charter authorises humanitarian intervention since it is not explicitly authorised as an exception to the prohibition on the use of force. But what if heinous crimes are being committed against a population? What of the cases of Rwanda, Bosnia, or Darfur, to mention just some of the more horrendous human rights violations committed in recent years[71] ? What if the SC does not determine the existence of a threat to the peace or breach of the peace? Or what if the SC cannot act because States will not commit the necessary troops for it to intervene? Must people then die in the name of the principles of sovereignty and non-intervention? These are perhaps some of the questions which have motivated others to claim that humanitarian intervention is in line with the purposes of the UN and/or that it does not threaten the territorial sovereignty and political independence of the state in which intervention takes place. It is further argued that when a State kills its own people:

> "it does not act in good faith under the obligations of the Charter. Therefore, the abusing State forfeits the benefit it derives as a sovereign under Article 2(4) and the balance swings towards promoting human rights. Thus, Article 2(4) cannot place an absolute ban on the unilateral use of force."[72]

Difficulties in embracing either position whole-heartedly arise owing to what can be loosely categorised as moral considerations. In the first case, there is a moral objection to letting the human rights of an entire population or people be violated in the name of a legal fiction called 'sovereignty'. In other words, intervention is legitimate—it is "just". In the second case, the risk is that intervention will not be on purely moral grounds but that the intervening State has a different agenda and is merely using the massive violation of human rights as a Trojan horse.

At issue is whether the motive of the intervening State is at all relevant and assuming that it is, the weight to be given to the intervening State's motive vs. the common interest in seeing the violations cease. Is it possible to ascertain the State's motive? What was the underlying rationale dictating intervention in Uganda by Tanzania, in East Pakistan by India, in Bosnia by NATO, or in Iraq by the US? In the event of an imminent attack by given State in the name of humanitarian intervention, could the State in whose territory the humanitarian intervention is to take place invoke a right of anticipatory self-defence? After all, as humanitarian intervention is an intrinsically moral, and therefore a subjective act, anticipatory self-defence is just as subjective. The state to be intervened in could argue that it was to be the subject of an act of aggression/armed attack. Would such potential controversies be avoided if the UN was involved in the humanitarian intervention equation at any stage? If so, in what capacity; at what stage; what criterion for intervention should then apply[73] ?

Returning to the humanitarian interventions mentioned above: were the considerations of the intervening States purely, or even predominantly humanitarian in these cases or were they subservient to geo-political and/or economic interests? Does it make a difference to the end result, i.e. the cessation of mass human rights violations, and to the way in which it is viewed?

These questions persist when, looking at the historical evidence more closely, it appears that there has been no humanitarian intervention in the West by non-Western States, at least since the end of the Second World War. Nor has any humanitarian intervention been carried out in the territory of a Permanent Member State of the Security Council.

Is this because their human rights record is so much better? Then what about Tibet or Chechnya[74] (to cite the most obvious)? And what about the widespread homelessness, permanent joblessness, urban squalor, drug culture, crime, the "new poverty", the exclusion of stateless people, minorities, women, etc, whose rights are violated daily and on a wide scale in the West? Do these violations not count? Or, do the people not count? Yet, are human rights not universal and all people born equal[75] ? Then again, are human rights truly universal? Where do they come from? Are they simply a Western creation to serve the purposes of *realpolitik?* How is one otherwise to understand the application of double standards, selectivity, and therefore the obviously cosy relationship between human rights and the politics of the mighty?

It would seem that the debate on humanitarian intervention and the twin issues of morality and human rights it necessarily throws up, are inevitably intertwined. After all, humanitarian intervention effectively justifies the use of force to prevent the use of force. Therefore, it legitimises the further suffering of the people it is designed to free from suffering. Must it always get worse before it can get better? Are the end and the means employed not antagonistic? How are they to be reconciled?

Collective Enforcement Action in the Name of HR

States with the potential to intervene in the defence of the Iraqi Shiite and Kurdish population did not have to face these complex issues since, as mentioned above, the Security Council itself seized the matter when it passed Resolution 688. The Resolution determined the existence of a threat to "international peace and security in the region", condemned the action, and required that "Iraq allow immediate access by international humanitarian organizations to all those in need of assistance in all parts of Iraq..." Although the Resolution did not name Chapter VII and did not authorize the use of force, the Resolution led to the creation, by the US and the UK, of "no-fly zones" and "safe havens" in Northern and Southern Iraq. These were later used as cover for further aerial and ground actions, including operations in 1998.

The most prominent question arising with regard to Resolution 688 is whether the zones and havens created by force were legal. Dinstein cautions:

> "In analyzing these events, it must be appreciated that the coalition forces have been acting in the course of an ongoing war in which hostilities had been merely suspended in a cease-fire."[76]

Yet this seems unsatisfactory as it does not address the crux of the matter: does the authorization of the use of force have to be stated explicitly in each and every Resolution pertaining to a given conflict? Or, can it be implied and if so, when? The proposition that an implied authorization to use force can be relied upon becomes untenable because if an authorization can be implied, it must be true also when the use of force is not or no longer authorized. Furthermore, if the authorization to use force can be implied, how can the spirit in which SC Resolutions are passed be preserved over time? In other words, how can subjective "interests", and self-serving interpretations be avoided? This in turn raises questions relating to the "death" of Resolutions. Do Resolutions have to be revoked expressly or can they be "revived" when the "need" arises? On a different but related note, what could the SC do in such instances, in theory and in practice? Whichever way one looks at it, simply because the two UN Members that created these zones and havens in Iraq are Permanent Members of the SC and/or one of them is the US, no action can or will be undertaken against them.

Anticipatory Self-defence

1. War in Iraq, 1993

In 1991, the US led a coalition acting in the name of a collective and acting subsequent to authorisation by the SC. In contrast, in 1993, the US once again used force against Iraq, this time in its individual capacity, pursuant to the right of anticipatory or pre-emptive self-defence. The US allegedly discovered a plot to kill former President Bush and proceeded to destroy the Iraqi intelligence establishment, killing a number of civilians in the process.

What is required to invoke the right of self-defence under Article 51, one of the two exceptions to the general prohibition on the use of force under the UN Charter? According to Dinstein:

> "The requirement of an armed attack as a condition of legitimate self-defence in accordance with Article 51 precludes not only threats. Recourse to self-defence under the Article is not vindicated by any violation of international law short of an armed attack. Even declarations of war, if it is evident that they are unaccompanied by deeds, are no enough. The notion that mere mobilisation or "bellicose utterances" as such may justify self-defence within the framework of Article 51 has no foundation"[77].

Does the plot to kill former President Bush constitute an "armed attack"? Does a plot to kill a former Head of State amount to an armed attack on the US State? Can the State of Iraq be held responsible for the actions of a group of individuals acting on or from its territory? Is there a duty to attempt to resolve the dispute through amicable means? In other words, how is one to evaluate whether the use of force in self-defence is *necessary*? And who evaluates this necessity? Was the requirement of *immediacy* fulfilled? When does a response fall out from the scope of immediacy and become retaliation? What is the difference between self-defence and retaliation? Does the same requirement of *proportionality* apply in terms of limiting the attacked State's response *vis-à-vis* the offending state?

Assuming that the killing of a former Head of State constitutes an armed attack triggering the right of self-defence, does Article 51 provide for a right to anticipatory self-defence? If yes, does it trigger the collective security system under the UN? If not, does it provide a right of anticipatory self-defence? Does a residual right of self-defence exist under customary law? After all, Article 51 states that "Nothing in the present Charter shall impair the *inherent* right of individual or collective self-defence if an armed attack occurs ..." [italics added]. If so, does this customary law right include anticipatory self-defence? What criteria are applicable in such cases?

2. *The War in Iraq, 2003*

As of August 1990, Iraq was subjected to a sanctions regime that is estimated to have caused the deaths of 5,000 children per month until its end in 2003 with the advent of a new war. The alleged non-compliance of Iraq with the UN weapons inspection programme triggered by Resolution 687 in 1991 was the justification given by the US for continuing the sanctions regime. In 2002, Resolution 1441 was passed holding Iraq in "material breach" of its obligations under previous resolutions and offering it a "final opportunity to comply" and cooperate with an enhanced inspection regime. An attempt by the US, followed by the UK, to pass a new SC Resolution authorising the use of military force in Iraq in 2003 failed. In March 2003, the US started waging war on Iraq justifying the use of force in the name of anticipatory self-defence. According to the landmark Caroline affair of 1837[78], anticipatory self-defence is justified only when the necessity for action is "instant, overwhelming, and leaving no choice of means, and no moment for deliberation". In other words, anticipatory self-defence must be in response to an imminent attack. On this basis, was the US justified in relying on anticipatory self-defence? Was Iraq capable of launching an armed attack against the US? Was it capable of doing so "imminently"? What about the US's knowledge that the vast majority of military facilities and military capability in Iraq had been destroyed by it from 1991 to 2003? What proof of "imminence" is required? Who assesses the information used to judge that an armed attack is imminent? Are distinctions between anticipatory self-defence, where an armed attack is merely foreseeable or even just conceivable, and "interceptive self-defence", where an armed attack is "imminent and practically unavoidable" useful in judging imminence? What about the US Defence Department's statement that Operation Iraqi Freedom was:

> "a preventive war, which traditionally has been indistinguishable from aggression, not a pre-emptive attack, which in contrast to preventive war has international legal sanction under strict

> conditions. Pre-emption is 'an attack initiated on the basis of incontrovertible evidence that an enemy attack is imminent'. Preventive war is 'a war initiated in the belief that military conflict, while not imminent, is inevitable, and that to delay would involve greater risk'."[79]

How do these categories differ from those above? Are these categories of self-defence helpful? Do they expand the doctrine of self-defence? And, as Abraham Sofaer, former Legal Adviser to the US State Department asks in the context of Afghanistan:

> "can and should the doctrine of pre-emption be expanded to reflect new technological and strategic realities? Can the concept of self-defence accommodate a role for pre-emption that satisfies the need for leaders to protect their people, without providing a ready basis for States to use pre-emption as an excuse for aggression?"[80]

Or should one simply avoid these fine distinctions, and, in the case of anticipatory self-defence, even

> "consider such action as *legally prohibited*, while admittedly knowing that there may be cases where breaches of the prohibition may be justified on moral and political grounds and the community will eventually condone them or mete out lenient condemnation"[81] ?

Perhaps, as asserted in the UN High Level Panel on Threats, Challenges and Change's 2004 report:

> "Article 51 needs neither extension nor restriction of its long-understood scope, and Chapter VII fully empowers the Security Council to deal with every kind of threat that States may confront. The task is not to find alternatives to the Security Council as a source of authority but to make it work better than it has... We do not favour the rewriting or reinterpretation of Article 51."[82]

What, if any, is the role of the SC in this process? What can the SC do if it finds a use of force in self-defence not necessitated post-facto? What action, if any, can it take against a Member State or against a Permanent Member of the Security Council in such cases? How do the two differ? Did the SC even question the US's assertion that its use of force was necessitated by the requirements of self-defence?

Despite the US's past history of intervention in Iraq, the arguable legality of its 2003 use of force as well as its arguable legitimacy in the eyes of the international community, there has been no monitoring of the US's compliance with the *jus in bello* since March 2003. Furthermore, although SC Resolution 1483 recognised the authority of the US and its allies in the war on Iraq as occupying powers under unified command and their "responsibilities and obligations under applicable international law", there has been no monitoring of the US's compliance with the Geneva Convention laws governing belligerent occupation. This is made perhaps even more urgent as, owing to their country having been invaded by foreign powers, the Iraqi people have a right under customary law to resist the occupation, making compliance with the rules more difficult. Additionally, information coming from Iraq on these counts is worrying and seems to warrant closer scrutiny of the US's behaviour in Iraq.

To name just a few clear violations of the Geneva Conventions governing belligerency, we are told that deaths in Iraq are a consequence less of collateral damage than of a failure to provide legally required support and humanitarian aid to civilians in occupied areas. We are told of operations designed to "send a message" and demonstrate fire power, of soldiers sitting by whilst property is looted and destroyed, and of the lack of observance of prisoners' rights to free and fair trials as well as the torture of prisoners in Abu Ghraib prison.

The Abu Ghraib scandal raises issues concerning the need to expand the scope of the laws of war to cover the acts of non-state actors. States, in particular the US, are increasingly resorting to hired mercenaries and private military companies to take over some of the work of regular troops, either as specialists or because regular armies cannot step into such sensitive situations. Holding such people accountable is well nigh impossible, let alone plausible, as it would contravene head-on the very rationale for hiring them in the first place. The Abu Ghraib scandal also forces us to question the veil of secrecy that covers the military apparatus and its structures:

> "Like with the Abu Ghraib torture scandal, the Bush administration will blame a few "bad apples" for the torture and murder of Iraqis. But the blame for these atrocities goes to the top. US President George Bush and Vice-President Dick Cheney, who waged a war based on manufactured evidence of "weapons of mass destruction"; Defence Secretary Donald Rumsfeld, who refused to allow detainees rights under the Geneva Conventions; Attorney General Alberto Gonzales, who literally wrote the memo on how to get away with torture—these are the real war criminals"[83].

Furthermore, money being used by the Coalition Provisional Authority—whether from the remains of the oil-for-food programme or from loans and aid packages received for Iraq's reconstruction — is not being accounted for, and no justification for it's spending is forthcoming. Yet, it is the state of Iraq that is contracting these debts and will therefore have to repay them. Meanwhile, US companies and those of its allies in the war against Iraq are receiving juicy contracts to rebuild Iraq's oil industry. Are occupying forces allowed to use Iraq's resources to "recycle" money by awarding their own companies contracts to rebuild Iraq's oil industry and economy? What arguments could the US use to prolong its presence indefinitely in Iraq and continue to "occupy" its economy? What are the difficulties raised by long-term belligerent occupation?

On the War on Iraq

The US war on Iraq throws up difficult legal questions that have to be balanced with political and moral considerations as well as the ever-evolving situation on the ground. At the same time, the US's war on Iraq is troubling. It is troubling because it shows the failure of the SC to maintain international peace and security, and this even in times when political cleavages between its Permanent Members have largely subsided and it is operating in the way it was initially designed to. It is troubling because it raises the spectre of imperialism, conquest, and colonialism. It is troubling because it seems to be just a pawn in a much larger and more ambitious project. It is troubling because it reveals the futility of laws to keep powerful in check, demonstrating instead the submission/servility of law to its master, politics, every time, in every age. It is troubling because it reflects a new era in which a lone superpower can "go it alone", at least for a while, and none can stop it. It is troubling because it sets a precedent for countries similarly inclined.

The Global War on Terror

On the 11th of September 2001, hijacked planes rammed into several buildings in the US killing thousands. On 12th September 2001, "France introduced and the Security Council unanimously passed Resolution 1368 (2001), which condemned the attacks and opened the way for United States-led military action against the

Taliban regime in self-defence"[84]. On the 20th of September 2001, President Bush declared his "global war on terror."[85]

A number of questions arise in this context. To cite just a few: what kind of war is the "war on terror"? If it only ends when "every terrorist group or global reach has been found, stopped, and defeated", can it ever end? Who does Bush have in mind when he refers to "the terrorists"? Who is considered to be "with the terrorists"? What are the practical consequences of being "with the terrorists"? What has been the global response to the US's declaration of a "war on terror"? What do the rules of the game dictated by the US bode for the future, for human rights and democracy as well as for the prospect of peace? What happens when the "war on terror" breeds more terrorism, extremism and fundamentalism? What are its implications on the proliferation of weapons of mass destruction? How do these elements affect the US's national security and how is the gap between the desired and actual impact of the "war on terror" in this respect to be bridged? How is the curtailment of civil liberties in the name of security in the US to be viewed?[86] Is a role for the UN and the Security Council foreseen at all in this "war on terror" and in the New World Order more generally?

Let us start with the "war on terror". Greenwood defines war as "a contention between two or more states through their armed forces for the purpose of overpowering each other and imposing such conditions of peace as the victor pleases"[87]. "Terror" on the other hand is "a general concept of emotionally enhanced fear" which results from the "terror-inspiring act" committed by a "terrorist"[88]. The very definition of "terror" therefore precludes Bush's "war on terror" from being understood in the legal sense of the term "war". Furthermore, "terrorism", in other words the strategies or processes of terror-violence, is addressed piece-meal in twelve international counter-terrorism conventions, but none of them comprehensively defines it. As the UN High-level Panel on Threats, Challenges and Change states in its 2004 report:

> "The search for an agreed definition usually stumbles on two issues. The first is the argument that any definition should include States' use of armed forces against civilians.... The second objection is that peoples under foreign occupation have a right to resistance and a definition of terrorism should not override this right"[89].

A final difficulty is that the denominations applied to given individuals, groups, or even states, change over time. During the Cold War, each superpower vied with the other to preserve and extend its sphere of influence. In order to set up "friendly" regimes and oust less malleable ones, the US pursued the so-called Reagan doctrine of destabilising regimes through covert and overt action. Latin American countries, in particular, are known to have been prey to this type of intervention, but the doctrine was rarely applied world-wide. In the process of "destabilising" regimes, the US aided military insurgencies, ousted or assassinated disfavoured leaders, and installed puppet governments[90]. Those whom the US then trained, aided, and supported were referred to as "freedom fighters".

Meanwhile, it is worth recalling that it is only in the 1970s that the threat or use of armed force against certain categories of civilians by the State was prohibited. Prior to this, States were free to deal with persons within their territory as they saw fit since the UN Charter did not prohibit the threat or use of force by States against peoples within their territory. The 1970s heralded the end of colonisation by prohibiting the use of force against peoples having a representative organisation, i.e. a national liberation movement, and falling within one of the categories entitled to self-determination, namely colonial peoples, peoples under foreign occupation, and peoples under racist regimes[91]. Cassesse[92] suggests that it is on account of their legitimate political goals that national liberation movements are given an international status; that States are allowed to provide them with humanitarian, economic, and military assistance short of sending armed troops, and conversely, that States are prohibited from assisting the State denying self-determination to these three categories of peoples. Self-determination therefore results in these liberation movements being given *a legal licence to use force against a State that denies them their right to self-determination*. Referring to the High-level Panel's 2004 report quoted above, it appears that it is the legitimacy of their goals and the right of resistance it affords them that distinguishes these groups from terrorists. The problem lies in the absence of any similar provision allowing specific groups, peoples or minorities the right to self-determination. Are their goals not legitimate? Are they "freedom fighters", "insurgents", "rebels", or "terrorists"? Are Palestinians "freedom fighters" or "terrorists"? What about the Chechens? Were Al Qaeda volunteers terrorists when they joined the US-financed war against the Soviet Union in Afghanistan? The answer lies in the eyes of the beholder as "what is terrorism to some is heroism to others".

In the absence of a comprehensive legal definition of "terrorism" or of a "terrorist', one may question the feasibility of the establishment, through the UN, of a special tribunal entrusted with the prosecution of those indicted for the crime of international terrorism, possibly starting with the apprehension and trial of Osama bin Laden, that is currently under discussion[93].

The War on Afghanistan

Afghanistan was the first country the US used force against after declaring its "war on terror". The US started its strikes on October 2001, almost a month after the 11th of September, in the name of self-defence. At issue is whether the State of Afghanistan can be held responsible for the acts of Al Qaeda, a non-state actor. The same questions which were raised regarding the US use of force in Iraq in 1993 have to be answered here. Was there an "armed attack" against the US[94]? When is a State (Afghanistan) responsible for the acts of a non-state actor (Al Qaeda) acting on or from its territory? Who is to judge whether the Taliban, as the government of the state of Afghanistan, exercised "effective control" over bin Laden, the terrorists, and Al-Qaeda? What is the doctrine of "effective control"? Did the US fulfil the self-defence requirements of immediacy, necessity, and proportionality?

Is the US abiding by the *jus in bello*? What is the legal status of Al Qaeda members captured by the US? Are they "prisoners of war" or rather "enemy combatants" as claimed by the US with respect to prisoners in Guantanamo Bay? Or, are they "terrorists"? How is their status to be determined and how does it affect the legal regime they fall under? Does the determination of their status depend on objective considerations or is there scope for subjective interpretation and therefore for politics to determine the answers? Are Taliban fighters considered "prisoners of war"? What are the likely consequences of the Supreme Court's judgement regarding the right of Guantanamo detainees to challenge their detention in court?

The US's treatment to date, of Al Qaeda members taken prisoner, is actually a cause for concern on several counts[95]. First, it points to a flagrant disregard by the US for the *jus in bello*[96]: freedom from torture is a non-derogable right. Second, it highlights the extent to which the US is willing to push legal interpretation and create legal fiction to suit various interests. Reference is being made to the US's non-abidance of *jus in bello* vis-à-vis prisoners in Guantanamo Bay because the area does not fall within the strict jurisdiction of the

US[97]. And third, through the concept of "broad jurisdiction", the US has granted itself the right to arrest anyone, worldwide, who is suspected of having links with Al Qaeda, without giving them a right to seek remedy. Thus, on the one hand, the lack of due process in such instances suggests a disturbing curtailment of hard-earned (universal) human rights in the name of national security[98]. On the other, the double standards in application are evident. The US refuses that its men should be hauled up before the courts, through the principle of universal jurisdiction, to be held to account for the alleged commission of mass violations, despite the legal safeguards provided. Such behaviour reflects a propensity by the US to "not regard [itself] as bound by international norms": the literal definition of a "rogue state"[99]. To this definition, Chomsky adds that "logic suggests that the most powerful states should tend to fall into [this] category unless internally constrained, an expectation that history confirms"[100] ... .

'Axis of Evil', WMD and Nuclear Proliferation

The war on Iraq in 2003 was justified in the name of anticipatory self-defence owing to weapons of mass destruction (WMD) which, it was alleged Saddam Hussein would either use to imminently attack the US or would only be too willing to give to Al Qaeda. US rhetoric changed over time as it became evident that there were no WMD in Iraq: "The President has switched seamlessly from proclaiming certainty about the weapons to certainty about the weapons programmes"[101]; and from there to the rhetoric of "just war"[102] claiming that Iraq had to be "freed". Whatever the rhetoric used, the point is that the US, the country with the greatest number of WMD in the world, went to war against Iraq to prevent it from developing its own WMD. Iraq was the first country on Bush's "Axis of Evil" list, and incidentally one of the two Muslim countries on the list. North Korea, in second place on the said list, announced the acceleration of its nuclear weapons programme, while the third member, Iran, revealed a potential nuclear programme that, it transpired, was more advanced than the international community had suspected.

The question is why did both countries make these announcements and revelations, especially with the wisdom of Iraq's experience? Is it conceivable that they did so in order to have a deterrent effect on the US[103]? Would their announcement actually have the desired effect by dissuading the US from waging a pre-emptive war against either of these countries? Is it possible that in this day, the best guarantee against US intervention is some form of nuclear capability? In that case, is it possible to reconcile the US's proclaimed intention to use WMD "in the future pursuit of [its] strategic interest" vs. the US statement that "some countries, the so-called 'Axis of Evil' countries, face war if they try to pursue their security by relying on this kind of weapon"[104]? Furthermore, if nuclear capability serves as an effective deterrent to an armed attack, is it not inevitable that attempts to develop WMD will proliferate? Will this, in turn, not undermine the Non-Proliferation Treaty (NPT) regime currently in operation? More dangerously, will this not force these attempts to be covert? Is the US capable of limiting these attempts through its pre-emptive attacks? Will it try to impose a blanket prohibition on such attempts or will it be selective in whom it targets? Can it effectively substitute the hitherto fairly successful NPT regime[105] through armed attacks? What does this mean with respect to the US's "war on terror"? Seemingly:

> "the conflation of rogue states, terrorism, and WMD, coupled with the administration's preventive war against Saddam Hussein's Iraq for the purpose of disarming that country, make the global war on terror as much a war on nuclear proliferators—at least ones the United States does not like—as it is a war against terrorism itself"[106]

In effect therefore, the US's "war on terror" is also a means of perpetuating the gap between the "have-WMD" and the "have-not-WMD", and therefore, of preserving its (unchallengeable) supremacy. It heralds a quasi-reign of terror. And it is "an approach based on double standards—one for ourselves and one for those whom we seek to govern".[107]

Changing Perceptions

The US's "war on terror" first targetted Afghanistan as there was "abundant incriminating evidence linking its government to Al Qaeda"[108], the terrorist organization behind the 11th of September violence. Whereas the US war on Afghanistan was widely viewed as legitimate[109] and generated wide-spread support, even amongst Arab countries[110], the US has since increasingly come to be seen as anti-Arab and anti-Muslim. Calls for a "crusade", the characterization of two Muslim countries as forming part of the "Axis of Evil", the waging of the war against a Muslim country (Iraq), and especially the support given to one of "us" (Israel) in its own war against one of "them" added fuel to the fire. Arab priorities and Bush's priorities were exactly opposite:

> "The daily suffering of Palestinians under Israeli occupation was the highest Arab priority, while it seemed to be President Bush's lowest. Conversely, the Iraqi threat was Bush's highest, and most urgent priority, but it was not considered either a priority or urgent by most Arabs. Moreover, to most Arabs, it looked as if President Bush was deliberately hostile to Arabs and Muslims (Palestinians, Iraqis, Iranians, and Afghans) while condoning Israeli actions"[111].

Parallels between the two situations started to be drawn: both Israel and the US espouse the doctrine of anticipatory self-defence.[112] Both have used the argument of anticipatory self-defence to destroy Iraq's nuclear capability. Both wage war against Muslim peoples. Both blur the distinction between enemy combatants and civilians. Both wage this war in the name of security. Both use the rhetoric of the "war on terror".[113] Both occupy foreign territory[114]. Both refuse the application of the rules of belligerent occupation, whether in theory or in practice.[115] Both use technology and military equipment that is far superior to that possessed by or available to their opponent[116].

One main difference between them lies in the past, with regard to their respective strikes on Iraq. In the case of Israel's 1981 strike against Iraq, the Security Council "strongly condemn[ed] the military attack by Israel in clear violation of the Charter of the United Nations and the norms of international conduct".[117] In the case of the US 2003 strike against Iraq, the SC simply legitimized the US's occupation of Iraq post-facto[118]. Yet, Israel staged a foray into Iraq to bomb the nuclear reactor whereas the US is an occupying power and, two years on, its forces are still very much present on the ground. Another difference is that whereas the US has found supporters amongst the Iraqi people, Israel has found none.

From the perspective of the Palestinians and Iraqis, both are fighting foreign occupation. Both are fighting for the sovereignty of their State. Both face a nuclear power. Both have inferior conventional weapons at their disposal. Both bear significant losses in human terms. Finally, both are labelled as terrorists—a designation that merely serves to reinforce the inequality between the protagonists and to highlight the use of double standards by seemingly exempting "state violence from moral and legal limitations, while insisting that such limitations apply to the violence of the terrorists"[119]

In the context of Palestine, Falk writes that:

> "the kinds of violence generated by Israeli oppression and Israel's refusal to uphold international law and human rights give rise to a politics of desperation that includes savage attacks on Israeli civilian society"[120].

Taking our cue from this statement, can one, by extension, argue that terrorism more generally, i.e. the commission of "savage attacks", against a "civilian society", is a reflection/manifestation of a "politics of desperation"? At first sight, this contention seems perfectly reasonable: "savage attacks" presumably inculcate terror owing to their savagery; and the "civilian society" element fits neatly into the current US national security strategy definition of terrorism as "premeditated, politically motivated violence against innocents"[121]. As regards the "politics of desperation", the issue is more ambiguous. Let us first consider terror-violence by the State[122], defined as the "strategy of violence that states, insurgent groups, and repressive regimes use against civilian populations and other protected persons and targets"[123]. If the "politics of desperation" is to apply to terror-violence by states, then we have to concede that these strategies are those of desperate states. If we are unwilling to do so, we risk falling into the trap of treating only anti-State violence as terrorism and viewing State-violence as "self-defence" and "security"[124].

Turning to the acts of individuals or groups, the focus of attention is usually the motivation, "the ideological motivation of the actor"[125], and the intention, "the political purpose, or power-outcome, contemplated by the act of violence"[126], or the intention "to coerce or intimidate governments or societies in pursuit of goals that are generally political, religious, or ideological"[127]. In short, the accent does not lie on the motor which propels a person to resort to violence as a means to an end. Can the propelling force of a "politics of desperation" be read into the acts of violence committed? Is the willingness of Palestinian and Iraqi suicide bombers, as well as the hijackers of the four commercial airplanes used on the 11th of September, to sacrifice their lives not a sign of desperation? What is the ideological motivation that compels these people to act in the way they do? What are they trying to achieve? Are the ends always legal and legitimate? Are the means employed bearing fruit? Does this justify them? Are "savage attacks" against a "civilian society" ever justified? Are they morally defensible? How is the assertion by the UN High-level Panel on Threats, Challenges and Change in its 2004 report that "terrorism is never an acceptable tactic even for the most defensible of causes" to be viewed? What other means can be employed to the same ends and are also available to those whom Record labels the "politically desperate and militarily helpless"[128] ? And if these acts are indeed propelled by a "politics of desperation", who is to be held responsible for them?

Although we shall not seek to comprehensively understand the "politics of desperation" as it is beyond the scope of this paper[129], we suggest that the case of Palestine reveals a combination of elements that could possibly explain the Palestinians' resort to "savage attacks" against a "civilian society", and by extension that of other "terrorists". The elements include: (1) asymmetric military capability; (2) rejection of/non-abidance by applicable international laws by the militarily more powerful party; (3) lack of action, including the lack of the use of force, by the SC; (4) subjugation/humiliation/sense of loss of dignity of the militarily weaker party and/or lack of respect of the people by the militarily powerful side; and, perhaps more importantly, (5) the engraving in stone of unequal power structures and more generally of structures of inequality.

Whether each of these elements is inelectably a part of the lethal combination which leads to terror-violence or whether further elements need to be added to complete the explosive mix remains to be tested. Assuming that at least some of these elements are indeed a motor of the "politics of desperation", it is worth noting that they cover all realms of life, from the legal to the socio-economical, from brute military force to power politics. Taking a closer look at the legal field, these elements can but undermine the legitimacy of both the law and the UN system. Where is the level playing field?

On the "War on Terror"

The US's "global war on terror" has forever relegated the Cold War era and its rules to the past while trumpeting the beginning of a new era of US hegemony. Some of the following elements, and more, should give us a clear portrayal of who is waging the "war on terror", against whom, for what reason, and to what end: the US's proclamation of the "war on terror"; its waging of war against

Afghanistan and Iraq in the name of the "war on terror"; its designation of Iran and North Korea as forming part of an "Axis of Evil"; its denouncement of neutrality in the war on terror[130] and its requirement that States choose between "us" and "them". Yet, as we have tried to highlight above, uncertainty prevails. What is clear is that the US dominates the scene and dictates the rules. It plays the role of arbiter with an iron fist, brooking no dissent. The US's game is one in which there are only two parties and these are diametrically opposed. A different set of rules applies to each party—there is no level playing field.

Concluding with Some Food for Thought

Throughout this paper we have spoken about war. War is the subject of a growing corpus of law that seeks to limit its resort as well as certain aspects of its conduct. Yet war continues. Thus laws proliferate.

Attempts to regulate the recourse to war and its conduct are rooted in the moral, religious, humanitarian, and legal fields. Since the 17th century, attempts to codify both the *jus ad bellum* and the *jus in bello* have been made at the multilateral level. Succeeding codes have always sought to address some of the weaknesses of the former, generally by expanding the coverage of existing legal regimes. Thus, in the *jus ad bellum*, for example, the threat and use of force rather than merely "wars" came to be regulated, whereas in the *jus in bello,* certain new weapons which were especially harmful were prohibited. It is interesting to try to understand the reason for the persistence of gaps and weaknesses, including in the currently applicable legal regime. It appears that some of these gaps are due to the differences between the geo-political environment and the available military technology and weapons, and those for which the given laws were intended. These gaps are therefore apparent in terms of their horizontal coverage and are due to time lags: they are unintentional. It also appears that other gaps are the trademark of each new legal regime. These pertain mostly to the limitations put on States to resort to war. Although the freedom of States to use force in inter-State relations is unarguably more restricted nowadays, States either retain the right to use force in specific (yet malleable) circumstances, or arrogate themselves the right to do so. States in the latter category are frequently the most powerful and thus, arguably, unfettered by the laws applying to others. Additionally, as the enforcement regime is invariably weak, resort to force by these States routinely goes unpunished. These gaps are apparent in the horizontal (non-coverage of all threats or use of force) as well as vertical (non-application to all States) coverage of the laws: they are intentional. In other words, powerful States are simply unwilling to give up their (discretionary) right to wage war. The experience of Iraq is used to test these propositions in practice and to give them some weight.

The war on Afghanistan in 2001 and the war on Iraq in 2003, waged in the context of the "global war on terror", exposes the purported "us" vs. "them" dichotomy that determines the application of standards: "One for ourselves and one for those whom we seek to govern"[131]. The phenomenon, as we saw above, is not new its explicitness is unique. The effect is two-fold. On the one hand, it poses a serious threat to the current legal regime governing wars. However, this challenge is one that the law has been tackling since its inception, with the "us" vs. "them" being reminiscent of the "just war" rhetoric. On the other hand, and more importantly perhaps, is the threat posed by the impact such a message can be expected to have on the "governed". On the "us" side, the envisioned response has engendered a tangible fear paranoia. In other words, there is an expectation, an anticipation that the "governed" will respond with terror-violence. The crucial question is why: why *must* they respond with *terror*-violence?

We do not seek to answer this question, nor do we wish to condone the use of terror violence, but simply point to the right to self-determination. The right to self-determination gives a legal license to peoples under colonial rule, under foreign occupation, and under racist regimes to use force against a State that denies them their right to self-determination. Is there a case for diluting the strict interpretation of the terms "colonial rule", "foreign occupation", and "racist rule", and applying the concept of self-determination at the global level? What is the outcome of such an exercise?

Furthermore, as we saw above, certain States appear to be unwilling to abide by the law and others appear to be unwilling or unable to force these detractors to do so. Should the focus of the law not simply shift from attempting to exert external pressure to regulating the behaviour of States through internal constraints? What types of constraints could be envisaged? Could they, *inter alia*, address the engendering of a "politics of desperation"?

Our task then is to face up to the threats inherent in the "us" vs. "them" dichotomy and to the application of double standards. Will we be more successful in this enterprise than our forefathers?

Notes

1. The full text of President Bush's address to a joint session of Congress and the nation, 20 September 2001: at http://www.washingtonpost.com/wp-srv/nation/specials/attacked/transcripts/bushaddress_092001.html
2. Dinstein, Yoram, *War, Aggression and Self-Defence*, 3rd ed. (Cambridge: Cambridge University Press, 2001) 59.
3. St. Augustine, *City of God*, trans. by H. Bettenson (London: Penguin, 1984); Aquinas, St. Thomas, *Summa Contra Gentiles*, ed. by A.C. Pegis, *et al.* (Notre Dame, N: University of Notre Dame Press, 1975); Vitorio, Francisco de., *Political Writings*, ed. by Anthony Pagden and Jeremy Lawrence (New York: Cambridge University Press, 1991); Grotius, Hugo, *The Rights* of *War and Peace*, ed. and trans. by A.C. Campbell (New York: M.W. Dunne, 1901); Grotius, Hugo, *The Law of War and Peace*, trans. F.W. Keisley, intro. J.B. Scott (New York: Bobbs-Merrill, 1925); Zouche, Richard, *Juris et judicii fecialis*, 2 Vols., ed. Thomas E. Holland, trans. J. L. Briefly (Washington, D.C: Carnegie Institution of Washington, 1911); Pufendorf, Samuel, *The Political Writings of Samuel Pufendorf*, ed. Craigl. Carr, trans. Michael J. Seidler (New York: Oxford University Press, 1927).
4. Mona Fixdal and Dan Smith, "Humanitarian Intervention and Just War", *Mershon International Studies Review* 42 (1998) 283-312 at http://www.mtholyoke.edu/acad/intrel/fixdal.html; Brother John Raymond, "The Just War Theory" at http://www.mtholyoke.edu/acad/intrel/pol116/justwar.htm
5. Cassesse, Antonio, *International Law* (Oxford: Oxford University Press, 2001) 21
6. *Ibid.*, pp. 27-28.
7. http://www.infoplease.com/ce6/people/A0809971.html, http://www.infoplease.com/ce6/people/A0816051.html
8. George B. Davis, "Doctor Francis Lieber's Instructions for the Government of Armies in the Field", *American Journal of International Law* 1 (1907) 13-25.
9. Meron, Theodore, *War Crimes Law Comes of Age* (Oxford: Clarendon Press, 1998) 156.
10. The Martens clause takes its name after a declaration read by Professor Martens, the Russian delegate at The Hague Peace Conferences of 1899. It was inserted into the Preamble to The Hague Convention II of 1899,

and Convention IV of 1907. It provided that, "Until a more complete code of the laws of war has been issued, the high contracting Parties deem it expedient to declare that, in cases not included in the Regulations adopted by them, the inhabitants and the belligerents remain under the protection and the rule of the principles of the law of nations, as they result from the usages established among civilized peoples, from the laws of humanity and the dictates of the public conscience." Although the Martens clause was devised to cope with disagreements among the parties to The Hague Peace Conferences regarding the status of resistance movements in occupied territory, it is today considered applicable to the whole of humanitarian law. For more information, see Rupert Ticehurst, "The Martens Clause and the Laws of Armed Conflict", *International Review of the Red Cross* 317 (1997) 125-134 or at http://www.icrc.org/Web/Eng/siteeng0.nsf/iwpList74 32AEA038821EA35EC1256B66005A747C

11. Covenant of the League of Nations, Article 10.
12. Although States did draw up a document designed to abolish the general right to go to war, namely the Geneva Protocol on the Pacific Settlement of International Disputes, Article 2, which was adopted by the Assembly of the League in 1924, it remained abortive.
13. Covenant of the League of Nations, Articles 12,13, and 15.
14. Dinstein, Yoram, *War, Aggression and Self-defence*, 3rd ed. Cambridge: Cambridge University Press, 2001) 75-77; Cassesse, Antonio, *International Law* (Oxford: Oxford University Press, 2001) 32-33.
15. Covenant of the League of Nations, Article 15(7).
16. *Ibid.*, Article 12.
17. *Ibid.*, Article 17.
18. Kellogg-Briand Pact, Article 1.
19. C. Greenwood, "The relationship between jus ad bellum and jus in bello", *Review of International Studies* 9 (1983) 221.
20. For general reading, see: B. Simma, "NATO, the UN, and the Use of Force: Legal Aspects", *EJIL* 10, 1 (1999); A. Cassesse, "Ex inuria jus oritur: Are We Moving Towards International Legitimization of Forcible Humanitarian Countermeasures in the World Community", *EJIL* 10, 1 (1999); Schachter, O., *Right vs. Might: International Law and the Use of Force*, 2nd ed. (Dordrecht: Nijhoff, 1991) 109; A. Cassesse, "The International Community's "Legal" Response to Terrorism", *International and Comparative Law Quarterly* 38 (1989); C. Greenwood, "The Concept of War in Modern International Law", *International and Comparative Law Quarterly* 36 (1987); A. Sofaer, "Terrorism and Law", *Foreign Affairs* 64 (1986) 901; T. Franck, "Who killed Article 2(4)?", *The American Journal of International Law,* 64 (1970) 809; Jarat Chopra, and Thomas G. Weiss, "Sovereignty is no longer sacrosanct: Codifying Humanitarian Intervention" at http://

hwproject.tufts.edu/publications/electronic/e_sinls.html

21. See the UN Declaration on Friendly Relations of 1970 and the Declaration on the Definition of Aggression 1974 for limitations on the use of force in non-international conflicts.
22. Economic coercion is envisaged in the UN Charter itself under Article 41. See Principles III of the UN Declaration on Friendly Relations of 1970, para. 2, for economic coercion amounting to a violation of the principle of non-intervention in internal affairs.
23. The Report of the High-level Panel on Threats, Challenges and Change "A more secure world: Our shared responsibility", United Nations, 2004, at point 249 for the principles to guide reform of the SC; points 249-260 for details of the proposed reform of the SC. The crux of the matter lies in the following statement "We recommend that under any reform proposal, there should be no expansion of the veto" in point 256. Will reform succeed to assuage the resentment caused by a handful of countries, not even dominant countries, taking binding decisions for 192 States? Or that of Muslims who will then be represented in the Security Council? See also Bowring, Philip, "UN power play drives China protests", *International Herald Tribune*, 12th of April 2005.
24. Dinstein, Yoram, *War, Aggression and Self-defence*, 3rd ed. (Cambridge: Cambridge University Press, 2001) 243-5, 257-9; Thailf Deen, "Flaws in UN's Moral Authority", *InterPress Service*, June 22, 1999; Stanley Hoffman, "Thoughts on the UN at Fifty", *EJIL* 6, 3 (1995); Martti Koskenniemi, "The Police in the Temple: Order, Justice and the UN—A Dialectical View", *EJIL* 6, 3 (1995); Rosalyn Higgins, "Peace and Security Achievements and Failures", *EJIL* 6, 3 (1995); "Envisioning the UN in the 21st century" at www.unu.edu/unupress/un21-report.html
25. For general reading see: C. Green, *The Contemporary Law of Armed Conflict*, 2n ed. (Manchester: University of Manchester Press, 2000); Adam Roberts and Richard Guelff, *Documents on the Laws of War*, 3rd ed. (New York: OUP, 2000); Marco Sassoli and Antoine A. Bouvier, *How does the Law protect in War? Cases, documents and teaching materials on contemporary practice in international humanitarian law* (Geneva: ICRC, 1999); Fleck Dieter, *The Handbook of Humanitarian Law in Armed Conflicts* (New York: OUP, 1995); Geoffrey Best, *War and Law since 1945* (New York: Columbia University Press, 1994); AJM Delissen and GJ Tanja, *Humanitarian Law of Armed Conflict* (Boston: Nijhoff, 1991); T. Meron, "The Geneva Conventions as Customary Law", *AJIL* 81 (1987); *Nicaragua vs. USA* at http://www.icj-cij.org/icjwww/icases/inus/inus_ijudgment/ inus_ijudgment_19860627.pdf; *Prosecutor vs. Tadic* at http://www.un.org/icty/tadic/trialc2/decision-e/100895.htm
26. The Convention for the Amelioration of the Condition of the Wounded and Sick in Armed Forces in the Field; the Convention for Armed Forces

at Sea; the Convention Relative to the Treatment of Prisoners of War; and the Convention Relative to the Protection of Civilian Persons in Time of War at http://www.yale.edu/lawweb/avalon/lawofwar/geneva05.htm—http://www.yale.edu/lawweb/avalon/lawofwar/geneva06.htm & http://www.yale.edu/lawweb/avalon/lawofwar/geneva07.htm

27. Protocol I Additional to the Geneva Conventions of the 12th of August 1949, and Relating to the Protection of Victims of International Armed Conflicts; Protocol II Additional to the Geneva Conventions of the 12th of August 1949, and Relating to the Protection of Victims of Non-International Armed Conflicts.
28. A state of war can exist in the technical and/or in the material sense. War in the technical sense "starts with a declaration of war"; war in the material sense "unfolds irrespective of any formal steps. Its occurrence is contingent only on the actual outbreak of comprehensive hostilities between two or more States". See Dinstein, Yoram, *War, Aggression, and Self-defence*, 3rd ed. (Cambridge: Cambridge University Press, 2001) 30-32.
29. For general reading see Boed, R., "The effect of a domestic amnesty on the ability of foreign States to prosecute alleged perpetrators of serious human rights violations", *Cornell International Law Journal* 33, 2 (2000); M.Griffin, "Ending impunity of perpetrators of human rights atrocities: A major challenge for international law in the 21st century", *International Review of the Red Cross* 838 (June 2000) 369-389; C. van den Wyngaert, "War crimes, genocide and crimes against humanity – are States taking national prosecution seriously?", in M. C. Bassiouni ed., *International Criminal Law*, Vol. 3, 2d ed., (New York: Transnational Publishers, 1999) 227-239; J. Garwood-Cutler, "Enforcing ICL violations with civil remedies: The US Alien Tort Claims Act", in M.C. Bassiouni, *International Law*, Vol. III: Enforcement, 2nd ed. (New York: Transnational Publishers Inc., 1999) 343-391, 597-636; Malanczuk, Akehurst, *Modern Introduction to International Law*, 7th rev. ed. (London, New York: Routledge, 1997); Malcolm N. Shaw,, International Law, 4th ed. (Cambridge: Cambridge University Press,1997).
30. Nuremburg Charter, Article 8.
31. Malanczuk, Akehurst's *Modern Introduction to International Law*, 7th rev. ed. (London, New York: Routledge, 1997) 118-123.
32. *Ibid.*, p. 42.
33. For statutory limitations, see the 1968 UN Convention on the Non-Applicability of Statutory Limitations for War Crimes and Crimes against Humanity, Article 1, and the Rome Statute of the ICC, Article 29.
34. Malanczuk, Akehurst's *Modern Introduction to International Law*, 7th rev. ed. (London, New York: Routledge, 1997) 110-113 for jurisdiction

principles; Restatement 3rd of the Foreign Relations Law of the US, 1987, para. 404, and *Kadic vs. Karadzic*, 70F. 3rd 232 (2d Cir. 1995), 240 for the universality principle giving jurisdiction to domestic courts in criminal and civil proceedings. For universal jurisdiction for war crimes and crimes against humanity, see UNGA Resolution of 1953, UNGA Resolution on the Question of Punishment of War Criminals and of Persons who have Committed Crimes against Humanity of 1971, UNGA Resolution on Principles of International Co-operation in the Detection, Arrest, Extradition and Punishment of Persons Guilty of War Crimes and Crimes Against Humanity of 1973, Rome Statute of the ICC of 1998. For universal jurisdiction for genocide, see the Convention on the Prevention and Punishment of the Crime of Genocide of 1948; Reservations to the Convention on Genocide Case (Adv. Op.) 1951 ICJ, 23; *Attorney General of Israel vs. Eichmann*, 36 ILR (Isr.DC.Jm. 1961) 18, 38-39; Restatement 3rd of the Foreign Relations Law of the US, 1987, para. 702. For universal jurisdiction for torture, see the Convention against Torture of 1984; for universal jurisdiction for torture as a crime against humanity, see *R v. Bow Street Metropolitan stipendiary Magistrates Court and Others*, ex parte Pinochet Ugarte (No. 3)[1999] 2 *All ER* 97, per Lord Browne-Wilkinson, 108, and Lord Millet, 178.

35. A duty to extradite or prosecute perpetrators of war crimes only applies to "grave breaches" (i.e. in international armed conflicts), and only binds States Parties [the four Geneva Conventions of 1949: Articles 49 I, 50 II, 129 II, 146 IV and Additional Protocol I of 1977] whereas the same duty only applies to States Parties to the Convention against Torture, 1984, in relation to torture. A duty to extradite or prosecute perpetrators of genocide exists both under treaty law [Genocide Convention, 1948] and under international customary law [Restatement 3rd of the Foreign Relations Law of the US, 1987, para. 702]. There is no such duty either by treaty or customarily for crimes against humanity.
36. See Borut Grgic, "Let the war crimes tribunal do its work", *International Herald Tribune*, 9th of March 2005 on the ICTY generally.
37. James Pringle, "Once there were killing fields", *International Herald Tribune*, 16-17th of April 2005; Cohen, Roger, "For Cambodia's dead, farce heaped on insult", *International Herald Tribune*, 2-3rd of April 2005.
38. In addition, the landmark arrest of Pinochet in the UK in October 1998 opened the floodgate for the prosecution of others, worldwide. See for example Sima Samar and Nader Nadery, "A cry for justice", *International Herald Tribune*, 3rd of February 2005 at http://www.iht.com/articles/2005/02/02/opinion/edsamar.php
39. Regarding justice for crimes committed in Darfur, the most recent locus

of mass violations, see for example Nicholas D. Kristof, "So we turn a blind eye to genocide, again", *International Herald Tribune*, 18th of April 2005; Stephanie Giry, "Darfur and the ICC II—A losing strategy on war crimes", *International Herald Tribune*, 12-13th of February 2005; "UN Denial on Darfur", *International Herald Tribune*, 8th of February 2005; Samantha Power, "Darfur and the International Criminal Court I – The court of first resort", *International Herald Tribune*, 12-13th of February 2005; Nicholas D. Kristof, "Bush puts ideology over lives in Sudan", *International Herald Tribune*, 3rd of February 2005.

40. See http://www.un.org/icty/indictment/english/mil-ai040421-e.htm- http://www.un.org/icty/indictment/english/mil-2ai020728e.htm— http:/ /www.un.org/icty/indictment/english/mil-2ai011029e.htm for details about the indictment and trial proceedings.
41. "Defiant Saddam rejects court, charges", 1st of July 2004 at http:// www.cnn.com/2004/WORLD/meast/07/01/iraq.saddam
42. See "Trial of Saddam Hussein" at www.sourcewatch.org/wiki.phtml? title=Trial_of_Saddam_Hussein
43. See "The Iraqi special tribunal: trying Saddam's regime", 15th of December 2004 at http://www.cbc.ca/news/background/iraq/ specialtribunal.html
44. Sudarsan Raghavan, "Iraqi War Crimes Tribunal could be used to settle old scores, some say", 10th of December 2003, at http:// www.commondreams.org/headlines03/1210-11.htm
45. "Iraqi Special Tribunal" at http://en.wikipedia.org/wiki/ Iraqi_Special_Tribunal
46. http://en.wikipedia.org/wiki/Universal_jurisdiction
47. "Belgium: Universal Jurisdiction Law·Repealed", Aug. 2003, at http:// www.hrw.org/press/2003/08/belgium080103.htm (Last visited on 10 Feb. 06); see also http://www.globalpolicy.org/intljustice/universal/ 2003/0613belgium.htm
48. *Ibid.*
49. "Under Article 12, the ICC may exercise such jurisdiction over anyone anywhere in the world, even in the absence of a referral by the Security Council, if either the state or the territory where the crime was committed or the state of the nationality of the accused consents. Ironically, the treaty exposes non-parties in ways that parties are not exposed.... It is simply and logically untenable to expose the largest deployed military force in the world, stationed across the globe to help maintain international peace and security and to defend U.S. allies and friends, to the jurisdiction of a criminal court the U.S. Government has not yet joined and whose authority over U.S. citizens the United States does not yet recognize", David J. Scheffer, "The United States and the International Criminal Court", *AJIL* 12, 93 (1999) 20. To be contrasted with Grant M. Dawson, "Defining Substantive Crimes Within the

Subject Matter Jurisdiction of the International Criminal Court: What Is the Crime of Aggression?", *New York Law School Journal International and Comparative Law* 413, 19 (2000): "... these concerns, however, are red herrings and belie the United States' continuing lack of commitment to compliance with international legal norms: the precondition of these concerns is the expectation that American soldiers will commit one of the core crimes. The focus of the United States should not be modification of the Rome Statute so that it is less able to insure justice, but rather to train its soldiers to insure that they will not commit genocide, crimes against humanity, and war crimes." For the Rome Statute of the ICC, 1998, see www.un.org/law/icc/statute/romefra.htm

50. See http://www.iccnow.org/documents/otherissuesimpunityagreem.html for a list of documents on the BIAs. See also http://www.hrw.org/campaigns/icc/docs/bilateralagreements.pdf for US domestic law on the matter.
51. See http://www.amicc.org/usinfo/administration_policy_BIAs.html
52. *Ibid.*; See http://www.amicc.org/docs/CGStableofBIAsbyICCstatus%2010-04.pdf for the amount of money withheld from certain countries.
53. *Ibid.*; "Status of US Bilateral Immunity Agreements" at http://www.amicc.org/docs/BIAsByRegion1Dec04.pdf
54. "UN SC refers Darfur to the ICC", 31st of March 2005 at http://hrw.org/english/docs/2005/03/31/sudan10408.htm
55. Judgments of the ICTY and ICTR have already contributed significantly to developments by expounding on applicable laws. Landmark cases include *inter alia* Tadic, ICTY (IT-94-1), and Akayesu, ICTR (ICTR-96-4).
56. Although reference throughout has been made to individual responsibility in criminal proceedings, it should be noted that the US is one of the more progressive countries in allowing victims of mass human rights violations to intervene either in criminal proceedings as "parties civiles" or to undertake private actions before civil courts. See, the Alien Tort Claims Act 28 USC para. 1350 (1994) and the Torture Victim Protection Act Pub L. No 102-256, 106 Stat. 73 (1992). For leading cases see *Forti v. Suarez-Mason*, 672 F. Supp. (N.D.Cal. 1987); *Kadic v. Karadzic*, 70 F. 3d 232 (2d. Cir. 1995) (genocide); *Filartiga v. Pena-Irala*, 630 F.2d 876 (2d Cir. 1980); *Abebe-Jira v. Negewo*, 72 F. 3d 844 (11th Cir. 1996) (torture); *Doe v. Islamic Salvation Front*, 993 F; Supp. 3 (D.D.C. 1998) (crimes against humanity).
57. At the time, Iraq was under pressure to pay debts accumulated during its war against Iran in the 1980s and was at the same time facing lowering oil prices due to over-production by Kuwait and other Gulf countries. Having tried to resolve the issue with Kuwait diplomatically, and

receiving mixed signals from the US, Iraq invaded Kuwait. Could it have argued the defence of survival of the state?

58. In the Korean War (SC Resolution 82 (1950)); Falkland Islands War (SC Resolution 502 (1982)); Iran-Iraq War (SC Resolution 598 (1987).
59. Resolution 661.
60. Other resolutions include 661, 665, 670.
61. Henry Kissinger, *Diplomacy* (New Work: Simon & Schuster, 1994). 384.
62. For the effects of economic sanctions on Iraq, see *The Bossuyt Report*, Economic and Social Council, E/CN.4 Sub.2/2000/33, June 21, 2000, pp. 59-73 at http://www.globalpolicy.org/security/sanction/unreports/bossuyt.htm
63. See for example D. Brown, "Independent panel recommended to oversee proof of Gulf War illness", *Washington Post*, 9th November 1997; P. Shenon, "Pentagon now says it knew of chemical weapons risk", *New York Times*, 26th of February 1997.
64. See for example Alim Yacoub, Imad Al-Sadoon, and Janan Hasan, "The evidence for causal association between exposure to depleted uranium and malignancies among children in Basrah by applying epidemiological criteria of causality" at http://www.irak.be/ned/archief/Depleted%20Uranium_bestanden/DU-CausalAssociation Basrah.htm
65. Ashis Nandy, "State", in The Development Dictionary, ed. Wolfgang Sachs (Hyderabad: Orient Longman, 2000).
66. Hugo Grotius [1583-1645], the chief magistrate of Rotterdam in 1613, was condemned to life imprisonment for speaking up against Calvinist Puritanism in 1619, but managed to escape to Sweden where he wrote *On the Law of War and Peace*, in 1625. The book is recognized as the foundational source for the international law of war. Grotius later served as the Swedish ambassador to France from 1635 until his death in 1645.
67. Byron F. Burmester, "On Humanitarian Intervention: The New World Order and Wars to Preserve Human Rights", *Utah Law Review* 269 (1994).
68. UN Charter, Article 1, para. 1.
69. UN Charter Article 24 para.1.
70. UN Charter, Preamble: "We the people of the United Nations determined... to reaffirm faith in fundamental human rights, in the dignity and worth of the human person, in the equal rights of men and women and of nations large and small".
71. These cases have to be viewed not only in the light of the international customary law duty to prevent and punish the crime of genocide, but also of the UN Report of the High-level Panel on Threats, Challenges and Change "A more secure world: Our shared responsibility", United Nations, 2004, allegation' at point 201 that "The principle of non-intervention in internal affairs cannot be used to protect genocidal acts or other atrocities, such as large-scale violations of international

humanitarian law or large-scale ethnic cleansing".

72. Christopher Greenwood, "The Concept of War in Modern International Law", *International and Comparative Law Quarterly* 283, 294, 36 (1987).
73. See the Report of the High-level Panel on Threats, Challenges and Change "A more secure world: Our shared responsibility", United Nations, 2004, points 199-209 on humanitarian intervention by the UN.
74. The European Court of Human Rights ruled unanimously in favor of the first complaints by Chechen civilians against the Russian armed forces during the second war in the breakaway Republic of Chechnya, March 2005. Steven Eke, "Russia committed Chechnya abuse", *BBC News, World Edition* at http://news.bbc.co.uk/2/hi/europe/4295249.stm
75. Universal Declaration on Human Rights (1948), Article 1: "All human beings are born free and equal in dignity and rights."
76. Dinstein, Yoram, *War, Aggression and Self-defence*, 3rd ed. (Cambridge: Cambridge University Press, 2001) 260-1.
77. *Ibid.*, p. 167.
78. See http://www.yale.edu/lawweb/avalon/diplomacy/britian/br-1842d.htm for details of the case.
79. Jeffrey Record, "Bounding the Global War on Terrorism", Strategic Studies Institute, December 2003 at http://www.mindfully.org/Reform/2003/Global-War-On-Terrorism-GWOTDec03.htm; See also Alan Bock, *Eye on the Empire*—"Preventive or Pre-emptive war?", 10th of Sept. 2002 at http://www.antiwar.com/bock/b091002.html
80. Abraham D. Sofaer, "On the necessity of pre-emption", *EJIL* 14, 2 (2003) 211.
81. Cassesse, Antonio, *International Law* (Oxford: Oxford University Press, 2001) 310-311.
82. Report of the High-level Panel on Threats, Challenges and Change "A more secure world: Our shared responsibility", United Nations, 2004, Synopsis to Part III and point 292.
83. Colson, Nicole, "United States: Pentagon's green light for murder" at http://www.socialistworker.org/2005-1/537/537_01_Green Light.shtm
84. Report of the High-level Panel on Threats, Challenges and Change, "A more secure world: Our shared responsibility", United Nations, 2004, point 14.
85. President Bush's address to a joint session of the Congress and the nation, 20th of September 2001 at http://douglassarchives.org/bush_c01.htm
86. See for example "Revising the Patriot Act to restore American liberties", *International Herald Tribune*, 11th of April 2005. This is to be contrasted with, for example, Eric Lichtblau, "Terror suspects finding it easy to buy guns in US—Federal laws have gaps, report alleges", *International Herald Tribune*, 9th of March 2005.

87. Christopher Greenwood in Byron F. Burmester, "On humanitarian intervention: the New World Order and wars to preserve human rights", *Utah Law Review* 269 (1994).
88. Bassiouni, Cherif, *International Terrorism: Multilateral Conventions (1937-2001)* (New York: Transnational Publishers, 2001).
89. Report of the High-level Panel on Threats, Challenges and Change "A more secure world: Our shared responsibility", United Nations, 2004, point 160. The Report nonetheless lists the elements which should be included in a definition of terrorism in point 164.
90. Eric S. O'Malley, "Destabilisation policy: Lessons from Reagan on International Law, revolution and dealing with pariah nations", *Vancouver Journal of International Law* 319, 43 (Winter 2003).
91. 1970 UN Declaration on Friendly Relations, 1974 Declaration on the Definition of Aggression.
92. Cassesse, Antonio, *International Law* (Oxford: Oxford University Press, 2001) 76, 107-8.
93. Richard A. Falk, "A just response", 20th of September 2001 at http://www.thenation.com/doc.mhtml?i=20011008&c=2&s=falk
94. Howard Zinn, "A just cause, not a just war", at http://www.commondreams.org/views01/1109-01.htm (Last visited on 10 February 2006): "The United States could have treated the September 11 attack as a horrific criminal act that calls for apprehending the culprits, using every device of intelligence and investigation possible. It could have gone to the United Nations to enlist the aid of other countries in the pursuit and apprehension of the terrorists. There was also the avenue of negotiations.... Before Bush ordered the bombers, the Taliban offered to put bin Laden on trial. This was ignored".
95. See also Maureen Dowd, "The women who torture", *International Herald Tribune*, 2nd of February 2005; "America looks the other way", *International Herald Tribune*, 4th of March 2005.
96. "Rights plea over Guantanamo Bay", 12th April 2004 at news.bbc.co.uk/1/hi/world/middle_east/3619055.stm
97. See "Guantanamo and the law", *International Herald Tribune*, 2nd of February 2005.
98. See also "Revising the Patriot Act to restore American liberties", *International Herald Tribune*, 11th of April 2005.
99. Chomsky, Noam, *Rogue States: the rule of force in world affairs* (New Delhi: India Research Press, 2000) 1.
100. *Ibid.*, 1.
101. Ellen Goodman, "An empire built on deception", *The Boston Globe*, June 26, 2003.
102. For discussions on the war on Iraq as a "just war", see Michael Novak, "Asymmetrical warfare and just war – A moral obligation", 10th of February 2003 at http://www.nationalreview.com/novak/novak021003.asp

103. See Stanley A. Weiss, "The principle is set, now what's the price – Nuclear Iran I", *International Herald Tribune*, 6th of April 2005: "Does Tehran see a nuclear weapon as an end in itself or as a bargaining chip for economic and security concessions from the West? Is the Bush administration willing to offer perhaps the only carrot for which the Islamic Republic might give up the bomb— meaningful US economic and security guarantees?"; George Perkovich, "The only way to change the rules—Nuclear Iran II", *International Herald Tribune*, 6th of April 2005; Cameron Khosrowshahi, "Iraqi Shiism could topple the mullahs—Dealing with Iran I", *International Herald Tribune*, 24th of March 2005: "The lesson the Iranian regime has drawn from Iraq is this: if you have the bomb, like North Korea, you are safe; it's better to build it, secretly if you have to, so you don't get caught short like Saddam Hussein."; See also Brian Knowlton, "Iran sends US a stern warning", *International Herald Tribune*, 14th of February 2005.
104. Richard Falk, "Rediscovering international law after September 11", *Temple International and Comparative Law* Journal 359,16 (Fall 2002).
105. Jeffrey Record, "Bounding the Global War on Terrorism", Strategic Studies Institute, December 2003 at http://www.mindfully.org/Reform/2003/Global-War-On-Terrorism-GWOTDec03.htm
106. *Ibid.*
107. Eric S. O'Malley, "Destabilization Policy: Lessons from Reagan on International Law, Revolutions and Dealing with Pariah Nations", *Vancouver Journal of International Law* 319, 43 (2003).
108. O'Malley, Eric S., "Destabilization Policy: Lessons from Reagan on International Law, Revolutions and Dealing with Pariah Nations", 43 Va. J. Int'l L. 319 (2003).
109. For discussions on the war on Afghanistan as "just", see Richard A. Falk, "In defence of 'just war' thinking", 6th of December 2001 at http://www.thenation.com/doc.mhtml?i=20011224&c=3&s=falk; Richard A. Falk, "Defining just war", 11th of October 2001 at http://www.thenation.com/doc.mhtml?i=20011029&s=falk; Richard A. Falk, "A just response", 20th of September 2001 at http://www.thenation.com/doc.mhtml?i=20011008&c=2&s=falk; Howard Zinn, "A just cause, not a just war" at http://www.commondreams.org/views01/1109-01.htm
110. William A. Rugh, "Iraq, US, and the War on Terror: Perceptions in the Arab World and Debates in Washington: Analyzing US Mideast Policy after September 11", *Fletcher Forum of World Affairs* 47, 27 (Winter/Spring 2003).
111. *Ibid.*
112. See for example Anthony D'Amato, "Israel's Air Strike Upon the Iraqi Nuclear Reactor", *American Journal of International Law* 584, 77 (1983).

113. For Israel, see Honderick, Ted, "After the terror", Spring 2002, at http://www.homepages.ucl.ac.uk/~uctytho/ATT1.html (Last visited on 10 February 2006).
114. On Israel, see generally "Sharon's new settlements set back Mideast progress", *International Herald Tribune*, 24th of March 2005; Greg Myre, "Israeli's plans unearth trouble—Expansion of West Bank settlement angers Palestinians", *International Herald Tribune*, 22nd of March 2005; Steven R. Weisman, "How hard can Bush push Israel? — Gaza pullout is a key to maintaining peace momentum", *International Herald Tribune*, 18th April 2005.
115. See generally Cohen, E., *Human Rights in the Israeli-Occupied Territories: 1967-1982* (Manchester: Manchester University Press, 1985); for the law of belligerent occupation see http://lawofwar.org/Occupation.htm. See also SC Resolution 799 (1949); and the Israel Year Book of Human Rights for court decisions concerning the Israel occupation.
116. It is worth mentioning the differential treatment between Israel and Iraq in relation to their nuclear capacity: Iraq is a party to the Non-Proliferation Treaty and has had its nuclear installations inspected on a regular basis by the International Atomic Energy Agency, whereas Israel has refused to place its own nuclear facilities under IAEA safeguards.
117. SC Resolution 487 (19th of June 1981).
118. SC Resolution 1511 (October 2003), preceded by SC Resolution 1483 (May 2003).
119. Richard A. Falk, "A just response", 20th of September 2001 at http://www.thenation.com/doc.mhtml?i=20011008&c=2&s=falk (Last visited on 10 February 2006). See also Jeffrey Record, "Bounding the Global War on Terror", Strategic Studies Institute, December 2003 at http://www.mindfully.org/Reform/2003/Global-War-On-Terrorism-GWOTDec03.htm
120. *Ibid.*
121. Jeffrey Record, "Bounding the Global War on Terror", http://www.mindfully.org/Reform/2003/Global-War-On-Terrorism-GWOTDec03.htm
122. Richard A. Falk in Jeffrey Record, "Bounding the Global War on Terror" Strategic Studies Institute, December 2003 at http://www.mindfully.org/Reform/2003/Global-War-On-Terrorism-GWOTDec03.htm notes that: "'Terrorism' as a word and concept became associated in US and Israeli discourse with anti-state forms of violence that were so criminal that any method of enforcement and retaliation was viewed as acceptable, and not subject to criticism. By so appropriating the meaning of this inflammatory term in such a self-serving manner, terrorism became detached from its primary historical association dating back to the French Revolution. In that formative setting, the state's own political violence against its citizens, violence calculated to induce widespread fear and achieve political goals, was labeled as terrorism".

123. Bassiouni, Cherif, *International Terrorism: Multilateral Conventions (1937-2001)* (New York: Transnational Publishers, 2001).
124. "Morass in the Middle East" at http://www.thenation.com/doc.mhtml?i=20020701&s=letter
125. Bassiouni, Cherif, *International Terrorism: Multilateral Conventions (1937-2001)* (New York: Transnational Publishers, 2001)
126. *Ibid.*, p. ?
127. Jeffrey Record, "Bounding the Global War on Terror", http://www.mindfully.org/Reform/2003/Global-War-On-Terrorism-GWOTDec03.htm
128. *Ibid.*
129. Some suggestions for readings which seek to explain terrorist violence by individuals or groups: William Lind, Bernard Lewis and Samuel Huntington on the "Clash of Civilizations" theory (culture); Mahmood Mamdani's *Good Muslim, Bad Muslim* (modernity); Ted Honderick's *Terrorism for Humanity*; Robert Kaplan in *The Coming Anarchy*; and generally Daniel Pipes at http://www.danielpipes.org/art/year/all
130. "You are either with us or against us", 6 November 2001 at http://archives.cnn.com/2001/US/11/06/gen.attack.on.terror/
131. Richard Falk, "Rediscovering international law after September 11", *Temple International and Comparative Law Journal* 359, 16 (Fall 2002).

Chapter Five

Of Nations and States

The discourse on State sovereignty, which has developed since the conclusion of the Cold War, conveys an interesting dichotomy. It has become fashionable to talk about the impending end of the Westphalian framework. Simultaneously, the States themselves have been regressing towards Thomas Hobbes' vision of *Leviathan* in empowering themselves against political discontent and insubordination. *Leviathan*, as we know, was a product of political anxieties of an aristocratic mind in England in mid-1600s about the revolutionary implications of the English Civil War. The resuscitation of the Hobbesean theory of sovereignty in the post Cold War world, which argues for powers of governance unencumbered by supposedly inalienable human rights, appears to have its origins in distinct but politically comparable sources of anxieties.

Firstly, there are anxieties about the defensibility of the violently engendered geography of Nation-States, born from the process of *transfer of power* at the end of World War II. The geography of Nation-States in previously colonized world is not the same as the locations of "identity formation" of the people residing within them by standards of their intergenerational memories. It also does not fulfil instrumentally effective standards of territoriality as viable and defensible demarcations. That should explain, at least partly, the internal wars or struggles for self-determination that raze across much of the debatable geography of States that emerged out of former European empires. The crumbling of the Soviet Union, as the culmination of the Cold-War, suddenly infected the States that had obtained their sovereign status by the reckonings of the Northern Empires with anxieties about the absence of democratic sanction for their territorial frontiers. Given the choice between negotiating the terms of legitimate authority with the people in conformity with the principles of self-determination and imposing it by force on the strength of a legal fiction that had accompanied the advent of European colonization, they preferred to opt for the latter. Ironically enough, this suited the victors of the Cold War.

The crumbling of the Soviet Union was a momentary triumph for the United States. Instantaneously, the triumph also generated a fretfulness attending on its self-recognition as a global power beyond competition and also on its understanding that a vast majority of peoples in the world would henceforth be more focused on the injustices hatched by its politics of hegemony.

Students of history and politics should not really be surprised at these theoretical reactions and their possible negative consequences on human rights. The breakdown of the monarchical systems in Central Europe and the simultaneous October 1917 Revolution in Russia produced similar anxieties that resulted in the constitutional theories of the State enunciated by Carl Schmitt and Hans Kelsen which culminated in the establishment of the Nazi hegemony in Europe. The theories of German nationalism and their agendas of 'purification' were false. But politically they worked and served to disguise the "final solution" programme under the doctrinal cloak of National Socialism. The constitutional and political theories of Carl Schmitt, premised on the categorization of the international and domestic political order according to the "friend and foe" binary, never ceased to guide the architectural principles of political realism in pursuit of power, self-interest and military might. The neo-conservative neo-imperialist lobby associated with Wolfowitz-Perle-Feith that guides the United States under President Bush is the spiritual offspring of political realists like Henry Kissinger and Robert McNamara who successfully conducted America's Cold War. The "red peril" has given way to the "green peril"; the war against communism has broadened into a "clash of civilizations". Projections of perils and civilizational theories in the service of a hegemonic agenda may again be false. But they may work politically to disguise the enterprises of power that may later be condemned for human wrongs they permit and promote. Democratic reinterpretations of people's struggles and their outcomes which become formal history generally belong to a realm of time in future we have little control over. What shall then become of identities outside States and nationalities that do not possess sovereign prerogatives in our own present?

The convergence of the American political enterprise against "terrorism" and India's own wars against "secessionist conspiracies" in its peripheries, for which the ubiquitous CIA used to previously take the blame, is an interesting development. President Clinton's March 2000 visit to India and the signing of a vision statement jointly with India's then Prime Minister are recognized as the visible high points of the changing world-order equations in the region. The BJP came to power by mobilizing explosive religious issues and seeking and confrontations with minority communities. The BJP drew its support from strongly nationalist constituencies that craved to see India join the superpower league. By deciding to make India openly nuclear, the party became the repository of their hopes. The supporters of the BJP view Pakistan as the creation of British perfidy. The BJP pursued a belligerent approach with regard to Pakistan. These perceptions also informed the dramatic transformation of relations between India and Israel. The cooperation between the two countries followed from their common antipathies towards "wellsprings of terrorism", "disguising as self-determination movements", in radical Islam. The new perceptions in New Delhi on Israel and Palestine mark a radical departure from the position, articulated by Mahatma Gandhi in 1938, that "Palestine belongs to the Arabs in the same sense that England belongs to the English or France to the French." These changes became possible because the BJP is not beholden to India's foreign policy traditions under Gandhi and Nehru. This also helps the US to pursue its policies in the Middle East with less obstacles and criticism in the international arenas, as well as to recognize that just as it underwrites Israel's superiority to maintain a regional balance in the Middle East, it should allow India to play its part as the dominant power to manage the security environment in South Asia. The BJP represents a political movement that permeates other political parties, including those belonging to the left side of the political spectrum which have been leading the Indian State on and off since 1977.

Way back in 1970s, the United States had used China to keep a check on the Soviet Union especially along their common borders in Central Asia. With the demise of the Soviet Union, China has emerged as a potential regional and world power. China is not yet a military threat to the United States, but its potential to become one is not discounted. In any case, it suits the United States and several countries within China's range of influence to remain wary and circumspect.

Several friends of the New Right in America argue that since it has not been politically possible to pressure China through trade policies, it would be expedient to pressurize it by creating an environment of military build-up in the region, compelling it to hike up its military expenditure and to slowly make it economically impracticable to pursue those policies, without political reforms. President Reagan used these tactics successfully against the Soviet Union. India, the largest democracy, can be an important strategic ally in implementing this approach to contain China, the most populous party dictatorship. Additionally, very influential elements within India's political establishment perceive China to be a threat just as Chinese political establishment, three decades ago, had considered the Soviet Union to be a threat.

Of course, implementation of this paradigm of partnership with India would require the United States to jettison some of its old postures. It would have to give up the ideological orthodoxy of non-proliferation in South Asia, or at least ignore it just as it disregarded the ABM Treaty while developing its missile defence system. In the same way, the United States could take a pragmatic view in assessing India's requirement to build an efficient nuclear deterrent to confront the Pakistani and Chinese threats. Also, the United States should assist in the development of the Indian defence industry. This would not only wean India away from Russia, but would also eventually help the US overcome its forward basing problems in South Asia and the Middle East. The political movement exemplified by the BJP accepts that the United States is potentially capable of ensuring political stability in Pakistan, retaining it as a buffer State against more rabid and reckless influences across its north-western frontiers. It also expects Uncle Sam to keep Pakistan away from teaming up with China to harass India's military management of political troubles in Kashmir and in the northeast. With the cessation of support for the secessionist causes, which the United States can ensure, India can become more capable of dealing with politically recalcitrant elements within the region that also harbour subversive sentiments against the hegemonic tendencies within the emergent world-order. Both India and the United States can then work more effectively together to intercept and disrupt the "Islamic terrorist networks" and their communication channels.

The post-Cold War international order is typified by the stirrings of new theories of the State which repudiate the understanding and arrangements of peace premised on the doctrine of State sovereignty that had been made when the religion-charged Thirty Years' War among and within the European nations formally ended in 1648. That is known as the Peace of Westphalia.

What was the Peace of Westphalia?

The agreement, conceived by Cardinal Richelieu of France who died six years before it was signed, conceded that a sovereign State can do virtually anything it likes with its people within its geographically defined territory. The arrangement, of course, applied essentially to mollify religious passions that had fired the war mainly within the German territories and it followed a previous arrangement attempted at Augsburg in 1555 A.D. based on the principle that each German territory must take the faith of its prince. The idea sounds ridiculous today. But in the context of the real history of the period, the Peace of Westphalia broke the power of the Holy Roman Empire and allowed various German States to become Protestant.

Soon, the historical purpose of the arrangement was forgotten and the Treaty of Westphalia became notionally synonymous with the sovereign prerogatives of States. During the 18th and 19th century-colonial era, the Westphalian principles were harnessed by the European imperial powers to paint the world map in their own colours without any respect for the sovereignty of indigenous people. During the Cold War arms race, the doctrine was worked by the American and Russian superpowers to rope in supposedly sovereign client States into their own camps, glued together by their representations of the threat of a nuclear Armageddon. The post-Westphalian idea, which claims to remedy these errors of history, is supposed to possess three distinct components: (1) What a sovereign does to his own people isn't necessarily his own business—and other States may rightfully intervene under certain conditions; (2) non-State entities such as international organizations, regional alliances, and non-governmental organizations have a place around the table that discusses and decides the issues of international governance; and (3) there are some universally applicable ideas that no one gets to reject, such as the inherent right of persons to fundamental human rights, the right of peoples to self-determination, and perhaps the right of everyone to democratic governance and environmental protection.

The experiment of the European Union, with a common currency and porous internal borders, is a positive manifestation of the so-called post-modern or post-Westphalian arrangement of interdependent States.

But the post-Westphalian world order has had other manifestations, for example, in the disintegration of the Soviet Union and of Yugoslavia. The process was welcomed by Western powers so long as it seemed to ensure the final death of Communism. But the principle of self-determination for ethnic and religious nationalities also threatened to upset the State-structures that had been raised largely in the age of the Northern Empires, as for example in the Middle East, which continue to serve the interests of Western capitalist powers. Western Europe, given its resources and political experience, was able to handle its own centrifugal dynamism rationally and efficiently to the advantage of political ideology it represents. The *Lega Nord* in Italy, Basque and Catalan separatist movements in northern Italy and northern Spain, and regionalism within the UK, which resulted in stronger regional assemblies in Wales, Scotland, and Northern Ireland, posed no major challenge to other European States. Outside Western Europe, State systems failed to develop a rational and efficient approach to deal with beleaguered nationalities, hungry for autonomy, without causing anxieties to the victors of the Cold War about their interests within the emergent world-order.

This constitutes an important challenge for the human rights community grappling with the issues of State violations and the violence that frequently accompanies peoples' struggles in previously colonized parts of the world. The challenge lies in the necessity of holding States accountable, to make them responsive to the genuine aspirations of the struggling people, and to wean them away from the culture of impunity without opening the doors to imperialist interventions. What should then be the way for us to educate the people and the politicians in our countries to resolve the apparent conflicts between the claims of sovereignty of States and the right to self-governance and self-determination of the people, spanning the guarantees under Articles 1 and 27 of the ICCPR through an internal, but internationally accountable, political process? What should be the strategy to develop international human rights solidarity and campaigns, which recognize the people living within the existing States as the actual referent of sovereignty and are also uncompromisingly committed against unilateral and hegemonic interventions of the kind that have taken place in Afghanistan and Iraq? What should be the strategy to confront the hypocrisy of the body of nations under the United Nations that silently acquiesces in the brutalities of Member States against their own people but endorses interventions in politically selective ways to fulfil hegemonic and imperialist objectives? These are some of the questions that must animate civil society initiatives in conflict-infested areas of South Asia.

Chapter Six

Rights-Based Approach to Development

Developmental scholars trace the modern history of "developmental engagement" to the speech that US President Truman made on 20th January, 1949, which announced the vision of "development based on the concepts of democratic fair dealing."[1] They refer to the tenacity of human rights abuses within the developing countries under political regimes that have ratified international human rights instruments and that sustain their economies on the strength of international aid, contractual loans, and project funds. They also refer to the tensions between the approaches that focus on "needs" and others that accord primacy to "rights". These are critical points of evaluation of developmental policies and practices that underlie the articulation of the rights-based-approach [RBA]; the United Nations Declaration on the Right to Development, 1986; and Article 10 of the Vienna Declaration on Human Rights, 1993.

A book by P. Springborg, *The Problem of Human Needs and the Critique of Civilization*,[2] takes in a good mix of theoretical and historical views on the centrality of "needs" within the European intellectual tradition. The footnote mentions other interesting works on the history of human bondage to "needs" manufactured by transient modernity. [3]

Several participants of the course connected with the developmental organizations active in conflict ridden countries like Nepal in South Asia have talked about their apparent failures to rectify the principal sources of social disparities; conditions of socio-economic exploitation; unequal opportunities; abortive, ineffective, or only partially realized schemes of welfare, empowerment and education of the people. Some of them have commented on how these failures feed into the existing social discontent about the bankruptcy of governance; political rancour about the developmental policies, envisioned and foisted upon governments and people by international agencies; and how these resentments feed into movements of violent resistance, bringing in their wake more distress, atrocities, and suffering.

It would be useful for those working in the areas of development in South Asia to engage more closely with the literature and ideas that examine "development" as a global intellectual matrix that rose from the ravages of World War II. The literature focuses on how this matrix of development is inseparably dependent on the technology of "competitive obsolescence"; on transnational financial control systems, the global politics of resource allocation and the attendant acquiescence in arrangements to exploit them, and the realities of market control in the name of free trade. The literature shows how this matrix of development perpetuates the conditions of inequity, injustice, and the abusive relations between governments and their people even after 'decolonization'. There is also a very useful book available in book shops in the region. It is called *The Development Dictionary*, edited by Wolfgang Sachs, and published by Orient Longman, Hyderabad, 1997, and is a compilation of writings on the subject by Gustavo Esteva, C. Douglas Lummis, Harianne Gronemeyer, Gerald Berthoud, Ivan Illich and others.

There are, of course, some very radical researchers and thinkers in the field who see the entire intellectual matrix of development as a political project to westernize the world with the inevitable logical corollary that non-western societies will be increasingly disadvantaged in all spheres of life, both physical and psychic. These critics of the dominant developmental model worry about the loss of diversity and cultural sumptuousness of non-western peoples and the vanishing respect for their traditions that attend on 'development'. More significantly, they refer to the standardization of "needs" and "aspirations for growth" that will substantially diminish the natural capacities of the world civilization to recoil from and readjust itself against calamities arising from cultural homogenization, technological monomania and the consequences of political and environmental management that mark the relationship among the dominant and the dependant. Professor Satish Kumar Jain from the Centre for Economic Studies and Planning, Jawaharlal Nehru University, New Delhi, is one such thinker. We requested him to write for us a paper exploring the relationships between the powerful economic processes globally underway and the concerns for the fulfilment of human rights that inform the "rights-based approach to development". His paper is titled "Globalization and Human Rights".

Notes

1. Harry S. Truman, "Inaugural Address on 20 January 1949", in Documents on American Foreign Relations, Connecticut: Princeton University Press, 1967.
2. London: Allen and Unwin, 1981.
3. (1) W. Leiss, The Limits to Satisfaction: An Essay on the Problem of Needs and Commodities, (Toronto: Toronto University Press, 1976), and (2) D. Baybrooke, "Let Needs Diminish that Preferences May Prosper", in N. Resher ed., Studies in Moral Philosophy, Oxford: Blackwell, 1968; (3) Ivan Illich, Towards a History of Needs, New York: Pantheon, 1978, and (4) M. Berman, Coming to Our Senses: Body and Spirit in the Hidden History of the West, New York: Simon & Schuster, 1989.

Chapter Seven

Globalization and Human Rights*

The main purpose of this paper is to explore, in the contemporary context, the relationship between globalization, which would be taken to stand for myriad and enormously powerful economic processes which are currently going on in the world with their associated social and political processes, and the fulfilment of human rights. For this purpose we carry out an analysis of the values underlying the process of globalization. The normative analysis shows that the values underlying the process of globalization are not always compatible with human rights; and that as the domain of application of these values expands, their incompatibility with human rights also expands. As the process of globalization can fundamentally be regarded as the process of expanding the domain of the values embodied in the idea of globalization, it follows that the incompatibility of the process with human rights will increase as its progression unfolds.

The most significant aspect of the contemporary international order is the predominance in it of the complex of economic rules having extraordinary reach. The proclaimed purpose or rationale of most of these economic rules is to increase wealth or enhance economic efficiency. The notion or rather notions of economic efficiency, though deceptively simple to state, are in fact exceedingly intricate. It is not easy to see their negative implications; and consequently, as normative values, they seldom raise controversy. Considering the nature and scale of economic processes in the contemporary context, involving massive negative externalities, particularly through the degradation of the environment, it should be clear that the deterioration in the living conditions for large numbers of people must inevitably result. This of course implies that, in the absence of action by the State or some other agency nullifying these negative effects, basic rights of anyone with a subsistence or marginal existence, whose living conditions deteriorate would be violated.

* Satish K. Jain

The commonly held conception of basic rights, suitably interpreted for appropriate treatment of externalities, then would entail a duty on the part of the State or the international order to regulate these processes, at least to the extent so as to remove the threats to others' basic rights or alternatively nullify their negative effects. Wealth-enhancing efficiency considerations, as they are understood nowadays, however, do not in general favour regulating economic processes and activities or undertaking of actions by the State to nullify their negative effects. In the absence of required regulation or action, there would be a violation of the rights of those with subsistence existence whose material and environmental conditions deteriorate as a consequence of these processes. It should be noted that apart from impinging on basic rights of the marginal and the marginalized people, the economic processes which result in the degradation of the environment imperil the basic rights of the future generations as well.

This paper is divided into four sections. Section 1 contains a formal analysis of the conception of human rights. The analysis focuses on the three constitutive and defining elements of the conception of human rights: State-centricity, inviolability and inalienability. It is argued that as in the contemporary world, the State is not the only source of rules, regulations and laws which have relevance from the perspective of basic rights. Rather the idea of basic rights being defined in relation to the State needs reformulation so as to include the relevant international organizations and transnational corporations among those with the power to violate human rights. In human rights literature a distinction is made between rights which require action by the State in order for them to be fulfilled and those rights for the fulfilment of which the State has to merely refrain from doing anything which would be violative of them. The reason for the importance of this distinction lies in the fact that while for the rights in the former category something akin to a welfare State might be necessary, the latter category of rights are consistent even with a minimal role for the State. It is contended in this paper that this way of classifying rights is fundamentally problematic and that analytically the correct position is that every right has both positive and negative aspects; positive aspects requiring action by the State for their realization and negative aspects merely requiring refraining by the State from doing anything against those aspects for their realization.

Consequently, a welfare State might turn out to be essential for the protection of rights if the positive aspects are such as to require substantial action on the part of the State. From this it follows that in the contemporary context, because of multifarious, pervasive, persistent, massive and widely diffused negative externalities of the economic processes, a welfare State would be essential for the protection of even rights like the right to life and liberty.

An important implication of the inviolability element of the conception of human rights is that normative considerations, no matter how persuasive, cannot be invoked to scuttle basic rights. The respect for basic rights must be treated as a prior constraint for the purpose of determining the domain of application of normative considerations, other than those relating to basic rights. In particular, normative criteria of an aggregative character, such as maximization of general welfare or social wealth, cannot be invoked over domains where their application might result in violation of basic rights.

In section 2 we discuss the philosophical and legal basis for human rights. In national constitutional law as well as in international law the status of laws and rules guaranteeing human rights is pre-eminent. In most countries, laws inconsistent with basic rights are treated as void. The situation in international law is analogous. Thus, both national constitutional law and international law are in harmony with the inviolability element of the conception of human rights. From a philosophical point of view it appears that the ideas of autonomy and equality of individuals are crucial for deriving human rights. In some philosophical systems, like Rawls' theory of justice, basic rights like liberty are derived from the core idea of individual rationality. These systems, it is argued, do not provide a firm basis for human rights because of realization problem. It is contended that in the absence of internalization of the values of basic rights or of more fundamental values from which they could be deduced, there, in general, would be no guarantee that the ideal of basic rights would be realized.

Section 3 contains a detailed analysis of the efficiency criteria, particularly from the perspective of their possible incompatibility with basic rights. Efficiency criteria provides the basis for assertions of the general desirability of free markets, of private ownership of resources over other forms of ownerships, and of avoidance of governmental, controls and regulations. Although there are several efficiency criteria, all of them are at least partly aggregative in character; and some are wholly so. Consequently they can easily conflict with basic rights if the domain of their application is not suitably restricted. An aggregative normative criterion would declare sacrificing the interests of one group of individuals for the benefit of another group of individuals ethically desirable, if by doing so the latter group can benefit to a greater extent than the extent of loss suffered by the former group. It is not that human rights cannot coexist with aggregative normative criteria; but they certainly cannot exist if normative criteria of aggregative character are allowed to override all other normative criteria. In other words, human rights cannot coexist with aggregative normative criteria if the domain of application of the aggregative criteria is so extensive as to include alternatives which might make the satisfaction of basic rights contingent on whether such satisfaction is in harmony with the aggregative criteria or not — as indeed is the case with the process of globalization. Exclusive reliance on aggregative normative criteria or accordance of pre-eminent position to a normative criterion of an aggregate character is inconsistent with any conception of human rights.

The next section of the paper is devoted to a consideration of the market ideology. An attempt is made to show that the market ideology, as it has developed, together with the expansion of ideas underlying the ideology to non-market institutions and systems like law, is fundamentally destructive of the values of preservation, advancement and realization for which these institutions were designed in the first place. We conclude with a few remarks on the wide divergence between the theory and practice of human rights.

1. The Conception of Human Rights

In this section an attempt is made to delineate the fundamental constitutive elements of the conception of human rights, as the notion is generally understood. An important and defining element of the traditional conception of human rights is that it is State-centric. Therefore, human rights are defined in relation to the State. Only the State can violate an individual's human rights. If an individual is tortured by another individual in his official capacity then the act of torture would be violative of the victim's human right to be free from torture. An act of torture by a private individual, in general, would merely constitute a crime and not a violation of human rights.

The State can violate human rights in many different ways. Violation of human rights can take place in accordance with the laws of the state as well as against them. For instance, the State laws may permit torture of suspects for eliciting information or of convicts as punishment. Even if the laws prohibit torture, it might be illegally resorted to and tolerated by the State officials. There might be no laws permitting torture and no instances of illegal torture by State officials, nevertheless the State would still be responsible for the violation of the human right to be free from torture, if the laws enacted by the State or their enforcement is such that they result in sanctioning torture of some individuals, by other individuals or that they fail to protect individuals from being tortured by other individuals. It would be incorrect in this context to make a distinction between actions and omissions by the State.

Whether the almost universally acknowledged State-centricity aspect of the conception of human rights is appropriate depends on whether the State has more or less of a monopoly on coercive powers in domains having relevance to human rights. If the State can be realistically assumed to have a monopoly on coercive powers in domains having relevance to human rights, then the rationale for State-centricity is immediate. On the other hand, if such is not the case then clearly entities other than the State have to be included among those with power and potential to violate human rights. If the state, voluntarily or otherwise, has surrendered some of its decision-making powers to international organizations or some other organizations together with a commitment to implement the decisions of these organizations; and if the implementation of these decisions results in violations of human rights, it is clear that the responsibility for these violations of human rights must devolve upon the organizations in question, in addition to falling upon the State. In fact, from the rationale of State-centricity to the traditional conception of human rights a general principle can be extracted, namely: Any entity, collective or otherwise, which has the power to make rules, in domains relevant to human rights, and has the power to enforce these rules, directly or through the state apparatus, must be held responsible for violation of human rights if the implementation of the rules framed by the entity is the cause of the violation.

This principle, implicit in the traditional conception of human rights, generalizes the idea as a results of which, in the traditional conception, human rights are considered only in relation to the State, application of it need not result in a complete identification of the entities responsible for violations of human rights. In the contemporary world, the power of transnational corporations to profoundly affect the lives, in myriad spheres, including those pertaining to human rights, of millions of people, is so great that any principle for identifying the violators of human rights which fails to hold them responsible for violations, even when the violations can be directly linked to the their actions and decisions, cannot be regarded as satisfactory.

It should be noted that the principle, extracted from the traditional or classical conception of human rights as stated above, linking power to make coercive rules in domains relevant to human rights with responsibility for violations of human rights in cases of their arising from the implementation of rules made using the coercive powers in question, always results in identifying the violators correctly; and consequently the shortcoming of the principle lies only in its possible incompleteness. To use a somewhat different language, the extracted principle states a sufficient condition for identifying violators of human rights. For completeness, in addition to correctness, what is required is a principle which states a condition both necessary and sufficient for identifying violators of human rights. As transnational corporations by themselves do not have power to make coercive rules the principle in question cannot take them into reckoning; even when the rules causing violations of human rights are enacted because of or under their influence. It is a cardinal principle of criminal law to hold an individual who induces, motivates or instigates another to commit a crime guilty, along with the actual perpetrators, conspirators, aiders and abettors. The relevance of criminal law principles for the purpose of locating an additional principle which, together with the extracted principle, can accurately and completely identify human rights violators should be obvious in view of the fact that all acts which constitute violations of human right, if committed by the state, are regarded, almost universally, as crimes if committed by individuals. Transnational corporations by their actions can cause serious damage to the environment and bring about deterioration in the living conditions of large numbers of people, rendering continuance of enjoyment of human rights by the affected individuals precarious or impossible. The laws and regulations under which the transnational corporations are able to inflict these harms in many instances are enacted or framed at their behest and in their interests only. And, it is clear that although transnational corporations are not coercive rule-making entities they must be held responsible for violations of human rights which result from their actions. The following modification of the principle under discussion can bring about the desired inclusion of such entities: If the implementation of a rule or action sanctioned by the rule is the cause of violation of some human right and if the rule has been framed by an entity, collective or otherwise, which has the power to make rules, in domains relevant to human rights, and has the power to enforce these rules, directly or through the State apparatus, then the entity and those responsible for implementing the rule or responsible for taking the action sanctioned by the rule, if any, must be held accountable for the violation in question.

One important implication of linking responsibility for violations of human rights with rule-making power is that in situations where the State has abdicated most of its rule-making powers to international organizations, it is the latter which primarily must bear the responsibility for violations caused by the rules framed by them.

Perhaps the most important human right is that of life and liberty. As far as this right is concerned, at one level, it seems that the State has only to refrain from doing anything for individuals to go on enjoying this right. It is actions by the State, not non-actions or omissions, which might imperil the continued enjoyment of the right. In other words, if one focuses on this human right then one might be tempted to conclude that violation of the right implies some action on the part of the State, that is to say that non-action on the part of the State implies that the right is not violated. Although this assertion is widely believed, it is not true as should be clear from the examples dealing with the right to be free from torture given at the beginning of this section. It might be helpful to consider another set of examples to clarify what is involved.

If a person dies of hunger because the state has confiscated all his property then the State would be responsible for violating the person's right to life. But if the person starves to death because all his property is destroyed in a natural calamity, the responsibility for his demise under the traditional conception of human rights does not lie with the State. The traditional conception of human rights is not as broad as some of the modern conceptions articulated in some of the international human rights instruments. Regardless of the entailment relations that might exist between deprivation and non-realization of rights, under the traditional conception of human rights, as long as deprivation has not been caused by the State or the social order, a violation of basic rights cannot be deduced. One may fault the state for not doing anything towards ameliorating the situation; but that is not the same thing as accusing it of violating human rights. Some care, however, is necessary while determining the causation. If the deprivation, material or environmental, threatening the right to life, is being caused as a consequence of activities undertaken by private individuals, with negative externalities for the affected directly or through environmental degradation, and the State or the social order fails to restrain these individuals from undertaking these activities or fails to make them undertake these activities with full compensation for the affected, then the State or the social order cannot evade the responsibility for the violations of basic rights caused by the deprivation in question. The case is analogous to the example considered earlier in the context of the right to be free from torture. If there is torture of some individuals by other individuals and the State fails to provide the necessary protection and deterrence, the State is bound to be considered to be in violation of its duty to guarantee the people the right to be free from torture. The State's failure to stop or regulate activities which would result, for some, in deprivation of an order leading to attenuation or violation of some or all of the basic rights, would render it in violation of its duty to uphold human rights.

In the human rights literature rights are often classified as negative or positive rights. A right is defined to be negative if, and only if, no action on the part of the State is required for the enjoyment of the right. Negative rights are violated only when the State takes actions to violate them. The most important example that is cited of a negative right is that of right to liberty. If the state does not deprive a person of his liberty then the person can go on enjoying his right to liberty. A violation of the right will take place only if the state acts to deprive the individual of his liberty. On the other hand, a right is defined to be positive if, and only if, some action on the part of the state is required for the right to be enjoyed by all in different possible circumstances. An example of such a right would be the right to food. It should be noted that a positive right does not necessarily require some action on the part of the state for realization of the right in every individual's case. If the right to food is guaranteed then, for its implementation, the State would have to take action only with respect to those individuals whose right to food would be in danger of being violated in the absence of such an action by the State. Furthermore, for enjoyment of a positive right some action on the part of the State is required not in every possible circumstance, but only in some circumstances. Even if the right to food is guaranteed no action on the part of the State might be required for its realization if all inhabitants happen to have incomes much above the poverty level. Thus, the essential difference between the two types of rights lies in negative rights never requiring any action by the state for their fulfilment, while positive rights require action by the State, at least for some individuals and in some circumstances.

Although the negative rights-positive rights distinction, corresponding to philosophical distinction between non-acts and acts, is quite pervasive and rather important in the human rights literature, analytically it does not seem to be a correct one as should be clear from the examples already considered. The analytically correct position is that every right has both positive and negative aspects. Whether one considers a right like the right to liberty, universally regarded as a negative right, or a right like the right to food, considered a positive right, enjoyment of it by everyone in every circumstance would involve, on the part of the State, both refraining from certain acts (negative aspects) and performing certain actions (positive aspects). For instance, for the realization of the right to free speech for all, the State must refrain from censorship (a negative aspect) as well as ensure that no group of individuals in the society, for whom certain ideas might be anathemas, is able to enforce non-articulation of these ideas on others (positive aspect).

Notwithstanding the fact that the negative rights-positive rights distinction suffers from logical infirmities, it might still be argued by some that the distinction, although not watertight, is nevertheless important in the sense that for the enjoyment of negative rights little action, if at all, on the part of the State, or for that matter, by any other entity is required, while for the realization of positive rights, in general, considerable activity on the part of the State or other organizations would be necessary. It is argued in this paper that this line of argument is quite misleading; and indeed is an important building block for a set of ideas, acceptance of which results in derecognition of violations of human rights of certain kinds as only violations.

If the idea that every right has both negative and positive aspects put forward here is accepted, then a very important inference can be made, namely that the scope and extent of the role of the State necessary for preservation of basic rights is not independent of the societal circumstances, particularly those relating to threats to human rights emanating from actions of non-State actors. If threats emanating from actions of non-State actors are massive and persistent, as we would argue is the case in the contemporary context, then a very substantial role on the part of the State might be necessary for warding off these threats or alternatively for taking measures for nullifying or ameliorating the negative effects of these actions. If it so happens that warding off these threats is not by and large a feasible option, as it would be argued is the case in the contemporary context, then the only way for preserving basic rights might be for the State to be a welfare State. From this it follows that the theories which establish the desirability of a minimal role for the State must be neglecting consideration of positive aspects of even the so-called negative rights like the right to life and liberty. Normally the idea of welfare State is associated with the so-called positive rights. But from what has been said here it should be clear that even if one exclusively focuses on rights, like the right to life and liberty, the welfare State might still be necessary for ensuring rights.

Possibly the most important defining element of the conception of human rights is that in relation to the State they are considered inviolable; that is to say that no violation by the State is regarded as legitimate or justifiable. The normative considerations, no matter how compelling, cannot be invoked by the State in justification of abridgment, attenuation, denial or violation of human rights. In particular, normative considerations of an aggregative character appealing to the greater good or prosperity of the society cannot be used in support of constraining or denying human rights. The inviolability of basic rights is a prior constraint which must be satisfied by any legal or social order to be eligible for being considered for adoption by the society. Another and equivalent way to state this characteristic of human rights is to say that in relation to the State human rights or fundamental rights are unconstrainable or illimitable. Unconstrainability or illimitability of basic or fundamental rights seems to be rooted in the philosophical premise of equality of all human beings and their autonomy. We will see later that it is because of this crucial characteristic of basic rights that globalization together with associated processes is inherently incompatible with human rights.

At one level, unconstrainability aspect of the conception of basic rights is an idealization. Even international human right instruments committing State parties to respecting basic rights routinely permit derogation from obligation to respect basic rights, in cases where the obligation conflicts with public order, morality etc. It is interesting, however, that International Covenant on Civil and Political Rights, while permitting derogation '*In time of public emergency which threatens the life of the nation and the existence of which is officially proclaimed*' (Article 4), does not permit derogations from Articles dealing with right to life, prohibition of torture, prohibition of slavery, and freedom of thought, conscience and religion, among others. It is rather remarkable that in the Convention against Torture and Other Cruel, Inhuman or Degrading Treatment or Punishment the prohibition against torture is absolute. Paragraph 2 of Article 2 says:

> No exceptional circumstances whatsoever, whether a state of war or a threat of war, internal political instability or any other public emergency, may be invoked as a justification of torture.

Similarly, the Convention for the Protection of Human Rights and Fundamental Freedoms while allowing derogation '*in time of war or other public emergency threatening the life of the nation*', does not permit derogation from certain articles or parts thereof. The articles or sections thereof from which no derogation is allowed deal with the right to life, prohibition of torture, prohibition of slavery and the right not to be punished without an act or omission which constitutes a criminal offence under national or international law during the time that it is being committed.

The Universal Declaration of Human Rights, in contrast, does not seem to be so unequivocally against making tradeoffs between human rights and general welfare. Article 29(2) of the Declaration reads:

> In the exercise of his rights and freedoms, everyone shall be subject only to such limitations as are determined by law solely for the purpose of securing due recognition and respect for the rights and freedoms of others and of meeting the just requirements of morality, public order and the general welfare in a democratic society.

In the context of analyzing of the defining elements of the conception of basic rights, there are at least four different ways to rationalize differences amongst different international human rights instruments. One could argue that the idea of inviolability of basic rights in relation to the state is essentially an idealization, although impossible to realize completely, towards which it is desirable for the society to move; and that the different international human rights instruments incorporate the ideal to different degrees. Alternatively, it could be argued that not all human rights can be treated on the same footing and that the notion of inviolability is relevant to only some of the rights which are included among human rights. The differences among instruments then could be reflective of this difference among human rights. It is also possible to contend that the idea of inviolability has been evolving progressively over the last six decades or so, since the coming into existence of the United Nations; and that the differences among international instruments could be reflective of this evolutionary process.

While in relation to the State, basic rights possessed by an individual are conceptualized, at least as an idealization, as illimitable; such is not the case in relation to other individuals. The clause "*In the exercise of his rights and freedoms, everyone shall be subject only to such limitations as are determined by law solely for the purpose of securing due recognition and respect for the rights and freedoms of others...*" 'appearing in The Universal Declaration of Human Rights (UDHR) in this connection is of great significance. One person's exercise or enjoyment of his or her rights can easily result in a situation which is not conducive for another to realize his or her rights. In fact it is easy to construct examples where one person's enjoyment of rights can be downright detrimental to another person's realization of rights. The question therefore arises as to what limitations require to be introduced in the conception of rights to take care of this problem.

It would be convenient in this context to introduce a technical term called 'externality'. If an action by a person has consequences for another person and these consequences are irrelevant to the former, an externality is said to exist. Externalities can be of both positive and negative kinds. If an action by a person has negative consequences for another person and these consequences are not a cost to the former, a negative externality is said to exist. Analogously, if an action by a person has positive consequences for another person and these positive consequences are not a benefit to the former, a positive externality is said to exist. The very existence of a society implies that, in general, there would be externalities. And the existence of negative externalities implies that individuals cannot treat rights in relation to each other as if there were no limits on them. In the context of conceptualizing the right to liberty, it is well recognized that without appropriate restrictions one person's right to liberty can easily be inconsistent with another person's right to liberty. The ideal way to deal with the problem seems to be that: (i) The rights should not be limited in any way whatsoever when the exercise of these rights does not impinge negatively on other persons' rights, i.e., when there are no negative externalities (ii) When the exercise of rights does impinge negatively on other persons' rights, the rights should be limited in a way such that they can be enjoyed to the maximum possible extent consistent with equal enjoyment by others of their rights. The classical conception of rights, in so far as it relates to basic rights like the right to life and liberty is essentially along these lines. The harmony of the above resolution with the philosophical premise of equality of all human beings and their autonomy should be noted.

The expressions like public order, morality, etc. appearing in clauses limiting rights are capable of being interpreted in a way that the limitations on account of them refer to only those limitations which are necessitated by the requirement that the exercise of rights by some does not result in denial of rights for others. Under this kind of interpretation there would not be any conflict between the inviolability feature and the limitations on account of interpreted objectives. However, these expressions can also be interpreted in a manner which would not be consistent with the inviolability feature. The expression 'general welfare', essentially connoting an aggregative idea, is unlikely to have an interpretation consistent with the inviolability feature.

Inalienability[1] is another fundamental and defining characteristic of basic rights. Human rights cannot be renounced, divested or bartered away. In this context, voluntariness or otherwise of the act of renunciation, divestment or barter is completely irrelevant. From this it follows that if an individual delegates some of his powers to another individual such delegation of powers can never include authorization for alienating basic rights. The claims of having people's mandate by elected representatives would be invalid if such claims were made for actions which in any way had the effect of curtailment, attenuation or abrogation of rights.

To sum up, in the stylized form, the conception of human rights, which we have been discussing and which has been variously called as classical, traditional or general conception of human rights, can be defined in terms of the following characteristics: (i) The rights are State-centric; and inviolable or unconstrainable in their relation to the State. The State-centricity entails both the absence of rules and practices leading to infringements of rights as well as existence of rules and practices to protect rights and to deter their infringements. The distinction between acts and omissions in this context is irrelevant; (ii) The rights should not be constrained in any way whatsoever when the exercise of rights does not impinge negatively on other persons' rights; and when the exercise of rights does impinge negatively on other persons' rights, the rights should be constrained in a way such that they can be enjoyed to the maximum possible extent consistent with like and equal enjoyment by others of their rights; and (iii) The basic rights are inalienable and consequently claims of mandates for curtailment, attenuation or abrogation of rights must be construed as invalid.

2. Philosophical and Legal Basis of Human Rights

Because of the inviolability characteristic of human rights, it is difficult to accommodate them within the framework of theories which exclusively employ normative criteria of an aggregative character; not to speak of deriving them from ideas and assumptions on which such theories rest. Utilitarianism is an example of a normative theory of an exclusively aggregative kind. Under utilitarianism, social alternatives are evaluated by comparing totals of utilities of all individuals under different alternatives. It is important that, in general, utilitarianism cannot be consistent with basic rights. When only a normative criterion of an aggregative character is used, violation of basic rights of an individual would be considered better than not violating his or her rights if such violation results in benefit to others of a larger magnitude than the magnitude of loss to the victim of the violation. The normative criteria used in economics are wholly or partly aggregative in character. A large part of law also makes use, although implicitly, of normative criteria of an aggregative character. On the other hand theories emphasizing the ideas of equality and autonomy of individuals hand are in greater harmony with the notion of human rights. It is important to note that the premises of equality and autonomy of human beings do not rule out normative criteria of aggregative kind altogether. What is ruled out by the two premises taken together is the exclusive reliance on the normative criteria of aggregative kind.

Although it is possible to argue that basic rights like liberty can be derived from the core idea of individual rationality by hypothesizing a primordial position, as Rawls does, it is not clear what significance is to be attached to such a derivation because of possible non-internalization of the derived principles. If individuals are solely motivated by self-interest, as they are in the Rawlsian construction, they might agree on a set of rules in a situation of complete ignorance as that of the Rawlsian initial situation; there is, however, no guarantee that these agreed upon rules would be implemented when the situation of complete ignorance no longer prevails. Agreeing to a normative principle in a collective context does not entail internalizing the principle as well. From the postulate of individual rationality it might be possible to derive basic rights; but it is unlikely that one would be able to demonstrate their realizability as well. There is a fundamental difference between individuals agreeing upon a principle because the principle is part of every individual's value-system; and everyone agreeing on the principle because it is the best that serves one's interests among those on which general agreement is possible. While in the former case there would be no realization problem; in the latter case, because of divergence between the course of action dictated by one's interests and the course of action dictated by the agreed upon principle in most instances, it is highly unlikely that the principle would in practice be realized.

In any case, in the absence of internalization of the principle, the core postulate of individual rationality would be contradicted if the agreed upon principle does get realized in all eventualities. It seems that for a satisfactory theory of rights what is required is that the individuals constituting the society must be committed to the normative idea of rights directly or must be committed to a set of normative ideas from which human rights could be obtained as derived norms.

In the contemporary world, almost all countries have constitutions laying down the rules by which they are to be governed. And almost invariably these constitutions guarantee and catalogue the fundamental rights to be enjoyed by everyone. This practice, however, does not mean that human rights are legally created. The dominant thinking, for some time, has been that human rights exist regardless of whether they are guaranteed by the constitution or some other law; or not. The State does not create rights; it can only transgress them. In the modern context it is doubtful if a State can claim legitimacy for itself if it does not constitutionally or legally respect basic rights. Spelling out in detail all the basic rights seems to have become a necessary condition for a constitution to be accepted as a legitimate instrument for governance. In theory, it is now widely recognized that laws inconsistent with fundamental rights cannot be regarded as valid laws even though their enactment might have followed the procedure as laid down in the constitution and other relevant laws determining the procedure for the making of laws. There is of course great divergence between the theory and practice in this respect; as indeed, is the case with almost every aspect of human rights.

In this connection it is of interest to note that the Indian Constitution in its original form specifically mentioned that all laws inconsistent with fundamental rights were to be treated as void, whether in existence prior to the commencement of the Constitution or enacted after the commencement. Although this feature is still there, it is no longer as categorical as it was in the original formulation because constitutional amendments are now excluded from its scope.

The theoretical position that has evolved with respect to political legitimacy of State can be summarized by saying that the State must be governed according to laws consistent with human rights defined broadly enough to include the right to democratic governance. Thus, respect for human rights is a necessary condition for legitimacy of the State.

In international law[2] also the developments relating to human rights which have taken place since the inception of the United Nations are along the same lines as those in the context of constitutional law. There is a large number of declarations, treaties, covenants, and conventions dealing with human rights. In most instances these instruments have been assented to, entered into, acceded to or ratified by a large number of countries. In addition, there is a large number of United Nations General Assembly resolutions dealing with human rights and related matters which were passed by acclamation or by an overwhelming majority. The most important instruments of international law relating to human rights include the Charter of the United Nations, Universal

Declaration of Human Rights, International Covenant on Civil and Political Rights, and International Covenant on Economic, Social and Cultural Rights, among others. The rights dealt with in these instruments can be classified into three broad categories: (i) civil and political rights, (ii) economic, social and cultural rights and (iii) collective rights.

The civil and political rights are usually described as negative rights and economic, social and cultural rights as positive rights. While most of the rights are defined in relation to individuals, the rights, like the right to self-determination and the right to permanent sovereignty over resources, are defined for collectives. A collective right is such that it is either satisfied for everyone or violated for everyone in the collective. In this respect, collective rights differ from individual rights where it is possible to violate rights of some individuals without necessarily violating them for all. Although the difference between individual rights and collective rights, in the sense just described, is quite sharp, it is not absolute. If one reflects on the nature of human rights, one realizes that even individual rights have a collective dimension. Freedom to express one's opinions does not amount to much if most individuals in the society are denied this right. Most civil rights also would lose much of their significance if denied to most people. The collective aspect of the individual right to vote in elections is so strong that it loses all meaning if denied to all others.

Human rights are an integral part of contemporary[3] international law[4]; any State violating human rights would be in breach of international law. Not only do human rights occupy an important place in international law, they are in fact part of *jus cogens* or peremptory international law.

Jus cogens is that part of international law from which no derogation is possible. While States may, by and within the limits of agreement between themselves, vary or dispense with most rules of international law, they are not allowed to derogate from those rules of international law which constitute the *jus cogens*. The Vienna Convention on the Law of Treaties[5] defines jus cogens as: "*accepted and recognized by the international community of states as a whole as a norm from which no derogation is permitted and which can be modified only by a subsequent norm of general international law having the same character.*"[6]. Although the boundary between *jus cogens* and the rest of international law is not finely drawn there is very little doubt that fundamental human rights, right to self-determination[7], prohibition of genocide, prohibition of aggression and crimes against humanity, among others, certainly belong to the category of *jus cogens*[8].

If a rule of customary international law conflicts with a rule of *jus cogens*, it cannot continue to exist as a rule of international law. According to the Law of Treaties, treaties inconsistent with a rule of *jus cogens*, are void to the extent of inconsistency. As derogation from *jus cogens* rules is not permitted, no act done in contravention of such a rule can be legitimated by any means including those of consent and acquiescence.

Thus, the status of human rights in international law is very similar to their status in most national legal systems. Just as laws inconsistent with basic rights are treated null and void in most national legal systems; so are the rules of international law inconsistent with human rights treated in International Law.

There is another important characteristic of international human rights law, apart from being part of *jus cogens*, namely, that it gives rise to obligations *erga omnes*, i.e., obligations to all States. One can distinguish between those rules of international law which, even though they may be of universal application, do not give rise to rights and obligations *erga omnes*, and those which do. Since the obligations of the law of human rights are *erga omnes*, violations of basic rights are violations of obligations to all other States and any State may, therefore, invoke the remedies available to a State when its rights under international law are violated. In particular, a State may invoke and pursue remedies for human rights violations, even if the individual victims were not nationals of the complaining State and the violations did not affect any interests whatsoever of the complaining State.

Thus, we see that both in international law and municipal law human rights occupy a pre-eminent position; rules inconsistent with basic rights being void in international law and laws inconsistent with basic rights being void in most legal systems. This, in effect, means that in national as well as international legal systems human rights are considered inviolable. This, indeed, is as it should be. The concept of human rights, having an intimate connection with the core idea of autonomy of individuals, would not have much of a meaning if the rights could be sacrificed for considerations of an aggregative character.

3. Normative Criteria of Efficiency and Human Rights

Globalization and the associated processes of liberalization and privatization find their ultimate justification in the normative criteria of efficiency. Notions of efficiency relate to social states, alternatives or outcomes. The social outcomes may come about as a consequence of individual actions in the context of some specific institutional setting or rules of the game. In social sciences, particularly economics, individuals are generally assumed to be rational. And, being rational generally includes having well-defined preferences. The individuals, however, are constrained to act in accordance with the rules of the game defined by the institutional setting. Market provides an example of an institutional setting in which individuals are constrained in their actions by private property rights. In economics, several different, though somewhat related notions of efficiency are used.[9] The most important notion of efficiency is that of Pareto-optimality, also called Pareto-efficiency, which is based on the Pareto-criterion. A social state x is defined to be Pareto-superior to another social state y if and only if it is the case that every individual in the society or the collective considers x to be at least as good as y, and at least one individual considers x to be better than y. According to the Pareto-criterion, alternative x is to be regarded socially better than alternative y if x is Pareto-superior to y. A social state is defined to be Pareto-optimal or Pareto-efficient if and only if there is no state which is Pareto-superior to it. In other words, a state of affairs is Pareto-efficient if and only if it is not possible to make some individual better-off without making anyone worse-off.

If alternative x is Pareto-superior to alternative y then, if the society moves from y to x, improvement would be unambiguous. As moving to a Pareto-superior position does not involve deterioration in the well-being of any individual, it follows that moving to a Pareto-superior position would not involve deterioration in the situation of any individual with respect to the enjoyment of basic rights unless the individual herself or himself is willing to forego partly or wholly the enjoyment of basic rights in exchange for something else. From this it follows that if individuals are assumed to value basic rights so much that they themselves would never be willing to forego them in exchange for other things, moving to a Pareto-superior position would not involve deterioration in the position of individuals with respect to basic rights. In particular, if the initial position from which a movement is being contemplated is such that everyone's basic rights are being respected fully, then they would continue to be fully respected even after a move has been made to a Pareto-superior position. In this context, the assumption that individuals value basic rights so much that they themselves would never be willing to forego them in exchange for other things is crucial. In the absence of this assumption one cannot conclude that moving to a Pareto-superior position would not involve any deterioration with respect to basic rights. Pareto-criterion is based on individuals' subjective judgments; and the notion of human rights is based on the fulfilment of certain objective criteria. It is this divergence because of which, in general, there is no entailment of non-deterioration in the status of individuals with respect to basic rights from movement to a Pareto-superior position. Thus, we see that although Pareto-criterion is in harmony with the ideas of equality and autonomy of individuals, it fails to be consistent, except under stringent conditions, with the inalienability aspect of human rights.

From the definition of Pareto-efficiency it is immediate that Pareto-inefficient alternatives are those corresponding to which Pareto-superior alternatives exist. If we agree to infer from the statement that 'x is Pareto-superior to y', the statement that 'x is socially better than y', then, if an alternative is Pareto-inefficient, it implies that among the feasible alternatives there is an alternative which is socially better than the Pareto-inefficient alternative in question. However, it would be erroneous to think that every Pareto-efficient alternative is better than every Pareto-inefficient alternative. An alternative can be Pareto-efficient and at the same time socially highly undesirable. It is clear that if one subscribes to the Pareto-criterion, one can recommend moving to a Pareto-superior alternative; but one cannot, in general, make a recommendation in favour of any arbitrary Pareto-efficient alternative.

Thus, recommending moving from a Pareto-inefficient status-quo to a Pareto-efficient situation, regardless of whether it is Pareto-superior or not, and regardless of any other considerations involving other values, involves a logical jump completely unjustified although frequently made. If one invariably recommends moving from a Pareto-inefficient state to a Pareto-efficient state, regardless of whether it is Pareto-superior or not, and regardless of any other considerations involving other values, then, in effect, one is making a value-judgment which would regard all Pareto-efficient states to be superior to all Pareto-inefficient states. This in turn is tantamount to saying that the normative criterion of efficiency has precedence over all other values. Such an approach to social change that accords pre-eminence to a single criterion universally, is bound to conflict with observance of basic rights in an essential way; indeed, it is bound to conflict in an essential way with any other societal value as well.

A very important implication follows from the point that one cannot, in general, make a recommendation in favour of moving to any arbitrary Pareto-efficient alternative, which is that: Even if institution A invariably gives rise to Pareto-efficient outcomes and institution B, by and large, or even invariably, yields Pareto-inefficient outcomes, simply on this basis one cannot infer that institution B is inferior to institution A. An institution which invariably gives rise to Pareto-efficient outcomes can be termed as Pareto-efficient institution; or simply an efficient institution. An institution which does not invariably gives rise to Pareto-efficient outcomes would be called a Pareto-inefficient institution or simply an inefficient institution. A large part of the contemporary economics, and increasingly of other social sciences as well, is devoted to analyzing Pareto-efficiency or otherwise of institutions. The preoccupation with efficiency analysis of institutions seems to be based on the erroneous belief that acceptance of Pareto-criterion implies that Pareto-efficient institutions are better than those institutions which are not Pareto-efficient. Thinking of efficient institutions as better than inefficient ones requires the same logical jump which was discussed above. No such conclusion can be derived from the Pareto-criterion alone. What is needed for such a conclusion is something much stronger namely, the value-judgment asserting the equally good character of all Pareto-efficient alternatives and their superiority over all Pareto-inefficient alternatives. In other words, for the conclusion that any efficient institution is better than any inefficient one, exclusion of all values other than efficiency is required.

It is important to note that, while the Pareto-criterion, being based on unanimity, is in harmony with the fundamental ideas of autonomy and equality of persons underlying the conception of human rights, the same cannot be said of Pareto-efficiency in so far as autonomy aspect is concerned. The idea of Pareto-efficiency is not compatible with the notion of autonomy, as it is understood in the context of basic rights. Another important point relates to the fact that, unlike the notion of Pareto-superiority, the Pareto-efficiency idea is independent of the status-quo. In the context of making distinctions between acts and omissions, the distinguished nature of the status-quo should be evident.

In connection with the idea of Pareto-efficiency it is important to remember that the idea relates to particular sets of individuals and social states. From the definition of Pareto-efficiency, it is clear that the answer to the question as to which alternatives are Pareto-efficient crucially depends on what the set of feasible alternatives is and which individuals constitute the society. It would be a serious error if one were to conclude the Pareto-inefficiency of an alternative by comparing it with an infeasible alternative. This point is particularly important in contexts where socio-political constraints make the set of feasible alternatives much smaller than what it would be in the absence of such constraints. The inefficiency of existing state of affairs, inferred under the assumption that socio-political constraints do not exist when in fact they do, needless to say, ought not to be of any significance. The usefulness of discourse however is often marred by an over-emphasis on the Pareto-inferiority of existing affairs in relation to some infeasible state of affairs. Pareto-inefficiency of an alternative when one is considering the preferences of a particular set of individuals, does not imply that it would remain Pareto-inefficient when one takes into account the preferences of a more inclusive set of individuals. In the context of environmental issues, the importance of this point cannot be overemphasized. If the set of individuals is enlarged to include future generations, many pro-environment but supposedly inefficient alternatives would in fact turn out to be efficient.

The Pareto-criterion is almost universally regarded as non-controversial. The non-controversial nature of the Pareto-criterion is explicated by asking the rhetorical question: Is there any sense in which one can say that a change is not better which makes some people better-off and none worse-off? Pareto-criterion, however, is non-committal if one has to make a choice from mutually exclusive Pareto-optimal social states. Such indeed is the case in most contexts, because of the basis of the Pareto-criterion lying in unanimity, a rather stringent requirement. In many contexts, therefore, the notion of efficiency that is used in economics is that of wealth-maximization. A change is considered better if it is wealth-increasing, i.e., if the gainers can compensate the losers and still be better-off. Actual compensation, however, need not be paid. It should also be noted that if actual compensation is not paid then there is no longer any unanimous basis to the change. The underlying, though often implicit, premise in using this notion of efficiency is that the questions of total wealth and its distribution can somehow be separated. Apart from the fact that there is no theoretical justification for this premise, the problems of incentives, which are invariably raised whenever the issue of redistribution is brought in, not only undermine the premise on which the notion is based but further mar the consensual basis for the criterion.

Wealth-maximization is of course an aggregative criterion[10]; and consequently can easily conflict with basic rights. Whether in a particular social context it would conflict with basic rights or not depends on the scope of the criterion. If the criterion is applied to only that subset of social alternatives which guarantee basic rights for all, there would not be any conflict between wealth-maximization and observance of basic rights. On the other hand, if it is applied over a set of social alternatives not all of which guarantee basic rights, then it is immediate that the wealth-maximization criterion can easily conflict with the requirement of universal observance of basic rights. Application of the criterion of wealth-maximization over the entire set of social alternatives is tantamount to relying on the criterion to the exclusion of all other normative considerations for evaluations of social states with differing total wealth. Other normative criteria can play a role, if at all, only with respect to social states with equal total wealth.[11]

Consider an activity which individual A can undertake and which has a negative externality for individual B. If undertaking of the activity on the part of individual A would result in a gain of 100 to him and a loss of 10 to B, then according to the criterion of wealth-maximization, the undertaking of the activity by individual A is socially better than his not undertaking the activity. The consequence of individual B suffering a loss of 10 without any fault of his might be regarded by some as unjust and therefore unacceptable. On the other hand, it might be argued by some others that while it is true that the undertaking of the activity in question by A involves harm for B without any fault of his, the fact remains that for the society as a whole the undertaking of the activity is enriching. The situation under consideration involves a trade-off between fairness considerations on the one hand and wealth considerations on the other. In social contexts such trade-offs are inevitable.

In the context of trade-offs between values, it is important to remember that by their very nature basic rights do not permit any trade-offs. Willingness to make a trade-off between wealth and fairness in some situations does not imply willingness to make a trade-off between wealth and basic rights. This follows from the fact that while every violation of basic rights implies a violation of norms of justice; not every violation of justice is a violation of basic rights. One may countenance the loss of 10 to B, for the sake of much bigger gain of 100 for A, if this loss of 10 is merely a material loss without any other serious consequences for B. If B is living a precarious existence, bordering on starvation, where a loss of 10 can make a difference of life or death, then obviously the situation is radically different and not at all appropriate for making any trade-off. One cannot make a recommendation for A undertaking the activity in a such a scenario.

This example makes it clear that the unmitigated pursuit of economic efficiency in a context like the contemporary one, where large number of people live a marginal existence and where economic activities have serious externalities, is bound to result in violations of human rights, particularly the right to life. At this juncture, one might interpose to assert that there is no conflict between efficiency and basic rights *per se* and that the reason why in the above example a conflict is emerging is due to the fact that the compensation for the loss to B due to the externality is not being considered. If B is compensated for the loss of 10, the apparent conflict between economic efficiency and basic rights vanishes. Indeed, one might argue that if those affected by negative externalities are fully compensated, then a conflict can never arise between economic efficiency and basic rights. As we show in what follows, which discusses the liability question in relation to economic efficiency, this would be a somewhat hasty conclusion. If the conclusions arrived at by economists in relation to the liability question[12] are correct, then the conflict between economic efficiency and basic rights would seem to be not amenable to any satisfactory resolution.

The question of liability arises in the context of actions involving harmful externalities. If an activity undertaken by individual A harms another individual B, whether individual A would compensate individual B, and if yes, then to what extent, depends on what the relevant laws are. Assuming individuals to be rational, as is generally assumed, the compensation to the victims of externalities would not exceed injurers' legal liability. In principle, the relevant laws could be of any kind; they might make the injurers fully liable or partly liable or even not at all liable for the harms inflicted on the victims as a consequence of their actions. The legal rule requiring full compensation to the victims by the injurers is called the 'rule of strict liability'. If no compensation to the victims is required by law then the 'rule of no liability' is said to prevail.

The liability of the injurers could also be made to depend on considerations other than that of causation. One important factor which is quite often taken into consideration is the conduct of the parties prior to the occurrence of harm. One of the most important legal rules for determining liability is that of the 'rule of negligence'. Under the rule of negligence, the injurer is made liable for victim's loss if and only if the level of care that the injurer took in conducting the activity, which gave rise to the harm to the victim, was deficient. The injurer is not liable at all in case the level of care that he took in conducting the activity involving externality was at least equal to a legally specified norm.

Like any rule or set of rules, the legal rules can also be examined, whether they invariably give rise to wealth-maximizing outcomes or not. That is to say, legal rules can be analyzed to find out whether they have the property of inducing individuals to act in a socially efficient manner. The rules of strict liability and negligence have been analyzed by economists from this perspective. These analyses show that while the rule of negligence is efficient; the rule of strict liability is not.

The inefficiency of the rule of strict liability is easy to see. Consider the example referred to earlier of an activity undertaken by individual A which gives him a gain of 100 with negative externality of 10 for individual B. Suppose furthermore that the harm to individual B can be entirely eliminated if care is taken either by the injurer or by the victim. Also suppose that taking care costs the victim 1 and the injurer 2. From the point of view of efficiency or wealth-maximization, it is clear that it is better that the care is taken by the victim rather than the injurer. Under the rule of strict liability the injurer is legally bound to fully compensate the victim; therefore it would be irrational on the part of the victim to spend anything on taking care. Knowing that a rational victim would not take any care under the regime of strict liability, the injurer in this example would take care to eliminate harm as it costs only 2 which is less than 10 that he would have to pay in case care is not taken and consequently harm to the victim of 10 takes place. It is of course possible to construct examples where the rule of strict liability would give rise to socially efficient outcomes. What this example shows is that it is possible for outcomes under the regime of strict liability to be inefficient. If the choice of rules is going to be confined to from among efficient rules only then the rule of strict liability goes out of reckoning.

If the legal regime is that of the rule of negligence, then the outcome in the context of the example considered above would be socially efficient if the legally specified level of care for the injurer is set at zero. A legally specified care level of zero for the injurer is tantamount to having the rule of no liability and therefore it follows that a rational injurer would undertake the activity without taking any care to eliminate the harm. Knowing this, a rational victim would take care which costs only 1 rather than suffer harm of 10 for which he would not receive any compensation. It can be shown that the outcomes under the rule of negligence are always socially efficient. In the example that we have been considering, taking care by either party completely eliminates harm to the victim. One can consider more complicated situations in which taking care, while effective in reducing harm, does not eliminate harm altogether. It may also be the case that for attaining a socially efficient outcome taking care by both the injurer and the victim might be required. The rule of negligence has the property of always inducing a socially efficient outcome regardless of whether taking care by one individual or both the individuals is required for social efficiency. As long as the legally specified due care level for the injurer is set at the socially efficient level, the rule of negligence would give rise to a socially efficient outcome.

On the relationship between liability rules and economic efficiency the following general result holds: A liability rule invariably gives rise to socially efficient outcomes if and only if its structure is such that: (i) whenever the injurer is non-negligent and the victim is negligent, the entire loss in case of accident is borne by the victim, and (ii) whenever the victim is non-negligent and the injurer is negligent, the entire loss in case of an accident is borne by the injurer. An individual is called non-negligent if and only if the level of care taken by him or her is greater than or equal to the legally specified level; otherwise he or she is called negligent. It is assumed that the legally specified due care levels are socially efficient.[13]

From the general result it is clear that economic efficiency at the very least requires from the victims socially efficient levels of care. If the victims in question are living a precarious existence, then the efficiency requirements would conflict with basic rights in an essential way.

When the negative externalities are pervasive, persistent and diffused over a large number of people, there is another aspect of the social and economic order which deserves special attention. If the social and economic order prohibits inflicting harm without compensation, the victims would not have to undertake measures, including legal ones, for obtaining the compensation due to them. On the other hand, if the social and economic order is such that it is the victims who would have to sue or take other measures for recovering compensation for the harm inflicted on them, as indeed is the case with the contemporary order, then the victims would be forced to expend resources in the undertaking of the required recovery measures. This means that even if the liability rule is that of strict liability, the actual compensation would be less than the harm, unless the recovery costs including legal costs are added to the judgment and there are no possibilities of errors in judgments, i.e., the probability of obtaining a correct court order awarding full compensation and all recovery costs is one.

Thus, it is clear that it is inherent in the nature of contemporary international order and national legal and social orders that violation of basic rights would take place for those who are living a subsistence existence and are exposed to the negative externalities of immensely powerful economic processes, unless the State or the international community takes countervailing measures. In view of the diffused and almost all-encompassing nature of the negative externalities of the contemporary economic processes, these countervailing measures for the protection of basic rights, at the very least, must consist of all that a welfare State would provide for the general welfare of the people.

4. Market Ideology and Basic Rights

The most important theoretical propositions linking competitive markets with efficiency are the fundamental theorems of welfare economics. Given the institutional setting of well-defined private property rights, under certain assumptions, including that of absence of externalities, it can be shown that interaction of self-interested and price-taking consumers and producers results in an equilibrium which is Pareto-efficient. The remarkable aspect of this result is twofold: Not only does the self-interested and decentralized decision-making on the part of numerous individuals not result in chaos, it actually gives rise to an unintended consequence of a positive character in that the outcome is efficient in the sense of Pareto. The elegance and rigour of the theorems establishing the existence of competitive equilibrium and linking Pareto-optimality with competitive equilibrium have played a significant role in establishing the pre-eminence of market ideology in the contemporary world, notwithstanding the extremely restrictive character of the assumptions on which these theorems are based.

Under ideal conditions, i.e., under the conditions which would guarantee that the allocation of resources achieved through the market mechanism would be efficient, there may or may not be a case for intervention in the markets on some ground or the other, but there would be no case for intervention in markets on efficiency considerations. If these ideal conditions do not prevail then in addition to other grounds for intervention, if any, there would be a case for intervention on efficiency considerations as well. The very existence of a society implies that there would be externalities in every domain including the economic domain. Externalities rupture the link between markets and efficiency. One way to restore this link would be through the intervention by the State in the form of taxing the activities with negative externalities and subsidizing the ones with positive externalities.

In an important contribution Coase showed that State intervention was not necessary even when externalities were present for restoring the link between markets and efficiency. The Coase theorem essentially says that in a setting of zero transaction costs, an efficient use of resources results from private bargaining, regardless of the legal assignment of property rights. Of course, when transaction costs are high enough to prevent bargaining, the efficient use of resources will depend on how property rights are assigned. The fundamental importance of the Coase theorem for the pro-market ideology arises from the fact that according to this formulation State intervention is neither necessary nor desirable for correcting problems associated with externalities, whereas prior to its formulation State intervention was considered both necessary and desirable in situations of market failures arising from the presence of externalities. As the efficient use of resources will depend on how property rights are assigned when transaction costs are high enough to prevent bargaining, the Coase theorem has normative implication for legal rules and institutions as well.

We can isolate three distinct, though related, elements of the market ideology. The market ideology the way it has evolved does not favour State intervention in the functioning of markets regardless of whether externalities are present or not. This, as has already been discussed in detail, is potentially violative of basic rights.

Secondly, in the process of studying the institution of market, a particular methodology has developed which consists of looking at institutions as ensembles of rules; assuming that individuals are rational, self-interested and constrained to act within the framework defined by the institutional setting; determining what outcomes would result as a consequence of actions undertaken by rational individuals constrained by the rules of the game; and analyzing the character of the outcomes thus generated, in particular asking whether these outcomes satisfy the normative criterion of economic efficiency. It is clear that in principle there is no reason why non-market institutions cannot be studied by using this methodology. Economists, for last few decades have been looking at non-market institutions within this broad methodological framework. Two areas where this methodology has been extensively applied to study institutions are law and political science. It is evident that regardless of the values for attainment of which these non-market institutions might have been designed, application of market methodology to study them can only result in substituting efficiency in place of the original values, or confusing the values for which the institutions were designed in the first place with efficiency. This, inevitably, would result in derecognition of whole classes of violations of basic rights.

Like the link between free markets and efficiency, there is also a link between private ownership of property and efficiency. In general, other forms like common ownership are not conducive for attaining efficiency. In the classical conception of human rights, private property was important, not so much for its own sake, but as a necessary enabling condition for realization of rights like the right to life and liberty. Assuming this link between private property and liberty to be a valid one, it is important to see how the efficiency considerations are impinging on this linkage.

It has already been discussed that rights like the right to liberty need constraining if one person's right to liberty is not to result in deprivation of the right to someone else. Such constraining is not only explicitly recognized in human rights discourses but also finds expression in the formulation of laws. It is in the context of the right to property that the treatment of externalities is conspicuous by its absence. As noted above, for the classical conception of human rights, the importance of the right to property arises from the fact that its existence is considered essential for the realization of the right to life and liberty. Consequently, whether the right to property in itself is considered a basic right or not is immaterial from the point of view of its inclusion in the ensemble of rights. The right to property, like any other right, if unconstrained, can result in one person's enjoyment of the right conflicting with another person's exercise of the right. Although in economics the awareness of externalities in the context of economic interactions and their systematic treatment has been there for a long time, surprisingly the externalities in relation to right to private property have not received any explicit and systematic treatment in the context of human rights. This omission is all the more surprising in view of the fact that the right to property after all, to a certain degree, receives its justification because of its supposed necessity for a meaningful exercise of the right to liberty, in the context of which there is explicit recognition of externalities. It is clear that it is essential that there be provision for constraining the right to property in case it conflicts with the basic rights of others. While, the right to private property, upto a certain level, might facilitate or be essential for the realization of basic rights, there is very little doubt that if unconstrained it would conflict with the basic rights of others.

Conversion of common property and state property into private property in general results in large numbers of individuals owning so little of private property as to cast serious doubts regarding their ability to continue to hold on to whatever rights they have. Thus efficiency considerations relating to private property seem to be in conflict with basic rights from both ends of the economic spectrum.

To sum up: The market ideology stands in sharp conflict with human rights both because of efficiency considerations corrupting the character of institutions and by destroying the enabling conditions for fulfilment of human rights. The most important aspect of the mainstream thought lies in the fact that a non-value concept, namely market, occupies a central place both in positive and normative analysis. Apart from the usual justification of market in terms of efficiency criteria, many pro-market philosophers tend to provide justification of market in terms of fundamental values like liberty. However, in contexts that place the market and those values in antagonistic relationships, it is not the market which is made to yield to the values. Rather, the very values which are invoked to justify the market in the first place must yield to it. It is inevitable that when a non-value concept is given centrality both in positive and normative analysis, even the most basic values would cease to be of much relevance in the shaping and designing of institutions, with regrettable consequences for the underprivileged. It is this curious reversal of roles between instruments and values that is characteristic of market ideology.

5. Concluding Remarks

One of the most paradoxical features of development of human rights discourse since the coming into existence of the United Nations has been its wide divergence with the practice of human rights. While the theory as well as law relating to human rights has made unprecedented progress, the progress regarding observance of human rights has not at all been commensurate. Throughout the period since the inception of the United Nations human rights violations have been rampant. Although, if one focuses on the magnitude and severity of violations of human rights, there would be little difference between the period from the inception of the United Nations to the collapse of the Soviet Union and the period from the collapse to date, there is one very important difference that needs to be noted. The pattern of human rights violations during the period from the inception of the United Nations to the collapse of the socialist bloc, by and large consisted of: Western countries, particularly U.S.A., to protect their economic and strategic interests, engineering coups in third-world countries resulting in the overthrow of democratically elected governments, installing extremely repressive regimes[14] completely dependent on western support; western countries denying or outright violating the rights of the non-white minorities; eastern block countries denying rights to their own peoples and violating the rights of dissidents; and satellites of socialist block in third-world countries replicating the behaviour. The few third-world countries, which were not de facto, part of the area of influence of either of the two major blocs and had democratic governments, resorted to repressive measures, leading to violations of basic rights, against ethnic and other minorities clamouring for independence or self-rule.

Notwithstanding the fact that during this period practically all countries were guilty of violations of rights, surprisingly it did not affect the development and the rhetoric of human rights discourse. But since the collapse of the socialist bloc the situation has fundamentally changed. Apart from the changes in the form of violations, the theory and rhetoric of human rights is also getting affected. The most important new form of violation of human rights is the new kind of genocide perpetrated in Iraq through sanctions. It is noteworthy that the genocide perpetrated through sanctions against the Iraqi people had the formal sanction of the United Nations. The most important development relating to the theory and the rhetoric of human rights consists the of derecognition of certain categories of violations as violations. This aspect has partly already been discussed. There is very little doubt that until the collapse of the Soviet Union the Permanent Sovereignty of Resources was part of customary international law, and possibly that of *jus cogens* as well. Not much has been heard of this right for the last one and a half decades. With the supremacy of the forces of globalization on the one hand and the occupation of Iraq, and the international community's capitulation on the issue of occupation on the other, it is doubtful if the concept of Permanent Sovereignty of Resources can survive as part of international law. Indeed, in the aftermath of Iraq it is doubtful if even the core ideas of prohibition of torture, prohibition of genocide and self-determination can survive for long as part of international law in any meaningful sense.

Notes

1. The Preamble of 1948 Universal Declaration of Human Rights begins as:

   Whereas recognition of the inherent dignity and of the equal and inalienable rights of all members of the human family is the foundation of freedom, justice and peace in the world,...

   Preambles of both International Covenant on Civil and Political Rights and International Covenant on Economic, Social and Cultural Rights begin as:

   Considering that, in accordance with the principles proclaimed in the

Charter of the United Nations, recognition of the inherent dignity and of the equal and inalienable rights of all members of the human family is the foundation of freedom, justice and peace in the world,...

2. On International Law relating to human rights generally see Crawford (2000), Brownlie (2003), Jennings (1992), Lauterpacht (1945) and Meron (1986).
3. Prior to the adoption of the Charter of the United Nations, international law did not recognize human rights.
4. The widespread acceptance of the authority of the Universal Declaration of Human Rights since its adoption has led to the opinion that notwithstanding the fact that the Declaration is not a treaty, its provisions must be regarded as embodiment of international law in the matter of human rights. See Jennings (1992).
5. On the Vienna Convention on the Law of Treaties see Reuter (1995) and Sinclair (1984).
6. See Article 53 of the Convention on the Law of Treaties.
7. The right of self-determination figures prominently in most important instruments relevant to human rights including the United Nations Charter; International Covenant on Civil and Political Rights; and International Covenant on Economic, Social and Cultural Rights. In the United Nations Charter the right of self-determination is mentioned in clause 2 of Article 1 which lays down the purposes of the organization. The clause reads:

   To develop friendly relations among nations based on respect for the principle of equal rights and self-determination of peoples, and to take other appropriate measures to strengthen universal peace;

   International Covenant on Civil and Political Rights and International Covenant on Economic, Social and Cultural Rights have identical Article 1 which reads:

   All peoples have the right of self-determination. By virtue of that right they freely determine their political status and freely pursue their economic, social and cultural development.

   Right to self-determination also figures in the Declaration on Principles of International Law concerning Friendly Relations and Cooperation among States 1970, GA Res 2625 (XXV). This declaration was adopted by the General Assembly of the United Nations by acclamation; and it authoritatively elaborates some of the basic principles embodied in the United Nations Charter. The seven principles contained in the declaration are of pre-eminent value in the International Law. The principles embodied in the Declaration were declared by the General Assembly to constitute 'basic principles of international law'. One of the seven principles lays down the right to self-determination. See Jennings (1992).
8. The International Law Commission, although it did not give any

examples of jus cogens in its draft Articles on the Law of Treaties, it did record that in this context mention had been made of the prohibition of trade in slaves, prohibition of genocide, the observance of human rights, and the principle of self-determination, among others.

9. On notions of economic efficiency see Arrow (1963), Jain (2003), Kaldor (1939), Scitovsky (1941) and Sen (1970), among others.
10. The evaluation of social states on the basis of wealth-maximization involves serious logical difficulties which we do not discuss here. See Kaldor (1939), Scitovsky (1941), Arrow (1963) and Sen (1970), among others.
11. A particularly explicit statement advocating the use of the criterion of wealth-maximization over the entire set of social states is to be found in Coase's enormously influential paper 'The Problem of Social Cost' (1960). The paper concludes with the following passage:
    'It would clearly be desirable if the only actions performed were those in which what was gained was worth more than what was lost. But in choosing between social arrangements within the context of which individual decisions are made, we have to bear in mind that a change in the existing system, which will lead to an improvement in some decisions may well lead to a worsening of others. Furthermore we have to take into account the costs involved in operating the various social arrangements (whether it be the working of a market or of a government department), as well as the costs involved in moving to a new system. In devising and choosing between social arrangements we should have regard for the total effect. This, above all, is the change in approach which I am advocating.'
12. On economic analysis of law in general, and tort law in particular see Barnes and Stout (1992), Burrows and Veljanovski (1981), Calabresi (1980), Calabresi (1991), Cooter and Ulen (1999), Landes and Posner (1987), Levmore (1994), Miceli (1997), Polinsky (1989), Posner (1975, 1992) and Shavell (1987) among others.
13. See Jain and Singh (2002).
14. Shah regime in Iran, Suharto regime in Indonesia and Pinochet regime in Chile were some of the worst examples.

References

Arrow, K.J., 1963. *Social Choice and Individual Values*, second edition, Wiley, New York.

Arrow, K.J. and Hahn, F.H., 1971. *General Competitive Analysis*, North-Holland, Amsterdam.

Barnes, David W. and Stout, Lynn A., 1992. *Economic Analysis of Tort Law*, West Publishing Company, St. Paul.

Brownlie, Ian, 2003. *Principles of Public International Law*, 6th edition, Oxford University Press, Oxford.

Burrows, P. and Veljanovski, C.G., 1981. 'Introduction: The Economic Approach to Law' in *The Economic Approach to Law ed.* by Burrows, P. and Veljanovski, C.G., Butterworths, London.

Calabresi, Guido, 1980. 'About Law and Economics: A Letter to Ronald Dworkin', 8 Hofstra Law Review.

Calabresi, Guido, 1991. 'The Pointlessness of Pareto: Carrying Coase Further', 100 Yale Law Journal.

Charter of the United Nations, June 26, 1945, 59 Stat. 1031, T.S. 993, 3 Bevans 1153, entered into force Oct. 24, 1945.

Coase, R.H., 1960. 'The Problem of Social Cost', 3 Journal of Law and Economics.

Convention against Torture and Other Cruel, Inhuman or Degrading Treatment or Punishment, G.A. res. 39/46, [annex, 39 U.N. GAOR Supp. (No. 51) at 197, U.N. Doc. A/39/51 (1984)], entered into force June 26, 1987.

Convention for the Protection of Human Rights and Fundamental Freedoms [213 U.N.T.S. 222, as amended by Protocols Nos. 3, 5, 8, and 11].

Cooter, Robert D. and Ulen, Thomas S., 1999. *Law and Economics*, third edition, Addison-Wesley, New York.

Crawford, James (ed.), 1988. *The Rights of Peoples*, Clarendon Press, Oxford.

Declaration on Principles of International Law concerning Friendly Relations and Cooperation among States, GA Res 2625 (XXV) (1975).

Declaration on the Protection of All Persons from Being Subjected to Torture and Other Cruel, Inhuman or Degrading Treatment or Punishment, G.A. res. 3452 (XXX), annex, 30 U.N. GAOR Supp. (No. 34) at 91, U.N. Doc. A/10034 (1975).

Donnelly, Jack, 1985. *The Concept of Human Rights*, Croom Helm, London.

Donnelly, Jack, (1989). *Universal Human Rights in Theory and Practice*, Cornell University Press, Cornell.

Dworkin, R., 1977. *Taking Rights Seriously*, Harvard University Press, Cambridge.

Dworkin, R., 1986. *Law's Empire*, Harvard University Press, Cambridge.

Harris, D.J., 1991. *Cases and Materials on International Law*, International Student Edition, Sweet and Maxwell, London.

Hart, H.L.A., 1961. *The Concept of Law*, Clarendon Press, Oxford.

Hayek, F., 1960. The Constitution of Liberty, Routledge and Kegan Paul, London.

Hossain, Kamal and Chowdhury, Subrata Roy (eds.), 1984. *Permanent Sovereignty over Natural Resources in International Law*, Frances Pinter, London.

International Covenant on Civil and Political Rights, G.A. res. 2200A (XXI), 21 U.N. GAOR Supp. (No. 16) at 52, U.N. Doc. A/6316 (1966), 999 U.N.T.S. 171, entered into force Mar. 23, 1976.

International Covenant on Economic, Social and Cultural Rights, G.A. res. 2200A (XXI), 21 U.N.GAOR Supp. (No. 16) at 49, U.N. Doc. A/6316 (1966), 993 U.N.T.S. 3, entered into force Jan. 3, 1976.

Jain, Satish K., 2003. 'Globalization, Legal Institutions and Values' in *Economic Institutions in India*, ed. by Parthasarathi Banerjee and Frank-Jürgen Richter, Palgrave Macmillan, London.

Jain, Satish K. and Singh, Ram (2002), 'Efficient Liability Rules: Complete Characterization', 75 Journal of Economics (Zeitschrift für Nationalökonomie), 105-124.

Jennings, Sir Robert and Watts, Sir Arthur, 1992. *Oppenheims's International Law*, Ninth Edition, Longman, Essex.

Kaldor, N., 1939. Welfare Propositions of Economics and Interpersonal Comparisons of Utility, 49 Economic Journal.

Landes, William M. and Posner, Richard A., 1987. *The Economic Structure of Tort Law*, Harvard University Press, Cambridge (MA).

Lauterpacht, H., 1945. *An International Bill of the Rights of Man*, Columbia University Press, N.Y.

Levmore, Saul, 1994. *Foundations of Tort Law*, Oxford University Press, Oxford.

Meron, T., 1986. *Human Rights Law-Making in the United Nations*, Oxford University Press, New York.

Miceli, Thomas J., 1997. *Economics of the Law: Torts, Contracts, Property, Litigation*, Oxford University Press, Oxford.

Permanent Sovereignty over Natural Resources, G.A. res. 1803 (XVII), 17 U.N. GAOR Supp. (No.17) at 15, U.N. Doc. A/5217 (1962).

Pigou, A.C., 1932. *The Economics of Welfare*, fourth edition, Macmillan, London.

Pogge, Thomas, 2000. The International Significance of Human Rights, 4 The Journal of Ethics, 45-69.

Polinsky, A. Mitchell, 1989. *An Introduction to Law and Economics*, second edition, Little, Brown and Company, Boston.

Posner, R.A., 1975. 'The Economic Approach to Law' 53 Texas Law Review.

Posner, Richard A., 1992. *Economic Analysis of Law*, fourth edition, Little, Brown and Company, Boston.

Rawls, J., 1971. *A Theory of Justice*, Harvard University Press, Cambridge.

Reuter, Paul, 1995. *Introduction to the Law of Treaties*, Kegan Paul.

Scitovsky, Tibor, 1941. 'A Note on Welfare Propositions in Economics', 9(1) Review of Economic Studies.

Sen, A.K., 1970. Collective Choice and Social Welfare, Holden-Day, San Francisco.

Shavell, Steven, 1987. *Economic Analysis of Accident Law*, Harvard University Press, Cambridge (MA).

Sinclair, I., 1984. The Vienna Convention on the Law of Treaties, 2nd revised ed., Manchester University Press.

Universal Declaration of Human Rights, G.A. res. 217A (III), U.N. Doc A/ 810 at 71 (1948).

Vienna Convention on the Law of Treaties, 1155 U.N.T.S. 331, entered into force January 27, 1980.

Chapter Eight

The Issues of Conflict in Nepal

In this paper, we shall take up the issues relating to the conditions of conflict in Nepal, their historical origins, the nature of political violence, the scale of State atrocities, and prospects for peace and the enforcement of fundamental human rights in the country that came up during the distance-learning exercises of our Human Rights and Peace Studies Course.

Four topics dominated the discussions on the subject. They are: (1) The conditions of the people known as the *Tharu* and *Madise* of the *Terai* region [the flat fertile extension of the northern Indian plains comprising 23 per cent of the Nepali territory] as well as of mid and western Nepal and their association with the Maoist insurgency; (2) failures of the democratic processes, especially after the supposed restoration of democracy in the 1990s, in addressing the people's aspirations, and their contribution in channelling the radical politics of reform in a violent direction; (3) failures of international human rights law mechanisms in preventing crimes against humanity or even in offering robust criticism against them; and (4) the dynamics of political violence employed by the Maoist insurgents in their so-called "People's War" and its impact on the most vulnerable sections of the population, especially women and children in the mid-western part of the country.

For the sake of concision and clarity, we shall make our comments under six headings. They are: (1) Some unique aspects of the modern political history of Nepal that contribute to the stagnation of citizenship within a medieval ethos while retaining the State as a platform for the power-games of its superannuated elites; (2) The connections between the monarchical centre of power in Kathmandu and the feudal elements in the mid-western hills; (3) Persistent realities of socio-economic and cultural exploitation, which have become the well-springs of the conflict currently ravaging the country; (4) The failures of democracy, restored through the so-called revolution of 1990; (5) The problems of enforcing the guarantees, within the domestic and international human rights law framework; and (6) The ethical concerns about the nature of Maoist violence that claims to be politically emancipatory.

Naturally, our comments can only echo some of the propositions already being discussed within the Nepalese civil society circles and raise a set of questions relevant to further research into a conflict that is not only politically unique in the whole of South Asia, but is also fast spiralling into a human catastrophe marked by extraordinary levels of violence and woe.

(1) Every text dealing with the history of modern Nepal inevitably dwells on the fact that it is the only country in South Asia that escaped the scourge of European colonization. Indeed, Nepal never became a British colony although it lost its wars against the British East India Company, fought from 1814 to 1816, and became a satellite of the British imperial interests. Under the Treaty of Sagauli, signed in 1816, the British acquired the right to recruit the hill tribes of Nepal known for their tenacity, courage, discipline and also ferocity, into its armies. The British identified all the hill tribes with the name of Gorkha, a tribe to which Prithvi Narayan Shah, the 1743 founder of the ruling dynasty of Hindu kings, belonged. By the time the British faced the Indian mutiny of 1857, Nepal had come under the virtual rule of the Ranas who had taken power from the Shahs through a palace massacre that took place on the 16th of September 1846 under the watchful eyes of a British resident. Gorkha soldiers of the British army played a major role in putting down the rebellion in India. In appreciation of its services, the British returned the fertile alluvial plains that they had captured between 1814 and 1816 to Nepal.

Under the Treaty of Sagauli, the British had forbidden the Gorkha kingdom of Nepal from making inroads into Kumaon and Garhwal to its west and Sikkim to its east. However, the "hill-station" of Darjeeling, taken on lease from Sikkim in 1839, soon became the nerve-centre of the tea-plantation industry and, once again, the British encouraged the Nepalese to come down and settle as plantation workers. The British also encouraged the Nepalese to migrate to Sikkim as well as to Bhutan, largely with the intention of diluting the Tibetan elements of the population in order to keep the two States away from the Chinese political influence in the long-run. The British suzerainty over Bhutan had become formal with the Treaty of Sinchula, signed on the 11th of November 1865. In December 1907, Ugyen Wagchuck, a warlord who had sided with the British against the Tibetan government during Younghusband's expedition of 1903-04, displaced the traditional Buddhist theocracy of Shabdrung and proclaimed himself as the hereditary king of Bhutan. The political change in Bhutan prompted the migration of Nepali hill people in the east, reeling under the burden of local rents and taxes, to southern Bhutan. They had probably been on the move already for some time, and the Bhutanese tolerated them as the new settlers brought much needed cash revenue for lands they cleared and cultivated. Within three decades, a British political officer concerned with the affairs of Sikkim and Bhutan, was remarking: "Both in Bhutan and Sikkim a very practical problem in politics is whether the local races are destined to be overwhelmed by the Nepalese."[1]

The expansion of the Nepali migration process to southern Bhutan in this period may have had some connection with the regional political ambitions of the Nepali Ranas. Michael Hutt, while researching accounts of refugees from Bhutan, discovered the legends surrounding Garjaman Gurung, a powerful Nepali Thekedar in the south-western district of Samchi. Garjaman Gurung allegedly joined a delegation going to Kathmandu to ensure that Chandra Shamsher Rana's government recognized the Wagchuck monarchy in Bhutan. According to some accounts, Garjaman began to issue local tax receipts written in Nepali in the name of "Samchi Garjaman State: Bhutan", and had a palace of 52 doors built for himself on a hilltop near Samchi Town. In some stories collected by Michael Hutt, it is said that Gurjaman wanted to proclaim himself as the representative of *3 Sirkar*, the honorific formula that refers to the Rana rule in Nepal. The Bhutanese governor of the region was offended and invited Garjaman to Paro, where he had him poisoned. The story may be apocryphal. But it shows that Rana rulers of Nepal remained interested in the Nepali settlements in Bhutan. It is also clear from independent British records that the Rana regime of Nepal was keen to retain the political allegiance of Nepalese who migrated outside its borders for livelihood and sustenance. The Nepali population in Bhutan, as also in Sikkim, was encouraged to seek guidance from the "Nepal Durbar" on sensitive political and caste matters. In 1929, Bhim Shamsher Rana tried hard to persuade the British that he should be allowed to assign official "Gurus" to live in the major centres of Nepali settlements not only to guide the people in religious and caste matters, but also to develop intelligence on political activities.[2]

Nepali soldiers of the British army remained notorious for their military ruthlessness. General Dyer used them in April 1919 to carry out a massacre of Indians who had gathered at Jalianwalla Bag in Amritsar, outside the Golden Temple, in defiance of a curfew order to demand the repeal of a black law known as the Rowlatt Act. Nepali soldiers fought for the British in the Afghan wars. More than 20,000 of them died during WW I. More than 2,00,000 Nepalese fought for the British in World War II and they were heavily deployed during the Malaya campaign to decimate the communist threat in the 1960s.[3] Nepalese soldiers also fought for India to quell internal rebellions and in its wars against China and Pakistan. The Indian army deployed them in 1984 to put down an uprising of Sikh soldiers that attended the Indian army's attack on the Golden Temple. All of this is known, and the salaries and pensions which Nepali soldiers receive constitute a fair share of the cash flow in the hilly regions of the country.

What is not so well-known is the role that these martial tribes of the Nepali hills continue to play in sustaining several private mercenary companies founded in the United States and the UK to carry out clandestine military operations as well as to train and organize militias in countries like Nigeria, Bulgaria, Taiwan and Equatorial Guinea, several countries in Latin America, and now in the Middle East. For example, a British private military company called Global Risk Strategies, operating in many of the aforementioned locations, mainly recruits Nepali mercenaries. In Sierra Leone, a diamond rich country thrown into anarchy by mining companies, the government of Captain Valentine Strasser was facing an implacable insurgency by the Revolutionary United Front [RUF], led by a former nightclub owner Foday Sankoh under the protection of Liberia's Charles Taylor, in 1992. Unable to handle the situation, Strasser's government engaged the services of the Gorkha Security Guards, a mercenary firm led by James Maynard and Andrew Myers, British nationals, in partnership with American Robert Mackenzie, son-in-law of former CIA deputy director Ray Cline. Gorkha Security Guards proved no match for the ruthless tactics of the RUF under Sankoh. The government of Sierra Leone had to call in Executive Outcomes, a South African company comprising veterans from the apartheid regime's elite forces, to stop the rebels from capturing Freetown.[4]

And what did this mercenary bond with the imperialistic and neo-imperialistic interests and their military objectives, developed and sustained over 188 years now, bring to the small Himalayan kingdom? It would be reasonable to assume that the connection would have brought not only cash and general economic prosperity but also the ideas of progress and material development encountered by Nepali soldiers in foreign lands. This has not been the case. It is generally agreed that Nepal remains one of the poorest countries in South Asia. Nearly half the population in the country lives in conditions of absolute poverty. The hilly terrains of Nepal have not seen progress in spite of a high level of foreign aid focusing on development, essential social services, community projects, livelihood security, forestry partnerships, poverty reduction, the redemption of bonded labour, family health, irrigation management, etc.[5]

(2) The heartland of the Maoist insurgency in Nepal's mid-western hills, including Rukum and Rolpa, is one of the exceptional regions in Nepal where the rulers belonging to local kingdoms predating the conquest and consolidation of Nepal as a Gorkha monarchy under Prithvi Narayan Shah retained considerable political influence and actually continued to deal with the kings of the Shah dynasty on a more or less equal footing to this day. For example, King Gyanendra's sister, Princess Shobha, who survived the June 2001 palace massacre is married to Prince Mohan Bahadur Shahi, a scion of the older Rukum-kot rulers. Gyanendra's other sister, Princess Sharada, was married to Prince Khadga Bikram Shah, a successor of the older Jumli royalty who was killed in the June 2001 palace massacre. Army General Vivek Shah, King Gyanendra's chief military advisor, is actually a descendant of the older Jajarkot royalty.

These are important connections between the powerful elite interests in Nepal's mid-western parts and Nepal's ruling monarchy, especially in order to understand why the same region has emerged as the heartland and the stronghold of the Maoist insurgency. The region is known to be the most retarded in terms of development and infrastructure even by Nepali standards. There is not even a single metalled road connecting its sub-district administrative headquarters. Thawang is a two-day walk along a mule track from the Rolpa district capital, Liwang. The first road in Rukum district was built by the Royal Nepal Army [RNA] in 2003, connecting Musikot, the district headquarters of Rukum, with an older road in Salyan district. Eastern Rukum did not possess even a rudimentary primary health care system until Dr. David Watters of the Summer Institute of Linguistics, a sister organization of the Wycliffe Bible Society, established a primary health care centre at Takasera in the late 1970s. He also introduced apple seedlings and the cultivation of potatoes in the region.

Dr. Watter's interests were primarily missionary in nature. Under his influence, some Kham-Magar speaking people converted to Christianity, a crime under the legal system of Nepal which prides itself as the only Hindu kingdom in the world despite the majority of its population being outside its pale. Dr. Watters and his family left Takasera in 1976. Nine close followers of Dr. Watters were jailed for one year and compelled to retract from the profession of their new faith. The alternative was six-year long term in jail. Hundreds of others were arrested for shorter periods and forced to recoil from Christianity. But a handful remained steadfast, and accepted imprisonment to demonstrate their courage of conviction. Christian organizations abroad collected money to support the families of the imprisoned. But the Christians of eastern Rukum used some of that money to purchase a Swiss-made water mill that could grind grain, press seeds for oil, and power a small sawmill. Carrying the mill to Takasera, to re-assemble it there, and to build a house to locate it were backbreaking exercises. But the small community of Christian Magars, under the inspiration of their newly acquired faith, managed them. Apparently, the mill served Christians and non-Christians alike and the surplus from a small payment collected for grain grinding and oil making was distributed to the poor half-yearly. In 1984, the Nepali government authorities ordered the mill to be shut down. The village headman of Takasera, a non-Christian, refused to carry out the order. The government dispatched a strong group of police personnel to dismantle the mill. The villagers trapped them on a mountain trail, disarmed them, forced them to undress, shaved off their moustaches, smeared their faces with animal excreta and binding them all with ropes, put them out on a procession through Takasera street to the accompaniment of the slogan: "Behold our government".[6] So, we see the first stirrings of what would soon become the "red insurgency."

It is noteworthy in this context that while the mid-western region of Nepal was in the middle of these throes of social upheaval, the government of Nepal held a so-called referendum on the future polity of the country, asking the people to either endorse the party-less *Panchayat* system or vote for a multi-party democracy. The referendum, held in May 1980, produced an endorsement for the status quo with 2.4 million people voting for it and 2 million voting for the change. Apparently, a majority of *janajatis* in the hilly areas of Nepal voted for the retention of the system. Well-known scholars interpreted the voting patterns in the hills as reflecting the stranglehold the feudal elements retained on largely illiterate people with no tradition of democratic political dissent. The iron grip that the medieval feudal elements maintained on the *janajatis* of the mid-western hills was the result of the conditions of underdevelopment, the social isolation of the people owing to the absence of infrastructure, and their abject dependence on personal favours and patronage even for the bare necessities of survival.[7]

Should it then be surprising that the same people, no longer able to endure the injustices and exploitation that saw no mitigation even under a supposedly democratic system of governance, become staunch supporters of the Maoists, who promise the advent of an egalitarian social order through a violent mobilization of popular aspirations?

(3) Nepal's *Terai* region is often referred to as the corridor between India and the Maoist strongholds in Western Nepal. Western *Terai*, one of the most fertile parts of the country, is also a textbook instance of exploitative relationships between the landlords and the actual cultivators. Two connected lines of inquiry commend themselves:

(a) Was the nature of the relationship between the people in western *Terai* and the State of Nepal during the Rana period any better than their relationship following the restoration of the monarchy at India's intervention in 1950? The royal family from Gorkha, which professes to have consolidated Nepal as a single kingdom, claims descent from a martial clan from Rajputana that, under Muslim pressure, chose to move out of Nepal in the early 15th century. The Ranas too have similar genealogies. It is possible, as Sudhindra Sharma suggests, that "this Rajput genealogy is contested" and that "vis-à-vis the local people the rulers identified themselves with the superior civilizing 'centre'".[8]

By the logic of this necessity to be the upholders of a true *Hindu Rajya*, the rulers of Nepal should have been more humane towards the people of western *Terai*, somewhat derogatorily identified as *Madise*, literally meaning those from the midlands, who—at least a majority of them—have been closer to the framework of Hindu *dharma* than the people of the hills.

(b) Does the common experience of socio-economic exploitation and of injustices without remedy under the monarchical system of governance, with and without a multiparty democratic façade, inspire the people across cultural, ethnic, and regional divisions in Nepal to take refuge in the utopia of emancipation, through force, that the Maoist mobilization represent?

A part of the western *Terai* around Nepalganj is known as *naya muluk* [new land] because, having been lost to the British under the Treaty of Sugauli, it was bestowed back to Nepal under the Ranas for the assistance they had rendered in putting down the 1857 mutiny in India. The restored area, comprising a total of 4,400 square kilometres that covered today's districts of Banke, Bardiya, Kailali and Kanchanpur, was highly wooded and virulently malarial.

The total population of Nepal at that time was probably less than 4 million since in 1911 it was estimated to be approximately 5.6 million. The hill population was much smaller and survived happily on the land and the forest resources that were then abundant. It was difficult to persuade the hill population to come down to the malarial plains where they would have to first burn down forests to clear the land for cultivation. The indigenous population, now known as *Tharus* and *Dhimals*, was small but had a greater immunity against malaria. But they had no standing within the caste society and were treated as untouchables. The Rana rulers were keen to develop *naya muluk* for agriculture but had no respect for the indigenous people who alone could have done it in a gradual, even if a slow, fashion. The evidence shows that the Rana rulers tried very hard, using extra inducements, to persuade the Nepalese domiciled in Bhutan and Sikkim to come down to the *Terai* and to take possession of the land. According to several 1932 reports from the British political officer in Sikkim, J.L.R. Weir, the Nepal government had been distributing "notifications" in Sikkim, Bhutan and Assam exhorting its "Gorkha subjects" to come down to the jungle lands of Nepal which were being opened for cultivation on extraordinarily propitious terms. The notifications promised free timber to build their dwellings, sweet water wells, good doctors, and exemption from taxes for a period of 10 years. The notifications even invited criminals convicted of murder to return if they had already spent 12 years outside, and others convicted for adultery. Only those outside the pale of the Hindu caste system were discouraged from responding to these notifications.[9]

Those who had migrated to Bhutan and Sikkim from the eastern hills generally did not respond to these appeals. Some of those who had moved from places at lower altitudes on the eastern side, like Jhapa and Morang districts, probably did. The Rana rulers also encouraged other hill people, embedded within the Hindu caste system, to become colonizers. Those who wanted to escape the conditions of life and servitude in Nepal preferred to enlist in the British army rather than risk their lives to reclaim land in the *Terai*. There were also other avenues of livelihood inside British India and Burma. Life conditions in plantations in the hilly terrains of West Bengal, Assam and Sikkim were preferable. Unable to develop new agricultural colonies in the *naya mulk* by inviting common settlers, the rulers began to lure the members of the aristocracy based in Kathmandu and other main centres of Rana power to get involved in the land development schemes by offering them large land grants, known as *birta* and *mauja* with inheritable rights. Members of the ruling elite and loyal military officers, especially *Brahmins* and *Khatris*, received much preference. The beneficiaries of these grants became absentee landlords. They employed local people to clear forests and to cultivate the land, themselves staying away from the heat of the plains and visiting their lands only in October or November when paddy was ready for harvesting. Forests were cut down indiscriminately to supply wood for the construction of the Indian railways and for building palaces for members of the aristocracy. Migration from the hills began in earnest only after USAID and the WHO started to pour in a lot of money in malaria eradication programmes, which relied heavily on the spraying of DDT.

We do not know much about the environmental impact of DDT-centered malaria eradication programme. But the fatality resulting from malaria was drastically reduced. New settlements began to develop in the late 1950s. Massive floods and landslides in the hills in the mid-fifties encouraged the process. Influential elements within the Nepali Congress also took the initiative in leading new hill settlers to the *Terai*, particularly in *Chitwan* areas. Other projects like the Rapti Valley Development Project, also funded by foreign donors, were seriously pursued. Landless people from Bihar and eastern Uttar Pradesh in India also came in substantial numbers. The story is long and interesting and plenty of literature is available on the subject.[10]

The eradication of malaria; the growth in population; the expansion of agriculture; the end of certain extra opportunities of employment in India and Burma; as well as the saturation of labour in the tea plantations etc., made the reclamation and ownership of land, by means fair and foul, increasingly attractive. There is enough literature documenting the process by which the owners of small land holdings lost their possessions.[11] Lione Caplan quotes a Limbu experience with a Brahmin land-grabber: "He would invite me to his house and offer me rice and meat. Then he made me put my thumbprints on papers. He would give me a few rupees and when I came some months later to return the money and take back my land, he would say: "This is not enough. Why do you bring me a few rupees and ask for your land back? The document says the amount of the mortgage is five hundred and you bring me five. What, am I a fool?" What can you do to such a man? They are all like that, the *Brahmins*. They are treacherous."[12]

Indebtedness and the inability of common peasants to redeem their lands mortgaged to moneylenders rapidly generated a large bonded-labour force, especially among the indigenous Tharus and Dhimals. Recipients of royal land grants, such as the *birta* and *mauja*, were already familiar with the system of exacting physical labour on a compulsory and free basis, called *jhara,* which had become an established political practice from the days of the military mobilization for the conquest and consolidation of all the territories of Nepal into a single kingdom under the Gorkha principality. Compulsory free labour to build palaces, temples and forts was also continuously exacted by the rulers of the Shah dynasty as well as by the Rana usurpers. The expanding State of Nepal, without a minimum monetary base, issued a royal order in May 1808 that allowed military officials to seize able-bodied persons and force them to carry loads. Thus, the system of exacting unpaid labour crept into non-agricultural sectors. Indirectly it contributed to the deterioration of productivity in agriculture and also to rural indebtedness and impoverishment of the peasantry simply because compulsory labour made it impossible for people to tend to their farms while the imperatives of survival compelled them to accumulate loans.[13]

Recipients of *birta* and *mauja* and others who emulated their ways found it easy to bring the Tharu and Dhimal natives under indebtedness—they would take over their lands and, over generations, convert them and their families into *kamaiya*, or a bonded labour force. The system of *Kamaiya* is generally associated with the Tharu people, indigenous to the far-western *Terai* region of Nepal, who, according to the 1991 population census, constituted the fourth largest ethnic group in Nepal—approximately 6.5 per cent of the total population.[14] BASE, a Tharu NGO, is reported to have done an impressive amount of work on the conditions of *Kamaiya* servitude as well as to build awareness and solidarity for legislative and administrative efforts for their redemption from bondage. In collaboration with BASE, the Informal Sector Service Centre, a human rights organization with its headquarters in Kathmandu, developed a draft of a central legislation granting debt relief which was finally enacted as the *Kamaiya Abolition Act* of July 2001. The government also made financial allocations for schemes that aimed to rehabilitate the freed bonded labourers by developing skills and providing them with alternative housing, small plots of land for agriculture, or an alternative vocation. But these schemes have not really been successful and many freed bonded labourers find themselves in impossible situations with no one to turn to.[15]

The *kamaiya* system of bonded labour is much talked about. But what about other systems of bondage or semi-bondage that have been practiced in different parts of Nepal and which also developed out of the same conditions of indebtedness of poor farmers? Some of these other systems are known as: (1) the *haruwari system*, under which a farmer under debt receives a plot of land to cultivate but is not given any substantial right of tenancy or even the produce from the land; (2) the *hali* system that is normally associated with the bonded-ness of entire families of low caste people, including their children and women, to varied forms of labour, and (3) the *dhakre* system that is associated with traders bringing their porters under debt and then using them for free labour. There are several other forms of bondage, including *khetala*, *jana*, *bali*, etc.[16]

These are the unchanging conditions of socio-economic exploitation and injustices under which the Maoist uprising developed. Article 25(2) of the Nepali Constitution, adopted in 1990, stipulates that: "The fundamental economic objective of the State shall be to transform the national economy into an independent and self-reliant system by preventing the available resources and means of the country from being concentrated within a limited section of society, by making arrangements for the equitable distribution of economic gains on the basis of social justice, by making such provisions as will prevent economic exploitation of any class or individual, and by giving preferential treatment and encouragement to national enterprises, both private and public."

Clearly, the vision of economic policies of the State encapsulated in Article 25(2) of the 1990 Constitution failed to take shape throughout Nepal because it remained a verbal statement and the political parties that steered the democratic ship of the State after 1990 had no commitment to it. The Maoist insurgency became widespread because it attempted to unite the underdogs throughout Nepal through a common awareness of their conditions of poverty, injustice, and the total absence of attention towards their needs that was characteristic of the governments before and after the democratic restoration.

Some participants of the course referred to the way in which the State of Nepal discriminates against the *Awadhi*-speaking Madises of the *Terai* in favour of new immigrants from the hills. The picture that we obtain of the conditions of socio-economic exploitation and deliberate underdevelopment of the mid-western hills, the heartland of the Maoist insurgency, suggests that the State of Nepal failed to transcend its feudal primitivism even after the so-called democratic revolution in 1990 and that it remains uniformly unjust towards all of its people who do not belong to its medieval network of privilege and power. It is quite possible that the State of Nepal finds it easy to use the hill migrants in the *Terai* to perpetuate its practices of exploitation of the indigenous people of the region. But clearly its practices towards the people of the hills, in their regions, are no better. The "rapid growth" of conflict in Nepal owes much to the prevalence of socio-economic injustice, to the exclusion of the most deprived from the developmental process, and to practices of governance without accountability. She also points out that a meaningful resolution of the conflict will elude until the fundamental causes from which it springs are honestly addressed.

(4) Failures of the 1990 democratic revolution in the country owing to its own internal shortcomings and the malpractices of power that quickly corrupted its promises and possibilities have contributed to the transference of the radical reformist politics into revolutionary channels. The constitutional deficiencies of the State that allow State institutions, including the judiciary, to actively or obliquely connive in human rights abuses and to rely on militarization to deal with expressions of popular discontent with impunity are obvious. Clearly, peace initiatives to resolve the current conflict between the State and the Maoists would be meaningful only if they confer pre-eminent attention to the issues of fundamental human rights.

In our view, the issues of the discourse on the nature of the Constitution in Nepal and of the controversies about the character and the magnitude of human rights abuses perpetrated by the State of Nepal are inseparably entangled.

Since the immediate discussion about human rights abuses in Nepal arises in the context of the conflict between the State and the Maoists, we should pay some attention to what constitutes as the core of Maoist demands. There is, of course, the 40-point Charter, which was submitted to the government for implementation before the Maoist group declared its "People's War" in February 1996. There is nothing fundamentally radical about the Charter. Its demands to remove "all unequal stipulations and agreements" from the 1950 Treaty between India and Nepal; to control the Nepal-India border; to close down the Gorkha recruiting centres; etc., are demands that have been made intermittently by leaders belonging to various political parties and groups. The main demand, under point 10, asks for "a new Constitution" to be drafted by the people's elected representatives. Under points 11 and 12, the Charter demands the end of "all the special rights and privileges of the king and his family", and requires that "the army, police and the administration should be under the people's control". Once again, these are promises and commitments that the Rana rulers and King Tribhuvan had made to the people of Nepal 54 years ago when they accepted the 8th December, 1950 memorandum from the Government of India initiating the negotiations that culminated in the Delhi Agreement of February 1951. The demand, under point 16, that the government should constitute a special investigating committee to determine the facts and the responsibilities for the disappearances of a number of people from police custody, at different times, is also the minimum any human rights organization must seek from the Nepali government, not only for the cases listed in the Charter, but for a myriad other cases of enforced disappearances and extra judicial executions that have since occurred. The demand, under point 18, that Nepal should be declared a secular State is an obligation that Nepal is subjected to after having adopted the Universal Declaration of Human Rights and also having ratified the International Covenant on Civil and Political Rights (ICCPR); the International Convention on the Elimination of All Forms of Racial Discrimination (ICERD); and the International Covenant on Economic, Social and Cultural Rights (ICESCR). Other demands, too, are liberal and democratic. Some of them are: To end exploitation and prejudices based on caste; gender discrimination in civil law; to guarantee the equality of all native languages and to offer the opportunity to be educated in the mother tongue until the middle-high school level; to ensure free speech and free press; to safeguard the autonomy of the communication media; to preserve academic freedom; to promote the decentralization of power. More radical demands correspond to the programmes of several mainstream socialist political parties in South Asia. They are: The right of ownership of land for those who actually cultivate it; a right to employment; minimum wage laws for workers in industry and agriculture; a protection against homelessness and the guarantee of shelter; the redemption of poor farmers from debt; support for small industry; ensuring fair prices for agricultural produce; relief to victims of flood and drought; the provision of drinking water, electricity and roads to all villages; measures against corruption in public life; and help and protection to orphans and the disabled.

Even the decision to declare a "people's war" after the government failed to respond to the Charter is not in any way unique if we examine it in the context of the modern political history of Nepal. The Nepali Congress itself has waged such wars, for the sake of democracy, in the past.

We can examine the war and its escalation separately. It is enough to recall that the submission of the 40-point Charter as well as the declaration of a "people's war" in the wake of a lack of response by the government in February 1996 is widely acknowledged to be the outcome of a sustained campaign against State terror from 1991 to 1996, under various democratic governments. The terror campaigns aimed to politically demoralize the people of the mid-western hills who had elected nine members of Parliament belonging to the United Popular Front of Nepal [UPFN]. According to a report by International Crisis Group,[17] "...efforts directed by the Congress Party leadership to suppress leftist political activity in the mountainous West, including through violent means such as the police-led Operation Romeo, only galvanized both the Maoists and a rising tide of localized resentment. An international official noted that, "the police reverted to the way they had behaved during the *panchayat* era because they had no other framework of experience", and even a senior Nepalese government official agreed that Operation Romeo was little more 'than the use of police for looting'. These heavy-handed police operations are widely seen in retrospect as a disaster that provided vital fuel for the insurgency."[18]

But we shall return to the issues of the war and violence after completing our point about the interconnectedness of the demands for human rights accountability and an end to impunity on the one hand and for a constitutional revision through an elected Constituent Assembly. Michael Hutt, a British scholar from the School of Oriental and African Studies at London, has documented the process of drafting the 1990 Constitution of Nepal in the wake of the so-called "Democratic Revolution". Apparently, it came to a successful conclusion with the truce in April 1990 between the political parties, mainly the Nepali Congress Party and the United Left Front spearheading the 'revolution', and the palace. The leaderships of the two parties have since been blamed for calling off their agitation without obtaining a clear abrogation of the 1962 Constitution, promulgated by King Mahendra, and without a commitment to elect a Constituent Assembly to draft a new Constitution. In April itself, a new government under Prime Minister Krishna Prasad Bhattarai, a Nepali Congress leader, and also including the ULF and others, took office. Several left wing political groups continued to insist that a new Constitution without an elected Constituent Assembly was meaningless. But the Nepali Congress justified its position by claiming that "the policy of national reconciliation between the palace and the people pursued by B.P. Koirala continues to be a part of Nepali Congress philosophy."[19] The Constitution Reforms Recommendation Commission, comprising seven members, was formed by King Birendra in May 1990. The Commission was asked to submit its recommendations within three months. Prime Minister Bhattarai disclosed that he had not been consulted about the formation of the Commission. A senior leader of the Nepali Congress, G.P. Koirala, described the process as "a great insult to the people of Nepal."[20] The Commission's Chairman, Justice Bishwanath Upadhyaya of the Supreme Court, resigned. Prime Minister Bhattarai announced the appointment of a new Commission, comprising nine members, once again with Justice Bishwanath Upadhyaya as the Chairman. On the 9th of July 1990, Justice Upadhyaya gave an interview in the course of which he expressed his concern about the procedure under way to develop a Constitution. He said: "The individual or institution who gives the Constitution is sovereign. The people will be sovereign if there is a Constituent Assembly, but we have not followed that path. If the Constitution is granted by the King, under what power should he do so?"[21]

On the 23rd of August 1990, Justice Upadhyaya announced that the draft of the Constitution would be submitted to King Birendra although there was no agreement among the Commission members on such critical issues as whether Nepal should remain a Hindu kingdom or should be declared a secular State. King Birendra received the draft of the Constitution from Justice Upadhyaha on the 10th of September 1990. The King returned the draft to the Prime Minister who, after making some changes at the recommendation of the Council of Ministers, resubmitted it to the King on the 11th of October. G.P. Koirala said that the process, which left the basic features of the Constitution in a state of uncertainty, was suicidal for democracy. The King said that he would study the draft of the Constitution to see to what extent it corresponded with his understanding of democracy.

Press reports throughout October talked about the strong differences between the palace and the Prime Minister about the language and the structure of the Constitution. Reports suggested that the King retained all the emergency powers that he possessed under the 1962 Constitution. Ganesh Man Singh reacted: "It is quite undemocratic to seek to promulgate a Constitution similar to that of 1962. No sane person can do it."[22] The Prime Minister offered to resign because "he would be unable to gain endorsement of the draft from the Congress party." [23] A press note from the palace said that "he had been fully consulted"[24] ; that it was only a "proposed draft" and that the new Constitution would be proclaimed on the 9th of November 1990. So, it was proclaimed.

Prime Minister Bhattarai hailed the new Constitution as a "historic document" which would never again allow Nepal to come under a "one-man rule." His prediction failed in October 2002 when King Gyanendra dismissed the Prime Minister and once again brought Nepal under his direct rule.

Clearly, the November 1990 Constitution of Nepal is the product of a compromise between the leaders of the "democratic revolution" and the "palace." It is very difficult to recognize anything democratic about the drafting procedure and the debates that followed before the Constitution took a final shape.[25]

We shall conclude this part of the discussion about the fundamentally undemocratic character of the Nepali Constitution with just one example about how it subordinates the concept of citizenship to the monarchic whims.

The 1962 constitution, under its Article 7, Part 2, defined citizenship in the following terms:

> "Every person who has his domicile in Nepal and — (a) who was born in Nepal; or (b) either of whose parents was born in Nepal; or who, as a woman, has any kind of relation with a citizen of Nepal constituting matrimony in accordance with the laws and customs of Nepal; or (d) who has already obtained a certificate of citizenship in accordance with the laws of Nepal; shall be a citizen of Nepal at the commencement of the Constitution." Article 8(3) of the same Constitution provided that "citizenship of a person may be terminated if — (a) he has raised arms or has made an attempt to raise arms against Nepal or has committed any other offence against the State; or (b) he has not served or avoids serving the State, during war or any other emergency, in the manner prescribed by law."

Article 7 of the 1962 Constitution remained valid until the promulgation of the November 1990 Constitution when the provisions for the annulment of citizenship were removed. However, Article 9(7) of the new Constitution says: "The termination of the citizenship of Nepal shall be as determined by law." And what is the law? The law is the *Nepal Citizenship Act, 1964* whose sections 10[2], (a) and (b) provide that Nepali citizenship may be terminated if a person raises arms or "attempts to raise arms" against the State and fails to serve the State during war or any other emergency. That is the law.[26]

As we know, a large number of Nepali people have taken up arms against the State and a still larger number of people, presumably, sympathize with the Maoist "people's war". Under the existing law of citizenship persons who have taken up arms can lose their citizenship. Once they lose their citizenship, they also lose the protective shield of fundamental human rights available to them as citizens under the Constitution. The significance of the loss of citizenship under the existing Constitution becomes more sinister if we view it in the light of the right against exile which the new Constitution provides under Article 21.

Let us try to visualize two different scenarios developing out of two different possible interpretations of the provisions: What happens to those who lose their citizenship by dint of their taking up arms against the State or due to their failure to assist it during a state of emergency? Do they still possess the fundamental human rights guaranteed to them under Part III of the Nepali Constitution (Articles 11 to 23)? Do they remain entitled to petition the Supreme Court for the enforcement of these rights? Can the Supreme Court exercise its power to issue writs including *habeas corpus, mandamus, certiorari, prohibition,* and *quo warranto* to compel the State to enforce the fundamental rights expressly available to citizens under the Constitution after the State has consciously stripped them of their citizenship? Can the State exile the people whose citizenship has been stripped? If not, what happens to the people who lose their citizenship and along with it the constitutional remedies against the deprivation of fundamental human rights within the institutional framework of Nepali polity? What meaning can the claim that "sovereignty resides in the people", as the Nepali Constitution under Articles 2 and 3 makes, have when the same Constitution authorizes the State institutions to divest the people of their citizenship and their rights?

The demand for an elected Constituent Assembly to write a new Constitution for Nepal, therefore, becomes a minimalist agenda that must unite all democratic forces in the country. The fact that this has not happened indicates that the political parties, that have been at the forefront of democratic reforms since King Mahendra dissolved the first elected government in December 1959 to assume totalitarian powers, are themselves rooted in the medieval ethos of power that guided the consolidation of Nepal as a Hindu kingdom under a Gorkha principality between 1742-1775. The Maoist demand for a Constituent Assembly is neither new nor radical. Nepal was rid of the Rana tyranny under the pledge that it would adopt a democratic Constitution drafted by an elected Constituent Assembly. The Maoist strategy of launching an armed struggle is also not new or radical. In April 1950, the Nepali Congress formed a liberation army and declared an armed struggle to rid the country of the Rana tyranny. King Tribhuvan and several members of his family, who aligned themselves with the call for liberation made by the Nepali Congress, were flown to Delhi in a special Indian Air Force plane on the 10th of November 1950, and the Nepali Congress captured most of the western *Terai* and declared it to be a liberated zone before the Rana regime agreed to abdicate it in February 1951. The current King of Nepal, King Gyanendra was then a 4-year-old infant and was anointed as the nominal King by the then Rana rulers to thwart the liberation struggle that the Nepali Congress had launched.

Gyanendra regained his kingship 51 years later following the royal massacre of June 2001. The armed struggle he faces today is more formidable than the struggle launched by the Nepali Congress in 1950. However, this is not the only example of attempts at armed struggle for democracy in Nepal. After King Mahendra dismissed the first elected government of Nepal under B.P. Koirala's prime ministry on the 15th of December 1960, the Nepali Congress again launched an armed struggle with covert Indian support that was withdrawn in the wake of the war between China and India, in October 1962.

(5) Several participants of the fifth course referred to the anomalies evident in the affirmation of the post-Cold War era as the age of human rights enforcement on the one hand, and the apparent realities of continuous human rights abuses committed against hapless people globally by States and other political agencies that pursue power through violence and with impunity. They also pointed out to the fact that whereas the Universal Declaration of Human Rights, adopted by the UN in 1948, is publicized as the universal law that transcends the laws and customs of independent sovereignty, the UN system is rarely able to challenge and effectively intervene against the rampant abuses of power that take place under the cloak of the sovereignty of nations. International interventions, when they occur, seem to happen on a politically selective basis whereby the principles of international human rights law take second place as against the political interests of the big powers who sponsor them. Taking stock of the conditions of the political conflict currently savaging Nepal, they asked: "So how do we go ahead? What does this mean for a young democracy like Nepal that is fighting its own 'insurgency' and where thousands of 'crimes against humanity' are taking place? Why has there not been more robust international criticism against such abuses? Who do the victims turn to for justice in the absence of national and international mechanisms of protection?" Can the International Criminal Court become the body to intervene in the internal affairs of sovereign States out of humanitarian necessity? Is there a way to strengthen regional treaty systems and their mechanisms to improve the track-record of enforcement of international human rights law in municipal courts throughout the world? Can South Asia develop some system of transnational governance different from the SAARC that will contribute to the democratization of States within the region as well as to improve the relations among them? Why

have the waves of democratization in South Asia not really been successful in establishing peace and development? How do we democratize democracy so that it may go hand in hand with justice, development, and peace?

These are difficult questions and our comments belong to the same spirit of inquiry for hard-to-find answers that pervade our participants' inquiries.

Talking about international human rights law, we should be aware that even Common Article 3 of the four Geneva Conventions of 1949, which binds the contracting States to "respect and ensure respect" for the provisions "in all circumstances", provides no mechanism for its implementation based on an appeal by victims of a violation. Common Article 3 affirms the principles of protection towards civilian populations in conflict situations irrespective of whether they are internal in nature or involve two independent countries.

What meaning can the principle have when access to international human rights mechanisms is exclusively limited to State actors? Even the International Humanitarian Fact-Finding Commission, established in 1991 to secure implementation of the Conventions, can initiate investigations only when the States concerned, and not their people, approach it for action. Regional forums like the European Court of Human Rights, which entertain individual complaints and have enforced the international standards of the laws of war in a number of cases, as for example in the case regarding the 1988 killing of three Irish suspects in Gibraltar by Special Air Service officials of the UK, have no jurisdiction over matters that involve violations committed outside the continent. The simple fact is that for people affected by State atrocities and political violence in Asia and Africa, there is no forum or mechanism to realize the right to remedy even when infringements involve binding obligations under international law *unless* State actors are willing to take action on their behalf. Frank Berman, the Legal Adviser to the Foreign and Commonwealth Office in the UK, sums up the problem in the following words: "It seems to many that the problem is not to discover what the law is, or how to apply it to the particular case, or even whether the existing rule is "satisfactory" or not, but rather how to secure or compel compliance with the law at all."[27]

The history of international human rights law is a history of conflict between rhetorical visions and the realities of power politics. Harold Hongj Koh, former Assistant Secretary of State for Democracy,

Human Rights and Labour in the USA from 1998 to 2001 and currently a professor of International Law at Yale, sums up the realistic perspective championed by many theorists and practitioners of international relations, like Hans Morgenthau and Henry Kissinger, in his own paraphrasing of Thucydides' wisdom: "the strong States do what they can, the weak suffer what they must, but in the end there is no real "obedience" of international law, only such coincidence between national conduct and international rules that results from power and coercion." This wisdom of political power not only steers the dominant theories and practices of international relations, but also the realities of the sovereign relations of States with their people. The rhetoric of the inalienability of human rights, accountability, and end of impunity that saturates political discourse worldwide has not been able to affect the realities.

But the questions that animate our discussions, seeking ways to enforce truth, justice, reparation, accountability, and an end to impunity within the framework of a universal human rights law, are premised on a view of power that stands feebly in its idealism in opposition to Thucydides' wisdom. It is a view that foresees eventual debacles for all sides when relations between the powerful and the powerless become bereft of human rights norms.

The challenges for those who stand for that spirit of idealism that cannot brook with Thucydides' wisdom are many. We cannot close our eyes to the dramatic changes underway since the beginning of the global war on terror that radically undermine the notions of inalienable rights. Within the framework of this war, all radical resistance has become banditry, terrorism, and zealotry. State representatives and the leaders of the so-called free media refer to violent resisters as 'terrorists'. Terrorism experts and political analysts, popular on TV talk shows, converse about the coming together of issues like "civilization versus the axis of evil", "terrorism versus global security." The proximate political objectives of the war remain uncertain. Certain, however, is their shattering impact on the glasshouse of human rights, raised largely in the interlude between World War II and the "global war on terror" proclaimed by the United States in the wake of the 11th of September 2001.

The cessation of dialogue between those who speak in the name of civilization on the one hand, and a great variety of discontented groups and individuals lurking beyond its frontiers in the shadowy realms of violence and chaos on the other, is probably the most, significant attribute of the polarity within the emergent world order. During the Cold War era, Marxist critiques of the capitalist world resonated widely. They even inspired vibrant and often sympathetic responses within the western world. The Marxist appeal for a revolutionary overthrow of an unjust social order received elegant rebuttals and thoughtful reflections on the origins and dynamics of inequalities in relations of production and the meaning of liberation in the age of technology. The new polarity, by unconditionally renouncing the path of dialogue, strikes a posture of intransigence whose implications are wide-ranging. Strategic concerns for security and stability within the emerging world order appear to be fixated by uncanny but unknowable dangers associated with the shadowy world of "terror," its perpetrators and its sponsors. Terrorists and their sponsors do not qualify for the legal respect and political protocol that were bestowed on the hostile and belligerent enemy within the bipolar world order. 'Terrorists' and their 'sponsors', no matter what their location within the State structures, lose the political standing necessary to enter mechanisms to peacefully resolve disputes. This situation conveys a growing subordination of politics to the power of the military that further destroys the meaning of the laws of war and of customary international human rights law.

We already referred to the failures of international human rights mechanisms in enforcing even the obligatory provisions of customary human rights law. The talk about the interventionist role of the United Nations, too, appears to be largely meaningless. The emergent world order has very clearly exposed the anomalies between the statement of objectives in the UN Charter and its organizational arrangements that allow the world's remaining Superpower to use the Security Council (UNSC) and its bureaucracy to further its foreign policy objectives. The UNSC is supposed to hold the Charter responsibility to save the world from the scourge of war, to ensure international peace, security, and human rights. Those who have paid attention to international politics, even cursorily, since the collapse of the iron curtain are not left with any doubt that the United Nations has moved beyond the hapless neutrality it maintained during the Cold War period to become an international political instrument of the remaining Superpower.

Reforming the United Nations has for long been a pet topic of those who tarry in its corridors but do not obtain access to the private chambers where privileged bureaucrats of the organization assemble and scheme. Their ideas of reform lack teeth and mostly do not amount to anything more than tickling a purring cat. The crimes of commission and omission, by the United Nations and the transformation of its role from ensuring peace and promoting human rights to providing foot-soldiers for global imperial projects, require a scrutiny that must originate in a more critical spirit. Can a world organization, led by the most powerful States that control the Security Council, be trusted to act in accordance with the noble principles of its Charter when it is not bound by any human rights treaty and convention? Is not the working of the Security Council genuinely undemocratic and almost always hostile to the principles and proposals that emanate from the General Assembly? Yet, the Security Council, its legislative fiats and commands for action, are supreme and beyond question. Is there any national or international court that can claim to possess jurisdiction over and the power to question and rescind Security Council decisions on the grounds of illegality? The United Nations is not a State. It is an organization of States. The United Nations does not possess juridical or criminal jurisdiction over sovereign States that are its members. Yet, its dictates are binding and unquestionable even as its actions remain uninhibited by laws and fears of institutional scrutiny. All its members are constitutional States that are sworn to respect and adhere to international laws and treaties. The UNSC operates as a body unshackled by any international laws and treaties.

A Security Council represents a global power-configuration that emerged half a century ago. It relies on the military might of the only Superpower in the world to obtain compliance with its resolutions that are completely self-governing and are not dependent on a normative framework of law. Yet, the body claims to represent a transnational moral authority. A General Assembly, with countries of less than a million and others of more than a billion commanding one vote each, also cannot be expected to set the norms of global democracy; not even in principle. Given the supine role of the UN in relation to the United States over the last years, it does not even enjoy the prestige of a rubber-stamp assembly. It has become more of a dust-bin into which States like the US discard their failed experiments, or those of which they tire, or which become too messy and too costly.

Yet, despite all its failings, no one is wishing or calling for a dismantling of the UN. That is because it seems to answer the need for international legislation and even in its mediocre role as an occasional peacekeeper it remains without replacement. Also, it functions as a natural focal point for mankind to speak with mankind. Hopefully, one day, following radical reforms, the forces of shared morality and shared values will feel stronger and more able, through the UN agency, to prevail over the military might and brutal logic of force and coercion that the word "realism" evokes today. But this will clearly take time and we can only hope that the reformers from within and those working outside the UN system will not tire.

Meanwhile, those who remain committed to peace, human rights, justice and democracy in a country like Nepal must show the courage to forge internally viable alternatives to international interventions and mediations. We believe that this is a precondition for the conflict to end and for the discovery of rules of governance that will genuinely address the long legacies of socio-economic injustices, cultural discrimination, and political subjugation of people, which is responsible for the consciousness of discontent and its eruption in violence.

This requires, first and foremost, an engagement of the civil society segments, themselves disinterested in the games of power, with the issues underlying the unrest and the insurgency in a spirit of truth, courage, and objective understanding. This engagement must be based on the courage and the capacity to generate a truthful, even if unpleasant, but rationally manageable discourse on the failures of the mainstream institutions, including the parliamentary parties, various organs of the State, the professional and business bodies, the INGO and NGO sectors, and the donor agencies, in living up to the expectations of the people.

All too often, "peace processes" and reconciliatory efforts in conflict situations tend to revolve around narrow politicians' concerns such as elections or the terms of power-sharing among various political groups. Experience shows that even if these arrangements work, the new governments remain weak and fail to come to grips with the basics of democratic rule. They spend all their time trying to consolidate their power base, or merely to retain it, at the expense of the real issues such as the revitalization of broken economies, the rebuilding of welfare institutions, legal reforms, and the redressal of socio-economic imbalances. As a result, even the superficial achievements brought about by reconciliation tend to break down. To pre-empt such failures, the search for peace should widen its attention to all issues of vital importance to the community, and explore possibilities of constructive engagement for political, economic, and legal justice. Joint projects for community development, educational and sensitization programmes, attention to human rights issues and redress of wrongs can also be of much help. The meaning of civil society initiatives, in ideal terms, is to make people recognize that they need not remain passive subjects of politics, tossed to and fro by forces infinitely beyond their control. Rather they may also, if they so choose, become active agents of history. Our historical and political inheritance, with the ideas and symbols that currently hold sway, neither exhausts reality, nor does it amount to a binding format for social action.

The success of civil society initiatives depends on their capacity to engage with the people caught in the state of conflict, in neutral and objective terms; to glean the primary data and the spectrum of perceptions of the concerned people about possible solutions, and to generate a discourse that aims at evolving flexible models of mediation. David Seddon and Karim Hussein, in their 2002 working paper titled "The Consequences of Conflict: Livelihoods and Development in Nepal", point out that "across Nepal, INGOs and NGOs, in particular, have valuable bodies of data collected but not adequately analyzed which would give the lie to the often repeated nostrum that relatively little is known about rural livelihoods—a lot is known but it seems not to be easily accessible."[28] This suggests insufficient interest or even lack of respect for empirical knowledge.

The success of such initiatives also depends on their honesty and the courage of conviction of specific individuals and organizations leading them. For example, international agencies and NGOs have, for long, been involved in a wide variety of developmental programmes with foreign donors contributing more than 60 percent of Nepal's developmental budget. Yet, the poorest, the most deprived and socially vulnerable groups of people remain outside their reach. In spite of much rhetoric about their schemes being guided by the rights-based approach, they have been unable to make much dent against "bonded labour, untouchability, gender discrimination, and other forms of exploitation, oppression and social injustices."[29]

Empirical research is also required to understand the apparatus of local governance, and "their distinctive forms of law and order", which the Maoists are reported to be establishing in "areas of their military and political control." They have reportedly been issuing codes of conduct or 'Directives' and also manuals, spelling out the rules, regulations, rights and responsibilities of their "People's Government." What exactly do these manuals and codes say and how helpful are they in introducing new practices of good governance? How fairly and "legally" do their "police" and "courts" function? The Maoists are reported to have established rural cooperative banks and credit institutions in some areas, ostensibly to support the poor and the needy with loans at low interest rates. How do these financial institutions function? Are they sustainable in the long-term? The Maoists are also collecting "contributions" and "tax" from people in areas under their control. Are these collections fair and bearable? Or, do they display extortionist tendencies? The Maoists have taken over a number of village schools to run their own indoctrination camps. Besides indoctrination, have the Maoists been able to communicate an approach to education and a curriculum that fulfils the requirements of basic education in rural areas by impartial standards?

The Maoists have been recruiting able-bodied young men and women for their guerrilla armies and People's Militia. Many young people are reportedly fleeing rural areas to avoid joining their ranks. How systematically coercive and brutal are the practices of the Maoists in forcing people, against their will, to join their ranks and what impact is this having on the capacities of rural families to secure livelihood?

The Maoists are also reported to have initiated a number of developmental projects, especially in cooperative farming; the pooling of skills in handicrafts and cottage industries; the construction of village roads; small irrigation scheme and drinking water facilities; etc. How viable and rational are these projects and how voluntary is the nature of the people's participation?

The purpose of these inquiries and research should be to generate a climate of attention on substantial issues that may have some influence on the dialogue process between the State and the rebellious groups. It should be possible for civil society initiatives to convey, with sufficient clarity and the force of public opinion, that to reject the road to peace only because the Maoists insist on a democratically elected Constituent Assembly is to perpetuate the error that has been the bane of democratic political life in Nepal since 1950. It should also be possible to make clear that using the rhetoric of emancipation, without a rational content and programmatic clarity, can have no relevance to resolving systemic political maladies with deep roots in history.

Civil society initiatives, if they proceed in this spirit of attention to the substantial issues underlying the discontent, of truth, and of courage of conviction, can certainly become a bulwark to protect the peace process against the forces of sabotage. These initiatives, in this spirit, can also prevail on all parties to the conflict to take the broadest possible view of "peace"—peace being not just the sheathing of daggers or the silencing of guns, but a quest for reconciliation, based on a sense of public purpose, a culture of dialogue and mediation, and a scrupulous recognition of everyone's rights. This leads us to the last point of this discussion on Nepal about the dynamics of political violence employed by the Maoist insurgents and its impact on the most vulnerable sections of the population, especially women and children.

(6) Students of armed struggles are very well aware of how these struggles tend to degenerate into organized criminality, notwithstanding their pre-natal idealism. The types of persons drawn to become armed fighters, by the very nature of their choice, tend to be violent, if not already with criminal propensities even if sublimated. Although it is difficult for us to say anything very definite in the absence of sufficient empirical exposure, it is clear that the Maoist insurgents, lacking in discipline and self-control to refrain from committing excesses, cannot for long retain their image as harbingers of a just society. Indeed, there can be no point in protesting against the violence wrought by the State if the protestors are merely going to augment these excesses with their own actions. Such actions can and should only arouse revulsion in morally sensitive people. Such excesses, apart from providing the State with an excuse to unleash atrocities on innocent people, cannot but corrupt the moral sensibilities of those very persons who may have joined the revolt with idealistic motives.

In the best of circumstances, perpetrators of such "revolutionary excesses" will be nagged by guilt; guilt will produce its usual antidote: cynicism. And, cynicism will eventually destroy the relevance of their ideas and the legitimacy of their actions. But the result may be something far worse than cynicism. The rebels guilty of excesses may become inured to guilt. They may acquire the automatism of self-justification in the name of "the Cause"; come to feel that they are above all rules, and develop into an unspeakable breed of players with the lives of others. By comparison, unadulterated criminality is less horrendous because, being unambiguous, it cannot confuse anyone.

This, of course, is a generalization. An absolute moral prohibition of violence has no meaning in a world that is often confronted with the evidence that non-violence, in specific historical contexts, can become the wellspring of catastrophe for the survival of humanity. For example, non-violence towards Hitler can also be described as acquiescence in the Holocaust. Ted Honderich, a well-known philosopher of the left, examines political violence, now universally identified as terrorism, in its less recognized aspects: "It is also an ongoing reply to State-terrorism, self-defence, defence of a homeland, freedom-fighting, liberation struggle, personal self-sacrifice in the hope of gaining great goods for others, defence against ethnic cleansing, a struggle of a people for their survival, terrorism for humanity."[30]

This is a possible, even if an embroidered, view of political violence. From our point of view, it is difficult to agree with the purity of a political intention that must systematically rely on the use of physical force that injures, violates, or destroys people; their lives and their notions of possibilities.

Notes

1. Hutt, Michael, *Unbecoming Citizens: Culture, Nationhood, and the Flight of Refugees from Bhutan* (New Delhi: Oxford University Press, 2003) 23-24; Report on a visit to Bhutan, Basil Gould, Political Officer Sikkim to Government of India, 26 August 1938, OIOC L/P&S/12/2222, quoted in Michael Hutt, ibid., p. 37.
2. Hutt, Michael, *Unbecoming Citizens*, supra, pp. 46-57; J.L.R. Weir, P.O. Sikkim, to GOI, letter 31(1)-P/29, 7 December 1929, OIOC Mss. Eur. L/P&S/12/3005, quoted in Michael Hutt, ibid., pp. 86-7
3. Colonel J.P. Cross, *The Call of Nepal*, (Kathmandu: Bibliotheca Himalayica, 1996).
4. Yeoman Barry, "Soldiers of good fortune", *Mother Jones* 28, 3 (1 May 2003); Shawcross, William, *Deliver Us from Evil: Warlords and Peacekeepers in a World of Endless Conflict* (London: Bloomsbury, 2000) 171-175.
5. David Seddon and Karim Hussein, "The Consequences of Conflict: Livelihoods and Development in Nepal", Working Paper 185, Overseas Development Institute, 111 Westminster Bridge Road, London, SE1 7 JD, UK, December 2002, Introduction, p. 3.
6. Robert Gersony, "Sowing the Wind: History and Dynamics of the Maoist Revolt in Nepal's Rapti Hills", Report submitted to Nancy Lindborg, Vice-President Mercy Corps International, October 2003, pp. 15-21.

7. David Seddon, "Democracy and Development in Nepal" in Michael Hutt ed. *Nepal in the Nineties* (New Delhi: Oxford University Press, 1993) 133.
8. Sudhindra Sharma, "The Hindu State and the state of Hinduism" in Kanak Mani Dixit and Shastri Ramachandaran ed. *State of Nepal* (Lalitpur, Nepal: Himal Books, 2002) 25.
9. Hutt, Michael, *Unbecoming Citizens: Culture, Nationhood, and the Flight of Refugees from Bhutan* (New Delhi: Oxford University Press, 2003) 86-89.
10. Blaikie, P., *et al.*, *Nepal in Crisis* (New York: Oxford University Press, 1980); Bolt, Davis., *Gurkhas* (London: Weidenfeld and Nicolson, 1967); Dahal, D.R., *et al.*, *Land and Migration in Far-Western Nepal* (Kathmandu: Institute of Nepal and Asian Studies, Tribhuvan University, 1977; Elder, J.W., *et al.*, *Planned Resettlement in Nepal* (Kathmandu: Institute of Nepal and Asian Studies, Tribhuvan University, 1974); Husain, A., *British India's Relations with the Kingdom of Nepal* (London: Allen and Unwin, 1970); Kansakar, V. B. S., *Effectiveness of Planned Resettlement Programmeme in Nepal* (Kathmandu: CEDA, 1979); V.B.S. Kansakar, "Land Resettlement Policy as a Population Distribution Strategy in Nepal", in L.A. Kosinski and K.M. Elahi eds., *Population Redistribution and Development in South Asia* (Amsterdam: Reidel, 1985); W. Ladejnsky, "Tenurial conditions in Nepal" in *Agrarian Reform as Unfinished Business: the Selected Papers of Wolf Ladejinsky*, ed. by L.J. Walinsky (New York: World Bank, 1977); Macfarlane, A., *Resources and Population: A Study of the Gurungs of Nepal* (London: Cambridge University Press, 1976); Mihaly, E.B., *Foreign Aid and Politics in Nepal* (London: Oxford University Press, 1965).
11. Caplan, L., *Land and Social Change in East Nepal* (Berkeley: University of California Press, 1970); Hitchcock, J.T., *The Magars of Banyan Hill* (New York: Holt & Co., 1961); Messerschmidt, D.A., *The Gurungs of Nepal* (Forest Grove: Aris and Phillips, 1976); and McDougal, C., *Villages and Household Economy in Western Nepal* (Kathmandu: Tribhuvan University Press, 1968).
12. Caplan, L., *Land and Social Change in East Nepal* (Berkeley: University of California Press, 1970) 64.
13. Regmi, M.C., *A Study of Nepali Economic History, 1868-1846* (Delhi: Majushri, 1971) 102-111.
14. Sharma, Shiva and Thakurathi, Manasa, *A Revisit to the Kamaiya System of Nepal* (Kathmandu: INSEC, 1998) 11.
15 "No Maghi for Freed Kamaiyas", *The Kathmandu Post*, January 11, 2001.
16. Omar Sattaur, Child *Labour in Nepal: A Report by Anti-Slavery International and Child Workers Nepal Concerned Centre* (Kathmandu:

SANN Research Institute, 1993) 44-45; Shiva Sharma and Manasa Thakurathi, *A Revisit to the Kamaiya System of Nepal* (Kathmandu: INSEC, 1998).

17. *Nepal Backgrounder: Ceasefire – Soft Landing Or Strategic Pause?*, Asia Report No. 50, (Kathmandu: Brussels: International Crisis Group) released on the 10th of April 2003 at http://www.crisisgroup.org/home/index.cfm?id=1642&l=1
18. *Ibid.*, p. 4.
19. Michael Hutt, "Drafting of the 1990 Constitution" in Michael Hutt ed. *Nepal in the Nineties* (New Delhi: Oxford University Press, 1993) 28-47.
20. *Ibid.*
21. *Ibid.*
22. *Ibid.*
23. *Ibid.*
24. *Ibid.*
25. *Ibid.*
26. Nepal Constitution at http://www.oefre.unibe.ch/law/icl/np00000_.html.
27. F.D. Berman in his Preface *Armed Conflict and the New Law*, eds. Hazel Fox and Michael Meyer (London: British Institute of International and Comparative Law, 1993) xii.
28. David Seddon and Karim Hussein, "The Consequences of Conflict: Livelihoods ad Development in Nepal", Working Paper 185, December 2002, Overseas Development Institute, 111 Westminster Bridge road, London, SE 1 7JD, UK, pp. 2, 12.
29. *Ibid.*, pp. 2, 12.
30. Honderich, Ted, *Terrorism for Humanity: Inquiries in Political Philosophy* (London: Pluto Press, 2003) 5.

Chapter Nine

Conflicts of History and Humanism in South Asia

During the distance learning period, the participants and the faculty discussed several interesting issues involving conflicts between historically hallowed systems of customary knowledge, which support traditional hierarchies of exploitation in South Asia, and the humanistic visions of emancipation and ideological enunciations that inform the movements for democracy, just peace, and human rights in the region. Several participants enumerated the conditions and the realities of life in South Asia that interfere with the fulfilment of moral claims about the inalienability of human rights: "Poverty, illiteracy, unemployment, unequal treatment of women, violence against women, pollution, exploitation of child labour, and religious fundamentalism." They also reflected on how the 20th century history of South Asia, despite its myriad diversities, remains unified by common elements of injustice, suffering, and strife. Many referred to the success of political classes in manipulating people's susceptibilities on communal and religious issues to destroy or marginalize their struggles for justice, democracy, and human dignity. Many participants also pointed to the fact that the struggles of women, working classes, *dalits*, indigenous people, and religious and cultural minorities, for the fulfilment of their legally acknowledged rights, remain weak under the orchestrations of false issues by those who control the levers of power.

Some participants tried to grapple with the problem of seemingly impressive gains made by our societies in the enunciatory realm that nearly always falter in the domain of practice. One participant drew attention to the baffling contradiction between the levels of attention that acts of political violence, irrespective of their cause, receive, and the near total indifference with which gargantuan injustices, dispossession, and the suffering of the people, noticeably arising from the practices of political power, are met.

Yet another participant discussed the plight of *dalits* within the Hindu caste stratification in Nepal, despite the stipulations of the ICERD to which Nepal is a signatory, and suggested the enactment of special legislations, as existing in India, to prevent caste atrocities and to enforce a reservation policy to ensure adequate representation of *dalits* in services, education, and politics in the country.

Some participants focused attention on the issues that affect the lives of nearly two million refugees and internally displaced people in South Asia, with political persecution by the States, communal and religious strife, political violence, unemployment, poverty, and other structural inequities contributing to the making of the phenomena. The discussions on refugees and internally displaced people also touched the issue of "uni-culturalism", a tool of political consolidation for the States that emerged out of the colonial era with their multicultural ethos scorched under the ordeals of partitions. Internal displacement through organized violence in places like Gujarat, Assam, Manipur, and Kashmir in India; the forcible eviction of more than 70,000 Muslims by Tamil armed groups from northern Sri Lanka; the Bhutanese refugees in Nepal and now the uprooting of the people of Nepal under the present conditions of conflict, convey, as several participants said, facets of antagonistic relations that exist between the nation-states and their people. One participant came out with a set of recommendations, which he believed to be necessary to resurrect the human rights of refugees in South Asia and to reinstate their citizenship.

These discussions converge around two common themes. They take note of the enigmas of history with their power of causal and structural determinism, which perpetuate the conditions of socio-economic, political, and cultural injustices. They also point out the failures of humanistic projects of emancipation, reflected in the Constitutional declarations of the States, in the international human rights covenants they have ratified, as well as in the manifestos and agendas of those who constitute a radical opposition to the State practices, in taming the manifestations of historical malevolence.

India's size and the influence it wields in various realms of life within the subcontinent are important points of the regional history.

Let us start with the reports of mass atrocities being committed by the State forces in India to deal with situations of conflict, political recalcitrance, and insurgency in various parts of the country. Unlike other States in South Asia, India calls itself a democracy with an enlightened Constitution that recognizes the inalienability of human rights, and independent institutions like the judiciary to ensure their enforcement and accountability. It is, however, known that the Indian State has been very consistent in using brutal force to stamp out political struggles that radically reject its claim of representing legitimate authority. The Naga insurgency and the Telangana uprising were stamped out brutally by the Indian army, without any reference to the rule of law, under Nehru's premiership. The Naxalite movement was eradicated largely under Indira Gandhi's leadership by the same methods. The mass atrocities that accompanied counter-insurgency operations of the Indian State in various peripheral parts of the country, including Punjab, Jammu and Kashmir, and in the northeast, under various governments over the last two decades, are well documented. The Constitution and its agencies remained intact even as pervasive atrocities occurred. No official agency formally approved of them; all silently acquiesced. The operations did not develop out of deliberations or policy decisions; but the legislators and members of Parliament knew what was happening in their constituencies. Judges and magistrates colluded with the torture and elimination of detainees by literally closing their eyes to the evidence and by uncritically accepting the official denials and lies. The media appeased the State by practicing self-censorship. Many journalists in the print, wire and electronic media supported the murderous operations of the security forces more directly. This was the climate of approval in which the atrocities occurred and unless we recognize and address these issues contributing to the state of impunity in India, our insistence on truth, accountability, and justice will remain meaningless and hypocritical. But what does this recognition entail? Is there anything new in our knowledge about the crimes against humanity, attributed to the security forces, which the contemporary human rights documentation in India reveals?

The reports about the brutalities committed by the security agencies in India convey an extraordinary repetitiousness from the very beginning of their creation. The following are some examples: On the 9th of September 1854, the Governor in Council of Fort St. George appointed a Commission "for the investigation of alleged cases of torture at Madras". The report was released on the 16th of April 1855 after the Commission examined 519 oral and 1,440 written complaints. The Commission found that the practice of torture for collecting revenue, for obtaining confessions, and, "now and then", for extorting money was rampant. The methods of torture were described by the Commission in its report: "Among the principal tortures in vogue ... we find the following: twisting a rope tightly around the entire arm or leg so as to impede blood circulation; lifting up by the moustache; suspending by the arms while tied behind the back; placing scratching insects, such as the carpenter beetle on the naval, scrotum, and other sensitive parts; dipping in wells and rivers till the party is half suffocated; squeezing the testicles; beating with sticks; prevention of sleep; nipping the flesh with pincers; putting pepper or red chillies in the eyes or introducing them into the private parts of men or women; these cruelties occasionally persevered until death sooner or later ensured."[1] Those who are familiar with the current methodology of third degree torture practiced by the security agencies in politically volatile parts of the country and throughout South Asia, know that many new innovations have been added to the methods of torture discovered by the Torture Commission of 1854.

The report precipitated a fervent discussion in official circles of the British government in India, resulting in a number of amendments to the Police Act of 1861, the Indian Evidence Act, and the Indian Penal Code [IPC] that created elaborate procedural and statutory safeguards against custodial crimes, made custodial confessions inadmissible as evidence, and prescribed stringent punishment for custodial torture by law enforcement officials. Sections 330 and 331 of the IPC, which remain part of the code, read: Section 330: "Whoever voluntarily causes hurt for the purpose of extorting from the sufferer, or any person interested in the sufferer, any confession or any information which may lead to the detection of an offence or misconduct, ... shall be punishable with imprisonment of either description for a term which may extend to seven years, and shall also be liable to fine." Section 331: "Whoever voluntarily causes grievous hurt for the purpose of extorting from the sufferer, or from any person interested in the sufferer, any confession or any information which may lead to the detection of an offence ... shall be punishable with imprisonment of either description for a term which may extend to ten years, and shall also be liable to fine." Section 44 of the Code defined "injury" to mean "any harm whatever illegally caused to any person, in body, mind, reputation or property."

The Second Police Commission was appointed in July 1902. New laws had been in effect for decades. Yet, the Indian Police Commission of 1902-3, also known as the Fraser Commission after its chairperson Andrew H.L. Fraser, then Chief Commissioner of the Central Provinces, found that the police force continued to follow third degree torture. Its report said: "What wonder is it that the people are said to dread the police, and to do all they can to avoid any connection with a police investigation? Deliberate association with criminals in their gains, deliberately false charges against innocent persons on the ground of private spite or village faction, deliberate torture of suspected persons and other most flagrant abuses occur …"[2]

India after independence has seen through nine State Police Commissions. The Punjab Police Commission of 1961-62, headed by a former Chief Justice of India, had many comments to make on the Central Investigation Agency [CIA] of Punjab: "The Commission is of the opinion that most of the investigating officers have no training in the use of scientific methods of investigation, and the only method of investigation known to them is that of third degree. Third degree methods are used by them in one form or the other to extract confession or else such statements as make the use of section 27 of the Indian Evidence Act possible. The CIA, a special branch of this organization charged with the duty of investigation of heinous crimes, has acquired notoriety in the public for third degree methods and is styled as the "butcher-khana". Instances of people dying as a result of torture by the police are not wanting and this is a big blot on the organization."[3]

The third All India Police Commission, also called the National Police Commission, appointed in November 1977 discussed the use of third degree methods in its Fourth Report released in June 1980, and regretted that several police officers under pressure of work and driven by a desire to achieve quick results use force on witnesses, suspects and the accused.

On the 26th of August 1994, the Law Commission of India, headed by former Chief Justice of the Supreme Court K.N. Singh, submitted its 152nd Report on Custodial Crimes to the Prime Minister with the remark that "revolted by the increasing number of reports of custodial torture and deaths, the Law Commission had taken up the subject *suo motu* for an in-depth study."[4] The Commission concluded that the anomalies and contradictions in the law of evidence, especially between sections 26 and 27 of the Evidence Act, have significantly contributed to the pervasiveness of custodial torture. Section 26 of the Act holds that "no confession made by any person whilst in the custody of a police officer, unless it be made in the immediate presence of a magistrate, shall be proved as against such person." The Commission pointed out that the safeguard provided by this section against custodial torture was nullified by the exemption available under section 27 of the Evidence Act. According to section 27: "Provided that, when any fact is deposed to as discovered in consequence of information received from a person accused of any offence, in the custody of a police officer, so much of such information, whether it amounts to a confession or not, as are related distinctly to the fact thereby discovered, may be proved." The Law Commission of India recommended the repeal of section 27.[5]

In constitutional terms, the protection against custodial torture is embedded in the fundamental guarantee to the 'Right to Life' under Article 21 of the Constitution.

In *Kharak Singh Vs. State of U.P.* 1963, Justice Ayyangar of the Supreme Court of India quoted an American Supreme Court judge: "By the term life, as here used, something more is meant than mere animal existence. The inhibition against its deprivation extends to all these limits and faculties by which life is enjoyed. The provision equally prohibits the mutilation of the body or amputation of an arm or leg or the putting out of an eye or the destruction of any other organ of the body through which the soul communicates with the outer world."[6]

A large number of subsequent cases decided by the Supreme Court have reinforced the injunction against torture, as a part of the right to life. Torture, as an element of punishment in any form and for any reason, is unconstitutional.[7] Even physical restrictions in custody that amount to physical or mental infliction of pain are impermissible.[8] The physical and mental restraint of prisoners, which is not warranted by the punishment awarded by the court and is in excess of the requirements of discipline, amounts to human degradation and cannot be tolerated.[9]

In a number of judgments, the Supreme Court has taken a strong stance against officials responsible for custodial torture. In 1932, while India was still a British colony, the Madras High Court ruled that no sanction for prosecution under section 197 of the Code of

Criminal Procedure was necessary when an officer of the state, who had the power to arrest and hold in custody persons suspected of offences, misused the power to torture him to obtain a confessional avowal.[10] In 1985, the Supreme Court of India ruled that in cases of custodial torture, where victims are left without any evidence except their own statements, the customary law of the burden of proof has to change and courts are free to infer guilt against accused officials.[11] The judgment inspired the Law Commission of India to recommend the insertion of a new section in the Indian Evidence Act. Although the recommendation has not resulted in the necessary amendment, the Supreme Court has upheld the principle in two other important cases. In a 1992 judgment, the Court ruled that "when the other evidence is convincing enough to establish that the deceased died because of injuries inflicted by the accused, the circumstances would only lead to an irresistible inference that the police personnel who caused his death must also have caused the disappearance of the body."[12] In yet another case involving a person found dead with injuries on his body after the police had taken him into their custody, the Supreme Court held that the "burden was on the State to establish how the victim came to sustain the injuries resulting in his death."[13]

We can go on illustrating the lofty principles with more quotations from the Supreme Court's judgments and parliamentary speeches. But, as we have already seen, the constitutional and judicial professions not only remain ineffective against pervasive practices, but are diametrically contradicted by them. The question is: what explains the imperturbability of the security establishment in India over the last hundred and fifty years despite the commissions, judicial indictments, and legislative reforms? Does not the persistence of the problem suggest that the matter has little to do with pious professions in the Constitution and the laws deriving from it?

The working of the elitist mind in India, throughout history, displays an extraordinary easiness in dealing with contradictions of profession and practice, and an uncanny felicity to spawn immaculate concepts of liberation in the realm of "pure spirit" even as life, in the world of dust and tears, continues to writhe in the abysm of misery. Is not such a radical dissociation between thought and reality a delusional aspect of social relations in which all glories go to the principal classes and all gloom and grief to the faceless masses?

Untouchability is an offence under the law. Yet every year, hundreds of *Harijans* are killed for daring to challenge the caste oppression. Bonded labour is abolished under the Constitution. According to the Bonded Liberation Front, an organization working for the emancipation of this wretched lot, at least five million people are still held in slavery under that system. *Sati* was abolished way back in 1824. However, not only do we hear of isolated incidents of *Sati*, but we witness, right under our eyes, in Indian metropolises, the steady rise of those gruesome "dowry deaths", which usually involve the burning alive of young wives by their husbands and mothers-in-law for their failing to bring sufficient dowry with them. In the year 1929, the Prohibition of Child Marriage Act, popularly known as the Sharada Act was passed. Even today we come across any number of baby-brides and baby-bridegrooms—unexceptionable toddlers—put through the rituals of marriage by their not so innocent parents. The Scheduled Castes or Tribes are supposed to have a fixed percentage of all available places reserved for them in government jobs and educational institutions. Almost all north Indian states regularly witness anti-reservation riots in which hundreds of these "backward" groups are killed by high-caste rowdies, often with the backing of the police or security forces who feel incensed over these small and largely unimplemented concessions. Most of the aboriginal tribes—the Santhals, Gonds, Mundas, Oraons, Bhils, etc.—have been brought to the verge of extinction. They are driven out of their natural abodes in forests, which are declared reserved for industrial monoculture or converted into game sanctuaries. We could go on cataloguing the manifestations of India's unremitting violence against the underprivileged, the outcastes, the minorities—the lower limbs of the social body as their scriptures describe them. Most of the people tortured or killed in State custody apart from the Sikhs, Muslims, and the Nagas; most of the women kidnapped, raped, or killed in the countryside by landlords and their henchmen; most of the prostitutes, prisoners, and beggars in the cities; all the human flotsam edged out to the fringes of society by the machinations of the privileged, are examples of India's relentless war against its own people.

The roots of this violence against those born meek and defenceless run deep. Striking at its contemporary manifestations without tracing their sources in the tradition can be like snipping the boughs and branches of a tree whose deep roots are left untouched and will soon send forth new sap up the trunk. Do not cosmetic and superficial reforms then become worse than being ineffective: exerting their own corrupting logic by breeding hypocrisy and spreading anaesthesia about the roots of the problems? Can there ever be a genuine reform unless politics becomes the instrument of the oppressed to dismantle the pipelines of primeval corruption that circulate ever-fresh poison into our contemporary perversions?

South Asia, as a colony and the vassal of the British Empire, was united in the struggle for independence from the foreign rule. More than five decades after attaining that independence, South Asia remains broken up, as nation-states floundering before the politics of hate and hostility in their external relations as well as in their dealings with their own people, which the ruling classes perpetuate to retain their hold on power and privilege. Old ideas of power, prerogatives, control, and domination, in ancient and new forms, permeate across geo-political demarcations and determine the conditions of injustice, human suffering, and the prodigious waste of human potential characterizing the state of affairs throughout South Asia. The discontented people, smarting before the malevolence of their history, remain powerless and unable to forge secular perspectives of solidarity and non-violent struggle that can unite religious minorities, indigenous people on the peripheries of the conquest States, and the majorities of downtrodden and oppressed people from the heartlands. With the subjugated lacking the power to enforce an acknowledgement of their experiences, their ordeals becoming more like mirages with no external confirmation, they themselves begin to lose a coherent sense of their syncopated reality.

With the coming together of the ruling classes at the local level and the harbingers of the global war on terror internationally, the discourse becomes more and more hegemonic, content in its exercises to comprehensively mutilate images of the vanquished and to eternally execrate their motives and their causes. Outside the opacity of this hegemonic history, an ideological summary of events for the powerful, the people saturated with their blood woes wait for their chances for redemption and revenge. It is in this bleak aftermath of the Cold War and the end of illusions that we must evaluate our pasts and postulate our goals for the future.

Bearing the imprints of history on our mantels are not pleasant. But we must face them and understand them if words like human rights, justice, accountability, peace, and democracy are to retain any meaning and efficacy for our futures.

Notes

1. Torture Commission Report, 1855, para. 67, Parliamentary Papers 420 1885, National Archives, New Delhi.
2. Report of the Indian Police Commission 1902-3, paras 24-25.
3. Report of the Punjab Police Commission, pp 64-65.
4. Law Commission of India, One Hundred and Fifty Second Report on Custodial Crimes, 1994, Chapter I, 1:2.
5. *Ibid*., Chapter 3, 3:29.
6. AIR 1963 Supreme Court 1295, para. 15; Field J, in *Munn Vs. Illinois*, 1876 94 US 113, p. 142.
7. *Sheela Barse Vs. State of Maharashtra*, *Javed Vs. State of Maharashtra*, AIR 1983 SC 378; AIR 1985 SC 231.
8. *Inderjeet Vs. State of Uttar Pradesh*, AIR 1975 SC 1867.
9. *Sunil Batra Vs. Delhi Adminsitration*, AIR 1968 SC 1775; *Sita Ram Vs. State of Uttar Pradesh*, AIR 1979 SC 745; *Sunil Batra Vs. Delhi Administration*, AIR 1988 SC 1579, para. 31, 42; *Javed Vs. State of Maharashtra*, AIR 1985 SC 231, para. 4, *Sher Singh Vs. State of Punjab*, AIR 1983 SC 465, para. 11.
10. *Ganapathy Gounder Vs. Emperor*, AIR 1932 Mad. 214, 215: 33 Cri. LJ 557.
11. *State of UP Vs. Ram Sagar Yadav*, AIR 1985 SC 416.
12. *Bhagwant Singh Vs. State of Punjab*, 1992, 3 SCC 249.
13. *Nilabati Behara Vs. State of Orissa*, 1993 2 SEC 746.

Chapter Ten

Universal Rights, Cultural Sensitivity, and Engagement with Religion

In this paper, we shall discuss some interesting points that came up during the distance learning period around the central theme of "cultural value systems" and the complex affinities they maintain with the visions and values of human rights as well as the matrix of social acquiescence towards the realities of their infringement. First, we shall briefly recapitulate the principal arguments on this theme that the participants developed.

One participant from Nepal argued: all religions through their teachings try to inculcate values such as "tolerance, understanding, respect, solidarity, and patience" in their adherents. Enforcement of human rights critically depends on the social and cultural receptiveness towards these values. Therefore, it may be important for human rights activists to try to "bring out/identify" the values that "our religions, cultures, and histories" have spoken about. The next task would be to figure out how to use them as tools of social dialogue and programmes of advocacy so that our societies and States become more sensitive towards human rights as the prerequisites of peace. As an example, the participant referred to "the great Hindu epic *Ramayana*" which in many instances, describes and commends the commitment and loyalty of King Rama and King Janak towards their people.

One participant from Pakistan marshalled several insightful examples about physically invisible, but psychically steadfast, effects of cultural value systems that hold the violators and the sufferers together in a state of naturalness and inexorability. He elaborated on the shadows of such effects on the entire edifice of institutionalism including the family, tribe, religion, sect and the State, interlocking abusiveness and suffering. Factors beyond the individual's capacity to determine, such as birth and belonging within specific social, political, ethnic, and religious or linguistic groups that are weak or demonized—even such coincidental but unchangeable occurrences as birth in politically sensitive or contested geographical areas—contribute to the deprivation of basic human rights. The Pakistani participant discussed the influences of ancestral attitudes, hierarchical equations, and the dynamics of superiority-subordination that characterizes the entire chain of relations within the primary social institution—the family—in inculcating attitudes, values, and ideational equations with larger institutions, including the State. Individual standing and status, within the hierarchical structure of the family, may vary and be dependent on "capacities" to command respect emanating from education, income, social recognition, and political affiliations of individuals within the chain of relations. However, these variations do not alter the constant nature of toleration of abusiveness and acquiescence to superiority-subordination principles that develops within the family itself. He also touched upon the issue of religion, which, in his view, contributes significantly to the success, or failure of all individual pursuits in South Asia. In his own words: "If a person is born in a minority religious group, almost fifty percent of that person's rights are denied in society at once without any justified reason." He also suggested that constitutional guarantees of equality of all before the law have no meaning in South Asian societies in which traditional and cultural values remain "more influential than written laws." In this context, he also referred to the predicament of *madrassa* students who join these institutions unconsciously and without the capacity to influence the choice exercised by their elders out of their own ideological and political calculations. The *Taliban* emerged through a process that reinforces the point about "social actors" being entrapped within "involuntariness" as a condition of life. The *Taliban* got "criminalized" under altered political conditions. The irony of it all is that the very forces that used the channel of a fundamentalist religious education to strategize a political mobilization in the region, which has since failed, are now at the helm of the system that aims to stamp out, torment, and persecute the foot-soldiers of their failed strategies.

One participant from Bhutan referred to the State policies in the country which have made a very large number of people of Nepali origin stateless over the last two decades. He referred to the enforcement of the *Driglam Namzha*—the compulsory dress code and the removal of the Nepali language from the school curriculum—to ask how dialogue, the essence of democracy, can resolve the issues of injustice and discrimination when a State is able to take away the right of almost forty percent of its population to be culturally and linguistically themselves.

A participant from the UK raised different set of propositions and questions around the problem of achieving a balance between cultural sensitivity and universal human rights. She provided several interesting examples to highlight the point about the absence of freedom and evident disrespect for personal choice in culturally different societies: "whilst in Afghanistan women were fighting against being forced to wear the *burka*, in England a young girl was recently fighting for her right to wear her *burka* to school. In these cases, the women's rights were being infringed in completely opposite ways—but, in neither instance was their right to choose being respected." A recommendation made by the participant merits reiteration: "dialogue is vital—between the State, activists, and the populace; between secular and religious groups; between countries; and between the East and the West."

These are the principal arguments that set the rational scope for us to examine the meaning and relevance of what we broadly recognize as the spectrum of cultural values, in interaction with the framework of enunciation or the constitutional-legal perspectives of human rights, and the manners in which their interaction becomes pertinent to our concerns about their implementation and enforcement.

The first introductory note included in this volume has a small note on Michel Foucault and his work. Those who have digested the note must know that Foucault engaged with the whole set of issues under discussion with a critical attention to the value systems responsible for our feeling of entrapment in history that leaves us powerless in our aspirations for emancipatory re-thinking, and in our projects of discursive politics to upset the established practices of power. We are aware that an influential segment of the human rights community in South Asia, knowing of Foucault from secondary sources, thinks of him and his work disdainfully as being connected to cranky causes, incomprehensibility, and narcissism. There may be some truth in that impression. But we strongly recommend the reading of at least two of his books: *The Archaeology of Knowledge*[1], and *Religion and Culture*.[2] We recommend these two books because they view these issues as belonging to the sphere of struggle between the established regimes of knowledge and the positions of radical inquiry that aim at new possibilities.

One participant referred to *Ramayana* as a textual resource for understanding the commitment and loyalty of kingship towards the people. The reference is problematic for a number of reasons. We shall identify only two of them here: (1) In our view, texts like *Ramayana* are more than texts; the power of creative interpretation they possess, when set free in different historical and social conditions, have served more than one system of values and accessory socio-political agendas. (2) Texts like *Ramayana* have been and perhaps can always be used as linguistic representations of a transcendental consciousness that falls within the realm of moral philosophy. But they are not open to investigative channels of knowledge about their actual meaning. This means that we lose logical control over the sense of values, feelings of truth, and the consciousness they create: the texts become points of transcendental intersection, repositories of psychological value that can simultaneously generate varied experiences and reactions. Political and juridical interpretations or interventions to explain their meaning, no matter how well-intentioned, can be both wrong and counter-productive.

We shall try to illustrate both the points. Let us first take up the textual issue. We really cannot know with certainty when the original version of *Ramayana,* attributed to Valmiki with its 24,000 Sanskrit verses, first appeared. We also cannot be certain about the transformations it has since undergone in the supposedly original text as well as in translations and renditions. Linguists and specialists of classical Sanskrit differ on the dates, but it is commonly agreed that together with *Mahabharata*, the second most important of the South Asian epics in Sanskrit attributed to Vyasa with its 2,20,000 lines, evolved and took shape over a long period of time spanning at least 800 years from 300 BC to A.D. 500.

There is no doubt that *Ramayana* has, throughout its history, served the purpose of instruction in the ideals of human behaviour. Its disseminative reach goes far beyond South Asia. Its centrality in South-eastern theatre and dance is an established fact. Its popularity through *Ram-Lila* is a phenomenon that will never cease to fascinate observers of popular culture in India. However, in our view it is impossible for us to recover from *Ramayana*, textually speaking, even a plausible understanding about the value systems and the connected projects of regimentation or resistance that its idealism of human behaviour serves. We speak of value systems with awareness that in *Ramayana* even if Rama is an ideal king, Sita is an ideal wife, Hanuman is an ideal follower, Laxman is an ideal brother, etc., the normative framework of struggle in life and its organization through dutifulness, faith, and obedience that the heroes, heroines, and villains epitomize are open to contradictory interpretations and uses.

Tulsi Das composed the most popular Hindi version of *Ramayana* known as *Ramacharitamanasa* in the second half of the sixteenth century. It extols the ideals of *Ramayana* that we have already identified. It also synthesizes various streams of devotional trends associated with the *Bhakti* movement. More significantly, Tulsi Das was also in touch with his contemporary luminaries belonging to other traditions including Mira Bai, the rebel poetess married to the eldest son of Rana Sanga of Mewar; Malik Muhammad Jayasi, the Sufi writer of an allegorical romance known as *Padmavat*; Surdas, the blind poet-saint supposedly patronized by Akbar; and, of course, Rahim, yet another devotional poet, who was also a General in the court of Akbar under the name of Abdur Rahim Khan-i-khanan. The apocryphal tradition of the *Bhakti* movement as well as a poem attributed to Tulsi Das, still very popular in northern India, actually suggest that Tulsi Das directly abetted Mira Bai's defiance of the *Rana* of Chittorgarh, and encouraged her to travel around Saurashtra in the company of other mendicants who did not respect the distinctions of caste or even formal religion.

Ramcharitmanasa has inspired millions of Hindi speaking people of north India for more than 400 years. It has also served as the main instrument to spread literacy in the Hindi heartland and in developing Hindi itself as the *lingua franca* of northern India in the same way as Martin Luther's translation of the Bible into German, in 1529, served to spread literacy in Germany, elevating German as a powerful language of philosophy and literature in the process.

In 1987, approximately 400 years after the composition of *Ramcharitmanasa*, the State-controlled television in India began to broadcast *Ramayana* as a serial watched by millions of people. The serial actually became the main instrument to mobilize a Hindu extremist movement resulting in the demolition of the Babri Masjid in Ayodha. The consequences, as all should agree, have been lethal to the constitutional framework of the Indian State, to the prospects for the harmonious coexistence of religious communities within its frontiers, etc. The carnage in Gujarat was, as all acknowledge, an offshoot of the process, and we don't know how it will all conclude.

This is what we mean by suggesting that the interpretative power of texts like *Ramayana* have been unleashed to serve more than one system of values and associated agendas of political regimentation and resistance.

The second point about a text like *Ramayana* actually becoming a point of transcendental intersection for varied experiences, sensations, and mystical feelings of consciousness that remain unavailable to logical recovery is more difficult to illustrate. In 1902, William James published *The Varieties of Religious Experience*.[3] We refer to this book primarily because William James talked about "faith as will" to emphasize his point about the moral quality of religious experience that develops only in freedom from the compulsion of belief and amid a genuine range of optional routes to faith. William James, also being a psychologist, posited the proposition that the quality of religious experience depends on varied capacities to believe in a divine power superior to the world of material evidence; a divine who, therefore, also becomes beyond recognition through normal cognitive faculties.

This is a point central and common to almost all transcendental perspectives including the most organized as well as more eclectic systems of religious faith. Some participants talked about "involuntariness" as a condition of life when those who have inherited a religion from birth become conscious of its negative influences. Many who are born to a given religious heritage may actually be content owing to the existential security it provides. Others approach religion from different positions of solicitude. For some, religion provides the consolation of happiness after death. For others, it is a path of quest to resolve difficult questions about the purposes and the meanings of existence, and for some it may be the route to the experience of bliss that obliterates all other existential anxieties. All, many, or some of these angles of faith intersect in texts that revolve around characters that are also objects of worship or deities; in texts with the personality of sacred stories; or in texts that are also linked to rituals, acts of worship, and religious ceremonies. The point of our argument is actually more complicated than the condensed principle by which we have tried to explain it. The requirement of brevity as well as the necessity to keep the intricacies of an interdisciplinary inquiry of this kind to a minimum dictates this approach. The principal points are two: (1) Texts Imbibed with religious value convey experiences and meaning that are not subject to rational discipline; and (2) the primacy of the transcendental and the dependence on the divine as the source and the authority of experience and meaning, which religious texts presuppose, preclude them for the purposes of a discourse on human rights that proceeds from an essentially mundane nature of concerns about human existence.

There are, no doubt, many extraordinary individuals who combine many angles of faith in approaching religious texts, worship, devotional ceremonies, and even rituals and come out with mystical experiences to reinforce the point some participants make about the unity of all religions in universal values.

Ramakrishna, better recognized with the epithet of *Paramahansa* that he received from his followers, lived in Bengal from 1836 to 1886. This was also the period in which South Asia, following much malevolent turmoil, was brought under complete subjugation by the British Empire. For the purpose of the illustration, we can only offer a brief sketch of his life. Books about his life and teachings are aplenty. The footnote mentions three books.[4]

Ramakrishna, a *Brahmin* mystic of Bengal devoted to *Kali*, a goddess representing the dance of death and the cosmic supremacy of the female within the *tantric* tradition, became a priest at a private temple in Calcutta dedicated to the goddess in 1855, when he was only 19. The mystical experiences he had while leading liturgical services at the temple were so radical that he was taken to have become insane and was brought back to his parental home, 100 kilometres northwest of Calcutta, where he got married to Sarada. Ramakrishna was then 23.

In 1860, one year after his marriage, Ramakrishna went back to Kali's temple in Calcutta. Over the next 14 years, Ramakrishna continued with his experiments in religious devotion, getting initiated into other faiths while remaining steadfast in his worship of Kali. Sarada, his wife, remained beside him as his spiritual companion. Ramakrishna explained his experience of Islam in the following words: "I devoutly repeated the name of *Allah*, and I said their prayers five times a day. I spent three days in that mood, and I had the full realization of the *sadhana* [discipline] of their faith." He described his empathy for Christianity in the following words: "This is Jesus

Christ, the great *Yogi*, the loving son of God, who was one with his Father, and who shed his heart's blood and suffered tortures for the salvation of mankind."

Equal respect for all religions remained a basic tenet of Ramakrishna's philosophy of faith. He explained: "It is not good to feel that one's own religion alone is true and all others are false. God is one only, and not two. Different people call on Him by different names: some as Allah, some as God, others as Krishna, Shiva and Brahman."

Ramakrishna's solution to the evils of the caste system was "the love of God". He said: "Lovers of God do not belong to any caste."

Surely, Ramakrishna's life is an example of syncretism of religious experience that can also be an inspiration for engagement with value systems, which, as a participant pointed out, become "the most serious barrier to effecting social change and acceptance of human rights."

We wish it had been possible for us to make a generalization on the basis of the example of Ramakrishna. Unfortunately, we cannot. Ramakrishna's experiences and teachings remained rooted in a transcendental sphere to which we can have no access and which, as a source of inspiration for the human rights movement, would never be available.

Also, very significantly, the missionary establishment around the iconic figure of Ramakrishna, which developed after his death under the leadership of Vivekananda, merely became an adjunct of the movement for the renaissance of a Hindu nationalism that is today so intolerant of the values Ramakrishna personified. The outcome supports the point we made earlier that political interpretations and interventions to explain mystical messages, no matter how well intentioned, can be both wrong and counter-productive.

But this is not a very optimistic note to close this topic about the possibility of and the basis on which to engage with religious and cultural systems that counteract the framework of universal human rights. So, we shall tarry along the concourse of rights and religion for just a while longer in the hope of finding a better position for engagement.

It should be reasonable to suggest that belief-systems that become directly responsible for the conditions of "involuntariness" in life are rehearsals of old habits rather than representations of a revelatory truth in any sense of the term. It should also be reasonable enough to admit that the enunciation of rights by powerless people from all cultures of the world, or the annunciation made on their behalf, is as much a result of an accumulated secular experience about what is pragmatically advantageous for all, as it is an appeal of a transcendental character that has met with a universal echo. The suggestion, if accepted as valid, becomes the proposition that fundamental human rights should have primacy over the value systems that contradict them. Their claim to primacy can be rooted in the pragmatic position that they advantage all, as well as in the argument that their universal approval suggests harmony at a higher level of consciousness. Rights become part of a higher truth that also works the world better, at least in terms of reducing conflicts and violence. Made as an argument for the prohibition against violations of fundamental human rights rather than as a contention that takes on the cloak of a new universal religion, it sounds like a ground good enough to begin the engagement. On a ground so carved out in philosophical humility, the "rights" argument would not be in contest with any authority at the plane of divinity. The ground would remain essentially secular. It would also admit agreement with a higher consciousness as a venture in harmonizing practices of power so as not to degrade human existence beneath minimal universal expectations of freedom, justice, and dignity. This is a proposition that can be developed and refined at both philosophical and juridical planes. For the moment, it is no more than a proposition for engagement with value systems, including religion. We don't adopt a religious tone in advancing our arguments. We only contest claims of transcendental legitimacy for practices that appear terrestrially abusive.

Notes

1. New York: Routledge, 1990.
2. Manchester: Manchester University Press, 1999.
3. (London: Penguin, 1983).
4. (1) Isherwood, Christopher, *Ramakrishna and his Disciples* (New York: Simon & Schuster, 1965); (2) Sadananda, Swami, *Sri Ramakrishna: The Great Master* (Calcutta: Sri Ramakrishna Math, 1970), and (3) Romain, Rolland, *The Life of Ramakrishna* (Calcutta: Advaita Ashrama, 1965).

Chapter Eleven

The Human Rights Discourse: Flaws, Weaknesses and Problems

This paper shall focus on the issues that emerged from our attempts to appraise the nature of the human rights discourse, its flaws, weaknesses, and problems. Some of the main arguments advanced by the participants require encapsulation.

One participant from Sri Lanka tried to trace the changing conceptions of the State, from Aristotle's vision of an institution aimed at the 'highest good', 'good life', and satisfying all the needs of men[1] to Max Weber's view of the State as "the sole source of the 'right' to use violence." The examination led him to argue that Aristotle's political theory in Book I and II of *Nicomachean Ethics* takes a functionalist approach to understanding social and political institutions, including the State. The approach was transformed, especially with the advent of modern capitalism, into a rational quest for an impersonal set of laws and regulations to guide the use of force. The transformation culminated in the establishment of State as the pivotal point of the human rights [HR] discourse. He further argued that the State-centric nature of the human rights discourse has allowed the institutions of political coercion to remain obsessed with the issues of power and politics, forever augmenting the monopolistic right to violence, to the detriment of economic, social, and cultural facets of life. He also suggested that the discourse will become increasingly irrelevant and illegitimate unless it is able to encompass non-State actors, such as multi-national companies (MNCs) and international financial institutions (IFIs) within its framework of accountability and, also, accord greater focus to economic, social, and cultural rights (ESCR), specifically to the issues of poverty and inequality.

One Pakistani participant drew attention to the parallel processes of the conceptualization of universal human rights and the rise of nationalism and the ensuing formation of Nation-States as the by-products of indigenous political response to colonialism. She pointed out that the rise of nationalism also led to efforts at homogenization which, in turn, served to justify partitions. The role of the State is to protect citizens, whether from outside interference or from interference from within the society itself. However, the State is not all-powerful: its sovereignty is encroached by non-State actors and international institutions. Its freedom of action is limited by rights that have the status of *jus cogens*, in other words, by peremptory norms, from which no derogation is allowed. Finally, its territorial integrity is threatened by groups struggling for self-determination. As a consequence, not only is the distinction between the international and the domestic blurred, but in practice, several sovereignties overlap. This leads to a domino effect whereby the State is affected by forces from within and without and this, in turn, has a bearing on the human rights situation within its territories. This helps to explain why there is frequently a gap between human rights theory and practice: States may simply be motivated by considerations other than human rights when they ratify international instruments. The gap tends to exacerbate group identities by the feelings of oppression and the economic, political, and cultural discrimination it generates. Claims of the right to self-determination are themselves plagued by the problem of "minorities within minorities", which emanates from the fissiparous tendency within the right to self-determination.

One participant from Bangladesh advanced the theory that "human rights", in the sense of moral principles governing relations amongst individuals, pre-existed the formation of Nation-States. He also suggested that the decline in group cohesion and 'socialization', as an attendant aspect of modernity, results in 'individualism', which accounts for the increasing clamour for human rights. In other words, human rights are not new: simply, more attention is being paid to them because of the individualistic shift in social relations. He pointed out that the same process of disintegration in relations among groups not only accounts for the escalation of self-determination movements within the nation-states, as exemplified by the separatist demands of tribes in Bangladesh, but also the breakdown of self-determination movements towards assertions of rights of "minorities within minorities".

Over-emphasis on the State in the Human Rights Discourse

All the three participants agreed that the State-centeredness of the HR discourse is misplaced: it leads to a narrow vision limited to civil and political rights, and it does not take into account the emergence of other actors who influence the understanding and actualization of human rights in their full range. Indeed, it is impossible to contest the argument. The post-colonial political experiences in South Asia clearly show that the success of a participatory democracy committed to secularism, pluralism, and human rights depends vitally on the genuineness of the political pledge of the State to secure economic, social, and cultural justice to historically underprivileged and marginalized sections of people. Without such a commitment on the part of the State, the vast majority of historically suppressed people in our societies can never meaningfully actualize their civil and political rights.

The attempt to trace the transformations in the understanding and the character of the State within the western intellectual traditions is interesting: the transformation from Aristotle's moral conceptualization of the State as an arrangement for the enhancement of human happiness to Hobbes' vision of an all-encompassing, all-regulating Leviathan on to its elevation as "the rational end of man's life" by Hegel, and finally its achievement of "the monopoly of the legitimate use of physical force within a given territory", is complex and varied.

Examples and references will proliferate unmanageably if we pursue the line of inquiry to outline the history of intellectualization of the State and its impact on the legitimization of coercive institutions of political power. Aristotle's political and ethical theories are supposed to be marked by his commitment to commonsense and the primacy he accords to the human being as a rational animal. By "aristocracy" he is supposed to have meant the rule of the best rather than the rule of the highborn. It is, however, known that Aristotle entered the service of Philip of Macedonia to teach philosophy to his son Alexander and returned to Athens to establish his own school when Alexander ascended the throne in 336 B.C. A follower of Plato and his student for 20 years until Plato's death, Aristotle repeated the mistakes of his master when trying to train capable rulers, or philosopher kings. Plato introduced his notion of "philosopher king" in his *Republic*, and attempted to influence a couple of tyrants like

Dionysos I of Syracuse and his son, and also Hermias of Aterneus in Asia Minor to become his archetypical "philosopher king." Plato was, of course, radically frustrated in his attempts. Aristotle's own school of philosophy in Athens was patronized by Macedonians and he had to flee the city–state to die miserably in Chalicis to escape persecution from the anti-Macedonia forces which became powerful after Alexander's death in 323 B.C.

In politics, Aristotle, like Plato, was an elitist with an absolutist temperament with nothing to say about Greek slavery, the aristocratic contempt for manual work, intellectual narcissism, the hierarchical organization of society, etc. No doubt, the State, for Aristotle, was a social arrangement to enhance the objective of human happiness. But his humanity, like Plato's, did not embrace the vast majority of the Athenian population: slaves, artisans, and women. The failure of Aristotle is largely that of political philosophy itself, which has, in much of its history, been chosen to be a handmaid of dominant social and economic interests.

We have already made our essential points about the philosophy of Thomas Hobbes and his *Elements of Law* [1640] and his *Leviathan* in the introductory notes. Hobbes' understanding of the "state of nature", the condition of human beings in the absence of political authority, is a historically conditioned view of an aristocratic mind about the revolutionary implications of the English Civil War. In Hobbes' "state of nature" there is no peace and the endemic conflict makes it very difficult to obtain the necessities and conveniences of life. This view of the "state of nature" was also, at least partly, shared by Locke and Kant, and it indirectly informs the theories of justice forged by such political philosophers as John Rawls, who basically subscribe to the social contract theory. The theory of the monopoly of force by the State was first articulated by Max Weber who published his *Protestant Ethic and the Spirit of Capitalism* in 1905. By then, the idea of superiority of the western civilization and the doctrine of the State founded on impersonal rules and procedures had gained ascendancy. The issue of justification of political authority became increasingly insignificant with the steady extension of the capitalist State under the European annexation of the world. Even Karl Marx, the most influential critique of the capitalist world order for over 150 years, since the publication of the *Communist Manifesto* in 1848, did not question either its historical legitimacy or its role. Marx waxed eloquent about alienation, injustice, and the horrors of exploitation.

However, the problem of human suffering, under the coercive power of the capitalist State, did not bother him much so long as it served the purpose of "historical progress" consequentially.

This comes out very clearly in Marx's articles on India, published in the *New York Daily Tribune* over the years 1853-57. There, Marx argued that by destroying the idyllic [a word he loads with irony] order of ancient India, no doubt at the price of great pain to the indigenous population, British rule was nonetheless performing a necessary and therefore salutary task. It was preparing the ground for a new, progressive civilization to take roots. To him, the pain caused by the crumbling of the ancient world counted for naught compared to the promise it held for the future.

Hobbes made an exception to the absolute power of the sovereign by permitting 'subjects' the right to defend their lives by rising against the sovereign, if necessary. The exception followed from the fact that the absolute power of the sovereign derives not from a divine bequest but from the covenant requiring the sovereign to protect the subjects from anarchic death.

Ironically enough, the modern philosophies of human rights and peace owe much to the ground of 'exceptionalism' that they recover from Hobbes' own "laws of nature". The first four 'laws of nature' postulates have been paraphrased by Kwame Anthony Appiah, a Professor of Philosophy at Princeton University, as follows:

1. You should seek peace wherever it is possible; but if you cannot achieve peace, you should defend yourself by all the means at your disposal.
2. You should give up the right to defend yourself to the extent that it is necessary to achieve peace, provided other people accept the same limitations.
3. You should keep your promises.
4. You should not give the people who keep their promises reason to regret doing so.[2]

Hobbes' laws of nature are "maxims of prudence" not "moral ideas." They do not originate in a divine wisdom but in a reasonable understanding of a utilitarian nature of human life forged through negotiations within civil society.

Robert Nozick, the author of *Anarchy, State and Utopia*[3], attempted to capture the rationality that results in the Hobbesian covenant that continues to inform the State-centric character of the human rights discourse in our own times: "A theory of state of nature that begins with fundamental general descriptions of morally permissible and impermissible actions, and of deeply based reasons why some persons in any society would violate those moral constraints, and goes on to describe how a State would arise from that state of nature will serve our explanatory purposes, even if no actual State ever arose in that way."

No State probably ever arose in that way. But any enunciation of justice and rights, in our own times, depends on the hope of our being able to make State institutions aware of the interests of all people, to defend them in reflective equilibrium, and to pay special attention to the underprivileged while engaging in the distribution of "inequality surpluses".

This is more or less what Rawls' theory of justice, with its roots in the utilitarian logic, contends. The argument, however, rests on the State's power to ensure distributive justice and, therefore, becomes exposed to criticism on at least two counts. Historically speaking, the State operates on the principles of differential entitlements and on the privileges of political loyalties in the past. To require it to shape its policies of "distributive justice" with special attention to the 'underprivileged' is like asking it to be especially genial towards its adversaries and opponents. This can never happen except as operations of political deception. In terms of utilitarian logic, the demand is absurd. It is better to increase the utilitarian advancement even if the process is afflicted by distributive inequalities and consequential injustices. Those who have paid for the life-saving drugs retain their right to keep them unused even when others in terminal need cannot obtain them for any price in the open market. The State cannot use its coercive force, without offending the fundamental right to property, to take life-saving drugs away from idle storage even to save human life at risk. Under the utilitarian logic of law, the State must use its coercive force to prevent and punish those who try to break into a house to obtain life-saving drugs in idle storage even to save human life at risk. That is the nature of the rule of law distinguishable from the anarchy in Hobbes' 'state of nature'. The laws enacted by the State capable of enforcing them by the use of force, described by the 19th century English legal scholar John Austin as the "commands of the sovereign", largely aim to defend private interests and attitudes even when their defiance invites the charge of sedition. Laws defend dominant private interests even when appearing to be socially impartial in nature. The racist and religiously discriminatory laws worldwide generate much political effervescence. Their remedies, however, seem to emerge through negotiations among the antagonists in the private sphere rather than through a blind confrontation between the aggrieved and the State. Martin Luther King successfully combated the laws of segregation in the United States avowedly on the basis that they contradict the basic tenets of its Constitution. Martin Luther King's success in combating the segregation laws in the United States followed, to a large measure, from his ability to win over an influential section of the white community leaders to his position.

State-centrism, as mentioned in the introductory note to Module 4, is also the overweening character of international law. Laws are developed by States to govern relations among themselves. Human rights law is, therefore, seen as a revolution in that it introduced a new subject of international law: the individual. A further novelty is the notion that individuals have rights against the State, which the State has a duty to "respect", "protect", and "fulfil." However, human rights posit the freedoms of the individual by reference to the State: civil and political rights (CPR) are mostly conceived in "negative" terms — they favour abstention by the State, — whereas economic, social, and cultural rights (ESCR) are mostly conceived in "positive" terms — they invite intervention by the State.[4] The entire human rights regime is thus based on the principle of State responsibility and is premised on a vision of State as the ultimate guardian of its population. The State rather than the individual therefore becomes the focus of attention. In David Kennedy's words:

> "Although the human rights vocabulary expresses relentless suspicion of the State, by structuring emancipation as a relationship between an individual right holder and the state, human rights vocabulary places the State at the centre of the emancipatory promise.... By consolidating human experience into the exercise of legal entitlement, the human rights vocabulary strengthens the national governmental structure and equates the structure of the State with the structure of freedom. To be free is ... to have an appropriately organized State. We might say that the right-holder imagines and experiences freedom only as a citizen."[5]

One implication of this statement is that the State structure is not only an end but also a means to be free. Secondly, individuals are never truly and totally free: they are only free within a State structure. And to fall within the State structure, they must be citizens. Thirdly, to the right-holder, the structure of the State is the single most important concern as it will determine the way in which he "imagines and experiences freedom".

What sort of a State structure are we referring to? Taking into consideration the origins of the notion of human rights, it may be assumed that the State structure envisaged is an offshoot of the western notion of liberty, and possesses the following characteristics: it is rationalist, secular, modern, and capitalist. In addition, this State structure is political and distinct from the economic sphere/market.

Of course, if one adheres to the above, it is not hard to see why human rights are so skewed towards CPR rather than towards ESCR.

This analysis of the State as being of such primordial importance to human rights as to sit in the place of honour, in the centre, tends to conceal the increasing role and influence of other actors and the resulting erosion of State power. Exclusive concern for the State simply serves to shield and absolve others of their responsibility. In order to move away from this State-centric paradigm, a legal framework must be developed with which to hold at least some non-State actors (NSAs) accountable for their role in poverty.

The difficulty in developing such a framework is that ultimately, the responsibility for its implementation once again lies with the State: States ratify legal instruments. They carry the primary responsibility for their implementation. States also bear the constitutional obligation to ensure the existence of a functioning, independent, and impartial judiciary capable of enforcing the rights contained in these instruments.

Ultimately, the State is involved in all stages of the legal process. This is true even of procedures allowing recourse to international fora by individuals, such as the European Court of Human Rights or the Optional Protocol to the International Covenant for Civil and Political Rights. Elaborating a framework that is non-State-centric would therefore require a radical change in the way in which international law is developed, implemented, and enforced. It would also require a shift towards a more dynamic vision of the state that is not constrained by "a false sense of rigidity and inevitability about social and political hierarchies and existing inequities".[6]

CPR and ESCR in the Human Rights Discourse

Concerns over inequality and poverty were amongst those that led to the elaboration of the Universal Declaration for Human Rights (UDHR). The UDHR was designed as a short, inspirational, and energizing document usable by common people as the foundational document for an international bill of human rights. However, the West and the East became separated by ideology before such an international bill could be drafted. In terms of human rights, this rift was translated into the West championing CPR and the East ESCR. As a consequence, rather than having a single legally binding document detailing the rights contained in the UDHR, two Covenants came into force in 1976: the International Covenant on Civil and Political Rights (ICCPR) and the International Covenant on Economic, Social and Cultural Rights (ICESCR).

Ten years later, a limited degree of consensus was formally reached in the Declaration on the Right to Development on the need for both sets of rights to be realized simultaneously:

> "The right to development is an inalienable human right by virtue of which every human person and all peoples are entitled to participate in, contribute to, and enjoy economic, social, cultural and political development, in which all human rights and fundamental freedoms can be fully realized".[7]

It should be noted that the Declaration on the Right to Development readily illustrates the point regarding States' differing motivations in signing up international treaties and how these motivations can affect their implementation. On the one hand, some countries viewed and still view the "right to development" as an oral weapon in a struggle for the transfer of resources to developing countries. These governments have been focusing on the international economic order and have thus been avoiding the uncomfortable issue of internal economic justice. On the other hand, the majority of Western countries supported the declaration because they recognized that development was an emotive issue for a vast majority of people living in the Third World. In any event, the main thrust of the Declaration that both sets of rights need to be realized together, was reaffirmed in the 1993 Vienna Declaration and Programme of Action. It stated that:

> "All human rights are universal, indivisible and interdependent and interrelated. The international community must treat human

> rights globally in a fair and equal manner, on the same footing, and with the same emphasis".[8]

A further step was taken with the development of the rights-based approach theory. The rights-based approach aims to keep human dignity at the forefront. Since dignity is closely connected with the satisfaction of the basic necessities of life and autonomy, it is concerned with poverty eradication. It is expressly linked to rights. It stresses participation and empowerment. It recognizes the principles of equality and non-discrimination; insists on democratic practices, including accountability; and requires the creation of a supportive social environment capable of fulfilling the aspiration of all people to dignity. The rights-based approach entails the realization of CPR as well as ESCR with the end-goal of realizing human dignity. Consequently, the rights-based approach should infuse all decision-making processes and not just those related to "development".

It is also argued that the protection of civil and political rights is a precondition for the fulfilment of ESCR and that the allocation and distribution of goods and resources, as well as determinations of entitlement to those goods and resources, are matters of political decisions and priorities. In Amartya Sen's words, "political and civil rights give people the opportunity to draw attention forcefully to general needs and to demand appropriate public action". Amartya Sen goes on to illustrate this point by reference to famines, noting that "no substantial famine has ever occurred in any independent and democratic country with a relatively free press".[9]

The instrumental role of CPR as a means of realizing ESCR is also very well illustrated by the *Right to Information Act* in India. Initially, a small NGO in Rajasthan started lobbying, at a very local level, for greater access to information. This gathered momentum and soon grew into a movement claiming the "right to information" that swept over the country. The right to information as a prerequisite to the enforcement of ESCR, through greater accountability and transparency of the administration, had to begin as a political initiative.

In both these examples, CPR stand out as the frontrunners of ESCR. We should then ask: is it at all possible to realize ESCR independently of CPR? Donor governments often seem to tie aid to CPR. Recipient governments, who accept the tie-up, often seem to accord greater lip service to ESCR. How come then that political persecution and violations of civil rights remain so pervasive? Why do poverty, inequality, and the denial of ESCR remain so ubiquitous and obdurate? We can only reiterate some of the explanations that rationalize the state of CPR and ESCR within the world today.

(a) *CPR and ESCR are Different*

One such explanation is that CPR and ESCR are different types of rights and that they do not belong to a symbiotic process of realization. It is thus argued that CPR can be implemented, given the will, more immediately: ESCR can only take the path of "progressive realization". CPR have clear cores and boundaries: the right not to be subject to deliberate infliction of pain is absolute. ESCR belong to a twilight zone in which the principles of entitlement as well as of responsibility for their deprivation are difficult to determine: as for example, with the right to education. Guaranteeing CPR, given the will, is "relatively cheap"; guaranteeing ESCR, despite intentions, is potentially "enormously costly" and time-consuming.

There are other arguments. It is, for example, said that ESCR concern themselves with the "basic satisfaction of certain core rights that are well within the means of developing nations to satisfy".[10] The argument cannot be dismissed lightly. Many countries with the majority of their people living in conditions of absolute squalor and deprivation of ESCR spend their scant financial resources on military establishments or, even worse, to acquire nuclear arsenal and to build the capacity to launch them from the air and from the sea.

Two relatively recent cases from the South African Constitutional Court illustrate the suggestion that a developing State's respect for socio-economic rights of its people is more a matter of political will than of fiscal capacity. The first case concerned Soobramoney's right to access health care.[11] Soobramoney, whose life could only be prolonged by an on-going dialysis treatment, was refused admission to a State hospital, which claimed a policy to allow such treatment if the patient fulfilled certain medical conditions that Soobramoney did not. Soobramoney asked for a court order directing the hospital to provide him with the requisite treatment. The Constitutional Court looked at a constitutional provision giving everyone the right of access to health care services. This provision required the State to take "reasonable legislative and other measures, within its available resources, to achieve the progressive realization of this right".[12] The Court indicated that "it would be slow to interfere with rational decisions taken in good faith by political organs and medical authorities whose responsibility it is to deal with such matters".[13] It took the view that the guidelines drawn up by the hospital authorities for determining patients who qualified for dialysis treatment were reasonable and, therefore, refused to order the provision of the treatment.

In the second case,[14] the Constitutional Court was required to consider the right to housing. The applicants had been evicted from a private land they were unlawfully occupying, and all their possessions and building material had been destroyed. They then camped on a sports field but could not erect adequate shelters owing to the destruction of their building materials. They, therefore, applied for an order requiring the government to provide them with adequate basic shelter or housing until they obtained permanent accommodation. The order was granted but the government appealed the decision. According to the Constitutional Court, the question was not whether socio-economic rights were justiciable under the Constitution, "but how to enforce them in a given case." This could not be decided in abstract, but would have to be "carefully explored on a case-by-case basis".[15] The State's duty with respect to the right to access to adequate housing was to "create the conditions for access to adequate housing for people at all economic levels of our society".[16] In cases in which it is argued that the State has failed to meet the positive obligations imposed on it, "the question will be whether the legislative and other measures taken by the State are reasonable." The Court emphasized that the housing programme should include measures that are reasonable both in their conception and in their implementation. The Court, then, proceeded to interpret "progressive realization" as imposing a duty on the State to progressively facilitate the accessibility of housing by examining legal, administrative, operational, and financial hurdles, and, where possible, lowering these over time. Housing should be made accessible "not only to a larger number of people but to a wider range of people as time progresses".[17] The phrase "within available resources" was interpreted to mean that "both the content of the obligation in relation to the rate at which it is achieved as well as the reasonableness of the measures employed to achieve the result are governed by the availability of resources".[18]

It is worth noting that in both the cases, the Court adopted a test of reasonableness. Furthermore, it would appear that the State's duty in guaranteeing ESCR is to "create the conditions" for the right to be realized. In other words, the State does not have to guarantee the right to housing or the right to access medical health or any other such right to each and every individual. Rather, it has to provide the groundwork for these rights to be attained.

(b) *Implementation vs. Enforcement*

Consideration of the jurisprudence of courts such as in the paragraph above leads us to our next point: whether or not judgments are, in fact, implemented and enforced. If they are not, the situation on the ground will obviously remain unchanged.

(c) *Motivation and "Rights Talk"*

On a more sceptical note, it may be assumed that the main reason for people being unable to enforce their ESCR today is that governments ratify international instruments and engage in "rights talk" but actually do very little towards implementing and enforcing human rights on the ground.

This is the argument that the Pakistani participant made, that there are several motivating factors which influence a government's decision to ratify, or not, a particular international instrument.

At a different level, this also reveals the power behind "rights talk": it convinces people that: (1) action is being taken; (2) action is laudable, though it merely comprises enunciation of objectives; (3) it is just a question of time before the promise of human rights transforms the world; and, therefore, (4) any criticism of the approach would be negative. "Human rights talk", thus, becomes a means of legitimizing the *status quo* and governmental inaction.

(d) *The Primacy of Commercial Interests*

A further explanation is that while Western governments, in tying development aid to human rights, profess to be working towards CPR and by extension towards ESCR, they turn a blind eye towards practices violating those rights when their own economic interests are at stake. The phenomenon of silent connivance is especially conspicuous in their relations with corporations and companies. It is partly for this reason that there is a felt need to design a legal framework to bring non-State actors, together with State actors, under a common system of accountability.

Non-State Actors (NSAs)

International law, with some notable exceptions, only recognizes a limited number of subjects, namely the State and the individual. The Geneva Conventions of 1949, for example, include provisions that seek to regulate the behaviour of insurgents and peoples struggling for self-determination. However, such provisions are too few to effectively meet the growing influence of non-State actors in all spheres of life. In particular, international financial institutions (IFIs) such as the World Bank and the International Monetary Fund (IMF), as well as multi-national corporations (MNCs), paramilitary organizations, armed political groups, and INGOs involved in the developmental sector should be held accountable for their acts of omission and commission which affect the human rights of people worldwide. We should not forget that non-governmental organizations, particularly those formed due to economic motivations, have been historically very important in establishing and extending the Northern Empires throughout the 17th, 18th, and 19th centuries. The English East India Company, which administered India until 1858; the Dutch East India Company, which colonized South Africa, and established the Dutch colonial Empire in Indonesia; and also the British South Africa Company, led by Rhodes, were all INGOs.

(a) *IFIs*

Projects funded by the IMF and the World Bank have often directly implicated violations of both CPR and ESCR. Structural Adjustment Programmes (SAPs) are notorious for the detrimental influence they often have on the social fabric. As Chris Jochnick points out, "the relative decline of national sovereignty and domestic control over local economic processes and resources and the corresponding growth in the level to which the international financial agencies directly influence domestic policy decisions are clearly aspects of the adjustment process which conclusively affect ESCR".[19] In the post-Washington Consensus era, the financial institutions tend to speak in the "rights language". For example, development is supposed to be 'people-centered'; a participatory approach to development the norm; and eradication of poverty the ultimate goal. This opportunistic use of the "rights language" can be misleading. The World Bank is actually said to view "participation" as "just a more efficient means of achieving its largely unchanged neo-liberal agenda—and not as a new and radical paradigm that demands some fundamental re-thinking of the Bank's core beliefs".[20]

The World Bank and the IMF concede their impact on human rights but refuse to be held accountable to human rights standards. This is allegedly on account of their Articles of Agreement that state that they shall not interfere in the political affairs of any country and that their policies shall be guided only by economic considerations.[21] According to these institutions, human rights are "political" and, thus, outside their purview. Both institutions have, however, broadened the interpretation of 'economic considerations' to include "good governance" on the grounds that this has an economic impact. Does not "good governance" come within the purview of politics? Is it being suggested that human rights violations do not have an economic impact? How can these institutions, designed as the economic counterpart of the UN, be free to impose any requirement on any nation, without a framework of human rights norms, in the name of 'development'? Does this situation not belie the claim that all rights are to be treated "in a fair and equal manner"?[22]

(b) *MNCs*

By contrast to IFIs, MNCs seem to be much more honest: they are after profit, nothing else, and everybody knows it.

The need to regulate and to impose some limits on the inordinate power of these multi-national companies has for long been recognized. MNCs generate revenues many times larger than the domestic economies of the countries in which they operate, acquiring, in the process, enormous clout and influence in shaping the human rights environment in which they operate. In order to attract investments, governments of developing countries are frequently willing to offer tax rebates, to establish tax havens, and to "forget" environmental laws or to turn a blind eye to violations of laws relating to working conditions, safety at work, and/or minimum wages. It has been established that Disney has been getting its tee-shirts, stitched by sweatshop seamstresses in Haiti on the wage of 28 cents an hour, sold at Wal-Mart for $ 11.95. Such MNCs as Nike, Gap, Wal-Mart, Tommy Hilfiger USA, Cutter & Buck, Bymboree, J. Crew, and Nordstrom are currently facing lawsuits alleging frequent verbal, physical, and sexual abuse of workers; the use of child labour; compulsory overtime; low wages; and polluting the environment.[23]

MNCs are also known to engage in more egregious human rights violations. Human Rights Watch has documented how Enron Power Corporation used illegal force to beat off and disperse a group of protesters who were staging a peaceful demonstration before its Dabhol power plant in the state of Maharashtra.[24] Former workers of an Exxon Mobile plant based in the Aceh provide of Indonesia filed a case under the *Alien Tort Claims Act* or ATCA before the district court of Columbia in the USA in July 2001 seeking restitution for serious human rights crimes committed by the MNC's officials. The American State Department has approached the court in writing to argue that the adjudication of complaints of abuses may demoralize the Indonesian government to the extent that it might cease to cooperate in its war against terrorism and also refuse lucrative business contracts to the US companies.[25]

Yet another illustrative example is the environmental damage and killing of the Ogoni people in Nigeria, subsequent to Shell's presence in the area. Shell discovered oil on Ogoni land in 1958 and coordinated with the government to obtain drilling rights. The oil company refuses to respect the land it is drilling, spilling thousands of barrels of crude oil each year, etc. The Ogoni people who brought their complaint to the government were arrested and killed. Their complaint said:

> "Shell Oil sees it fit to ... emphasize education, the arts, environment, health, and welfare in her areas of operation in Australia and other parts of Europe and America by the establishment of the Shell Foundation. But she does not consider the people of Ogoni and the Niger Delta human enough to enjoy such benefits ... Shell Oil has gotten over $32 billion dollars in revenue receipts [by the year 2000] from operating in Ogoni land since 1958".[26]

In response, Royal Dutch Petroleum and Shell Transport and Trading Company not only recruited the Nigerian military forces to suppress all political opposition to their activities in the region, but also had Ken Saro-Wiwa, a well-known poet and environmental activist, and his colleagues John Kpuinen and Saro Wiwa arrested under false charges and, after an unfair trial, had them executed.[27]

The stories of the Ogoni and Acehan people obviously raise several questions about the government's treatment of its own people, and about what a people can do when their own States are co-opted into allowing human rights violations by foreign MNCs. They also reveal the real necessity of a legal framework that requires the governments to insist that MNCs adhere to certain non-negotiable principles.

The aforementioned examples depict a victimized people at the mercy of "negatively active" governments and all-powerful MNCs whose freedom of action remains totally unfettered by domestic and international law. There are other examples that illustrate how governments themselves take up the battle against MNCs operating within their own territory. One such example comes from South Africa whose government took up a pro-active role in defending the interests of its people against those of Western pharmaceutical companies.

In 1997, South Africa introduced a law permitting its government to circumvent patented AIDS drugs by allowing the import or manufacture of their generic versions. In response, 39 pharmaceutical companies joined hands to bring a court case against the government in an attempt to block the law claiming that it violated their ownership of drug patents and their intellectual property rights and that such an infringement could undermine the funding of scientific research in the future. The South African government argued that it was not in a position to afford prohibitively high costs of patented medication to deal with the HIV crisis in the country and that the proposed law was essential for the authorities to meet their constitutional duty to provide affordable and sustainable health care to citizens. The case became a public relations disaster for the pharmaceutical companies amidst accusations that they put profit before the lives of millions of people.[28] In April 2001, the companies decided to drop the case.

These cases, representing some drops in the ocean of violations committed by Western MNCs against the populations of developing countries, clearly bring to light the magnitude of the problem in trying to regulate such companies. What form should a legal framework for holding MNCs accountable for human rights violations take? Could one envisage a tiered legal approach whereby in the case of a "collision" of laws as, for example, between pharmaceutical companies' patent rights and the right to health care of individuals, human rights law should always have primacy? Would this be feasible at all? How could the workings of such a system be guaranteed and realized in practice?

In recognition of the need to regulate MNCs in terms of their impact on human rights, numerous codes and declarations have been drawn up. These include, the UN Commission on TNCs, the Rio

Declaration, the Copenhagen Declaration, the Commission on Human Rights, and the Global Compact.[29] Although a number of these documents seem impressive at first sight, the content and the legal obligations which go with them are much less so. Not only are these codes largely voluntary but a number of them were actually established through corporate initiative. This means they do not impinge on corporate interests and do not address substantial human rights, especially ESCR. To a large extent, the purpose of signing up to these codes seems to be, once again, motivated by the lure of greater profits, when labelled an "ethical" company.

(c) *Private Military Companies*

Soldiers of fortune and mercenary organizations are not new to history. Theresa Whelan, US Deputy Assistant Secretary of Defence for African Affairs, made a speech referring to Napoleon's use of civilian contractors to support his garrison on the march, and to the role of the merchant marines in providing critical support to the US navy during WW II. The speech was made on the 19th of November 2003 during a Washington DC dinner hosted by International Peace Operations Association, an advocacy group that works to promote private military firms for security operations worldwide. Theresa Whelan's speech explains how the necessity was driving the United State's policy to enlist private military companies for training, logistical, and operational purposes in Africa and elsewhere.[30] This was a promotional speech that referred to examples of private military deployment in Somalia, Liberia, Sierra Leone, the Ivory Coast, and other places. It is common knowledge that many covert military actions during the Cold War were led by obscure commandos with uncanny connections to the Pentagon, and even such companies as Executive Outcomes (South Africa) and Military Professional Resources, Inc., (USA) continue to bid for overseas military contracts in consultation with their governments to carry out their foreign policy aims. The governments pay substantial amounts of money to buy plausible deniability of responsibility in politically sensitive covert operations.

According to the United Nations Special Rapporteur on Mercenaries, Enrique Bernales Ballesteros: "In practice what is happening is that a process of international restructuring has begun in which the end of bipolarity has left exposed and vulnerable areas formerly in liege to one of the two axes of world power. The disappearance of decisive ideological influence, the cutting-off of economic assistance, and the withdrawal of military control forces have given rise, almost naturally, to complex processes of rearrangement and transition."[31] These histories and the rationalization of the processes developing from the end of bipolarity can be of little help to understand the modern proliferation of private military companies. The forms and functions that they have obtained in our age of unipolar hegemony are likely to influence the sovereign capacities of soft States in ways that would have been inconceivable in previous times.

In 2002, Blackwater USA, a private company based in Moyock, North Carolina, signed a $35.7 million contract with the Pentagon to train 10,000 sailors in "force protection" for special operations. The Blackwater USA website says that since its inception, the company has trained over 50,000 military and law enforcement personnel in different parts of the world. The company has other contracts that are more secretive in nature. The website claims that Blackwater has the people to execute any requirement. Gary Jackson, who retired from the US Navy as a Chief Warrant Officer-4, is the President of the Company. And, who are their personnel? An investigation carried out by Yeoman Barry for *Mother Jones Magazine* provides one example: Tony Torres retired from the US Navy after a tough nine-year career performing search-and-rescue and anti-terrorism operations in life-threatening situations. Following his retirement from the Navy, Tony Torres joined Blackwater USA as a trainer for special operations. Many like Tony also volunteer for hazardous operations for satisfactory payments. The four Americans killed in Iraq on the 31st of March 2004 by an irate mob near Fallujah were actually such recruits working for Blackwater USA. Their killing, as described by Robert Fisk, was brutal: "They had been dragged from their cars, mutilated, stoned, burnt, beaten with iron pipes. One of them was decapitated, then dragged through the streets behind a car". The corpses were, then, hung on an old railway bridge across the Euphrates river, from girders six feet above the road. The incident shows, as Oakland Ross writing in *The Toronto Star* explains, that the largest single ally of the US military force in Iraq is the corporate world of frontline mercenaries. With more than 15,000 personnel on the ground, the private military industry in Iraq is stronger than the 9,000 troops of the British contingent, a strength that must have some bearing on a reconstructed Iraq. A short obituary hosted on http://

www.blackwatersecurity.com/ seeks contributions payable by check to a memorial fund that the company claims to have established to support the families of their "assets" whose mutilated bodied ended up hanging from a bridge over the Euphrates.

Not all the private military companies publicly advertise their losses. A British company called Olive Security lost two of its "assets", Andy Bradsell and Christopher McDonald, when a hostile crowd near Mosul waylaid a convoy they had been engaged to protect. The company has not put up an obituary to ask for contributions.[32] Blackwater USA and several other private organizations, that are in the business of war for profit also, worked for the Pentagon during the Gulf War to provide logistical support to troops on the front lines. The business boomed after September 11th 2001. Soldiery for profit suddenly found previously unexpected channels.

The President of Afghanistan does not feel safe enough with the security services available to him in his sovereign country and is protected by bodyguards who work for DynCorp. Former Haitian President Jean-Bertrand Aristide, likewise, had a contract with Steele Foundation, a California-based private military company, to ensure his physical protection. The company has also stationed about 500 special agents in Iraq. Another British military company called Global Risk Strategies has 1,200 personnel, mostly Nepali Gorkhas and former soldiers from the Fiji islands, deployed in Iraq. These companies are specially licensed by the State department to train and organize militaries in Nigeria, Bulgaria, Taiwan and Equatorial Guinea, several countries in Latin America and now in Asia.

Since the late 1990s, the US has been paying private military companies an estimated $1.2 billion to help the Colombian army fight rebels and their drug trade. In 1994, Military Professional Resources Inc. (MPRI), which calls itself a professional services company engaged in defence-related contracting in the US and international markets, provided military training to the Croatian army under Franjo Tudjman, when the country was under the UN embargo. In August 1995, the Croatian army launched Operation Storm to take back the disputed Kranjina region from the Serbs. The assault was accompanied by bloody acts of ethnic cleansing, summary executions, and indiscriminate shelling of civilian targets, leaving hundreds dead and more than 1,50,000 homeless. Afterwards, Croatians thanked MPRI for the help and the training that made the operation possible. Incorporated by eight former senior military officers in 1988, with its headquarters in Alexandria, Virginia, MPRI has gone on to create a subsidiary called Alexandria Group in November 2000, headed by retired FBI Assistant Director Joseph R. Wolfinger.[33]

Military Professional Resources Inc. boasts that it can call on 12,500 veterans with expertise in everything from nuclear operations to submarine attacks. MPRI provides its personnel to run recruitment centres for the US army, train soldiers for special tasks in many countries, including Korea, South Africa, Kuwait, and now Iraq. The Company is led by General Carl Vuono, who served as the Chief of the Army during the US invasion of Panama and the Gulf War. His team in the firm includes General Crosbie Saint, former commander of the US Army in Europe; Lt. General Harry Soyster, former head of the Defence Intelligence Agency; and General Ron Griffith, former Army Vice Chief of Staff. Colin Powell describes General Vuono as "one of my dearest friends". An investigation by Mother Jones Magazine showed that 17 leading private military firms have invested more than $12.4 million in congressional and presidential campaigns since 1999. DynCorp, a Virginia-based military and technology company that receives nearly $2 billion in annual revenues from the US federal government, regularly pays contributions to the Republican National Committee and others involved in key positions at the Capitol Hill.[34]

Two DynCorp employees exposed a sex slavery business, their Company had been promoting in Bosnia, in the course of helping the American military with peacekeeping operations. The company employees bought and sold local Bosnian girls, some as young as 13, for use as sex slaves, often confiscating their passports so that they would not escape. The supervisor of the Company had himself filmed engaging in sexual intercourse with two such girls, apparently for promotional purposes. When the scandal broke out, the company recalled the persons involved and fired the whistle-blowers.

International Charter Inc., a military company based in Salem, Oregon, and led by Brian Boquist, has provided air transportation for peacekeeping operations in Liberia, Haiti, Sierra Leone, Nigeria, Sudan, and several other counties in Africa and outside.[35] In 1996, Brian Boquist hired DynCorp to fly helicopters for international peacekeepers in Liberia. When rebels spilled into the capital city of Monrovia, shooting and killing people indiscriminately, DynCorp employees fled without even informing Brian Boquist. Boquist and his colleagues bought weapons on the black market and defended the embassy until US reinforcements arrived. Even then, DynCorp is heavily involved in Iraq. Already in March 2003, the company employed more than 1,000 persons to prepare for the war against Iraq. The industry also maintains an advocacy group called International Peace Operations Associations, which specializes in promoting private military firms for security and peace operations in difficult and remote areas. Doug Brooks is the Director of the group.[36]

In 2001, an Alabama-based firm called Aviation Development Corp., which provided reconnaissance for the CIA in South America, misidentified an errant plane as belonging to cocaine traffickers. The Peruvian air force shot down the aircraft, in which Veronica Bowers, a Baptist missionary, and her seven-month-old daughter Charity were travelling. The State Department and the CIA blocked all information on the episode.[37]

Northrop Grumman Corp, a large military contractor, has many subsidiaries, like Vinnell Corp that has for long been involved in training and organizing the Saudi Arabian army and has also won a contract for special duties and training programmes in Iraq. Northrop Grumman has another subsidiary, California Microwave Systems, which is also involved in special operations in Columbia. In February 2003, a private aircraft carrying three former US military officers employed by California Microwave Systems, one Colombian soldier, another American member of the reconnaissance mission, and the pilot was brought down under fire by a left-wing rebel group. One American died following the crash. The pilot and the Colombian soldier were killed in the skirmish with the rebels that followed the crash. The three former American officers, who worked for California Microwave Systems, were taken hostages and have not yet been released. The incident has not generated sufficient publicity or public concern within the US because it involved a private military company.[38]

All these private companies have been involved in sensitive functions in preparing for the current war in Iraq. The list of tasks includes supplying essential support to forward military bases; running mess halls; providing armed guards at the US Army base in Qatar; training soldiers at Camp Doha in Kuwait; and maintaining an array of weapons systems, including the B-2 bombers, F-117 stealth fighter, Apache helicopters, KC-10 refuelling tanks, U-2 reconnaissance planes, and unmanned Global Hawk reconnaissance units. It is estimated that more than 20,000 private contractors are currently working with the US military establishment in the region. It is a multibillion-dollar business and big companies like Halliburton, Brown and Root Services, Lockheed Martin, and Raytheon are also involved. Retired military officers, with good connections within the Pentagon, lead these companies and carry out clandestine operations in soft States to relieve the United States government of direct responsibility.[39]

P.W. Singer, an advocate of privatization of military operations connected with the Hoover Institution, argues that these private firms do what regular armies cannot do. They get hired to establish protected safe havens, facilitate international aid by providing security, etc., when regular armies and UN peacekeepers cannot step in. Singer points out that these private military firms are already operating in more than 100 countries in six continents, making over $100 billion in annual revenue.

In Sierra Leone, a diamond rich country thrown into anarchy by the mining companies, the government of Joseph Momoh faced an implacable insurgency by the Revolutionary United Front (RUF), led by a former nightclub owner Foday Sankoh under protection from Liberia's Charles Taylor. The government was unable to handle the situation and was replaced, in a *coup d'etat*, by 27-year-old Captain Valentine Strasser in May 1992. Strasser was unable to handle the situation and hired the services of the Gorkha Security Guards, a mercenary firm led by James Maynard and Andrew Myers, British nationals, in partnership with American Robert Mackenzie, son-in-law of former CIA deputy director Ray Cline. RUF wiped out the mercenary band, including Robert Mackenzie, and was very close to capturing Freetown, when in early 1995 Strasser's government hired the services of Executive Outcomes, a South African company comprising veterans from the South African apartheid regime's elite forces. The government had the support of multinational mining companies, including Ohio-based Sierra Rutile, which provided the money for the hiring of the mercenary organization.

Executive Outcomes deployed a battalion-sized unit of assault infantry, supported by combat helicopters, and armoured vehicles to defeat the RUF within some weeks of gaining the assignment. The successful operation allowed the government of Sierra Leone to hold its first ever elections in February 1996. Executive Outcomes, which received $35 million and mining concessions for friendly companies for its services, withdrew; and the situation again got out of control.

In 1999, the UN went in but the peace could be restored briefly only after the government signed a peace agreement with Sankoh in prison and under death sentence, offering him not just an amnesty but also the control over the diamond trade and the country's vice-presidency. The UN remained embroiled in the bloody mess for a number of years, but failed to establish order.[40]

P.W. Singer cites this as an example to show what good soldiers of profit can do for humanitarian causes. Of course, no one knows the tactics and operational details of the Executive Outcomes' interventions. But many world leaders are impressed. Apparently in 1994, Kofi Annan commissioned a British company to do a study about the merits of sub-contracting a private security service, preferably Executive Outcomes, to run refugee camps in Rwanda in which murderous leaders of the genocide were hiding.[41]

The British government, too, is reportedly getting enthusiastic about what Singer describes as the twenty-first-century business solution to all pervasive security problems. Singer recommends linking international aid agencies with private military firms to provide them with the necessary security to operate in difficult regions. Singer talks about their use for rapid reaction operations, with an emphasis on combat efficiency, when recalcitrant armed groups create trouble. He also talks about their use in situations of genocidal crises that cannot be controlled by local government agencies and before international interventions can authoritatively occur. The option was actually considered by various governments and the UN peacekeeping department monitoring the situation in eastern Zaire in 1996. According to Singer, the plan could not be implemented because of disputes over who would have to pay. He suggests that the issue of payment will gradually become secondary when governments and the UN recognize that it would be more sensible to use soldiers of profit to establish order in places like Mogadishu before their peacekeepers get involved.

Discussing the matter businesslike, Singer suggests that Executive Outcomes would have been able to intervene in Rwanda in 1994, deploying no more than 1,500 of its soldiers supported by air and fire support within 14 days of its hire, and to stop the genocide over the next six months for no more than $150 million. Singer points out that the UN relief operation that followed the genocide cost approximately $3 million a day and it would have been wiser in terms of cost effectiveness to follow the private option.

Of course, Singer is aware that accountability would suffer if private military firms are hired in such circumstances. Many notorious and ruthless military officers of the Soviet and apartheid regimes, who act without any respect for human rights, dominate the industry. The firms would not turn over their employees to the local authorities for justice. Their contracts include provisions for their anonymous withdrawal from the scene if things get dirty. According to Singer, the UN peacekeepers themselves engage in atrocities that mostly go unreported.[42]

Under the circumstances, interested powers are taking a look at the military labour and knowledge that has begun to circulate as commodities to be bought and sold in the world market. Mercenaries may "align" themselves with a State and offer their services for pay. However, they do not embrace the political ideology of the State and do not offer themselves for sacrificial acts in terms of the duties and obligations of citizenship. Mercenaries are there for business in blood and bring their skills in managing and deploying their power of violence for pay. Mercenaries, former soldiers, pilfer the military training and specialized skills and employ them to constitute a new military profession for profit without carrying other ideological ballast. The mercenary companies also constitute the most serious challenge to the established political wisdom that States alone hold the monopoly over the use of force.

We know that the situation is not entirely unique. It has been reported that in the period between 1300 A.D., and 1900 A.D., privateers, mercantile companies, and mercenaries were, like casual labourers, alienable commodity in the international market. Mercenary soldiers in Europe constituted a major export trade throughout the Middle Ages. They were common in Renaissance Italy. Charles VII of France integrated large groups of mercenary gangs into his standing army in 1445 A.D. Also, during the eighteenth century, most European States enrolled foreign mercenaries into their troops. Britain engaged more than 18,000 privates to deal with the US War of Independence. In the thirteenth century, it relied on private military adventurers to undertake foreign ventures, including establishing its colonies. It is only in the nineteenth century that States interfered to set up a centralized control over private violence and to establish a hierarchical order with a legal façade.[43]

With the return of the medieval conditions of a mercenary market in our own age, it is necessary to examine the role of laws in evaluating their operations. In *United States v. Terrel*, the United States was charged with shipping and transporting weapons to the Nicaraguan Contras. The US district court ruled that the United States was not at peace with Nicaragua but the Contras were funding the operations themselves with the objective to overthrow the Sandinista government. The United States shared this objective but was not under any obligation to occupy the killing fields in a low-intensity situation of warfare and the court further added that mercenaries can act with impunity to assist the covert operations in which the United States had a stake. The court's interpretation of the US neutrality law showed that the United States could deploy mercenaries to block the application of the laws of war.[44]

Let us briefly examine the existing legal response to the growing challenge of the global mercenary trade. In 1972, the Organization of African Unity Convention for the Elimination of Mercenaries in Africa prohibited the use of mercenaries by insurgent groups. But the Convention did not forbid States from hiring them. Thus, the African States appropriated the pool of military manpower available for sale only for their own purposes.[45]

The Protocol Additional to the Geneva Convention of the 12th of August 1949 and Relating to the Protection of Victims of International Armed Conflicts (Protocol I) does not prohibit the use of mercenaries by States or other entities. It simply deprives mercenaries of the status of combatants in armed conflicts, and denies them protections afforded to other combatants, including the right to be treated as a prisoner of war when captured.[46]

The 1989 International Convention Against the Recruitment, Use, Financing and Training of Mercenaries defines them as people who "participate in a concerted act of violence aimed at … overthrowing a government or otherwise undermining the constitutional order of a State or undermining the territorial integrity of a State".[47] It also focuses on the financial motivations of such mercenaries who "receive material compensation substantially in excess of that promised or paid to combatants of similar rank and functions in the armed forces of that party".[48] Clearly, the Convention does not interfere with the State's freedom to engage mercenary companies for its own purposes.

The customary international law, mainly the Hague Convention of 1907 on the Rights and Duties of Neutral Powers and Persons in War on Land, imposes mild restrictions on the circulation of private military labour and on their recruitment within their territory against other nations. It also says that "corps of combatants cannot be formed nor recruiting agencies opened on the territory of a neutral power to assist the belligerents." However, Article 6 of the Hague Convention also states that the "responsibility of the neutral power is not engaged by the fact of persons crossing the frontier secretly to offer their services to one of the belligerents."[49]

Clearly, the loopholes within customary law permit sufficient scope to States to permit a black-market in military labour; to draw from and exploit it according to their needs; and to prohibit its benefits to rebel and insurgent groups.

The Special Rapporteur on Mercenaries released a report in 1997 to point out that many countries were recruiting private mercenary companies registered in foreign countries to provide internal security services, safeguard public order, and even to end internal armed conflicts. The report notes: "If such contracts are, indeed, being concluded, the governments signing them must be doing so on the basis of a sovereign decision; but is it not the responsibility for a country's internal order and security, an inalienable obligation that a State fulfils through its police and armed forces? Is it not a grave infringement of that State's sovereignty to hand over such responsibilities to companies registered in third countries which sell security services staffed by foreigners, presumably mercenaries? Who will be responsible for any repressive excesses that the security companies may commit against the civilian population, especially when representatives of the political opposition are concerned? Who will take responsibility for any violations of international humanitarian law or human rights they may commit?"[50]

(d) *Armed Opposition Groups and Individuals "Involved" in Armed Conflict in a Private Capacity*

Although the Geneva Conventions of 1949 seek to regulate the conduct of armed opposition groups, they remain largely outside the framework of international human rights obligations for the simple reason that, lacking in the governmental status, they are not invited to sign up to international human rights instruments. The First Protocol to the Geneva Convention on the Laws of War, which applies to international armed conflicts, accords special status to armed opposition groups that engage in fighting against colonial domination, alien occupation, and racist regimes. Within the terms of the Protocol, members of such groups are to be treated, when captured, as prisoners of war, and cannot be prosecuted for acts of combat.[51]

We do not know if Polisario, widely recognized as the legitimate representative of the people of Western Sahara, effectively under the control of Morocco, and the P.L.O., universally acknowledged as the body representing the Palestinian people, are signatories to the First Protocol. We suspect that they have not formally applied. The Naga people in the north-eastern peripheries of India have been engaged in a national liberation struggle since 1947. The government of India has been formally negotiating a peaceful political settlement, unconditionally, with the National Social Council of Nagalim (NSCN) under a ceasefire agreement signed in 1997. But the NSCN is not a signatory to the First Protocol and is not recognized internationally as a national liberation movement.

Although liberation or self-determination movements cannot ratify Additional Protocol I (AP I), one would generally expect them to lobby the UN for recognition of their status and for access to international law mechanisms if the governments that have signed API begin to violate its terms.

Similarly, in the case of internal conflicts, Additional Protocol II (AP II) can apply only if the affected government has ratified it. In the event that the government has ratified APII, the government itself decides whether or not the threshold for the application of APII has been met. Governments are generally reluctant to assert that this threshold has been met, and that an armed opposition group controls enough territory to be able to carry out sustained military operations.

In reality, many such armed groups effectively control large territories and rule their inhabitants with force to obtain loyalty and revenue. The rule of force inevitably results in acts of abuse without there being a normative framework or a legitimate system to enforce accountability. Ironically enough, most of these armed opposition groups represent themselves as liberation or self-determination movements and rely on the rhetoric of human rights, justice, and human dignity to convey their political objectives.

Most governments use the excuse of uncontrollable political violence, all-encompassingly branded as terrorism in our own times, to sanction or silently acquiesce in atrocities committed by their own armed forces. Enforced disappearances, extra-judicial killings, and custodial torture are pervasive. Human rights groups worldwide spend most of their time and resources documenting and exposing such atrocities and in seeking truth, justice, and reparation, often in vain.

The problem clearly requires a remedy within a binding framework of international norms and a system of monitoring, accountability, and enforcement. Measures are required to hold governments as well as armed opposition groups accountable for atrocities they respectively commit.

The problem was taken up for discussion at the 1990 session of the Commission on Human Rights held in Geneva, with Peru and Columbia proposing the creation of special mechanisms under the UN to monitor, report on, and work for the cessation of violent crimes perpetrated by armed opposition groups. The initiative failed due to arguments advanced by several participants that the governments were well-equipped with special legislation to use force to curb violent crime, and that the focus on human rights abuses committed by armed opposition groups would only assist governments in concealing their own failures and abuses. Eventually, the Commission adopted a modified resolution that required the existing Special Rapporteurs and Working Groups under the Commission on Human Rights to pay special attention to atrocities committed by armed opposition groups.[52] The requirement can have meaning only if the Commission engages with the armed opposition groups and accords them a status, subject to scrutiny, within the terms of the First Protocol. The requirement of monitoring is important especially with regard to those armed opposition groups which stand some chance of gaining control over the State. If they succeed, they should be retrospectively judged and made to account for their actions. If they continue to commit atrocities, without any regard for international human rights norms, they should forfeit their status as a group enjoying recognition within the terms of the First Protocol.

The principles of responsibility for human rights crimes involving non-State actors are not altogether alien to the modern history of human rights accountability. The Nuremberg trials implicated several persons who did have a formal position of authority under the Third Reich. Especially notable are the cases of Flick, I.G. Farben, Krupp and Zyklon B. The Nuremberg tribunal sentenced two civilian industrialists belonging to Zyklon B., a chemical company, to death for supplying asphyxiating gas to kill inmates in Hitler's concentration camps. Flick, a steel industrialist, was convicted to seven years of imprisonment for using slave labour in his factories. In his case, the

Tribunal clearly pronounced: "Acts adjudged criminal when done by an officer of the government are criminal also when done by a private individual. The guilt differs in magnitude, not in quality. The offender in either case is charged with personal wrong, and punishment falls on the offender in *propria persona* (for one's self). There is no justification for a limitation of responsibility to public officials." The Tribunal applied the same reasoning to convict the industrialists in charge of I.G. Farben and Krupp.[53] We propose that the same standards of accountability should apply to recognized armed opposition groups that aim to capture State power and to govern their people.

(e) *NGOs*

Non-governmental organizations cannot claim any exception to the principles of accountability. Like IFIs and MNCs, NGOs significantly influence human rights and set the rights agendas. The difference is that in the public mind, NGOs are generally associated with positives: they influence the human rights situation of a given place or peoples positively and use "rights talk" to do so. Unfortunately, such generalizations are not always useful. Many activities undertaken in the name of "development" have later been recognized as ill-conceived and perhaps even counter-productive in human rights terms. Furthermore, it is not clear that the NGOs truly represent democratic constituencies and that they observe democratic norms in their decision-making processes. In this context, we must ask: Are human rights NGOs themselves democratic? Do they act transparently? To whom are they accountable? Where do they get their legitimacy from? Are the causes they champion always worthy? Are they really independent and impartial? NGOs are often dependent for financial support on governments and other international institutions. Do they, therefore, really offer solutions or do they simply assuage people's pain and, thus, perpetuate current systems of governance and, thus, violations? How do they use human rights and to what end, theoretically and practically? Furthermore, do NGOs not absolve the State of some of its obligations towards its people by entering spaces vacated by the State, such as by providing health care, education, training opportunities, etc.? Is such behaviour not an incentive for governments to further abdicate their responsibilities in such areas with the knowledge that NGOs will take over the job? Do NGOs, therefore, provide governments with a safety net or a cushion, by fulfilling their obligations? And since, most of the areas

NGOs have now "occupied" are in the field of ESCR, are they not, to a certain extent, "forcing" governments to focus on CPR? Do NGOs contribute to the problems of HR discourse or, are they actually a part of the problem?

Obviously, answers to these questions are not easy and clear-cut. Professor Winston P. Nagan, professor of law at the University of Florida College of Law and former Chair of Amnesty International, USA, who has been involved with a number of major INGOs, has the following to say while discussing the issue of the role of INGOs in the making and application of human rights law and practice:

> "In point of fact, not every INGO is an operation that seeks benign and ideal humanitarian and human rights goals. Some INGOs may well be in the business of doing everything possible to disparage world order and human dignity as, for example, in those non-governmental operations that are specialized in organized crime, terrorism, paramilitary, proto-fascist, hate and violence groups, and so on. Other INGOs may be the quintessential representatives of powerful political and economic interests, and whose basic orientation is not the vindication of the common interest humanity has in human dignity, but rather to special interest concerns that may or may not coincide with some version of the human dignity objective. In other words, we have to be cautious about the power vacuum produced by an uncritical proliferation of the global institutions of civil society, recognizing that some of these institutions of civil society are critical to the struggle for human rights, while others are critical to the struggle against human rights."[54]

HR Discourse as a Controlling, Hegemonic Discourse

Throughout this note, constant reference has been made to "rights talk". As we have seen, "rights talk" is used by governments, IFIs, MNCs, NGOs, basically, by virtually everybody. Why? How come?

On the one hand, the use of the discourse of human rights may be necessary or expedient to articulate claims and aims. First, it serves as an internationally understood, recognized, and legitimate vehicle of certain values, claims, and goals. Secondly, it serves to rename peoples' experience in rights terms—a problem becomes a "violation", people become "victims"—and thereby, people become the holders of a certain category of rights and the violations suffered become intolerable and unacceptable. Because a violation has been suffered, right-holders have entitlements that fall within the realm of legal obligations rather than that of charity or generosity. On the other hand, all players must use the same discourse because, as Ashis Nandy has put it, "both the game and the game rules are set by the West, so even the opposition must be in the same language and vocabulary as the West, for the West is still the ultimate arbiter of categories. Debate, if it is carried out, must be in terms of these categories or it is not legitimate".[55] The result is that the voices of the oppressed and the oppressors become indistinguishable. Furthermore, by using the same discourse, the oppressed lose "the opportunity of voicing a genuine challenge to the hegemonic values and policies (that the language and values of rights) entail."[56]

The lack of choice of the oppressed further extends to "emancipatory projects" which "must be expressed in the vocabulary of 'rights' to be heard", whereas "good policies that are not framed that way go unattended". In sum, "efforts that cannot be articulated in the vocabulary of 'rights' seem less legitimate, less practical, less worth the effort".[57] The consequence is that the discourse of human rights crowds out efforts to come up with other, alternative discourses, projects, policies, ways of doing, etc, as well as resources and legitimacy.

The human rights discourse is, thus, indeed a controlling discourse. It controls the values talked about; the language in which they are talked about; the projects and policies designed to "implement" them, and frames the choices of people as well as governments and, therefore, the way in which they view themselves and others. Yet, within the realm of reality, "rights talk" appears to have only a marginal influence. What explains this gap between enunciation and action; language and reality? Clearly, the problem is at least partly intrinsic to the nature of the discourse.

From the very beginning, claims of rights have relied on arguments of a transcendental morality and an intellectually envisioned rationality of nature that have consciously placed themselves outside the positivistic tradition. The discourse presupposes inherent virtues, ethical awareness, the capacity for freedom, and inter-subjective tolerance in a "universal" humanity with little patience for the processes of empirical verification and even less faith in the potentials of social engineering. Various shades of social contract theories, which explain the relations between the State and citizens, see the source of moral obligations in individual autonomy and expect it to survive the pressures of antithetical motivations such as the urge for power, possession, economic greed, covetousness, malice, unruliness, anger, and violence in individuals and human collectives. The dichotomy between the spirit and the matter or the soul and the body, which informed metaphysical speculations of idealistic philosophies, is replicated within the human rights discourse in its formulation of the paradox between the State and the citizens. Theories of social contract tend to be as ahistorical and mythically oriented as the speculations about the divine origins of sovereignty. The concept of justice is so primarily tied to the utilitarian enterprise of striving for the best results that justice ceases to have an objective value. Hair-splitting of the law, pitilessly in moralistic and positivistic terms, often fails to recognize that law can serve other purposes as well. It fails to see that the law can be simultaneously stereotyping as well as used for indoctrination, elaboration, and justification for the established interests. The discourse becomes a prey to the law's empty incantations, remaining alienated from the norm-building activities within the civil society. It fails to recognize that the practices of power are not bound by a set of immutable principles or by a watertight system of procedures, but by the insuperability of democratic opinion. The human rights discourse often fails to recognize that the uncertain promises of the law are realized by claiming them against the hazards of political repression. "Rights talk", which has become increasingly entangled in legalism, baulks at the recognition that the basic rationality of law is not 'right' or 'morality' but social preservations and that the due process and the power of judicial review, necessary to defend substantive human entitlements, cannot by themselves alter the socio-economic and political conditions responsible for their deprivation. "Rights talk" has become generally inattentive to the complexity of the human struggle for dignity and to the predicaments of conscientious judgment about the rightness of reactions and resistance to the practices of power in the world.

The realities of the world are there before us all to see. Fifty-six years after the adoption of the UDHR, the world remains trapped within familiar and persistent trends of human disparities; suffering from squalor and denial of the minimum requirements of survival; political repression and tyranny; and conflict, violence, and the pervasive destruction of the environment. Thousands of civilians are regularly exterminated in religious, ethnic, and political conflicts throughout the world. Millions of people remain bonded and compelled into conditions of human servitude without remuneration and dignity. Human trafficking for prostitution has become a major issue. Not only the exploitation of child labour, but also the forced recruitment of child soldiers appears to be beyond actual remedy. Developed countries are witnessing a steady rise in the levels of violence against people of colour, especially those of the Middle Eastern origins. The law enforcement agencies brazenly admit to racial profiling of suspect foreign-looking people, resulting in malicious prosecutions. Despite the growing evidence of a high percentage of death penalty mistakes and the evident disparity in death sentencing, advocacy for executions has only become more strident. The global war on terror appears to have become a camouflage for the establishment of a trans-hemispheric hegemony of the only Superpower across the globe, unleashing new horrors of conflict, chaos, instability, violence, human rights violations, and bloody repression.

Notwithstanding the hype around globalization, socio-economic conditions in the developing world, especially in Africa, have become dismal as never before. Despite the clamour of developing countries for a more equitable share of the world's resources, captured in the draft of the New International Economic Order adopted by the United Nations General Assembly in 1974, international financial institutions remain obsessed with structural-adjustment approaches. The 1999 United Nations Development Programme (UNDP) Human Development Report offers some glimpses into the nature of the problems of inequality. The report points out that:

1. By the late 1990s, the top one-fifth of the world's people lived in the highest income countries and had 86 percent of the world's Gross Domestic Product, against the bottom fifth's just 1 percent.
2. The assets of the top three billionaires total more than the combined Gross National Product of all the least developed countries and their 600 million people. The highest income countries possessed 74 percent of the world's telephone lines; constituted 93.3 percent of the world's Internet users; and consumed 84 percent of the world's paper.
3. Although only 10 percent of the people worldwide speak English, 80 percent of Internet websites appear in English.[58]

So, what can the human rights movement do in this situation made further distraught by the global conservative backlash? What can it do to improve the daily material conditions of people's lives? How can it liberate their resources of mind and spirit towards higher pursuits through poverty alleviation?

Probably, the movement needs to revive the traditions of protest and struggle when legal methods fail. The human rights movement, largely manipulated by INGOs and NGOs dependent on foreign funding, has veered towards top-down approaches, law-focused activism, and lobbying at high political levels without developing sufficient participation from the affected constituencies.

Notes

1. "The state is the highest form of community and aims at the highest good. The state aims at satisfying all the needs of men. Men form states to secure a bare subsistence; but the ultimate object of the state is the good life" at http://www.mdx.ac.uk/www/study/xarianal.htm
2. Appiah, Kwame Anthony, *Thinking it Through* (New York: Oxford University Press, 2003) 226.
3. New York: Basic Books, 1977.
4. Chris Jochnick, "Confronting the Impunity of Non-State Actors: New Fields for the Promotion of Human Rights", *Human Rights Quarterly* 21,1 (1999) 56-79.
5. David Kennedy, "The International Human Rights Movement: Part of the Problem?", *Harvard Human Rights Journal* 15 (Spring 2002) 113.
6. Chris Jochnick, "Confronting the Impunity of Non-State Actors: New Fields for the Promotion of Human Rights", *Human Rights Quarterly* 21, 1 (1999) 56-79.
7. Declaration on the Right to Development, adopted by the General Assembly through Resolution 41/128 of 4th of December 1986, Article 1(1) at http://www.unhchr.ch/html/menu3/b/74.htm
8. Vienna Declaration and Programme of Action, adopted by the World Conference on Human Rights on 25th of June 1993, Article 5 at http://www.unhchr.ch/huridocda/huridoca.nsf/(Symbol)/A.CONF.157.23.En?OpenDocument.
9. Amartya Sen, "Human Rights and Asian Values", *The New Republic*, July 14-July 21, 1997.
10. Report of the Round-Table on the Draft Optional Protocol to the ICESCR, 30 November 2001 at www.icj.org/IMG/pdf/doc-55.pdf
11. *Soobramoney Vs Minister of Health*, KwaZulu-Natal 1998 (1) SA 765 (CC).

12. Constitution of the Republic of South Africa, Section 27 (1.2).
13. *Soobramoney Vs Minister of Health*, KwaZulu-Natal 1998 (1) SA 765 (CC), para. 29.
14. *Government of the Republic of South Africa and Others Vs. Grootboom* (Grootboom) 2001 (1) SA 46 (CC).
15. *Ibid.*, para. 20.
16. *Ibid.*, para. 35.
17. *Ibid.*, para. 45.
18. *Ibid.*, para. 46.
19. Chris Jochnick, "Confronting the Impunity of Non-State Actors: New Fields for the Promotion of Human Rights", *Human Rights Quarterly* 21, 1 (1999) 56-79.
20. Emma Mawdsley and Jonathan Rigg, "The World Development Report Series II: Continuity and Change in Development Orthodoxies", *Progress in Development Studies* 3,4 (2003) 271-286.
21. "...with due attention to considerations of economy and efficiency and without regard to political or other non-economic influences or considerations", IBRD, Articles of Agreement III, Section 5.
22. Vienna Declaration and Programme of Action, 1993.
23. Cristina Baez, Michele Dearing, Margaret Delatour, and Christine Dixon, "Multinational Enterprises and Human Rights", *B.B. International Law* 183, 239, 8 (1999/2000); Claudia R. Brewster, "Restoring Childhood: Saving the World's Children from Toiling in Textile Sweatshops", *Journal of Law and Commerce* 191-192, 16 (1997); Jonathan Wide, "The Marbor Man in Asia: U.S. Tobacco and Human Rights", *Vancouver Journal of Transnational Law* 329, 29 (1996); Mark B. Baker, "Tightening the Toothless Vise: Codes of Conduct and the American Multinational Enterprise, *Wisconsin International Law Journal* 89, 20 (2001); Jack Donnelly, "Human Rights Globalization and the State" in Monique Castermans-Holleman, Fried van Hoof and Jacqueline Smith eds., *The Role of the Nation-State in the 21st Century: Human Rights, International Organizations and Foreign Policy* 201, 407 (1998).
24. "The Enron Corporation: Corporate Complicity in Human Rights Violations", *Human Rights Watch* 104-11 (1999).
25. *Doe Vs Exxon Mobile Corp.*, No. 01-CV-1357, D.D.C., filed 19 July 2001; Kenneth Roth, "US Hypocrisy in Indonesia", *International Herald Tribune*, 14th of August 2002; Peter Waldman and Timothy Mapes, "White House sets new hurdles for suits over rights abuses", *Wall Street Journal*, 7 August 2002.
26. Rift with Shell Oil Can't be Healed Without Justice - Gateway Green Alliance/Green Party of St. Louis, February 2000 at http://www.greens.org/s-r/gga/ogoni.html
27. Ariande K. Sacharoff, "Multinationals in Host Countries: Can they be

held liable under the Alien Tort Claims Act for Human Rights Violations?", *Journal of International Law* 927, 958-64, 22 (1998).

28. www.news.bbc.co.uk/hi/english/world/africa/newsid_1284000/1284633.stm.
29. The Global Compact is an initiative of the Secretary-General of the UN. It was first proposed in 1999 and contains principles derived from international instruments, including, inter alia, from the UDHR and ILO provisions.
30. Theresa Whelan, Deputy Assistant Secretary of Defence for African Affairs, Remarks to IPOA Dinner, 19 November 2003, Washington, DC at http://www.defenselink.mil/policy/sections/policy_offices/isa/africa/IPOA.htm
31. Report on the Question of the Use of Mercenaries as a Means of Violating Human Rights and Impending the Exercise and the Right of Peoples to Self-Determination, U.N. ESCOR, 50th Session at 15, UN Doc. E/CN.4/1994/23/1994.
32. Blackwater at http://www.blackwaterusa.com/; Yeoman Barry, "Soldiers of Good Fortune", *Mother Jones* 28, 3 (1 May 2003) 38. Also at http://www.motherjones.com/news/feature/2003/05/ma_365_01.html; Robert Fisk, "Atrocity in Fallujah", *The Independent*, 1 April 2004; Oakland Ross, "Rise of the Private-Sector Soldier: Falluja Killings put Spotlight on Corporate Cadres, *The Toronto Star*, 4 April 2004; "Military Planners Say Price Right for Neo-Mercenaries" at http://www.lubrinco.com/articles/Toronto% 20Star%204%20April%202004.pdf
33. MPRI—Taking Expertise Around the World at http://www.mpri.com/channels/about.html; Yeoman Barry, "Soldiers of Good Fortune", *Mother Jones* 28, 3 (1 May 2003) 38. Also at http://www.motherjones.com/news/feature/2003/05/ma_365_01.html; Oakland Ross, "Rise of the Private-Sector Soldier: Falluja Killings put Spotlight on.Corporate Cadres, *The Toronto Star*, 4 April 2004; "Military Planners Say Price Right for Neo-Mercenaries" http://www.lubrinco.com/articles/Toronto%20Star%204%20April% 202004.pdf; "Second Class Citizens: The Serbs of Croatia", *Human Rights Watch*, index no. D1103, 1 March 1999.
34. Yeoman Barry, "Soldiers of Good Fortune", *Mother Jones* 28, 3 (1 May 2003) 38. Also at http://www.motherjones.com/news/feature/2003/05/ma_365_01.html
35. International Charter Incorporated of Oregon at http://www.icioregon.com/aviation.htm (Last visited on 10 February 2006)
36. Yeoman Barry, "Soldiers of Good Fortune", *Mother Jones* 28, 3 (1 May 2003) 38. Also at http://www.motherjones.com/news/feature/2003/05/ma_365_01.html; International Peace Operations Associations Association at http://www.ipoaonline.org/

37. Yeoman Barry, "Soldiers of Good Fortune", *Mother Jones* 28, 3 (1 May 2003) 38. Also at http://www.motherjones.com/news/feature/2003/05/ma_365_01.html; Wayne Madsen, "Peruvian No-Fly Zone: Case of the Missionaries Shot Down in Peru", *The Progressive*, June 2001; Cynthia Cotts, "Spooked in Peru", *Village Voice*, May 2-8, 2001. Also at http://www.villagevoice.com/issues/0118/cotts.php
38. Oakland Ross, "Rise of the Private-Sector Soldier: Falluja Killings put Spotlight on Corporate Cadres, *The Toronto Star*, 4 April 2004; "Military Planners Say Price Right for Neo-Mercenaries" at http://auto_sol.tao.ca/node/view/127?PHPSESSID=2303a5274564f7f4eb63715020714386
39. Borzou Daragahi, "Use of Private Security Firms in Iraq Draws Concerns", *The Washington Times*, 6 October 2003. Aslo at http://washingtontimes.com/world/20031006-122420-5426r.htm
40. Shawcross, William, *Deliver Us from Evil: Warlords and Peacekeepers in a World of Endless Conflict* (London: Bloomsbury, 2000) 171-175; Sue Cullinan, "Time Trail: Sierra Leone" at http://www.time.com/time/europe/timetrails/sierraleone/; "Militarization and Minerals Tour: Sierra Leone" at http://www.moles.org/ProjectUnderground/mil/sleone.html
41. Shawcross, William, *Deliver Us from Evil: Warlords and Peacekeepers in a World of Endless Conflict* (London: Bloomsbury, 2000) 122-3.
42. P.W. Singer, "Private Militaty Corporations", Policy Review Online, No.119, June-July 2003. Also at http://www.policyreview.org/jun03/singer_print.html; Dr. Abdel Fatau Musah, "Mercenaries are Part of the Problem", *Africa Analysis* (1 May 2001); Dr. Musah, Abdel Fatau, *Mercenaries: An African Security Dilemma* (London: Pluto Press, 2000).
43. Thompson, Janice E., *Mercenaries, Pirates, and Sovereigns: State-Building and Extraterritorial Violence in Early Modern Europe* (Princeton: Princeton University Press, 1994); Huntington, Samuel, *The Soldier and the State: The Theory and Politics of Civil-Military Relations* (Cambridge: Harvard University Press, 1957); Charles Tilly, "Theories of Political Transformation" in Charles Tilly ed., *The Formation of Nation-States in Western Europe* (Princeton: Princeton University Press, 1975) 638; V. G. Kieman, "Foreign Mercenaries and Absolute Monarchy" in Trevor Aston ed., *Crisis in Europe 1560-1660* (London: Routledge and Kegan Paul, 1965) 121; Ingrao, Charles W., *The Hessian Mercenary State: Ideas, Institutions, and Reform under Frederick II, 1760-1785* (Cambridge: Cambridge University Press, 1987); Thomas J. Wertenbaker, "Virginia Under the Stuarts, 1607-1688" (Princeton: Princeton University Press,1914) 29-30.
44. *United States Vs.Terrel*, 731 F. Supp.. At 476.
45. Organization of African Unity Convention for the Elimination of Mercenaries in Africa, OAU. Doc. CM/433/Rev. L. Annex 1, 1972.
46. Protocol Additional to the Geneva Conventions of 12th of August 1949

and Relating to the Protection of Victims of International Armed Conflict [Protocol I], Article 47(1) adopted on 8th of June, 1977, 1125 UNTS 3, 16ILM 1391.

47. International Convention against the Recruitment, Use, Financing and Training of Mercenaries, 4th of December 1989, Article 1.1 at http://www.un.org/documents/ga/res/44/a44r034.htm
48. International Convention against the Recruitment, Use, Financing and Training of Mercenaries, G.A. Res. A/44/34 UN GAOR 44th Session, Annex., Agenda Item 144 UN Doc. A/Res/44/34, 1989.
49. Convention Respecting the Rights and Duties of Neutral Powers and Persons on Land adopted on 18th of October, 1907, 36 Stat. 231, T.S. No. 540.
50. 1997 Report on the Question of the Use of Mercenaries, p. 93, UN ESCOR, 53rd Session, Annex. Agenda Item 7, UN Doc. E/CN.4/1997/24, 1997.
51. Protocol Additional to the Geneva Conventions of 12th of August 1949, opened for signature on 12th of December, 1977, U.N. Doc. A/32/144, Annex I (1977), reprinted in 16 I.L.M. 1442 (1977).
52. Summary Record of the 1st Part – Public – of the 54th Meeting, held at the Palais des Nations, Geneva, 7th of March 1990: Commission on Human Rights, 46th Session; UN Document E/CN4/1990/SR54.
53. Law Reports of the Trials of War Criminals, L.R.W.T.C., Vol. 5, p. 59; History of the U.N. War Crimes Commission, 1948; *Ibid.*, Vol. 11, pp. 1-18; L.R.W.T.C., Vol. 15, p. 60.
54. Winston P. Nagan, "Human Rights and Non-State Actors", *Pace International Law Review* 209, 11 (Spring 1999).
55. Nandy, Ashish, "Human Rights and Western Dominance" in Chandra Muzaffar, ed., *Human Wrongs: Reflections on Western Global Dominance and its Impact upon Human Rights* (Penang: Just World Trust, 1996) 139.
56. David Kennedy, "The International Human Rights Movement: Part of the Problem?", *Harvard Human Rights Journal* 15 (Spring 2002).
57. *Ibid.*, p. 108.
58. Human Development Report, UNDP, pp. 2-6, U.N. Sales No. 99. III. B. 43, 1999.

Chapter Twelve

The War on Terror, Islam and Wahabi Fundamentalism

The distance learning period of the 5th course witnessed a serious engagement between the participants and the faculty on several sensitive issues connected with the developing global perceptions about the Islamic threat to the legitimacy of modern values and the manner in which they influence political-military mobilizations against various autonomous movements under the clarion call of a war against "terrorism" and "fundamentalism". The participants' inquiries reflected the moral and political predicaments which the artificial spectre of a global Islamic threat has introduced into the kaleidoscopic world of national, ethnic, political, and human rights movements ranging across countries in which Muslims, with nothing in common but a shared aspiration to transcend the inequities of history, predominate.

One Bangladeshi participant pointed out how the US reactions to 9/11, originating in prejudices, hubris of power, mistrust, and fear of widespread discontent within the Muslim world against the injustices of the trans-hemispheric hegemony, have merely reinforced and magnified existing problems of violence and strife. He explained how the stereotyping of Muslims as "terrorists and fundamentalists" has resulted in innocent Muslims worldwide, "especially the young people", becoming victims of human rights abuses. He also discussed how atrocious States worldwide have begun to use the fog of war against terrorism to violently stamp out legitimate struggles of peoples. The participant from Bangladesh made yet another significant point. According to him, even as "Muslims as the catalysts of violence" receive the imprimatur of headlines within the world media, it becomes "a mundane duty of every follower of Islam to make it crystal clear to every other non-Muslim citizen of the world that Islam is indeed the greatest promoter of peace on earth."

One participant from the northern areas of Pakistan commented on a paper, included in the list of essential reading, about the workings of tribal councils in the country by Mary D. Castetter, which appeared in *Indiana International and Comparative Law Review*, 2003. The participant sounded distressed by the framework adopted by the author to analyze the dispensation of justice by the Pakistani tribal councils. Whereas the author sees the Pakistani tribal councils as constituting an unofficial organism of justice parallel to the formal court system in the country, in the participant's view, this simply leads to the unhappy conclusion of Pakistan being "a primitive rather than a civilized State". The participant also disagreed with the value-judgmental implications behind the author's inference that "in Pakistani society, men's honour resides in the actions of the women of his family", giving rise to severe penalties against women suspected of "honour crimes". The Pakistani participant suggested that being "the carrier of the family honour" should actually be flattering to women. The participant also disagreed with the author's discussion of rape within the context of the "code of honour" and finds it "to be exaggerated". According to the participant, prohibition on adultery, which is common to many religious systems, is essential to maintain societal coherence and harmony and "to shake the religious values of any religion" in itself amounts to a violation of human rights. The participant also objected to what he believes to be the negative insinuations behind the author's description that "the standard amount of compensation for the murder of a man is Rs. 2,00,000 while the murder of a woman fetches Rs. 4,00,000." According to him, the example shows, if anything, that the "principle of equality is crossed in favour of women."

The participant, however, seemed to agree with the analysis and the recommendations in the conclusive part of Castetter's paper which cites inefficiency, tardiness, high financial costs, and corruption of the official criminal justice system in Pakistan to argue that systemic reforms rather than an outright abolition of the tribal councils must be the way forward.

One Muslim participant from Sri Lanka tried to explain the roots of the long-drawn conflict, violence, and trauma within the country in terms of racial, religious, and linguistic intolerance, political misunderstandings, and the propensity to violence in all sections of society. The participant pointed out that Sri Lankan armed groups—themselves victims of Sinhalese tyranny, intolerance, and injustice—

did not hesitate to ruthlessly uproot and drive away more than 70,000 Muslim inhabitants from the northern part of Sri Lanka in 1990. Since then, no government in Sri Lanka, let alone the Tamil armed groups, has cared to pay attention to the plight of these unfortunate people who once lived a life of dignity and economic self-sufficiency. For the last 14 years, these unfortunate Muslims from the northern part of Sri Lanka have been living in make-shift shelters without the essentials of life; like food, water, health, hygiene, and education. The Sri Lankan participant wondered what meaning the international humanitarian and human rights law can claim to have when even peace mediators from different parts of the world fail to take note of the plight of the Muslim minority in the country arising out of their internal displacement.

In our view, the arguments of the Bangladeshi participant offer an extraordinarily genteel reproach to the uncanny combination of military violence, imperialistic arrogance, cultural bigotry, and disdain for the facts of history that characterize the response of the United States and its allies to the events of 9/11. The President of the United States has been speaking to explain its rationale.

Some quotations are necessary. On the 20th of September 2001, President Bush announced his agenda of the 'war on terror' before a joint session of the Congress: "Our war on terror begins with Al Qaeda, but it does not end there. It will not end until every terrorist group of global reach has been found, stopped and defeated... They are the heirs of all the murderous ideologies of the 20th century. By sacrificing human life to serve their radical visions, by abandoning every value except the will to power, they follow in the path of fascism, Marxism and totalitarianism. And they will follow that path all the way to where it ends in history's unmarked grave of discarded lies... We will direct every resource at our command—every means of diplomacy, every tool of intelligence, every instrument of law enforcement, every financial influence, and every necessary weapon of war—to the destruction and to the defeat of the global terror network... Our response involves far more than instant retaliation and isolated strikes. Americans should not expect one battle, but a lengthy campaign unlike any other we have ever seen. It may include dramatic strikes visible on TV and covert operations secret even in success... Every nation in every region now has a decision to make: either you are with us, or you are with the terrorists."[1]

The speech also made it clear that any sovereign State that chose not to be with the United States in its resolve is to be regarded as a hostile regime. The President elaborated the point unambiguously in his West Point Address delivered on the 3rd of June 2002: "America has, and intends to keep, military strengths beyond challenges". And, "ready to strike at a moment's notice in any dark corner of the world". Terror cells had to be uncovered in "60 or more countries, using every tool of finance, intelligence and law enforcement". The President pointed out: "Some nations need military training to fight terror, and we will provide it. Other nations oppose terror, but tolerate the hatred that leads to terror—and that must change... All nations that decide for aggression and terror will pay a price... We will lift this dark threat from our country and from the world."[2]

Surely, this is an agenda of trans-hemispheric hegemony and the declaration of an imperial project even surpassing in its reach and its emphasis on military power the November 1st 1858 proclamation by the British Queen in Council to the Princes, Chiefs, and people of India.[3]

And just as surely, the hegemonic project of these dimensions, whether or not it eventually succeeds, is bound to inspire aversion and resistance, both peaceful and militant.

The horrific violence of 9/11 was attributed to Al Qaeda, especially its supposed leader Osama bin Laden. President Bush lost no time in serving an open ultimatum on the Taliban regime in Afghanistan to turn over bin Laden and his cohorts or face military action for its overthrow. When the Taliban asked for evidence to show Osama bin Laden's connection with the 11th of September 2001 attacks, it received disdain: as a pariah of the international community, it had no choice but to carry out America's bidding without demur. The Taliban deliberated on the situation and first offered to put Osama bin Laden on trial within Afghanistan and to later hand him over to a third neutral country, if America showed any evidence against him. But America turned down the offer, and refused to let an independent body examine and determine the merits of the offer. President Bush told a joint session of the Congress on 22nd of September, 2001 that "the Taliban must act and act immediately. They will hand over the terrorists or they will share their fate... Our grief has turned to anger, and anger to resolution...". President Bush told the Taliban: "If you cough him up and his people today... we will reconsider what we are doing to your country. You will have a second chance. Bring him in.

And bring his leaders and lieutenants and other thugs and criminals with him."[4]

The intemperance of the language showed that America did not really care about nabbing Osama bin Laden and was simply determined to take the opportunity not only to eliminate him but also to use its guided missiles, 'smart' munitions, global positioning systems, free-flight rockets with multiple warheads, and sophisticated data communications systems to militarily destroy Taliban with the knowledge that the hapless Afghani people will be the worst victims. In a comment in *The New Republic*, it was stated that the main purpose of this war is to defend the United States. This objective will be accomplished if, as a result of this war, Afghanistan is left in a chaos that will make it impossible for it to be used as a base for terrorist operations. *The New Republic* comment went on to explain: "This time we are not making the world safe for democracy. We are making the world safe for Americans. That, too, is a meritorious enterprise."[5]

Another advocate of vengeance as the main objective of this war said: "Whether by overt or covert means, the U.S. is entitled to its pound of flesh. It is entitled to retribution for 7,000 civilians murdered. That might be just one element within the war on terrorism that President George W. Bush has sworn to wage... but the September 11 victims must not be allowed to fade away, eclipsed by a larger purpose, nor by geopolitical considerations... Afghans, who have known precious little peace for all their days, will suffer and they will probably die... But the peace and security of a nation's people is the primary responsibility of its own government. That is true in Iraq, in Sudan, in Algeria and every other country where warlords and belligerent regimes plot against international stability, or where the objective is to export Islamic militancy and terrorism. Civilians always pay the price for zealots and megalomaniacs—from Dresden to Coventry to Hiroshima to Kabul."[6]

If the US diplomacy in the wake of 9/11 has, by turning Clauswitz on his head, become the continuation of war by different means, and no longer an independent phenomenon, we must, then, withhold the temptation to carry out a purely political evaluation of the way in which the United States fights its wars. When war becomes a strategic instrument and a political necessity of a long-term objective of domination, then the success of diplomacy and politics consists merely in bringing "the enemies" under the spotlight. Milton Bearden, a former CIA field officer in Afghanistan, accused the United States of oversimplifying and exaggerating the power and the reach of Al Qaeda and its leader bin Laden by "linking him to every known terrorist act in the last decade" and making him "the North Star of fundamentalist Islam" by creating this "bin Laden mythology". But Milton Bearden also understood the purpose it served: "We haven't had a national enemy since *the evil empire* (our italics!) slipped beneath the waves in 1991. And I think we kind of like it this way."[7]

The war in Afghanistan continues to seethe even as bin Laden remains outside the reach of the coalition forces. But the American military presence in the region is firmly established. The focus of orchestrated publicity as the "enemy of civilization" soon shifted from bin Laden to Saddam Hussein with much emphasis on his secret weapons of mass destruction (WMD) and the danger of his passing them on to the terrorist groups that had carried out the September 11th 2001 attacks. This was the line US Vice President Cheney and British Prime Minister Blair jointly took at a press conference in London addressed by them on the March 11th 2002, a year before the invasion of Iraq was launched on that ground.[8]

Hans Blix, the Chief of the UN Monitoring, Verification and Inspection Commission (UNMOVIC) created in December 1999 under UNSC Resolution 1284, later revealed that Saddam Hussein's Iraq did not possess weapons of mass destruction for 10 years before the war and that both Washington and London over-interpreted their own intelligence reports to launch an unjustified war that had been planned much in advance. Mohamed El-Baradei, Chief of the International Atomic Energy Agency, said that his team hadn't found any evidence of prohibited nuclear activities and that there was no evidence to show a revival of a nuclear weapons programme since its elimination in the 1990s.[9]

Saddam Hussein and his WMD have ceased to be the issues of discussion on the war on Iraq. The American forces are there to stay no matter what the formal arrangements for the local administration. President Bush repeatedly explains: "We did not charge hundreds of miles into the heart of Iraq and pay a bitter cost of casualties and liberate 25 million people only to retreat before a band of thugs and assassins."[10] Most independent observers of the situation in Iraq suspect that the American gift of a post-Saddam regime in Iraq may not fare any better than the Hashemite monarchy created under the British Mandate from 1914 to 1932 had. But who is bothered so long as the US remains confident of being able to keep the local administration subordinated to US foreign policy interests through the institutionalization of violence, American military control over the region, and the politics of patronage?

Meanwhile, the United States and its allies have other agendas to pursue in the region. The taming of Iran is one. Helping Israel attain its objectives in the region is yet another. It cannot really be a coincidence that even as Iraq remained caught in a violent upheaval around the issues of a caretaker government under American military control, with the UN envoy Lakhdar Brahimi refusing to condemn the American military atrocities, President Bush received Israeli Prime Minister Ariel Sharon in Washington to endorse his "go-it alone" plan. Sharon announced his decision to withdraw from approximately 7,500 Jewish settlements within the Gaza strip, a 215 square-mile strip of land bordering the Mediterranean Sea on the south western edges of Egypt, but to retain more than 230,000 settlements in the West Bank, bordering Jordan.

Israel occupied both the West Bank and the Gaza Strip during the 1967 war. Ed Abington, a former US consul general in Jerusalem, describes Gaza as a "basket case" of abject poverty with no value to Israel: "nothing but a throwaway." Israel's determination to protect its West Bank settlements has for sometime been evident from its programme to build a security wall, which cost the country at least $300 million just in the last year. Sharon also made it clear that the abandonment of settlements in the Gaza Strip would not mean the end of Israel's control over its air, water, and land passages. While Sharon announced the proposal in Washington, his Chief of Staff, Lt. General Moshe Yaalon talked to the press in Jerusalem to say that Israel will re-enter the Gaza Strip if terrorism continues: "If there is terrorism in Lebanon we act, if there is terrorism stemming from Syria we act, and if there is terrorism from the Gaza Strip or Nablus we will respond."[11]

President Bush endorsed Sharon's plan enthusiastically and described the Israeli West Bank settlements as "facts on the ground". He also made it clear that the Palestinians displaced since 1948 under Israeli aggression, approximately 4 million people, cannot claim the right to return, but will have to live in a Palestinian State that may yet materialize out of his "road map". These pronouncements place President Bush's stamp of approval, in bold letters, on the Israeli annexation of the Palestinian lands in the period between 1949 and 1967. As the first official American endorsement of the Israeli occupation of the Palestinian territory, it cancels out the formal position it maintained so far that the location of borders, the future of Jewish settlements in the West Bank and the Gaza Strip, the status of Jerusalem, and the fate of Palestinian refugees are issues that need to be resolved through direct negotiations between Israel and Palestinians. A triumphant Sharon told an Israeli newspaper that the American endorsement of his proposals closed the door to substantive negotiations with the Palestinians. In his assessment: "It will bring their dreams to an end."[12]

The Palestinian authority calls the agreement between Sharon and Bush a "new Balfour Declaration." Saeb Erekat, the Palestinian minister formally responsible for the negotiations with Israel, points out that the settlement between Sharon and Bush is as invalid as any settlement he might make "sitting with Tony Blair" and "agreeing on giving Texas to China" would be. Not all Arab leaders appeared as unequivocal. Hosni Mubarak of Egypt met Bush at his Texas ranch in Crawford to offer what sounded like tentative support for the Israeli proposal.[13]

These developments in Iraq and Palestine, belonging to the agenda of *reconquista*, seem interconnected in ways that may not be immediately apparent. Rashid Khalidi, a scholar from Columbia University, points out that Sharon's proclamation in Washington mirrors a post-Iraq war realism that allows the militarily victorious to dictate what happens to the vanquished without any reference to facts of history or merits in international law. By endorsing Israel's unilateral offer of withdrawal from the Gaza Strip, its decision to keep choice settlements in the West Bank contiguous to Jerusalem, traditionally described as "obstacles to peace", and its rejection of the Palestinian "right to return", the United States has cleared the road for a new era of peace that will depend on the military power of enforcement rather than on the diplomatic skills to obtain agreement. Those who feel threatened by the dispossessed and the discontented of the world rejoice. Thomas L. Friedman, writing in *The New York Times* points out that the Israeli decision to pull out of Gaza without a bilateral agreement provides a unique opportunity to saddle the rebellious Palestinian leaders down with the responsibility to administer the region and to make them dependent on donors while they remain aware that Israel has not given up military options to enforce order. Friedman also sees a lesson for Iraq. According to him, Iraq's nascent leaders "will act in a concerted and responsible fashion" only when they obtain the burden of responsibility.[14]

Does this reasoning not, at least partly, explain why the Americans went out of their way to establish an illegitimate government in Kabul even as much of Afghanistan continued to reel under its special operations? Does it not also explain why the American Viceroy in Baghdad and the UN Secretary-General's Special Envoy for Iraq insisted on transferring notional sovereignty to an unrepresentative body without entering into a formal process of consultation and agreement with the Iraqi people? Does the political experiment underway in Iraq not closely emulate the example of unilateralism that Israel has so deftly employed against the people of Palestine, improved only by the fact that the coalition forces can dictate terms to the United Nations? The Likud in Israel managed to convince the American political establishment that the Palestinian authority cannot be a negotiating partner for peace in the Middle East because it remains mixed up with America's enemies in the global war on terror. The principal effect of the Israeli position is, in Sharon's own words: "My plan poses difficulties for the Palestinians—a critical blow… In the unilateral process there is no Palestinian State…"[15]

In the same way, the popular representatives of both the *Shia* and the *Sunni* segments of the population in Iraq oppose the occupation and are mixed up with the armed resistance against the coalition forces. Therefore, the coalition decides not to negotiate with them. It also wants to be rid of its obligations and responsibilities under the law of occupation, which explains its eagerness to transfer formal sovereignty to a group of essentially Iraqi expatriates, groomed and promoted by the Pentagon, the CIA, and the State Department for years. As their ability to maintain political order and stability, necessary to pursue the strategic interests that precipitated the invasion, remains the exact obverse of their commitment to rule *sans* popular support, the coalition must retain its military capacities on the ground to keep them in the saddle.

These parallels between the developments in Iraq and in Palestine establish the ideological centrality that Israel has assumed in Middle Eastern affairs and the way it has been able to mould the framework of the world order under the American tutelage. The fact that President Bush, so deeply mired in the chaos, bloodshed, and the discovery of lies behind his arguments for Iraq's invasion, can still afford to stand next to Sharon and share responsibility for further mutilating the Middle Eastern peace process, shows the grip that the Likud has acquired on the White House. Perhaps, the timing reflects the political impatience of a President, who has clearly failed to show any meaningful results in his war on terror, to win over to his side the evangelical and pro-Israeli segments of the electorate whose voting choices would not be adversely affected by television images of the US troops killing Iraqis or by the knowledge of the Israeli troops, "equipped with US weapons, destroying Palestinian homes and killing children."[16]

From the Muslim point of view, the contrast between the treatments meted out to Iraq, essentially for defying the United States since 1991, and the overweening position of power which Israel has been able to obtain, in spite of its crimes, on the strength of its strategic relationship with the United States, makes the Palestinian and the Iraqi issues, and a discussion of their future, inseparable. Iraq has been famished and disarmed for more than a decade, then attacked, bombed and occupied on the charges of having arms it clearly does not possess, for posing a threat it patently does not pose, for breaching UN resolutions it does not really breach, and which are arbitrary anyway. The other country, next door, is allowed to sit on one of the world's mightiest nuclear-chemical-biological arsenals; to get away with defying and subverting each and every one of over seventy UN resolutions, and to occupy, torment, dispossess, and harass the local population which it displaced. It benefits from an uninterrupted flow of economic and military assistance from the US, from a cosy sharing of intelligence, and from unconditional, unflinching diplomatic support. And, now comes the Sharon-Bush decree on the Gaza Strip and the West Bank, declaring the Israeli annexation of the Palestinian land a *fait accompli*, terminating the right of the uprooted to return, and making the establishment of a viable Palestinian State through bilateral negotiations with reference to facts of history and merits in international law virtually impossible.

It is evident that the spirit of imperialistic hubris that has possessed the United States will not allow it to back away from its "civilizational mission" in the Middle East humanely and without more savagery. This is tragic for the Iraqi and the Palestinian people who have had to cope with an uninterruptedly malevolent history of internal tyranny, external aggression, wars and violence since the British first appeared in their land promising freedom and self-determination from the Ottoman yoke.

The last decade and a half, since the end of the ruinous war with Iran, has been especially calamitous for the Iraqi and the Palestinian people, for both the material conditions of life as well as their idealistic framework of political endeavours. It is, indeed, remarkable that the malevolence of history can actually become so tangible an impediment against a people's existential choices in the present and the possibilities of the future. Passive submission to foreign invasion and domination inspired by imperialistic voracity is morally indefensible. Armed resistance against a physically insuperable occupation is prospectively unrewarding. Non-violent mobilization, as a mode of political bargaining, presupposes a cohesive perspective on the socio-political order that has emerged from an internally democratic and intellectually rational process of debating and developing agreement on substantial issues of State and society. Without a perspective on these issues and without a common political programme, it would not be possible even for revolutionary nationalist groups to coordinate their strategies of resistance towards meaningful objectives.

In the 1960s and '70s, the visions of "Arab awakening", that were both secular and fiercely anti-colonial, drew many young, idealistic, and talented people to join the political process. That process became a victim of the Cold War. The Baath Party in Iraq, with Saddam Hussein as a key agent, was used by the American secret service establishment to carry out anti-communist purges within the country. The narcissistic streak in leaders, like Gamal Abdel Nasser, and the anti-democratic methods they adopted to advance their political objectives eventually destroyed the very ideas of Arab unity, modernity, and anti-imperialism they championed. In Iraq, the vision of coexistence and the people's partnership in nation-building to rectify the shortcomings of a system of State in the colonial mould died along with Abd as-Salam Aref when his helicopter crashed mysteriously on the 15th of August 1966. The world of oil and its inducements and political disorientation resulting from Israel's ruthless expansionism and militarism, which ensured the Arab defeat in the famous Six-Day War in June 1967, came together to emasculate the secular dreams of Arab destiny. The Wahabis of Saudi Arabia, with American support and their oil wealth, set themselves against the Pan-Arab agenda. The remaining Hashemite royalty of Jordan, with its all-consuming dedication to self-perpetuation, became yet another dependable American ally in the region. Syria, smarting under its own share of historical malevolence and the tyranny of the Baath Party under Assad, consigned itself to converting Lebanon, known as the land of Arab enlightenment, into a terrain of communal carnage.

The oil enclaves of Kuwait and the UAE, managed almost entirely by immigrant workers, devoured the remaining Arab talent, education, and enterprise in sustaining their phantasmagoria of lavishness and luxury. The rise of Ayatollah Khomeini in Iran, the corruption within the Palestinian liberation movement, the decade long war between Iran and Iraq in which one million people perished, the decimation of Kurds under Saddam Hussein, with America and its allies acquiescing, further traumatized the Arab soul.

The conclusive and the decisive phase of the Cold War, fought in Afghanistan, brought Wahabi fundamentalism and Arab-Afghan tribalism into a long-term alliance under the banner of an Islamic *jihad.* With the political, financial, and military support which the United States and its Cold War partners poured into the crusade, the warlords in Afghanistan, and their Arab mentors like Osama bin Laden were able to inflict a morally exhausting defeat on the Soviet Union. The withdrawal of its forces paved the way for the rise of the Taliban, initially endorsed by the United States out of its eagerness to find non-Arabic outlets for Central Asian oil and gas resources. The American flirtation with the Taliban failed because of the stronger pull which its Arab mentors like Osama bin Laden held on its leaders as well as on the rank and file. Bin Laden became emblematic of Islamic Arab grievances with modern history, indistinguishable from the advent of Western hegemony, in the same way as Ayatollah Ruhollah Khomeini was for the *Shia* sense of wrongs. Like Khomeini, but with a larger agenda, he established himself as the Muslim avenger. The culmination of the Cold War with the disintegration of the Soviet Union changed the regional equations in ways that left the United States, the leader of the Cold War, as the common enemy of all disgruntled elements.

In the five independent Republics of Central Asia, the United States quickly adopted the old KGB-communist apparatus of repression that the Soviet Union had left behind to deal with Islamic militants who had, until then, been its allies. The United States had drawn its fighting force in Afghanistan from the ranks of radical Islamic dissidents in Turkmenistan, Tajikistan, and Uzbekistan who had been branded as "*basmachis*", meaning bandits, by the old communist regime. For decades under the Soviet Union, reformist Muslims of Central Asia known as *Jadids*, who drew their inspirations from the strong Sufi traditions, had dreamt and fought for religious freedom and political autonomy. The Fergana valley, which covers

Kyrgyztan, Tajikistan, and Uzbekistan, had been their stronghold. Independence from the Soviet Union brought them no relief from its ways of tyranny. The new Republics, led by the same old communist bosses, cracked down on them with greater ferocity. The government of Uzbekistan under Karimov passed a law on Freedom of Conscience and Religious Organizations, which made public offering of prayers and the wearing of *hijab*, the head covering of women, punishable offences. In Tajikistan, with its total population of 6 million, at least 50,000 persons are reported to have died in the conflict between the State and the Islamic opposition in the period from 1991 to 1997. Tahir Yuldeshev and other leaders of the Islamic revolution in Uzbekistan and other Central Asian republics are reported to have become friends of Osama bin Laden and to have taken shelter in Afghanistan to continue with their crusades.

Zalmay Kahlilzad, himself a born Afghani, and other neo-cons who shaped the American policies in the region, understood little beyond the material value of Central Asian oil and gas resources and the strategic benefits of political partnership with Israel in the Middle East. Their approach on Central Asian resources, guided by a single-minded commitment to keep Iran and other Arab countries of the Middle East out of the loop, substantially contributed to the development of the later cultural war theory.

In a paper that appeared in the September 1991 issue of *Foreign Policy*, William Lind, Director of the Centre for Cultural Conservativism in Washington, discussed the World Wars I and II and the Cold War as self-dissipating "civil wars" of the "Christendom". According to him, the cycle of civil wars has cost the Western world a lot of its vigour and a loss of its internal values, while "other cultures", poor in technology but commanding the destiny of demography, developed aspirations of conquest and revenge. In his paper, William Lind talked about the Islamic threats and challenges, including to "the Western-created system of nation-states". By invading Kuwait, Saddam Hussein was rejecting its legitimacy as an arbitrary demarcation in the sand, maintained by the West. It was possible for the Western coalition to defeat Iraq, Lind argued, because it included those Muslims who had abiding interests in preserving the "general *status quo* allied with Western powers": "But such alliances may become weak with the growing belligerence between the cultures". Lind went on to talk about the great danger to "the right flank of the Western world stretching from the Black Sea to Vladivostok", if Central Asia became Islamic. He warned the Western world not to underestimate its enemies because of their backwardness in technology and modern weaponry: whereas Americans pay almost $1 billion for each "stealth bomber", their enemies can drive truck loads of explosives into their targets, killing hundreds of people. He drew up a scenario: "Imagine a truck armed not with several hundred pounds of high explosives, but with a genetically engineered weapon, a bomb that would spew out a cross of the toxins in cholera with a benign bacterium normally found in the human body." The enemies of the Western world will not appear openly armed in battle fatigues. They will come in secretly as immigrants and terrorists, indistinguishable from others. The defence of Western culture abroad, as also at home, will require exceptional methods and greater attention to the values of national security than to those of freedom and justice. These ideas, propagated by William Lind, who is also a leader of the military reform movement in America, have since witnessed much development in both the theories and practices of the cultural war; in preemptive military strategies against "backlash" and "rogue" States; in the hunt for WMD; and in regime changes currently converging against the Muslim societies of the world.[17]

These, in our view, are some of the elements of the hegemonic thinking which inform the crusade, masquerading as a war on terror under the leadership of the United States, that is currently underway even as the people of the Middle East, Central and South Asia, and parts of Africa, most of them being Muslim, struggle to find an exit from the 20th century history of political unbecoming that became their lot.

Several groups in Iraq and elsewhere are trying to resist the advent of a new global Empire with violent means and it is difficult to condemn their struggle as illegitimate by the standards of those who denounce their use for doctrinal political objectives and imaginations. However, an aesthetic stance about the legitimacy and morality of violence does not really help. That is where the insistence on non-violence, which is reflected in the arguments of the Bangladeshi participant, acquires special significance. History has repeatedly shown that the dynamics of violence inevitably interfere with the development of a genuine alternative to the doctrine of "Might is Right". Thus, we find ourselves in agreement with the prescription of one of our participants that there is no substitute for resistance through the thoughtful mobilization of people, based on a critical understanding of the nature of the hegemonic world order and its crimes against humanity.

We are, however, slightly uneasy with the advice made by the participant, that even as the protagonists of the established world order continue to portray Muslims as the "catalysts of violence", it becomes "a mundane duty of every follower of Islam to make it crystal clear to every other non-Muslim citizen of the world that Islam is indeed the greatest promoter of peace on earth." We understand the spirit in which the suggestion is made. However, we feel that it not only imposes an unreasonable obligation on all Muslims, since it appears to be impossible to fulfil, but also seems to allow those who have been trampling the acknowledged rights of the powerless with total impunity to further mortify their victims by having them explain themselves.

For example, let us look at the plight of the Palestinian people, which we have already referred to. The Palestinian right to self-determination was the basis for the League of Nations' mandate conferred on Britain immediately after WW I. It is almost universally forgotten that Article 22(4) of the Covenant of the League of Nations, which sanctioned the detachment of Palestine from the Ottoman Empire, "provisionally recognized" the Palestinian people as an independent nation. Article 22(4) of the Covenant of the League of Nations stated: "Certain communities formerly belonging to the Turkish Empire have reached a stage of development where their existence as independent nations can be provisionally recognized subject to the rendering of administrative advice and assistance by a Mandatory until such time as they are able to stand alone."[18] The United Nations has since confirmed that the sovereignty of Palestine emerged out of this mandate that could not be alienated by the Mandatory Power.[19]

The history of Israel is not so ancient as to obscure its origins in terror and political blackmail. The Balfour Declaration of 1917, as we know, did not come out of a process of democratic consultation involving inhabitants in the region. Morally speaking, Israel should have been established in a part of Germany, as a measure of reparation for the genocide that had been inflicted on the Jews within its territories. The eastern part of Germany was allowed to disappear behind the Iron Curtain. This was to appease Stalin. The holocaust took place in Nazi Germany. And, Israel arose in Palestine, as an imperial bequest to the descendants of Abraham, to decimate the Palestinian people's right to exist. In 1947, the United States prevailed against the will of the General Assembly to force a partition of Palestine, without consulting its people or their representatives. In doing so, the United Nations relied on the postulates of ethnic divide within the land that had gained strength from a legally meaningless document called the "Balfour Declaration".[20] It has been argued that the resolution was fundamentally *ultra vires* because the body did not possess the competence to create sovereign entities at the expense of the inalienable right to self-determination of a people under the League's mandate. The United Nations' power of action is limited by Article 14 of the Charter which only allows the General Assembly to recommend measures for the peaceful adjustment of any situation "which it deems likely to impair the general welfare or friendly relations among nations." A Sub-Committee of the General Assembly's Ad Hoc Committee on the Palestine Question clearly said that "the General Assembly is not competent to recommend, still less to enforce any solution other than the recognition of the independence of Palestine", and that "the settlement of the future government of Palestine is a matter solely for the people of Palestine." The Sub-Committee further said that "partition involves the alienation of territory and the destruction of the integrity of the State of Palestine. The United Nations cannot make a disposition or alienation of territory, nor can it deprive the majority of the people of Palestine of their territory and transfer it to the exclusive use of a minority in the country..."[21]

Under pressure from the United States, the General Assembly also rejected, with a narrow margin of 21 to 20 votes, a draft resolution presented by the Ad Hoc Committee on the 24th of November 1947, that asked for a legal evaluation of the proposal to partition Palestine within the statutory framework of the United Nations by the International Court of Justice. The proposed resolution said: "The General Assembly... resolves to request the International Court of Justice to give an advisory opinion under Article 96 of the Charter and Chapter VI of the Statute of the Court on the following questions:... Whether the United Nations, or any of its Member States, is competent to enforce or recommend the enforcement of any proposal concerning the constitution and future government of Palestine, in particular any plan of partition which is contrary to the wishes, or adopted without the consent, of the inhabitants of Palestine..."

The Security Council asked the General Assembly to discuss and develop a government for Palestine. The Jewish Agency for Palestine scuttled the process by unilaterally proclaiming the State of Israel on the 14th of May 1948. The United States immediately recognized Israel and, thus, destroyed the UN's efforts to establish an interim trustee administration in the area to accommodate the aspirations of both the settlers and the Palestinians.[22]

Golda Meir had no hesitation in plainly stating that "there is no such thing as a Palestinian people..." She was saying this after the 1967 war, when Israel further occupied the Sinai Peninsula, the Gaza Strip, and the West Bank of the Jordan river with crucial support from the United States.[23]

Since then, the Palestinian people in these lands have been subjected to collective punishments, locality confinements, deportations, arbitrary arrests, custodial torture, and killings. Between 1967 and 1988, more than 300,000 Palestinians have been arrested, interrogated, and tortured for creating or plotting troubles for Israel.[24]

Since September 2000, a total of about 2,100 Palestinians, out of a population of about 3.4 million, have been killed. Out of these, it is admitted that about 1,650 were "innocent civilians". In the same period, a total of about 700 Israelis, out of a population of about 6 million, have been killed. It is not clear how many of them were non-combatants.[25]

Sustained Palestinian protests, called Intifada or uprising, started in December 1987. The protests abated in 1991 and altogether ceased with the commencement of the Oslo peace process in the middle of 1993. The second phase of the Intifada, which started in September 2000, is marked by the participation of a large number of stone-throwing teenagers who have since been dying under Israeli bullets. About 100 children under the age of 13 have been killed. Israel condemns the participation of children in these protests as terrorism.[26]

Israel is the only country in the world that uses the argument of 'State necessity' to permit the use of custodial torture under its Penal Law. When the High Court of Justice in Israel held the methods of physical and psychological force widely employed by members of the General Secret Service against suspects under interrogation to be impermissible, the government established a Commission under Justice Landau which decided that interrogators are entitled to use torture if they can justify it under the criminal law defence of necessity.[27]

Numerous Security Council resolutions, beginning with Resolution 237 adopted on the 14th of June 1967, have condemned the Israeli occupation of the Palestinian and Arab territories. These resolutions hold the occupation to be legally invalid and to constitute a serious obstruction to "achieving a comprehensive, just and lasting peace in the Middle East." They also urge Israel to "rescind" the occupation and other actions that change the legal status, the geographical nature, and the demographic composition of the Arab and Palestinian territories, including Jerusalem, and to scrupulously respect the human rights of the Palestinian people in the occupied territories. Several Security Council resolutions call on all Member States "not to provide Israel with any assistance to be used specifically in connection with settlements in the occupied territories."[28]

On the 13th of September 1993, the government of Israel, led by Prime Minister Yitzhak Rabin, and the Palestine Liberation Organization (PLO) under Arafat's leadership, signed the "Declaration of Principles on Interim Self-Government Arrangements" on the lawns of the White House. The process, initiated in the wake of the 1991 Gulf War, is known as Oslo Accords because the negotiations had started in Oslo, Norway.[29] Under the Accords, the PLO recognized the right of the State of Israel to exist in peace and security, and committed itself to pursue a peaceful resolution of the conflict and to resolve all outstanding issues through negotiations. Israel recognized the PLO as the representative of the Palestinian people and promised to engage in a comprehensive peace process. Thus, the *de facto* Israeli sovereignty and its military supremacy in the region became the pivotal aspects of the Oslo framework. The White House ceremony was followed by a number of other agreements involving an arrangement over the Gaza Strip, the Jericho areas, and the West Bank, the preparatory transfer of powers and responsibilities, a memorandum on the sharing of Wye river resources, and a timeline agreement for the resumption of permanent status negotiations. All these agreements were signed between the 4th of May 1994 and the 4th of September 1999.[30]

The process, even when formally on, was known to have been a failure. Its open-ended vision without any definiteness about the final objectives, and the compromises that would have to be made to achieve them, left both sides with very little in terms of concrete ideas. Extremists became suspicious of the process that moved forward on the basis of a spirit of compromise but without being able to specify the goals. Terrorist campaigns and military retaliations, resulting in hundreds of deaths, continued. The West Bank and Gaza remained occupied. When Arafat threatened to resume the Intifada, Israeli Foreign Minister Ariel Sharon called on the Jewish settlers to "capture as many hills as possible." Between 1993 and 2002, Israel nearly doubled the number of its settlers in the occupied territories. The Palestinians were convinced that Israel had no plans for them but to extinguish their aspirations through force.[31]

Israel objected to various clauses in the PLO's Charter that questioned the establishment of Israel through a partition of Palestine and declared the eradication of the Zionist presence in the land as an objective. On the 14th of December 1998, President Clinton attended and addressed a meeting of the Palestine National Council, convened in Gaza, which endorsed Arafat's recommendation to amend the Charter to Israel's satisfaction. The next day, Israeli Prime Minister Netanyahu announced his satisfaction.[32] But the peace process made no progress. Bill Clinton, despite all his charm and dynamism at Camp David, could not bring Ehud Barak and Yasser Arafat to resolve the thorny issues of Jerusalem, the settlements, and the refugees.[33]

The Oslo process formally died when President Bush made a speech on the 24th of June 2002 to announce that "peace requires a new and different Palestinian leadership." He also accused the Palestinian authorities of encouraging terrorism. The speech heralded the end of a disingenuous bilateralism that had begun in September 1993.[34]

We shall not go into the story of "the road map" announced by President Bush in December 2002, which is worse than nothing and merely adds insult and derision to injury as well as oppression because it is set within a framework of Israeli tutelage and its hegemony over the Palestinian territories. The conditions of a meaningful peace process in the Middle East, as any fair person should agree, must include an unambiguous proclamation of the Palestinian right to self-determination, a belated acknowledgement of the Palestinian sovereignty, and a guarantee of the right of Palestinians to return to their land. Instead, the Palestinian people are constantly berated as terrorists. Should they respond to the charge and to the exhortation that they are wedded to terrorism which they must renounce, change their leadership at the command of Israel and the United States, and stop their children from throwing stones at Israeli armoured vehicles? If yes, how should they do so?

In our view, it is morally wrong to shame the Palestinian people by requiring them to respond to invectives that only represent the arrogance of power and its capacity to manipulate all discourse for the hegemonic objectives. In our view, atrocious criminals are not entitled to interrogate their victims about their inner feelings on what they can do to make the world morally better. The forces of the far-right, the evangelicals, and the fundamentalist Christian fringe, the pro-Likud lobby, economic conservatism, big business, and the ever-hungry industrial-military complex that control the "civilizational project" behind the "global war on terrorism" have a lot in common with Wahabi fundamentalists in terms of their narrow missionary commitments, their fierce militancy, their confrontational attitudes, the lowliness of intellectual and spiritual content of their respective traditions, etc. The forces behind the global war on terror certainly surpass the Wahabi fundamentalists in their power to inflict violence and material and moral depravity. The global war on terror is being waged by an extraordinary bunch of truly ignorant but politically arrogant persons and others who have a lot to account for.

There are sufficient indications that their current control of the neo-cons and theo-cons on global affairs represent decades of doggedly methodical propaganda and patient ideological and organizational effort. Their initiatives can be traced to a memorandum circulated by Lewis Powell in 1971, first among America's business leaders and among a wider circle of conservatives in the United States. This was the time when the liberal left dominated the political discourse worldwide mainly in opposition to the Vietnam war. Lewis Powell was appointed a Supreme Court judge by President Nixon exactly one month after he circulated the memo. The memo drew a grim picture of the world dominated by pacifists, communists, libertarians, and assorted leftists and proposed an ambitious plan to stem the tide, to reclaim lost positions, and to secure a firm, lasting hold on American politics through the creation of organizations with clear objectives, clear strategies, and the finances to achieve them. The memo also called for the creation of research organizations, and the launching of newspapers and media outlets to counter the leftist wave.

Christopher de Muth, later the President of the American Enterprise Institute, shared Powell's vision and joined the team to lead the long march of the American far-right. The presidencies of Reagan and then of Bush-senior provided helpful, encouraging interludes to these forces and the foretaste of their triumphs in the offing. Men like Richard Scaife Mellon, who inherited a colossal fortune from his banker grandfather Andrew Mellon, and several richly endowed foundations including the Sarah Foundation, Allegheny Foundation, and Carthage Foundation, became the money-bags behind the conservative revolution.

A series of new foundations, including the Scaife Family Foundation, the Heritage Foundation, the American Enterprise Institute, the Free Congress Foundation, the Olin Foundation, the Linde and Harry Bratley Foundation, the Hoover Institute, and the Cato Institute emerged on the American political horizon as the neo-con think-tanks. These foundations have been led by such bright stars of the neo-con lobby as Irving Kristol; Richard Perle; Lynn Cheney, the Vice-President's wife; Dinesh D'Souza, an ethnic Indian who leads the "race and society" theory; Condoleeza Rice; Donald Rumsfeld; Douglas Feith; Elliot Abrams; Ari Fleischer; and others.

Leaders of the far-right like Nelson Bunker Hunt, Richard de Vos, William Coors, and others concentrated their efforts on supporting the evangelicals in building political organizations. The Olin Foundation, supported by the revenues of an industrial dynasty in control of chemicals and ammunitions, went out of its way to create and build conservative academics like Allan Bloom of Chicago University and the political guru Paul Wolfowitz, who created the John M. Olin Centre for Research on the Theory and Practice of Democracy. The Olin Foundation also supported another noted hawk, Irving Kristol. Rupert Murdoch opened up his coffers when Irving Kristol's son, William Kristol, became the editor of *Weekly Standard.* The Bradley Foundation funded the National Empowerment Television (NET), which was the foremost propaganda machine of the far-right before Murdoch established FOX News.

The Linde and Harry Bratley Foundation funded the campaigns led by the John Birch Society, the notorious evangelical group so paranoid and extremist in its outlook that it to denounced denounced President Eisenhower as a secret communist agent, and also Fred Schwartz, who led the Christian Anticommunist Crusade. Billy Graham, the spiritual advisor of half a dozen American presidents including Richard Nixon and Tim LaHaye, the most influential figure on the evangelical scene in the United States today, led the fantastic interpretations of biblical prophesies, revolving intensely around Iraq and the Muslim world in the Middle East, portraying men like Saddam Hussein as agents of Satan and the forerunners of the Antichrist. LaHaye has a direct pipeline to the White House and is reported to have been guiding President Bush on issues like abortion, judicial appointments, education, and religious freedom since his days as the Governor of Texas. Hundreds of leaders of the Christian right, from TV preachers and talk-show hosts to Bible Belt pulpit pounders, supported the Bush-Cheney ticket in 2000. Michael Gerson, the leader of the team of speech writers at the White House, is a follower of LaHaye and literally believes in an impending Armageddon, a place in Palestine mentioned in the Bible where the decisive last battle before the Christ's second coming is to be fought. It is hardly a coincidence that President Bush's speeches echo apocalyptic visions of conflict between the good and evil to such an extent that Rev. C. Welton Gaddy of the Interfaith Alliance was compelled to address a formal letter to the President asking him to "please, assure the American people that you are not developing foreign policy on the basis of a fundamentalist biblical theology that requires cataclysm in Israel in order to guarantee the return of Christ."[35]

In our view, the Muslims of the world owe no apology or explanation to the weird bunch of fundamentalists and cynics who revel in their visions of global domination and who pursue them without qualms about the magnitude of violence, human suffering, death and depravity they inflict on the vast masses of powerless people.

Powers of the Pakistani Tribal Councils

The Pakistani participant's comments about Mary D. Castetter's paper on the workings of the tribal councils in Pakistan raise yet another set of sensitive issues. Castetter's paper starts with an example of a sentence delivered by a tribal council at Meerwala in the southern part of Punjab in June 2002, which we shall briefly recapitulate:

A twelve-year old boy belonging to the *Gujjar* tribe was accused of having an illicit affair with an older woman of the *Mastoi* caste. The boy was abducted, manhandled, sodomized, and held a prisoner by men related to the *Mastoi* woman. The matter went before the tribal council, also known as the *panchayat*, when the *Gujjar* boy's uncle asked for an adjudication and resolution of the dispute. Since

Punjab is not a federally recognized tribal area, the tribal council had no legal status. This made no difference to its time-honoured authority. The boy pleaded innocence and his sister testified in his support. The council decided that the family honour of the *Mastoi* woman would be considered restored only after her tribesmen disgraced a female member of the boy's family. Immediately, the boy's sister, who had come to testify in her brother's favour, was dragged away by four *Mastoi* men to a nearby hut and gang-raped. She was, then, compelled to walk back to her house without clothes. The aftermath of the incident, which received wide-publicity, is not important for our discussion here.[36]

There is no dearth of literature on the workings of informal justice in Pakistan, its outrages, and the violence against women committed, with the State institutions silently conniving, in the name of "crimes of honour".

The problems discussed in Castetter's paper are not unique to Pakistan. The following are some examples from Saudi Arabia. In the middle of March 2002, Saudi newspapers reported an incident of fire in a girl's public school in Mecca. At least 14 girl students died from burns and asphyxiation. They died not because there was no way for them to escape. They died because a deployment of religious police, called *mutawwa'un*, outside the school, forced them back into the building when they tried to run away from the fire without being able to cover themselves under veils. The religious police forbade fire-fighters and civil defence personnel from entering the building since physical contact between unmarried men and women is forbidden under the Saudi Islamic law. Known as the Committee for the Promotion of Virtue and the Prevention of Vice, the Saudi religious police enjoy absolute power over other branches of the civil defence forces. The incendiary doom of the 14 girl students forced by the *mutawwa'un* was reported in Saudi newspapers, including the *Saudi Gazette* and *Al-Iqtisadiyya*. Crown Prince Abdullah promised an investigation. Three days later, the government ordered all newspapers to stop publishing anything about the accident. No one knows what happened to the investigation. No official has been charged or prosecuted.[37]

Elsewhere, we have discussed the issues concerning the conditions of persecution of Ahmadiyas and other religious dissenters and minorities in Pakistan and Bangladesh. The following two examples are from Saudi Arabia: a Syrian citizen, Abd al-Karim al-

Naqshabandi, worked for Prince Salman bin Sa'ud bin 'Abd al-Aziz, a nephew of King Fahd. Abd al-Karim al-Naqshabandi was executed on the 13th of December 1996 after the religious police discovered an amulet, inscribed with verses of the Koran, on his body and some books on Sufism in his possession. His mother in Syria had given the amulet to him as a protection against bad luck. The religious police prosecuted him on charges of heresy and practicing sorcery, and sentenced him to death.[38]

A prominent human rights activist Abdullah al Hudhaif was executed on the 11th of August 1995 following his conviction on the charges of sedition and heresy. As a member of the Committee for the Defence of Legitimate Rights, he had published reports that criticized the government for abusing human rights. In May 1995, al Hudhaif was tried and sentenced to twenty years in prison. The Ministry of Interior appealed before a *shari'a* court to argue that the sentence was very light. The court upheld the argument and enhanced al Hudhaif's sentence to death.[39]

Before the period of its decline beginning in the late 18th century, Islam had been the most powerful force on the stage of world history, not only in its capacity to build empires, but also in its capacity to inspire and disseminate science, philosophy, arts, architecture, and literature and ways of life that became the standard for the refined and the sophisticated worldwide. Its scholars and philosophers like Al-Arabi, Avicenna, and Averroes were the standard-bearers of objective thinking and its chivalric heroes like Saladin exemplified the ideals that the world of warriors aspired to emulate. Despite the crusades and its barbarities, Islam as a faith and as the carrier of political order successfully resisted both conquest and conversion and, with short pauses, witnessed astonishing expansion.

Surely, its capacity to accommodate cultural diversity and intellectual differences (*ikhtilaf*) played its part, as Abu Hanifah, one of the most celebrated Muslim jurists who died in 767 A.D. pointed out. Theodore Zeldin, in *An Intimate History of Humanity*, quotes the standards of generosity and tolerance from the writings of the Brothers of Purity of Basra: "The ideal and perfect man should be of East Persian origin, Arabic in faith, of Iraqi education, a Hebrew in astuteness, a disciple of Christ in conduct, as pious as a Syrian monk, a Greek in individual sciences, an Indian in the interpretation of all mysteries, but lastly and especially a Sufi in his whole spiritual life."[40]

With this kind of an approach to divergence, Islam's external standing and internal fortunes survived slander and hateful vilification by leaders of the Catholic Church. Fantastic stories about Islam as an instrument of the Anti-christ looked ridiculous in the face of clear evidence of its civilizational verve and appeal.

Crusaders became gleeful at the advent of the Mongols and, when Baghdad was sacked in 1258 A.D., they fantasized about the arrival of a Christian army led by King David or Prester John. Missions to Mongolia to convert Mongols to Christianity failed. The sacking of Baghdad by Hulagu in 1258 A.D. was a calamity, but soon the Mongols embraced Islam and were sufficiently civilized by it to establish new empires, like the Mughal Empire in India.

The entire Mediterranean was a Muslim sea and Arabs controlled trade across Asia, Africa, and Europe. The Muslim rulers in South Asia, in the territories under the Ottoman Empire, in Muslim Spain, and elsewhere, were more cosmopolitan and tolerant of cultural and religious variety than their Christian counterparts. The thousand flowers of literature, arts, syncretistic devotionalism, and political and cultural partnerships that flowered under Akbar's rule in South Asia probably constitute an unparalleled phenomenon in the political history of the world.

Women played a prominent role within different traditions of Islam. This was but natural, given the role of leadership Prophet Mohammad's own wives had assumed in the early days of his mission. Zainab, Prophet Mohammad's granddaughter, personified feminist liberation in a wholesome sense that is rare in that period of history. Legends about the women warriors who fought alongside Prophet Mohammad in the first decisive battles of Islam, like Nasibah bin Ka'b al-Maziniyyah and Umm 'Umarah, who supposedly turned the tide of battle at Uhud, abound. According to a legend, Umm 'Umarah became a prominent warrior in the Muslim army and led many battles under the Caliphate of Abu Bakr. The first woman ruler in South Asia was probably Razia Sultana, an able successor of Altamash, put to death by her own brother in October 1240 A.D. Shagrat al-Durr, a contemporary of Razia Sultana and the wife of the Sultan of Egypt, became the Head of State after the death of Sultan in 1250 A.D. Shagrat-al Durr was not only a Sultana but also a military leader who headed the Mamluk army in the battle against the crusaders. Originally a slave from Turkemenistan, Shagrat al-Durr is the founder of the Mamluk dynasty in Egypt. Rejected by the Caliphate at Baghdad, Shagrat al-Durr too, like Razia Sultana, met a violent end.

The role of women in Islam was not limited to political affairs. They also figure among the most celebrated Sufi saints. Rabi'a of Basra is still remembered as one of the greatest mystics within the Islamic tradition. Rabi'a is not an isolated example. Kharajist tradition insists that women are as naturally ordained to lead the faithful as men.[41] Is it not then unfortunate that the barbaric practices of the kind described in Mary D. Castetter's paper are defended in the name of Islam?

Internally Displaced Muslims in Sri Lanka

The plight of internally displaced Muslims in Sri Lanka is the last point of this paper. Despite their insignificant numbers, Muslims of Sri Lanka, like their counterparts in the rest of South Asia, contributed immensely to the cultural, political, and economic achievements of the region, including to the history of the struggle for decolonization. The spirit of resistance that in formed their attitude to the British Empire and generally to the western domination placed them at a distinct disadvantage compared to others who had more easily adopted the Western ways.

The arguments of the participant from Sri Lanka showed that a community that has suffered and resisted majoritarian tyranny persistently, even if violently, and which has done so with an astonishing degree of visible success, fails to empathize with the aspirations of the rights to dignity of yet another, more vulnerable minority. The Muslims of Sri Lanka are being forced to live with the injustices perpetrated by both Sinhalese and Tamil political power blocks.

The demography of the island country of Sri Lanka, with its approximately 17.7 million people, is overwhelmingly dominated by nearly 74 percent of Sinhalese whereas Tamils comprise only 18 percent and the Muslims just 7 percent of the population. The Tamils were driven to extremism by the suppression of their legitimate political, cultural, and economic rights under the Sinhalese majoritarian tyranny. Now that the LTTE is powerful and able to force its terms of negotiations on the Sinhalese-dominated State, Tamil extremists are trying to take advantage of the fog of a global war on terror to inflict injustices on the hapless Muslim population by pretending to fight Muslim extremism.

The tendency to stereotype is evident in the fact that all Muslims are often referred to as an ethnic group. It is important to remember that the Muslims of Sri Lanka are not an ethnic but a religious group, comprising people of mixed Arab descent, commonly referred to as Moors; people of Malay, Bengali and Malayali descent; as well as Memons, Borah, and others who migrated from the northwestern fringes of South Asia. The Muslims of mixed Arab descent, who once dominated maritime trade, have been settled in Sri Lanka for more than one thousand years. Many Arab adventurers married local women, and intermingling is supposed to have been very easy and genial—especially in the time of King Rajasinha II, in the seventeenth century. These Muslims are known today as Akurana Moors. Sri Lanka can be genuinely proud of its peace-loving Muslims throughout its history.

The Norwegian facilitators of the peace process have so completely concentrated on getting the Sri Lankan government and the LTTE to continue with their dialogue that they apparently see no point in raising these issues with sufficient force. The same can be said for sections of the Sri Lankan civil society, otherwise involved in the peace process. Instead of showing sympathy and support, many actually coax the Muslims and their representative body called the Sri Lanka Muslim Congress (SLMC) not to rock the boat and to sacrifice themselves for the sake of peace and prosperity for the rest of Sri Lankans.

Nearly 100,000 Muslims who lived in Jaffna and Mannar for more than five hundred years have been living the life of refugees for the last ten years and no one is bothered about it. The violence against the Muslims in the northern part of Sri Lanka has not been the last of Tamil extremist intolerance in the country. Since then, clashes, killings, and the displacement of Muslims have been witnessed in the eastern parts also, particularly in the districts of Batticaloa, Amparai, parts of Trincomalee and Muttur.

In the face of this callousness, it is natural for some Muslim leaders to raise the demand for the constitution of a separate administrative unit, as has been done by a SLMC leader, Rauff Hakeem. He has spoken about an autonomous South-Eastern Council comprising the Muslim majority electorates of Pottuvil, Sammanthurai and Digamadulla. These are disturbing developments for a country that has already been savaged by nearly two decades of brutal war between the Sinhalese-dominated governments of Sri Lanka and the

Tamil militants, especially the LTTE. If the governments and the groups involved in the current peace process, including the facilitators belonging to the international community, continue to treat the humanitarian and political concerns of the Muslims as disdainfully as they have done so far, we may not be far off the mark in saying that "only the dead have seen the end of war."

Notes

1. The full text of President Bush's address to a joint session of Congress and the nation, 20th of September 2001 at http://www.washingtonpost.com/wp-srv/nation/specials/attacked/transcripts/bushaddress_092001.html
2. Complete text of the West Point Address, 3rd of June 2002 at http://www.newsmax.com/archives/articles/2002/6/2/81354.shtml
3. Proclamation by the Queen in Council, to the Princes, Chiefs and People of India, Monday, 1st of November 1858 at http://www.movinghere.org.uk/deliveryfiles/BL/025MSSEURD00620U00000001/0/1.pdf
4. "Taliban Must Act Now: Bush", *The Hindu*, 22nd of September 2001. Also at http://www.hinduonnet.com/thehindu/2001/09/22/stories/01220008.htm; "Bush Gives Another Chance, Taliban Mock at Offer", *The Hindu*, 13 October 2001. Also at http://www.hinduonnet.com/thehindu/2001/10/13/stories/01130004.htm
5. "Our Reasons", *The New Republic*. 5th of November 2001.
6. Rosie DiManno, "U.S. is Restrained Toward Afghans", *The Toronto Star*, 1st of October 2001.
7. "Hunting bin Laden: Interview: Milton Bearden" at www.pbs.org/wgbh/pages/frontline/shows/binladen/interviews/bearden.html
8. "Transcript: Cheney, Blair warn of weapons in hands of terrorists, Iraqis", London, 11th of March 2002. Aslo at http://www.usembassy-israel.org.il/publish/press/visits/march02/cheney2.html
9. "Blix: Iraq was not justified" at http://www.mg.co.za/Content/13.asp?ao=20680; "War planned 'long in advance'", *News 24*, 4th of September 2003 at http://www.news24.com/News24/World/Iraq/0,,2-10-1460_1345303,00.html
10. Barry Rubin, "Bush pushes Mideast Democracy", *The Jerusalem Post*, 11 November 2003.
11. Megan Goldin, "Sharon seeks support for Gaza pull-out plan", *Sun Herald*, Sydney, 11th of April 2004; Greg Myre, "Sharon promises to retain 5 big settlements in West Bank", *The New York Times*, 13th of April 2004; Timothy M. Phelps, "Bush on Mideast", *Newsday*, New

York, 15th of April 2004; Suzanne Goldenberg, "How Sharon won US backing for Gaza strategy", *The Guardian*, London, 15th of April 2004; Mark Matthews, "US backs Israeli pullout plan", *The Baltimore Sun*, 15th of April 2004; Margot Dudkevitch and David Rudge, "Israeli Iraq abductee is Canadian citizen", *The Jerusalem Post*, 11th of April 2004.

12. Mitch Potter, "Sharon buoyed by US support", *The Toronto Star*, Ontario edition, 15th of April 2004; John Ward Anderson, "Party to vote on Sharon's proposal to leave Gaza", *The Washington Post*, 12th of April 2004; Donald MacIntyre, "Sharon and Bush reach their own settlement on Israel", *The Independent*, London, 15th of April 2004; "Peace Understandings in Works", *The Seattle Times*, 12th of April 2004; James Bennet, "Sharon Coup: U. S. Go-Ahead", *The New York Times*, 15th of April 2004.
13. Joel Greenberg, "Palestinians upset with Bush", *Chicago Tribune*, 15th of April 2004; Suzanne Goldenberg, "Bush rips up the road map", *The Guardian*, London, 15th of April 2004; Khaled Abu Toameh, "PA warns against US giving 'new Balfour Declaration", *The Jerusalem Post*, 13th of April 2004; Joel Greenberg, "Palestinians upset with Bush", *Chicago Tribune*, 15th of April 2004.
14. Suzanne Goldenberg, "Bush rips up the road map", *The Guardian*, London, 15th of April 2004; Maura Reynold and Mary Curtius, "In Shift, Bush backs Sharon on West Bank", *Los Angeles Times*, 15th of April 2004; Thomas L. Friedman, "From Gaza to Baghdad", *The New York Times*, 15th of April 2004.
15. Suzanne Goldenberg, "How Sharon won US backing for Gaza strategy", *The Guardian*, London, 15th of April 2004; Laura King, "Sharon aims to retain some settlements in disengagement", *Los Angeles Times*, 13th of April 2004.
16. Donald MacIntyre, "How Israel persuaded leader of the free world to see West Bank entirely their way", *The Independent*, London, 15th of April 2004; Margaret Coker, "US-Israeli link outrages Arabs", *The Atlanta Journal-Constitution*, 14th of April 2004; Adrian Hamilton, "No wonder we are seen as colonial powers", *The Independent*, London, 15th of April 2004; Maura Reynolds and Mary Curtius, "In Shift, Bush back Sharon on West Bank", *Los Angeles Times*, 15th of April 2004; Khaled Abu Toameh, "Palestinians urge holy war against the US", *The Jerusalem Post*, 11 April 2004.
17. William S. Lind, "Defending Western Culture", *Foreign Policy*, 1 September 1991.
18. The Covenant of the League of Nations, including amendments adopted to December, 1924 at http://www.yale.edu/lawweb/avalon/leagcov.htm#art22.
19. The Origins and Evolution of the Palestine Problem 1917-1988, prepared for, and under the guidance of, the Committee on the Exercise of the

Inalienable Rights of the Palestinian People. United Nations, New York, 1990, p. 56.

20. United Nations General Assembly Resolution 181, 29th of November 1947 at http://www.yale.edu/lawweb/avalon/un/res181.htm
21. Cattan, Henry, *Palestine and International Law: The Legal Aspects of the Arab-Israeli Conflict* (London: Longman, 1973) 42; Dr. Hans Koechler, "The Palestine Problem in the Framework of International Law", a paper presented at the International Conference on "1991-2000: The Palestinian-Israeli Peace Process", Madrid, 30 September-1 October 2000; Appendix I to Report of Sub-Committee 2 to the Ad Hoc Commission on the Palestine Question, Records of the General Assembly, Second Session, Doc. A/AC 14/32 [1947], pp. 276-304.
22. Palumbo, Michael, *The Palestinian Catastrophe: The 1948 Expulsion of a People from their Homeland* (London: Faber and Faber, 1978) 31; Letter from Dean Rusk, Secretary of State to the Historical Office, 13th of June 1974, recalling the General Assembly reaction to the US recognition of Israel on 14th of May 1948 in [5 part 2] of Foreign Relation of the United States, 1948, Department of State, ed., 1976, p. 993; Memorandum of Conversation/1/Glassboro, New Jersey, 23rd of June 1967, Subject: Middle East, Participants: Secretary Dean Rusk, Foreign Minister Gromyko, Foreign Relations, 1964-1968, Volume XIX, Arab-Israeli Crisis and War, 1967, Released by the Office of the Historian, Documents 320-344, US Department of State at http://www.state.gov/r/pa/ho/frus/johnsonlb/xix/28063.htm
23. Tony Judt's reply to Louise Weinberg's comments on "America, the War, and Israel: An Exchange", *The New York Review of Books* 49, 1 (17 January 2002). Also at http://www.nybooks.com/articles/15115 (Last visited on 11 February 2006); Rubenberg, Cheryl, *Israel and the American National Interest: A Critical Examination* (Chicago: University of Illinois Press, 1986) 106-20.
24. Don Peretz, "Intifadeh: The Palestinian Uprising", *Foreign Affairs* (1988 Summer) 964.
25. Ted Honderich, "Terrorism for Humanity", lecture to the International Social Philosophy Conference at Northeastern university in Boston, 4th of March 2004 at http://www.ucl.ac.uk/~uctytho/terrforhum.html
26. Justus Reid Weiner, "The Use of Palestinian Children in the Al-Azsa Intifadeh: A Legal and Political Analysis", *Temple International and Comparative Law Journal* 43, 16 (Spring 2002); Hugh Dellios, "Holy Sites Sees Day of Rage", *Chicago Tribune*, 30th of July 2001; Mohamad Bazzi, "10 dead in Mideast fights: Bloodiest day in over 2 weeks", *Newsday*, 9th of December 2000; Alex Safian, "Excessive Force and Hypocrisy", *Jerusalem Times*, 10th of November 2000; "Israel Condemns Terrorism at Security Council", *Jerusalem Post*, 24th of November 2000; Mellisa Radler, "PA Ads encouraging child violence

slammed", *Jerusalem Post*, 11th of May 2001.

27. H.C. 5100/94, The Public Committee against Torture in *Israel Vs. The State of Israel*, 53 (4) P.D. 817 at http://www.derechos.org/human-rights/mena/doc/torture.html
28. Resolution 237 (1967) of 14th of June 1967 at http://domino.un.org/UNISPAL.NSF/0/e02b4f9d23b2eff3852560c3005cb95a?OpenDocument; UNSC Resolution 446 (1979) of 22nd of March 1979 at http://domino.un.org/UNISPAL.NSF/0/ba123cded3ea84a5852560e50077c2dc?OpenDocument; Resolution 465 (1980) adopted by the Security Council at its 2203rd meeting on 1st of March 1980 at http://domino.un.org/UNISPAL.NSF/0/5aa254a1c8f8b1cb852560e50075d7d5?OpenDocument; The UNSC resolution 242 adopted on 22nd of November 1967, which has been cited in the preambles to the Oslo Accords, requires an Israeli withdrawal from all the occupied territories as part of any final settlement. Resolution 242 (1967) of 22nd of November 1967 at http://domino.un.org/unispal.nsf/0/59210ce6d04aef61852560c3005da209?OpenDocument
29. Footnote 3 in Orde F. Kittrie, "Intellectual Relations- More Process than Peace: Legitimacy, Compliance and the Oslo Accords", *Michgan Law Review* 1661, 101 (May 2003).
30. Watson, Geoffrey R., *The Oslo Accords: International Law and the Israeli-Palestinian Peace Agreements* (Oxford: Oxford University Press, 2000) 315-390.
31. Saeb Erekat, "Saving the Two-State solution", *The New York Times*, 20th of December 2002; Dennis Ross, "Mapping out peace in the Mideast", *Los Angeles Times*, 20th of December 2002; Justus R. Weiner, "An analysis of the Oslo II Agreement in light of expectations of Shimon Peres and Mahmoud Abbas, *Michigan Journal of International Law* 667, 699, 17 (1996); "Arafat Warns: Our Rifles are Ready", *Jerusalem Post*, 17th of November 1998.
32. The Palestine National Charter (1968) available at http://www.palestine-un.org/plo/frindex.html and http://www.palestine-net.com/politics; Deborah Sontag, "Clinton watches as Palestinians drop call for Israel's destruction", *The New York Times*, 15th of December 1998; Deborah Sontag, "Israel won't meet Friday timetable for next pullout", *The New York Times*, 16th of December 1998.
33. "Sharon's Surprise", *The Economist*, 7th of February 2004.
34. "President Bush calls for new Palestinian leadership", Press release, White House, 24th of June 2002, at http://www.whitehouse.gov/news/releases/2002/06/20020624-3.html
35. Jerry M. Landay, "The Powell Manifesto: How a Prominent Lawyer's Attack Memo Changed America", August 2002 http://www.mediatransparency.org/story.php?storyID=21; Tom Carver, "Bush puts God on his side", *BBC News*, 6th of April 2003 at http://

news.bbc.co.uk/2/hi/americas/2921345.stm; Robert Dreyfuss, "Reverend Doomsday" at http://www.rollingstone.com/politics/story/_/id/5939999?rnd=1090028394515&has-player=true&version=6.0.10.505&; Nathaniel Helle, M. Asif Ismail, Erin Bartels, Brenda R. Mayrack and Josey Ballenger, "The Bush Team", Center for Public Integrity, Washington D. C., 2001 at http://notes.ire.org/ireresources.nsf/0/848c03d2bf3ce94586256b5200604e1e?OpenDocument; Maureen Farrell, "On a Mission from God: The Religious Right and the Emerging American Theocracy" at http://www.buzzflash.com/farrell/04/03/far04007.html; Stan Crock, "Bush, the Bible, and Iraq", Middle East Information Center, 7th of March 2003 at http://middleeastinfo.org/article2155.html; Chip Berlet, "Clinton, Conspiracism and the Continuing Culture War", *The Public Eye* 13, 1 (Spring 1999) 1. Also at http://www.publiceye.org/magazine/v13n1/PE_V13_N1.pdf Dana Milbank, "Religious Rights Find its Center in the Oval Office", *Washington Post*, 24th of December 2001. Also at http://www.washingtonpost.com/ac2/wp-dyn/A19253-2001Dec23?language=printer;; Francine Kiefer, "The Private Faith of a Public Man", *Christian Science Monitor*, 6th of September 2002 at http://www.csmonitor.com/2002/0906/p01s03-uspo.html; Marc J. Ambinder, "Vast, Right-Wing Cabal?", *ABC News*, 2nd of May 2002 at http://www.freerepublic.com/focus/news/678326/posts; Matthew Engel, "Meet the New Zionists", *The Guardian*, 28th of October 2002. Also at http://www.guardian.co.uk/israel/Story/0,2763, 820528,00.html; Julian Borger, "Staff cry poetic injustice as singing Ashcroft introduces patriot games", The Guardian, 4th of March 2002. Also at http://www.guardian.co.uk/bush/story/0,7369, 661458,00.html; "Robertson: God says it is Bush in a 'blowout' in November", *USA Today*, 1st of February 2004. Also at http://www.usatoday.com/news/politicselections/nation/2004-01-02-god-bush_x.htm

36. Brian Bennett, "A Violation of Justice", *Time - Asia Magazine*, 15th of July 2002. Also at http://www.time.com/time/asia/magazine/article/0,13673,501020715-300692,00.html
37. "Saudi Police Stopped Fire Rescue", *BBC News*, 15th of March 2002 at http://news.bbc.co.uk/2/hi/middle_east/1874471.stm; Tarek Al-Issawi, "Saudi School Girls' Fire Death Decried", *Washington Times*, 18th of March 2002; Mona Eltahwy, "They Died for Lack of a Head Scarf", *Washington Post*, 19th of March 2002.
38. Simons, Geoff, *Saudi Arabia: The Shape of Client Feudalism* (New York: St. Martin's Press, 1998) 48; Clarisa Bencorno, *Flawed Justice: The Execution of Abd al-Karum Mara'I al-Naqshabani* (New York: Human Rights Watch/Middle East, 1997).
39. El Fadl, Khaled Abou, *Rebellion and Violence in Islamic Law* (New York: Cambridge University Press, 2001).

40. Zeldin, Theodore, *An Intimate History of Humanity* (New Delhi: Penguin Books, 1999) 377.
41. Smith, Margaret, *Rabi'a: The Life and Work of Rabi'a and Other Women Mystics of Islam* (Oxford: Oneworld, 1994) 32-33.

Index

Contributors

I.A. Rehman is the Director of Human Rights Commission of Pakistan.

Rita Manchanda, former Gender Advisor to the Government of Sri Lanka, is a SAFHR expert on media and gender issues.

Satish K. Jain is a Professor of Economics at Jawaharlal Nehru University, New Delhi. His teaching and research interests include social choice theory, law and economics and methodology and philosophy of economics.

Tapan K. Bose, the Secretary General of the South Asia Forum for Human Rights, has been an eminent documentary filmmaker, human rights and peace activist and a writer with several international and national awards winning films to his credit.

Uma Chakravrty is a well-known feminist historian and the former teacher of history at Miranda House, Delhi University.

SOUTH ASIAN ORIENTATION COURSE IN HUMAN RIGHTS AND PEACE STUDIES

■ THE CONCEPTUAL FRAMEWORK

Human rights, peace and democracy are the main areas of concern of the South Asia Forum for Human Rights [SAFHR], a regional forum established in 1990. In the strife torn region of South Asia, SAFHR is committed to the promotion of inter linkages between human rights, peace and substantive democracy. SAFHR's initiative in developing a framework for the South Asian Orientation Course in Human Rights and Peace Studies [HRPS] followed the Vienna Declaration of 1993, which devotes its Articles 33, 34, 36, 38, 78-82 to stress the importance of human rights education and to call on the governments to establish programmes to impart it. The initiative was based on the recognition that human rights and peace education should not become a monopoly of the States, which not only commit widespread human rights violations but also stimulate, with their socio-political, economic and military policies, endemic situations of violent conflict and wars within the region.

SAFHR believes that human rights as aspirations and human yearning for peace, pluralism, substantive democracy and justice are indeed universal. However, the practices of power that thwart and injure these aspirations and yearnings also seem to be universal and, regrettably, there is no general theory to explain why those practices of power so pervasively have their way. Having remained engaged with human rights, peace and justice as the issues of research and education at the regional level as well as having taken part in the practical work of human rights documentation, public interest litigation, advocacy, building solidarity networks and civil society initiatives in all the countries of South Asia, SAFHR holds the view that aspirations for human rights and peace as also the realities of abuse of authority, violent strife and suffering have very complex local contexts that are not always obvious to all the votaries of universalism. SAFHR believes that the ideals and standards contained in the Universal Declaration of

Human Rights, drafted nearly 6 decades ago, stand better chances of realization if they move from the local to regional on to the global plane. SAFHR also believes that knowledgeable initiatives for the protection and promotion of justice, democracy, development, human rights and plural peace within the local contexts of all the countries of South Asia become effective only when they are able to draw support from a wider environment of similar initiatives in their neighbourhood in harmony with the universal objectives. That is the *raison d'etre* of SAFHR's HRPS Programme.

The Programme is designed to be research and action oriented. Grounded in participatory principles of pedagogy, their epistemological assumptions, curricula and methodologies have been adapted to serve the dual purpose of generating critical knowledge about the issues under inquiry as well as to interrogate the systems of knowledge in ways that may lead to mutations in policies and practices of power through social action. Inevitably, the programme is experimental in nature and tends to evolve in close consultation with the participant-collaborators, partner organizations and friends. Prevailing socio-economic conditions and conditions of human rights violations and situations of conflict within the countries in the region tend to influence its content and the focus.

Tentative timeline of the course is as following:

- February : The course advertisement to invite applications.
- April : Final selection of the participants.
- May/June/July : Distance learning.
- August : The field work.
- September : Direct Orientation.

The distance-learning is conducted on SAFHR's secure e-learning platform. Participants also receive the course material on CDs. However, familiarity with e-learning skills and proficiency in the English language are essential. Six compulsory modules of the course are: 1. Basic Concepts of Human Rights; 2. Constitution, Laws and Justice; 3. Conflicts and the Politics of Peace; 4. "The Global War on Terror"; 5. Globalization, Politics of Technology and Environmental Justice; and 6. Media and Conflict.

- **CLINICALS AND THE FIELD WORK**

  The three-month long distance learning period is followed by a month long partnership between the participants and the members of the permanent faculty in joint audit exercises with strong emphasis on the field work. The number of such audit exercises, as the clinical component of the HRPS, their themes, the nature of cooperation between the country-teams and their methodologies develop out of the distance learning engagement.

- **THE DIRECT ORIENTATION PROGRAMME**

  The course culminates in a three-week long direct orientation period that brings the participants, members of the permanent faculty and expert resource persons face to face for intense class-room interactions and evaluations. The structural pre-planning for these sessions takes into account the quality and the content of engagements during the distance learning and the clinical periods.

- **CRITERIA FOR THE SELECTION OF PARTICIPANTS**

  Between thirty to thirty-five participants are selected for the course every year on the basis of their involvement with the issues of human rights, peace, democracy and development. Each applicant is required to send a filled in application form with two references, and a 1,000-word essay explaining the relation of the applicant's work to human rights and peace studies and the reason for applying for the course. The selection process is guided by the necessity to have a balanced representation of participants from all the countries in the region, women activists, refugee activists, media practitioners, members of minority groups, researchers, academics and policy makers, leaders of non-governmental organizations and government officials. A maximum of four participants from outside South Asia are selected.

For Information, Address

South Asia Forum for Human Rights
GPO Box 12855, Kathmandu, Nepal
Tel.: 00977-1-5541026, 0091-11-41682841/42
E-mail: desk@safhr.org, south@safhr.org
Website: www.safhr.org, www.safhr-hrps.org